Environmental stress

Environmental stress

Edited by

GARY W. EVANS

Program in Social Ecology and
The Public Policy Research Organization
University of California, Irvine

The right of the
University of Cambridge
to print and sell
all manner of books
was granted by
Henry VIII in 1534.
The University has printed
and published continuously
since 1584.

CAMBRIDGE UNIVERSITY PRESS

Cambridge
London   New York   New Rochelle
Melbourne   Sydney

Published by the Press Syndicate of the University of Cambridge
The Pitt Building, Trumpington Street, Cambridge CB2 1RP
32 East 57th Street, New York, NY 10022, USA
296 Beaconsfield Parade, Middle Park, Melbourne 3206, Australia

© Cambridge University Press 1982

First published 1982
First paperback edition 1984

Printed in the United States of America

Library of Congress Cataloging in Publication Data
Main entry under title:
Environmental stress.
Includes indexes.
1. Environmental psychology.   2. Stress
(Psychology)   3. Stress (Physiology)
I. Evans, Gary W. (Gary William), 1948–
BF353.E56   155.9'1   82-1336   AACR 2
ISBN 0 521 24636 9 hardcover
ISBN 0 521 31859 9 paperback

For Geordie

Contents

Contributors

Sherry Ahrentzen
Program in Social Ecology
University of California
Irvine, California 92717

Andrew Baum
Uniformed Services University
  of the Health Services
Department of Defense
Bethesda, Maryland 20014

Carlene S. Baum
Uniformed Services University
  of the Health Services
Department of Defense
Bethesda, Maryland 20014

Paul A. Bell
Department of Psychology
Colorado State University
Fort Collins, Colorado 80523

Sheldon Cohen
Psychology Department
Carnegie–Mellon University
Pittsburgh, Pennsylvania 15213

Joseph F. DiMento
Program in Social Ecology
University of California
Irvine, California 92717

Yakov M. Epstein
Department of Psychology
University College
Rutgers University
New Brunswick, New Jersey 08903

Gary W. Evans
Program in Social Ecology
University of California
Irvine, California 92717

Thomas C. Greene
Department of Psychology
St. Lawrence University
Canton, New York 13617

Stephen V. Jacobs
Department of Psychology and
  Social Relations
Harvard University
Cambridge, Massachusetts 02138

Gregory M. Jue
Program in Social Ecology
University of California
Irvine, California 92717

Janet E. Reizenstein
Office of Hospital Planning,
  Research and Development
The University of Michigan
  Hospitals
Ann Arbor, Michigan 48109

Sally Ann Shumaker
Department of Psychology and
  Center for Metropolitan
  Planning and Research
Johns Hopkins University
Baltimore, Maryland 21218

Jerome E. Singer
Uniformed Services University
  of the Health Services
Department of Defense
Bethesda, Maryland 20014

Mary Anne Skorpanich
Program in Social Ecology
University of California
Irvine, California 92717

Ralph B. Taylor
Center for Metropolitan Planning
  and Research
Johns Hopkins University
Baltimore, Maryland 21218

Neil Weinstein
Department of Human Ecology and
  Social Sciences
Cook College
Rutgers University
New Brunswick, New Jersey 08903

Jean D. Wineman
College of Architecture
Georgia Institute of Technology
Atlanta, Georgia 30332

Craig Zimring
College of Architecture
Georgia Institute of Technology
Atlanta, Georgia 30332

Foreword

Traditionally, the president of the Society for the Psychological Study of Social Issues (SPSSI) contributes a foreword for SPSSI-sponsored books published during his or her presidential year. This honor should have been Clara Mayo's. Her untimely death during her first few months of office has led me, as past president of SPSSI, to write in her stead.

I believe that this book represents the best of both theoretical and applied work on environmental stress. It offers a conceptual integration of research on stress, reviews what is known about specific environmental stressors – noise, crowding, temperature and air pollution – and examines stress in a diverse array of specific environments – hospitals, schools, office buildings, and neighborhoods. The authors' multivariate approach helps to bring about much-needed convergence between laboratory and field studies. The book dovetails applied problem-solving with theoretical concerns. It will play a useful role in helping societies and individuals to understand, and to seek solutions to, the impelling problems of stress and poor environmental design. SPSSI is pleased to sponsor this volume, in the best tradition of research on the psychological aspects of important social issues.

Leonard Bickman
Vanderbilt University

Editorial preface

The relationship between human behavior and the physical environment assumes two basic forms. On the one hand, our behavior affects environmental quality: The amount of energy we consume, the products we buy, and the economic and political policies we support affect environmental conditions. On the other hand, the quality of our physical surroundings affects our mental and physical health. In this book we focus on the latter relationship by examining what happens when individuals are exposed to suboptimal environments.

This book has four specific objectives. The first is to provide some conceptual integration across several environmental problem areas by utilizing the concept of stress as a unifying theme. Noise, heat, air pollution, and crowding can all be viewed as nonoptimal environmental conditions that may elicit behaviors designed to modify that suboptimal human–environment relationship.

The second objective is to demonstrate how the stress concept can be used to understand human behavior in designed environments. Most research on human responses to the built environment has been atheoretical, focusing on postoccupancy assessments of user satisfaction. Following a general introduction to the ways in which the stress concept can describe dysfunction between human needs and the designed environment, sources of stress are discussed in four specific settings: medical hospitals, schools, offices, and neighborhoods.

Third, we review existing knowledge about the effects on human behavior of four environmental stressors: noise, heat, air pollution, and crowding. As is apparent in the various chapters in this volume, there is considerable variety in what, and how much, we know about these stressors. Although some environmental conditions such as air pollution have received scant attention from behavioral scientists, other sources of environmental stress such as crowding and noise have received considerable coverage. Empirical findings about each stressor are organized, in general, around three main areas of impact: health and physiology, performance, and affect and social behavior. Research on designed settings is also reviewed, with an emphasis on physical features that influence user satisfaction. The impact of environmental design on health and performance has received relatively little research attention, however.

Our final objective is to stimulate thinking about the ways in which research on behavioral aspects of environmental problems can be integrated into decision-making processes. A central feature of the National Environmental Policy Act of 1969 was the creation of the environmental impact review process, which mandates the assessment of environmental impacts of any federal action that could significantly affect environmental quality. Since this Act, over one-half of the states have extended the environmental impact review process to their own actions as well. Interestingly, in their report on the environmental impact review process, entitled *Planning for Environmental Indices*, the National Academy of Sciences and the National Academy of Engineering conclude that a major shortcoming of the environmental impact review process is inadequate assessment of environmental change on human health and well-being (Washington, D.C.: Environmental Studies Board, 1975).

Support and guidance for the preparation of this book came from many sources. The book evolved from a volume of the *Journal of Social Issues* on the same topic. The papers from that issue were expanded, and four chapters on specific designed settings were added. I am particularly grateful to James McGrath for his excellent stewardship as Editor of the *Journal of Social Issues*. I appreciate the sponsorship of this book by the Society for the Psychological Study of Social Issues and thank Marilynn Brewer and Jeffrey Rubin for their help. All royalties from this book are donated to the Society.

I thank Joseph DiMento, Director of the Program in Social Ecology, University of California, Irvine, and M. N. Palsane, Head of the Department of Experimental Psychology, University of Poona, Ganeshkind, Pune, India, for providing institutional and personal support during the preparation of this book. Susan Milmoe and the editorial staff at Cambridge University Press have provided considerable expertise that has helped shape and refine this book. I thank Jill Vidas for assistance with the manuscript and Mary Anne Skorpanich for preparation of the indexes. Finally, I am grateful for support from a Fulbright award that enriched my sabbatical year in India, and for grant support from the National Science Foundation (BNS 77-08576), the National Institute of Environmental Health Sciences (1 R01 ES0176401 DBR), Southern California Edison Health Effects Research Division (B-2058902, J-1909902), and the Focused Research Program on Stress, University of California, Irvine.

GARY W. EVANS

Irvine, California

General introduction

Gary W. Evans

This book evolved out of a need to more fully understand the ways in which suboptimal environmental conditions affect human health and behavior. The environmentalism and ecological concern of the 1960s helped to generate scholarly interest in the effects of environmental problems on human health. Much of the initial work in this area was done by biological scientists.

In the late 1960s and early 1970s, a few behavioral scientists became interested in these effects. Early research efforts in the new field of human–environment studies focused on two broad topics: design and user satisfaction, and human responses to pollution and overpopulation (Craik, 1973; Kates & Wohlwill, 1966).

In some respects, the emergence of human–environment studies represented a convergence of two relatively distinct intellectual paradigms: (1) environmental sciences, which focus primarily on the conditions of the biosphere, and (2) the study of human behavior, conducted by psychologists and other social scientists. Human–environment studies emphasize the transaction between these two perspectives and focus on two key questions: How does variation in the physical environment affect human behavior?; and How does variation in human behavior affect environmental quality?

This book illustrates how the transactional construct of stress can be used to understand this interaction. Stress is defined broadly as any situation in which the environmental demands on individuals exceed their abilities to respond. There are many definitions of stress and considerable controversy about which are proper definitions. The reader interested in this problem should see Appley and Trumbull (1967); Lazarus (1966), McGrath (1970), and Selye (1956). Definitions vary in their specificity and the extent to which they emphasize physiological or psychological processes.

Limitations in biological models of human–environment interaction

Biological models of the human–environment interface derive from animal models and emphasize interactions between environmental constituents and the physiological response of the organism. Although the biological perspective has undoubtedly made enormous contributions to understanding the human–environment interface, it has important limitations. Some of these led to the emergence of human–environment studies as a focus of inquiry for social scientists.

Direct effects

One limitation of the biological perspective is the emphasis of biological models on direct, environmental effects on human health. Rene Dubos (1965) was among the first biologists to note the role of cognitive mediators between physical stimuli and human responses. Human beings, to a much greater extent than other animals, interact with the symbolic, cognitively constructed world. The contexts in which stressors occur have important influences on our cognitive appraisals of events. The distinction between noise and sound may serve as an example. Human reactions to sound levels of a given physical intensity (e.g., decibel levels) are mediated by a host of individual and contextual variables. Reactions ranging from cardiovascular changes to annoyance are strongly linked, for example, to individual judgments of the importance of the noise source, or perceptions of personal control over the noise (Cohen & Weinstein, Chap. 2, this volume). One person's music may be another's noise.

Pathogenic outcomes

A second limitation of the biological perspective on environmental health is the overemphasis of biological models on pathogenic outcomes. Toxicologists, epidemiologists, and other health-related scientists tend to concentrate on serious, catastrophic measures of health. Mortality and morbidity, although of paramount importance, are not the only health indexes worthy of examination. Irritability, depression, anxiety, and other indicators of mental health can be affected by changes in environmental quality. Affect, mood, and interpersonal relationships can also be impacted by physical surroundings. Furthermore, as increasing evidence shows, the susceptibility of the host organism to disease is drastically altered by psychological factors (Monat & Lazarus, 1977). Psychosomatic diseases are no longer a small, specialized area of medicine. Stress has been implicated in a wide array of health problems. Thus, psychological variables play important roles both as final outcome measures and as mediators that can predispose us to react more severely to environmental insults.

Methodological limitations

Both biological and ecological research strategies have been criticized on methodological grounds. Many biological studies of environmental influences on human health use the traditional experimental paradigm with laboratory-based controls and isolation of key causal variables. Although this approach to scientific research has many strengths (cf. Platt, 1964), it comes at a cost of limited generalizability. Do isolated, highly controlled reactions occur in the same way in the "real" world as they do in the lab? Field research, on the other hand, also has limitations. Aggregate-level associations of "real" phenomena often leave the researcher with vague descriptions of causal processes that are subject to reasonable alternative explanations.

As the research reviewed in this volume indicates, it is possible to combine experimental rigor with the realism provided by naturalistic studies conducted in the field. Among the strategies employed in environmental stress research to achieve this meshing of the two approaches are longitudinal studies of individual respondents and cross-validation studies of experimental and naturalistic findings. Nevertheless, researchers of environmental stressors have by no means solved the difficult problems related to experimental and nonexperimental research methodologies. Moreover, although there are several serious methodological problems specific to stress research (discussed later), *some* research on environmental stress does illustrate the possibility of rigorous, externally valid research.

Models of stress

Two dominant models of stress influence the research discussed in this book. These emphasize, respectively, physiological and psychological processes in the reactions of organisms to environmental intrusions and demands. Both models are described in detail in Chapter 1 by Baum, Singer, and Baum. Thus, we provide only a short overview of the two approaches here.

Physiological models

Physiological responses to stressors were described by Hans Selye (1956) in his efforts to explain various nonspecific reactions of the pituitary–adrenal axis to pathogenic insults. Selye noted that when rats were exposed to a variety of environmental insults, a common pattern of bodily reactions consistently occurred regardless of the particular insult the body encountered. Selye termed this pattern of nonspecific responses the General Adaptation Syndrome, which includes a sequence of alarm, resistance, and exhaustion that is characterized by certain physical events. Briefly, these events include ACTH-mediated adrenocortical activity that causes glucocorticosteroid secretion (anti-inflammatory agents) from the adrenal cortex and other areas. This in turn triggers catecholamine output (e.g., adrenaline) from the adrenal medulla. If resistance to the pathogen is successful, adaptation to the stressor occurs and this somatic sequence ceases. If somatic defense becomes depleted, exhaustion occurs, and the body loses its capacity to respond to attack by external pathogens. Work by Mason, Lacey, and others has challenged the nonspecificity hypothesis of Selye's model, but the general pattern of somatic responses is well accepted in the stress literature (Lacey, 1967; Mason, Maher, Hartley, Mougey, Perlow, & Jones, 1976).

Two aspects of Selye's model have strongly influenced work on environmental stress. Many stress researchers accept, in principle, that the body has a finite amount of adaptive energy available to cope with stress. Depletion of this energy reserve is viewed as harmful to the organism as it leads to serious disequilibrium. There is also an implied homeostatic model of bodily function with coping processes viewed as efforts to maintain internal stability (Cannon, 1963). Second, the processes involved in coping are seen as having negative effects independent of the harmful impacts of the stressor (Cohen, Krantz, Stokols, & Evans, in press).

Psychological models

Psychological models of stress emphasize cognitive interpretations of environmental conditions. Work in this tradition has been heavily influenced by Richard Lazarus's research on psychological stress (Lazarus, 1966; Lazarus & Launier, 1978). According to Lazarus, individuals appraise how threatening events are. The extent to which an event will be seen as threatening is dependent upon a constellation of personal and contextual features. Individual attitudes about a stressor, prior experience with it, knowledge of its costs, and evaluations of alternative courses of action can all influence how an event is appraised. Furthermore, the severity and chronicity of the stressor itself can influence this assessment. An appraisal of no threat, for example, is more likely to occur when the individual believes the stressor is marginal, short-lived, or relatively familiar.

Once an event has been appraised as worthy of response, coping processes ensue. Secondary appraisal encompasses an accounting of one's coping resources and generally is manifested by either instrumental or palliative coping. Instrumental coping involves direct action to remove the stressor, efforts to learn more about it, or strategies to filter its impact on the individual. Thus, instrumental coping with noise, for example, might include asking your neighbor to turn the stereo down, calling the airport to complain or to obtain more information about jet overflights, or wearing ear protectors while on the job. Palliative or intrapsychic coping entails reappraisal of the stressor by psychological means such as defense mechanisms. One might cope with air pollution by deciding that your neighborhood, in comparison to adjacent areas, is relatively pollution free. Alternatively you may feel that bad air quality has little effect on your own health because you have not experienced any respiratory problems where you live. Finally, poor visibility may be attributed to fog or other "natural" causes rather than to smog or air pollution.

Limitations of the stress construct

Several limitations of the stress construct are also of concern to environmental researchers and are discussed by the chapter authors. One of the major conceptual difficulties is the lack of convergence between psychological and physiological perspectives on stress. Little theoretical or empirical work has addressed this difficulty, but some progress has been made recently on two aspects of this problem.

First, Mason and his colleagues recently argued that psychological threat is a necessary prerequisite for activation of the pituitary–adrenal, somatic responses characteristic of the General Adaptation Syndrome (Mason, 1975). Selye disputes this position, and the issue currently stands at a point of controversy (Selye, 1975). Second, some research indicates that stressors have some direct physiological effects (e.g., elevated heart rate) that are distinct from physiological effects due to coping efforts (e.g., increased catecholamine output) (Frankenhaeuser & Lundberg, 1977; Lundberg & Frankenhaeuser, 1978).

The largely distinct influence of the psychological and physiological perspectives on stress has led to two additional problems. One is the relative importance of objective and subjective stressors for human health and behavior. It is unclear which are more crucial in determining human reactions: the actual physical parameters of stressors, or subjective appraisals of stressors. It is also possible that the issue is more complex. Perhaps some physiological outcomes are more sensitive to objective characteristics of the stressor, whereas other behaviors are more reactive to subjective appraisals of threat or harm. Although there is much discussion about the importance of distinguishing between, for example, sound and noise or density and crowding, remarkably little research has focused directly on how well objective versus subjective stressors predict human behavior.

The second problem stemming from the dual influences of the physiological and psychological perspectives on stress concerns the coping process. Many of the immediate effects of stressors on human beings may go undetected because of the adaptive resources available to the individual for coping. Many early studies of environmental stressors and task performance, for example, concluded that stressors such as noise and crowding had no negative effects on human task performance. As we now know, these conclusions were premature because stressor effects on task performance are very subtle and are masked to a large degree by individual efforts to maintain normal performance levels. Current views of stress and human performance suggest that stressors can degrade performance on certain kinds of complex tasks or cause negative aftereffects in performance. Tasks with multiple signals, rapid signal presentation, or low probability signals are disrupted by environmental stressors such as noise (Hockey, 1979) and crowding (Evans, 1978). After periods of exposure to these stressors, performance on tasks suffers when the stressor is no longer present (Cohen, 1980). Individuals can perform at normal levels on many cognitive tasks during stress. With the use of measures that have sufficient task complexity, or that measure aftereffects, the costs of coping efforts can be detected.

Another conceptual limitation of the stress construct is confusion about what physiological indexes of stress and coping should be used in research. One aspect of this limitation centers on the definition of stress as a nonspecific set of physiological adaptations, described earlier (Selye's General Adaptation Syndrome). There is disagreement over which physiological indexes to monitor, and whether they should be highly correlated or form stressor-specific patterns. This controversy is further complicated by the fact that when attention is paid to external stimuli, a different physiological pattern (directional fractionation) occurs than when efforts are made to inhibit external sensory input (Kahneman, 1973; Lacey, 1967). Thus, when measuring the effects of stressors on task performance, the researcher must take into account that the individual's attention to task cues has some physiological consequences. Furthermore, efforts involved in coping with stressors have their own effects on physiological states, which are distinct from the effects of the stressor. All of these additional variables, plus parameters of the stressor itself, can affect human physiological responses. Understandably, there is now a good deal of confusion about how to interpret physiological measures in stress studies.

Large individual differences are often noted in response to stressors. A statistical implication of this fact is that many tests for stress effects have low statistical power because of large, unexplained within-groups variance. The existence of individual differences also relates to the objective-subjective issue already raised. Many studies of environmental stressors may have large intragroup variances because of varying personal appraisals of stressors. Some of the more promising individual difference variables noted to date are the extent of previous experience with the stressor, the individual's age, and the expectancy or set of the individual, particularly with regard to control over the stressor and the environment in general. Efforts to identify a general stress-prone personality variable have proven unsuccessful so far.

Finally, the knotty problem of how stressors interrelate is still largely unresolved. Curiously, although many early volumes on stress noted the importance of this issue (Appley & Trumbull, 1967; Lazarus, 1966; McGrath, 1970), little research on this topic has ensued. The problem is interesting for several reasons. Conceptually the issue relates to the integrity of the stress construct itself. If various kinds of changes in physical conditions can be conceptualized as stressful, then they must share some common mechanism or process. One way to explore shared processes is to create additive formulations. Broadbent (1971), for example, has invoked this approach to study the feasibility of an arousal explanation of stress. He noted that noise and sleep deprivation in combination canceled out one another's individual negative effects on task performance. Because noise increases arousal and sleep deprivation reduces it, Broadbent argued that this cancellation effect supported an arousal mechanism for stress effects on performance.

The issue of multiple stressors is also important from a policy perspective. If stressors have interactive effects, is what we learn about an isolated stressor in the laboratory applicable to our daily encounters with multiple stressors? There is a great need for more research on the interactive effects of environmental stressors on human health and behavior.

In summary, we have noted six controversies about the stress construct that center around the following issues: (1) conceptual convergence between the physiological and psychological models of stress, (2) the relative importance of objective and subjective measures of stressors for health and behavioral outcomes, (3) the influence of coping on reactions to stress, (4) problems in physiological measurement of stress, (5) individual differences in response to stressors, and (6) interrelationships among multiple stressors. All are touched on in the chapters that follow.

Central themes of the book

Three major themes can be discerned in the chapters. All of the authors are concerned with the role of processes mediating between the environment and the individual's response. They are concerned also with the limitations of laboratory research, and with the lack of conceptual clarity of the stress construct.

Related to these themes is a frequent call for more multivariate research with greater convergence between laboratory and field investigations. Few research programs have systematically cross-validated lab and field findings. This kind of approach to research would allow stress researchers to maximize the trade-offs between internal validity (isolation of causal variables) and external validity (generalizability of results across persons and settings) (Cohen, Evans, Krantz, & Stokols, 1980; Cook & Campbell, 1976).

Mediating processes

Concern with subjective appraisals of environmental conditions and subsequent coping strategies is evident in all of the chapters. Attributions and expectancies about the cause and importance of stressors are important in mediating the relationship between stressor state and organismic response. Individual perceptions of control over stressors are also discussed at length

as a mediating variable. In addition, several authors describe the production of stress through dysfunction between individual needs and environmental opportunities. This approach is particularly germane to the chapters
on ambient stress in designed settings.

Limitations of laboratory-based research

Several of the chapter authors express concern about the limitations of
laboratory research on environmental stressors. Cohen (1981) has presented
a concise summary of several of these limitations. His basic premise is that
a number of factors in laboratory settings reduce an individual's perceptions of stressors as threatening. This reduction minimizes psychological
stress since threat appraisal is an important component of the stress response.

Threat in laboratory settings is minimized by the subject's awareness
that the stressor will only last for a short time, and that no serious harmful
effects could occur because he or she is under the experimenter's care. In
addition, subjects for laboratory experiments are usually volunteers and
frequently are informed that they can remove themselves at any time from
the experiment without penalty. By providing choice and some degree of
subject control, the experimenter removes some of the potentially threatening aspects of the stressor (Gardner, 1978). Finally, some of the annoying,
interruptive aspects of stressors may be legitimized by the laboratory context. For example, the experimental subject may view the situation as important and necessary because it is part of a university research program.

There is also some discussion in this book of the limitations of field
studies of environmental stressors. Less attention is paid to this topic,
however. The major questions raised have to do with subject self-selection,
with the existence of confounding variables, and with an overreliance on
subject self-report measures of stress.

Conceptual clarity

If one can accept for the moment that there is sufficient evidence to maintain the stress construct as a viable model of human responses to suboptimal
environmental conditions, a fundamental issue still remains. What is/are
the mechanism(s) or process(es) that makes certain environmental conditions stressful? Several models of environmental stress are offered in this
volume.

One of the earliest and still predominant models of stress is *arousal*.
According to this model, changes in the physical environment can affect
activity levels in the reticular activating system in the brain. These changes
are manifested on a behavioral continuum ranging from sleep to frenetic
excitement. Arousal theory posits an inverted U-shaped function between
arousal level and measures of comfort and performance. Thus, environmental conditions that lower or raise arousal levels beyond some optimal

range cause stress. More detailed descriptions of the arousal model as it has been applied to environmental sources of stress can be found in Broadbent (1971), Evans (1978), and Mehrabian and Russell (1974).

Another model of stress that has influenced several of the chapters is *overload*. According to this model, too much information causes stress by taxing the limited information-processing system of the organism. In order to deal with information overload, various adaptive strategies are employed: filtering out low-priority inputs, blocking inputs, increasing routinized, habitual behavior, and attempting to redefine the source of information, for example. Aftereffects from stressors have been interpreted as indicative of adaptive costs or cognitive fatigue resulting from dealing with information overload. Further discussion of overload models of environmental stress can be found in Cohen (1978), Milgram (1970), and Wohlwill (1974).

A final set of models of environmental stress can be characterized as systems models. These models emphasize congruence between personal needs and environmental resources. When individual needs are thwarted by environmental conditions, stress may result if goals cannot be readjusted or sufficient resources located. Examples of systems models of environmental stress are discussed by Altman (1975), Michelson (1970), and Stokols (1979).

Subsumed within systems models of environmental stressors are theories about the role of personal control and stress. Several theorists have argued that environmental conditions are stressful to the extent they interfere with individuals needs for control over their environment. This concept has been developed in connection with environmental stressors by Baron and Rodin (1978), Baum and Valins (1977), and Glass and Singer (1972).

Researchers working on environmental stress need to evaluate the implicit models of stress that they use in their research. Unfortunately, not enough careful thought has been given to the empirical and conceptual implications of these various models. There are other possible explanations of the environmental stress process, but the arousal, overload, and systems approaches represent the major models used in research on environmental stress.

References

Altman, I. *The environment and social behavior: Privacy, territoriality, crowding, and personal space*. Monterey, Calif.: Brooks Cole, 1975.

Appley, M., & Trumbull, R. (Eds.). *Psychological stress*. New York: Appleton-Century-Crofts, 1967.

Baron, R.M., & Rodin, J. Personal control as a mediator of crowding. In A. Baum, J. Singer, & S. Valins (Eds.), *Advances in environmental psychology* (Vol. 1). Hillsdale, N.J.: Erlbaum, 1978.

Baum, A., & Valins, S. *Architecture and social behavior: Psychological studies of social density*. Hillsdale, N.J.: Erlbaum, 1977.

Broadbent, D. *Decision and stress*. New York: Academic Press, 1971.

Cannon, W.B. *The wisdom of the body*. New York: Norton, 1963.

Cohen, S. Environmental load and the allocation of attention. In A. Baum, J. Singer, & S. Valins (Eds.), *Advances in environmental psychology* (Vol. 1). Hillsdale, N.J.: Erlbaum, 1978.

Cohen, S. Aftereffects of stress on human performance and social behavior: A review of research and theory. *Psychological Bulletin*, 1980, *88*, 82–108.

Cohen, S. Cognitive processes as determinants of environmental stress. In I. Sarason & C. Spielberger (Eds.), *Stress and anxiety* (Vol. 7). New York: Hemisphere, 1981.

Cohen, S., Evans, G.W., Krantz, D.S., & Stokols, D. Physiological, motivational, and cognitive effects of aircraft noise on children: Moving from the laboratory to the field. *American Psychologist*, 1980, *35*, 231–243.

Cohen, S., Krantz, D.S., Stokols, D., & Evans, G.W. *Behavior, health, and environmental stress*. New York: Plenum, in press.

Cook, T., & Campbell, D.T. The design and conduct of quasi-experiments and true experiments in field settings. In M. Dunnette (Ed.), *Handbook of industrial and organizational psychology*. Skokie, Ill.: Rand McNally, 1976.

Craik, K. Environmental psychology. *Annual Review of Psychology*, 1973, *24*, 403–422.

Dubos, R. *Man adapting*. New Haven, Conn.: Yale University Press, 1965.

Evans, G.W. Human spatial behavior: The arousal model. In A. Baum & Y. Epstein (Eds.), *Human responses to crowding*. Hillsdale, N.J.: Erlbaum, 1978.

Frankenhaeuser, M., & Lundberg, U. The influence of cognitive set on performance and arousal under different noise loads. *Motivation and Emotion*, 1977, *1*, 139–149.

Gardner, G. Effects of federal human subjects regulations on data obtained in environmental stressor research. *Journal of Personality and Social Psychology*, 1978, *36*, 628–634.

Glass, D., & Singer, J. *Urban Stress*. New York: Academic Press, 1972.

Hockey, R. Stress and the cognitive components of skilled performance. In V. Hamilton & D. Warburton (Eds.), *Human stress and cognition*. New York: Wiley, 1979.

Kahneman, D. *Attention and effort*. Englewood Cliffs, N.J.: Prentice-Hall, 1973.

Kates, R., & Wohlwill, J. Man's response to the physical environment. *Journal of Social Issues*, 1966, *22*, 1–140.

Lacey, J. Somatic response patterning and stress: Some revisions of activation theory. In M. Appley & R. Trumbull (Eds.), *Psychological stress*. New York: Appleton-Century-Crofts, 1967.

Lazarus, R. *Psychological stress and the coping process*. New York: McGraw-Hill, 1966.

Lazarus, R., & Launier, R. Stress-related transactions between person and environment. In L. Pervin & M. Lewis (Eds.), *Perspectives in interactional psychology*. New York: Plenum, 1978.

Lundberg, U., & Frankenhaeuser, M. Psychophysiological reactions to noise as modified by personal control over noise intensity. *Biological Psychology*, 1978, *6*, 51–60.

McGrath, J. (Ed.), *Social and psychological factors in stress*. New York: Holt, Rinehart, and Winston, 1970.

McGrath, J. Stress and behavior in organizations. In M. Dunnette (Ed.), *Handbook of industrial and organizational psychology*. Skokie, Ill.: Rand McNally, 1976.

Mason, J. A historical view of the stress field, Part 1. *Journal of Human Stress*, 1975, *1*, 6–12. Part 2, 1975, *1*, 22–36.

Mason, J., Maher, J., Hartley, L., Mougey, E., Perlow, M., & Jones, L. Selectivity of corticosteroid and catecholamine responses to various natural stimuli. In G. Serban (Ed.), *Psychopathology of human adaptation*. New York: Plenum, 1976.

Mehrabian, A., & Russell, J. *An approach to environmental psychology*. Cambridge, Mass.: MIT Press, 1974.

Michelson, W. *Man and his urban environment*. Reading, Mass.: Addison-Wesley, 1970.

Milgram, S. The experience of living in cities. *Science*, 1970, *167*, 1461–1468.

Monat, S., & Lazarus, R. *Stress and coping*. New York: Columbia University Press, 1977.

Platt, J.R. Strong inference. *Science*, 1964, *146*, 347–353.

Selye, H. *The stress of life*. New York: McGraw-Hill, 1956.

Selye, H. Confusion and controversy in the stress field. *Journal of Human Stress*, 1975, *1*, 37–44.

Stokols, D. A congruence analysis of stress. In I. Sarason & C. Spielberger (Eds.), *Stress and anxiety* (Vol. 6). New York: Hemisphere, 1979.

Wohlwill, J. Human response to levels of environmental stimulation. *Human Ecology*, 1974, *2*, 127–147.

Part I

Environmental stressors

The first part of this volume begins with an overview of the stress construct. Baum, Singer, and Baum argue the merits and deficiencies of the stress concept as a tool for analyzing the various environmental stressors. They draw from a conceptual framework developed in attitude change research and suggest that environmental stress can be understood in terms of three factors: the physical stressor itself (e.g., noise), the appraisal of the stressor (i.e., the extent to which the person perceives the stressor as threatening), and the impact of the stressor on the organism (e.g., physiological impact).

Each author discusses the effects of a particular environmental stressor on health and physiology, cognition, and affect and social behavior. Consistent with Baum, Singer, and Baum's appraisal factor, the various papers on specific environmental stressors note the importance of intervening psychological variables that mediate the impact of stressors on human behavior. It is noteworthy that in one of the earliest books on the environmental crisis, *Man adapting*, biologist Rene Dubos criticized traditional biological models of human–environment interaction for not adequately acknowledging the critical role of cognition in this transactional process (New Haven, Conn.: Yale University Press, 1965). Both the physical condition of our environs and our images of those conditions affect our responses to that environment.

Cohen and Weinstein's chapter on noise and Epstein's chapter on crowding both address the importance of threat and control as mediating constructs between physical environmental conditions and behavioral outcomes. On the other hand, Bell and Greene's chapter on temperature focuses more on the direct effects of heat and cold on behavior, noting the general absence of research on mediating variables. Bell and Greene also provide considerably more detail on the physical characteristics of the stressors themselves than do the other authors, since several features of temperature conditions (e.g., relative humidity) markedly affect its impact on human health and well-being.

Evans and Jacobs introduce a topic area that has generally been ignored by psychologists: effects of air pollution on behavior. They draw more heavily on survey research data than do the other authors. Evans and Jacobs also emphasize the need to examine how people cope with chronic environmental stressors like air pollution.

One environmental source of stress notably absent from this volume is water pollution. Unfortunately, with the exception of a few attitudinal studies, no behavioral research has been conducted on water pollution. All of the major environmental pollutants – noise, temperature, crowding, and air and water pollution – have important psychological factors.

1. Stress and the environment

Andrew Baum, Jerome E. Singer, and Carlene S. Baum

Stress has become a popular concept for explaining a wide variety of outcomes, mostly negative, that otherwise seem to defy explanation. In the
scientific realm, stress has been used as a psychological precursor of illness, as a result of any number of conditions, or as a catchall for anxiety
reactions, discomfort, and the like. It is also fashionable to attribute erratic
or unexplainable behavior of friends and acquaintances to the fact that
"they are under a lot of stress." From a cursory reading of psychological
and medical texts and from simply listening to people, one can derive a
fairly broad definition of stress. Yet, despite its general use, stress refers to
a process that is not only specific, but also central to the relationship
between people and their surroundings.

Stress is the process by which environmental events or forces, called
stressors, threaten an organism's existence and well-being and by which
the organism responds to this threat. The stress reaction, replete with
commonly known symptoms such as fear, anxiety, and anger, is only part
of this process. It is probably the most easily recognized, but in many cases
it may simply represent "side effects" of the main attraction – perceiving a
threat, coping with it, and adapting to it. This adaptation sequence is
almost a daily routine: Our lives can be characterized as constant adaptation to sudden change or gradual evolution of our surroundings. Sometimes these changes are minor and we can adapt to them without even
being aware of them. At other times, however, these changes can be severe
and clearly threatening.

In this chapter, we will briefly review some of the major models of stress,
some of which characterize stress as a natural bodily defense against physical threat and others that focus on stress as a psychologically mediated
response to psychological or environmental dangers. By considering both
physiological and psychological threats to well-being, we will attempt to
draw these different perspectives together, recognizing both the impor-

tance of the biological context in which we function and the contribution of appraisal and expectation in the interpretation of stressful events. We will also consider the differences and commonalities among various stressors, and the organism's response to them. Finally, we draw some conclusions about the nature of environmental stress, examining what, if anything, sets it apart from what has generally been termed stress.

Models of stress

Selye and the physiological stress model

The first systematic treatments of stress were those provided by Selye (1978) and were based upon a triad of physiological responses that accompanied physiological challenge. When extracts were injected into laboratory animals, he found that their adrenal glands were enlarged, that their thymus and lymph glands had shrunk, and that they had developed gastrointestinal ulcers.

Selye's *General Adaptation Syndrome* (GAS) is based upon the idea that the body can cope with stress but that this coping has costs for subsequent coping. Long-term exposure to stress or repeated instances of adaptive demand can deplete the organism's adaptive reserves and lead to physical dysfunction. When first exposed to a stressor, the body responds by mobilizing its coping abilities; this *alarm reaction* represents preparation for resistance. When these reserves are made ready, the body enters a *stage of resistance,* applying various coping mechanisms and typically achieving suitable adaptation. When these reactions are repeated often or when coping is not successful, however, adaptive reserves are depleted and the organism enters a *stage of exhaustion*. At this point resistance declines, physiological breakdown occurs, and the body becomes highly susceptible to disease.

This description of stress is primarily a "pathogen model" in which threats to the organism are physiological and response is based on mobilization to fight off this infection or disease. As the presence of a pathogen is recognized, the endocrine system responds by producing and secreting adrenal corticosteroids. As the invasion is turned away and the threatening substance is overcome, adaptation is achieved and adrenal activity returns to normal levels. When invasion is not overcome, or when threats are repeated after only brief intervals, the organism will remain in a state of resistance until the threat disappears or until adaptive reserves are depleted and the body becomes exhausted.

Selye's work also allowed for psychological activation of the GAS. However, this was not a major part of the theory and made no attempt to discriminate between responses to psychological and physiological stressors. Subsequent research provided support for Selye's view that the stress response was governed by the pituitary–adrenal axis and also provided the impetus for research on psychoendocrine response to stressors. Mason (1968, 1975) has argued that, contrary to Selye's notion of nonspecific stress responses, the relationship between physiological response and emotional arousal or distress is specific, at least as far as patterns of endocrine activity are concerned. Evidence of mediation by the specific demands of different situations and by different coping styles has been reported, as have indications that normal adjustments involved in routine daily life are reflected by hormonal changes (e.g., Rose, Poe, & Mason, 1968). Recently, Mason (1975) has also suggested that psychological threats are necessary for adrenal activity in the stress response, contrary to Selye's position that pathogens are sufficient for pituitary–adrenal arousal.

A somewhat parallel line of research has considered the stress-relevant activity of sympathetic arousal focusing on the adrenal medulla rather than the cortex. Cannon (1928) described emotional stress as a syndrome involving activation of the adrenal medulla and the subsequent release of catecholamines. The emergency function of one of these substances (epinephrine) was one of readying an organism for "fight or flight." When danger was encountered, sympathetic arousal, supported and extended by elevation of circulating epinephrine, prepared the organism to cope.

Frankenhaeuser (1975) and her associates (e.g., Lundberg, 1979) have studied catecholamine response to a variety of physical and psychological stressors and have fairly well established it as a characteristic of stress. Thus, at least two systems appear to be involved in a physiological response during stress. Mason (1975) suggests that other systems may be involved as well, noting the patterning of insulin and other substances during periods of stress.

Although they differ in focus as well as the degree to which psychological factors are viewed as necessarily involved in stress, the biological models of Selye, Cannon, and Mason are similar in an important and basic way. In these views, stress is generated by threatened curtailment of needs central to organismic survival. Most are based on the notion of homeostasis and whether the threatened needs are emotional or molecular. The key to understanding stress is to understand the adjustments the organism makes to maintain positive balance. Despite Mason's important work on psychological factors and Cannon's recognition of emotional factors in stress, it fell largely to psychologists to add detailed consideration of ongoing appraisal, coping, and compensatory defenses to the stress process.

Psychological stress

Increasingly, the impact of psychological variables on stress has been considered. These variables have been incorporated into stress theory as both mediators of physical stressors and as stressors in their own right. Generally, psychological variables have been viewed as instrumental in the onset of stress and are associated with the appraisal of environmental events (e.g., Lazarus, 1966). In some instances, psychological variables mediate response to stressors, as in the case of perceived control (e.g., Glass & Singer, 1972). In other cases, appraisal of events leads directly to stress. Thus, loss of a job or interpretation of the nature of one's daily work may generate stress (e.g., Frankenhaeuser, 1978; Kasl & Cobb, 1970). But the importance of psychological perspectives is only partly reflected in this appraisal process; it also suggests reasons for our heightened susceptibility to stress. We respond not only to dangers or threats that have materialized; we are equally affected by expectations of these events and by symbols of danger experienced previously (Wolf & Goodell, 1968). And it is here that linkages with physiological mechanisms are evident, as psychosocial variables evoke stress responses that may ultimately be more damaging to the organism than the aversive event itself. Psychological stressors may precede the physical event, last longer than the event, and continue to evoke stress after it is past. Indeed, psychologically induced stress may occur in anticipation of physical events that never come to pass. Studies of anticipated crowding, for example, have suggested that people will experience stress when expecting to be crowded, even if the crowding never actually materializes (e.g., Baum & Greenberg, 1975).

Psychological perspectives on stress emphasize the role of interpretation of stressors in the stress response. Response to stressors is determined by the degree to which an event is perceived as threatening, harmful, or challenging (Lazarus, 1966). Internal demands that challenge or surpass one's ability to adapt to them are likely to result in an interpretation of the demands as being stressful. The appraisal of each stressor will depend upon a number of factors, including attitudes toward the stressor, prior experience with it, knowledge of its consequences, and evaluation of its apparent costs. Thus, annoyance caused by transportation noise is mediated by attitudes toward the source of the noise, and response to loss of a job will depend on whether other jobs are available and on the perceived consequences of unemployment. Consistent with more general models of health behavior (e.g., Rosenstock, 1966), response will be mediated by a costs–rewards analysis, the perceived severity of a stressor, and the judged likelihood of the stressor's consequences having an effect on the individual.

A series of studies conducted by Lazarus and his associates provided support for this perspective. In one study (Lazarus, Opton, Norrikos, & Rankin, 1965) subjects were shown a stressful film depicting woodshop accidents such as a worker cutting off a finger or being killed by a wooden plank being driven through his body. Some subjects were told that the events had been staged and that no one was really being hurt, whereas others believed that the events were real but that the film would help improve safety in such settings. A third group of subjects was given no explanation.

Both sets of instructions were effective in reducing arousal during the film, presumably because they allowed appraisal of the film in a less threatening way. These results were similar to those of an earlier study (Speisman, Lazarus, Mordkoff, & Davison, 1964) in which subjects were shown a stress-inducing film depicting primitive initiation rites that included rather unpleasant genital surgery. Subjects saw the film accompanied by one of three soundtracks. One group heard narration emphasizing pain and possible disease consequences (trauma condition), another group heard a script in which the pain and consequences were denied and the participants in the rites were depicted as willing and happy (denial condition), and a third group heard a detached description of the rites from an anthropological perspective (intellectualization condition).

The results showed that stress responses were reduced for subjects in the denial and intellectualization conditions, relative to subjects in the trauma group. The instructions in the second and third conditions allowed subjects to appraise the situation as less threatening, and the instructions provided to trauma subjects emphasized those aspects of the film that were most likely to be seen as threatening.

More recently, Lazarus and his associates (e.g., Coyne & Lazarus, in press; Folkman & Lazarus, in press; Lazarus & Launier, 1978) have considered distinctions among appraisals concerned with anticipated impacts, that is, the degree to which an event is seen as causing disruption or danger in the future. Harm–loss interpretations, on the other hand, are concerned with "damage already sustained." Coyne and Lazarus (in press) point out that these kinds of appraisals "can occur as alternating or concurrent themes as the person appraises and reappraises harm that has occurred and threats to well-being that are apt to result from the harm." Thus, evaluation of air pollution during a prolonged period of unhealthy air quality may be concerned with present danger or subsequent danger or both at any given time. The degree to which either is salient may help to determine the kind of response evoked; temporary avoidance of the pollution, either by staying indoors or leaving town, is more likely when attention is focused on harm or loss issues. Activity in pollution abatement programs or decisions to move to a less polluted area follow from future-oriented appraisals of threat. Concurrent appraisals of threat and harm–loss are likely to result in ameliorative behaviors directed both at reducing immediate risk and at preventing the situation in the future.

Challenge is somewhat different from either of these two appraisals. First, challenge interpretations are characterized by a belief that the stressor can be dealt with effectively. Stressors that are taxing but that can be overcome are more likely to generate challenge appraisals than interpretations involving threat or harm and loss. Second, challenges may be positive or negative: They may be gain experiences as well as losses. Attending a newborn infant is taxing and disruptive but is neither a threat nor a loss. Rather, it is a positively toned challenge: It can be dealt with and is clearly a constructive event.

Third, although most people make all three kinds of appraisals, the tendency toward making challenge versus threat appraisals may be a useful individual differences construct. It is likely that people predisposed to view stressors as a challenge, that is, those who have great confidence in their ability to adapt to disruptive events, will cope differently than those who tend to view events as more threatening. These differences are no doubt linked to self-esteem, motivational states, and other processes, and, if stable, offer potentially useful tools in understanding factors that make people more or less vulnerable to stress.

Finally, it is evident that different situations may make challenge or threat appraisals more or less adaptive. In highly threatening situations, for example, both denial of one's inability to cope and interpretation of the event as challenging can facilitate adaptation (e.g., Gentry, Foster, & Harvey, 1972; Lazarus, 1966). In other situations, selective use of denial and challenge appears more adaptive (Vaillant, 1979). And in other situations, flight in the face of threat may be better than resistance to challenge (e.g., Baum & Valins, 1977).

Lazarus's conceptualizations have proven to be an important contribution to the study of stress. When exposed to potentially stressful situations, people appraise the setting and make judgments about how threatening, harmful, or challenging it is. If a situation is judged to be stressful, *secondary appraisals* are made. No longer concerned with assessment of danger, people turn their attention to the dangers or benefits of different modes of coping with perceived threats. The perception of danger motivates a search for coping responses that will reduce this threat. And, as part of an appraisal process, these interpretations are intimately linked to primary appraisal of the environment.

Coping behavior is therefore an important part of the stress response. Lazarus (1966) proposed that these responses can take manipulative or accommodative forms. They may be *direct action* responses, where the individual tries to directly manipulate or alter his or her relationship to the stressful situation. Thus, people may change the setting, flee, or otherwise remove the physical presence of the stressor. When this is not possible, *palliative* coping may be necessary. Here, the individual accommodates the stressful situation by altering his or her "internal environment." Taking drugs, using alcohol, learning to relax, creating or using psychological defense mechanisms, or engaging in meditation are examples of this kind of coping.

This account of coping appraisals has been extended to include a number of options that may be considered in the face of threat. Secondary appraisals may affect the degree to which an event is perceived as threatening, challenging, or irrelevant (e.g., Lazarus & Launier, 1978). A person who does not view himself or herself as an effective coper – who does not possess extensive coping skills or resources – may be more likely to make threat interpretations. Appraisals of coping alternatives in this case would not yield much hope of overcoming the stressor. Someone with more confidence would be more likely to evaluate it as challenging. And if a person's coping reserves are sufficient, the stressor may not even be challenging, and the person decides it can be dismissed as neither a threat nor a challenge.

The processes involved in these appraisals and the give and take between them are complex and dependent on a number of factors. They can lead to a number of alternative courses of action, each with associated advantages and drawbacks. The degree to which any of these alternatives results is a function of appraisals of individual estimates of threat or challenge and the demands posed by the situation (Baum, Fisher, & Solomon, 1981). As was indicated by initial discussions of coping, response may be directed toward the environment (direct action) or toward the self (palliation). Further, depending upon the nature of primary appraisal, response can be directed at the present or the future. Within these contexts any of several modes of coping may be considered (Lazarus & Launier, 1978).

One of these modes is information seeking. Both in terms of avoiding future difficulties and dealing with present ones, the predictability gained through information can facilitate adaptation. A number of studies have demonstrated the value of such information as it applies to regulation of emotion or of the environment (e.g., Baum et al., 1981; Johnson, 1973; Johnson & Leventhal, 1974; Langer & Saegert, 1977; Paulus & Matthews, 1980). Additionally, information may increase one's sense of control and confidence in coping efficacy, or it may reinforce one's appraisals of the situation (e.g., Janis, 1968). Response to environmental crises, such as extreme temperature or weather, provides some further evidence of the use of this coping mode. In the face of storms, prolonged heat waves, tornadoes, and the like, people seek information from the media or their friends in an attempt to predict and gain some sense of control over the stressor's effects.

When information seeking is blunted, the effects may be negative, especially if other modes of coping are less preferred. During the Three Mile Island emergency, many people sought information about what was occurring, what they could do, how dangerous the situation was, and so on (Baum, Gatchel, Streufert, Baum, Fleming, & Singer, 1980). However, information provided by the Nuclear Regulatory Commission, by the utility operating the reactor, and by other sources was rated by many residents as being confusing, inadequate, contradictory, and often useless (e.g., Flynn, 1979). It is possible that the failure of information seeking to provide any real increment in the predictability of the situation may have exacerbated stress among these residents.

Direct action, as already noted, refers to coping that deals with the stressor directly. Evacuation during the Three Mile Island emergency is one example of this; turning on air conditioning during a heat wave, seeking shelter in the path of a tornado, adding sound insulation to one's home in a noisy neighborhood, or altering the arrangement of space in crowded settings are other examples of such responses. Conversely, some situations may lead people to do nothing – to ride out the storm or let things happen as they may. Such inhibition of action is also a mode of coping with stress and will quite clearly be more or less effective in different settings.

‹   Intrapsychic coping modes are similar to those noted earlier as palliative coping. These responses are directed toward emotional regulation, designed to make people feel better or experience less discomfort. They are accommodative and may include cognitive reappraisal of a stressful situation (e.g., "Being poor isn't so bad," or, "It isn't really that noisy here") or insulation from a stressor through use of defense mechanisms or drugs. At Three Mile Island, intrapsychic coping was marked, probably because other modes were less feasible (many people could not evacuate) or ineffective (e.g., Houts, Miller, Tokuhata, & Ham, 1980).

'   Coping is more likely to be successful when the stressor is one that is familiar, is definite in time and space, and for which the individual has knowledge of the efficacy of previous coping strategies and responses (e.g., McGrath, 1970). Thus, having accurate expectations of what may occur has been related to reduction of crowding stress. Vague, indistinct, or novel stressors may pose the greatest difficulty to an individual. Anxiety about an impending future event or stress generated by indistinct threats may be difficult to reduce because the individual gets no feedback on the effectiveness of his or her coping attempts.

Stress paradigms and levels of study

The descriptions of stress provided by Selye and by Lazarus share commonalities just as they diverge in many ways. Both models indicate a process of coping and adaptation motivated and facilitated by the stress response. Yet, each has been associated with a "tradition" of research that is very different from the other. They view different phases of the process in varying detail, emphasizing or focusing on one or another aspect of stress. Viewing the phases of stress within a framework frequently used by social psychologists enables us to link these traditions.

Research on attitude change has viewed persuasion as a function of at least three levels of study: the source of the persuasive message, the transmission of the message, and the audience or recipient of the message (e.g., Hovland & Janis, 1959). Attitude change can be affected at these three levels: (1) source of the communication (i.e., whether the source is credible, trustworthy, etc.), (2) the way in which the message is transmitted (i.e., characteristics of the media by which the message is presented or structural characteristics of the message itself), and (3) by the characteristics of the person or persons to whom the message is directed. If we think of stress as having source, transmission, and audience "levels" of analysis, the different ways of studying stress may be placed in clearer perspective. Sources of stress (stressors) have been studied by researchers in many disciplines, most notably by psychologists, sociologists, and epidemiologists, whose emphasis is on defining and distinguishing from among the myriad of agents or events that require adaptation. At another level, the appraisal or interpretation of stressors has been studied, primarily by psychologists. Here, the key issue is transmission: Will an event or agent be perceived as threatening? Is it apprehended and comprehended? Finally, the recipient/audience level has been considered, primarily by biologists and psychobiologists. Here, the responses by the organism are crucial, and important variables include those that make an individual more or less vulnerable to stress.

Sources of stress

Lazarus and Cohen (1977) have considered three general classes of stressors. The first, cataclysmic phenomena, refers to sudden, unique, and powerful single events or clusters of related occurrences affecting large numbers of people. Many of these have been studied, including natural disaster (Baker & Chapman, 1962; Sims & Baumann, 1974) and relocation (Fried, 1963; Schulz, 1976). These fairly obvious examples do not represent an exhaustive listing; one could consider the Arab oil embargo of 1973–1974 or the present gasoline shortages as stressors of this magnitude.

A second class of stressors includes those powerful events that challenge adaptive abilities in the same way as cataclysmic events but that affect fewer people. This distinction is important, since affiliative and socially comparative behaviors have been identified as styles of coping with a focused, specific threat (e.g., McGrath, 1970; Schachter, 1959), and social support has been shown to moderate the effect of stress (e.g., Cobb, 1976). In the first category, people were able to share distress with others undergoing the same difficulties. In this case, fewer people are involved, resulting in fewer people with whom to share. These events include response to illness, death, or significant loss (e.g., Greene, 1966; Parkes, 1972; Hackett & Weisman, 1964) or losing one's job (Kasl & Cobb, 1970).

Lazarus and Cohen refer to the third group of stressors as "daily hassles," that is, those stable and repetitive problems encountered in daily life that typically do not present great adaptive difficulty. Many of these are more chronic than the stressors already described, including job dissatisfaction (Kahn & French, 1970; Frankenhaeuser & Gardell, 1976), neighborhood problems (Harburg, Erfrut, Chaperi, Nauenstein, Schull, & Schork, 1973), and commuting (Singer, Lundberg, & Frankenhaeuser, 1978). Crowding, especially that encountered in one's neighborhood, in transportation settings, and in residential buildings, may also be considered to be chronic or often repeated stressors (see Epstein, 1981). In dormitory settings, for example, it is unlikely that a single episode of unwanted contact presents severe adaptive demands. Rather, the cumulation of instances of unwanted contact and loss of control appears to be responsible for stress and withdrawal that have been observed (e.g., Baum & Valins, 1977). Similarly, people can cope with individual episodes of noise even if it is uncontrollable (e.g., Glass & Singer, 1972), but the cumulative effects of chronic exposure to noise appear to be more severe (see S. Cohen, 1980).

These distinctions involve differences on a number of dimensions; some stressors are acute, affect large numbers of people, and require major adaptive responses. Other stressors may be more chronic, but may still tend to be short-term, require more adaptive energy, affect large numbers of people *but on an individual basis*, and do not require great amounts of adaptive energy. They may not even be readily identifiable, as in the case of air pollution (see Evans & Jacobs, 1981). Yet, the chronicity of this last group may result in these stressors' having deceptively severe consequences. Because of regular and prolonged exposure to them, they may not be perceived as severe, but they may require far more adaptive responses *over time* than other stressors. If we think of these background stressors as generally pushing an individual's adaptive abilities toward their limit or committing people to make allocations of resources that are not easily changed, they may gradually reduce an individual's ability to cope with subsequent, acute stressors.

Kiretz and Moos (1974) have proposed other ways of viewing stressors. They consider the magnitude of adjustment required, but they also view the kind of adjustment, perceptions of control, and valence as important mediators of stress. *Kind of adjustment* refers to "the kinds of coping processes, emotions or illnesses they (stressors) generate." For example, some stressors, such as severe weather or the Three Mile Island crisis, are not directly available to change by an individual; one cannot manipulate or change these stressors so as to reduce their effect. Responses to these kinds of stress are more likely to lead to accommodative responses such as staying indoors or leaving the Harrisburg area.

Perceptions of control, or the degree to which a stressor is seen as being under an individual's control, are also important in the appraisal of threat. Cataclysmic events, illness, and the like are not under an individual's control; they are neither predictable nor modifiable by individual action. When control is not perceived as feasible or when a stressor is seen as unpredictable, greater costs will be exacted (e.g., Glass & Singer, 1972). However, this relationship is mediated by variables such as success in controlling the effects of a stressor. When control is available and is used effectively by some people but not by others, stress may be even greater. In the recent gasoline crisis, some people were able to avoid serious consequences by exerting control over the situation; by "shopping around" for service stations with short lines, by reducing their driving, and by modifying habits slightly, they were able to cope fairly successfully with the problems presented. Others, for a variety of reasons, could not exert this kind of control (e.g., they did not have many service stations available, had long commutes, etc.), and their *comparative* failure may have exacerbated the problems they experienced.

Finally, valence is considered an important mediator of stress. Some events are stressors in that they require adaptive response, but they are not *loss* experiences. *Gain* experiences that require coping are more positive and include marriage, the birth of a child, or beginning a new job.

One thing that is apparent in this listing of ways to classify stressors is that some are instrusive, physical, and universally threatening (such as natural disaster), whereas others are more culturally determined, less universal, and more psychosocial in nature. Crowding and spatial invasion, for example, are culture bound in that responses to varying densities and proximities are specific to cultural norms and meanings (e.g., Aiello & Thompson, 1980; Hall, 1966). Similarly, Frankenhaeuser and Gardell (1978) have found that certain aspects of different occupations and work settings, such as the degree of control, responsibility, or redundancy in the job, can evoke stress. These kinds of stressors are clearly more imbedded in the psychological processes involved in appraisal and less universal than such things as earthquakes or floods. The psychosocial medium in which some events are conveyed makes them different and, in some cases, more destructive.

Not surprisingly, these various ways of classifying stressors do not always work. To different degrees, some stressors cut across a number of these distinctions. For example, where does one place the continuing difficulties at Three Mile Island? Is it a cataclysmic event? It was certainly sudden and powerful, but not acute. Problems persist there 2 years and more after the accident. More importantly, it differs from disasters such as tornadoes and hurricanes in that it has never reached a clear point of *most significant impact*. When a storm strikes a community, it does specific damage and requires specific rebuilding after its departure. The most significant impact occurs and is then over, and those affected can go about the task of recovery. There is a specific point at which the "worst" has passed, people can be thankful for what did not happen and can grieve over those losses that did occur. Recovery can proceed as the likelihood of further destruction recedes.

At Three Mile Island, however, this has not been the case. Although the accident and emergency period were significant and acute, it is not clear that people in the area have been able to breathe easily since. Continued fear and stress among many residents suggest that for them, the worst may still be to come. It is not difficult for us to understand why many of these people are not convinced that the brunt of the problems is in the past. In the years since the accident, they have had to contend with perceived threats related to repeated accidental leaks of radioactive gas and water, hearings on the restarting of the undamaged reactor, venting of radioactivity into the atmosphere, proposals to release more than 400,000 gallons of contaminated and treated "accident" water into a river that supplies drinking water, and other incidents that suggest "more to come." Many of the residents with whom we have talked are not confident that the reactor will not experience further difficulties, and some believe that explosions or massive radiation releases are still possible. Thus, residents of the Three Mile Island area experienced an acute accident and emergency period, but perceptions of threat did not go away when these events ended. Chronic concern has plagued many, inhibiting recovery and apparently causing wear and tear on physiological and psychological response systems.

It is therefore important to distinguish between physical and psychological stressors. Clearly, physical agents such as pollution, climate, and temperature have direct effects on us although the relation between such effects and the physical agent may be complex, as in the case of heat stress (cf. Bell, 1981). At the same time, however, stress responses can be evoked by changes and challenges that are experienced in daily life by disruption of one's habits (e.g., by crowding or unpredictable noise) or culturally governed mores, by obstacles and hindrances placed before us through malfunction of social systems, or by deprivation or loss experienced in life. In short, a noxious agent may be anything from a virus to a vicissitude.

Appraisal of stressors

As one would expect of "transmission" variables, factors that mediate interpretation of stress are both environmental and psychological in nature. For example, individuals with a great wealth of resources for coping (e.g., money, friends, material) may be less likely to appraise events as threatening and, as a result, be less affected by the stressor. Thus, the upper middle class resident of a large city may be less likely to experience difficulty as a result of urban stressors than will a poorer resident of the same city or may be less likely to be exposed to these aversive urban conditions at all. Although the availability of resources often provides a buffer between the individual and the stressor, Evans and Jacobs (1981) note that concern about air pollution is positively correlated with socioeconomic status. Since higher SES persons are generally more insulated from many highly visible urban stressors, they may have more freedom to concern themselves with less intrusive ones.

Attitudes toward the sources of stress will also mediate responses; if we believe that a stressor will cause no permanent harm, our response will probably be less extreme than if its danger carries the threat of lasting harm. At a more psychological level, perceptions of control, social support, and other characteristics of the person exposed to the stressor will affect the appraisal of different stressors. Although an exhaustive review of these mediating factors will not be attempted here, we will selectively consider some of the variables that affect the transmission of stress and, in effect, link the source with the response by the recipient.

Attitudes toward stressors. Attitudes and beliefs about stressors are important filters in the perception and appraisal of stressors. In early studies of psychological stress, for example, Lazarus and his colleagues (e.g., Lazarus et al., 1965; Speisman et al., 1964) were able to affect the appraisal of stressful stimuli by manipulating information that caused subjects to have different beliefs about what they were viewing. Similarly, opinions about the limitations fostered by stressors and the consequences of demands they impose will mediate response. By briefly viewing the role of attitudes and beliefs in response to some stressors, this may be made clearer.

High levels of noise are generally regarded as potent environmental stressors (e.g., S. Cohen, 1980; Glass & Singer, 1972). Although noise levels in areas surrounding airports are highly correlated with noise annoyance reported by residents of these areas and exposure to airport noise has been shown to have deleterious effects on children (e.g., Cohen, Krantz, Evans, & Stokols, 1980), the direct relationship between noise and annoyance is generally not strong (Wilson, 1963). Tracor (1971) found that individual annoyance ratings were more highly correlated with several attitudinal measures than they were with various indexes of physical exposure to noise. Moreover, in his review of the literature, Davis (1975) notes that noise levels alone can only explain between one-tenth and one-third of the variability in individual annoyance. Several studies suggest that the addition of attitudinal measures increases the predictability of annoyance to between 58% and 65% (Tracor, Inc., 1971; Leonard & Borsky, 1973).

Manipulation of people's attitudes toward aircraft noise has also been shown to affect annoyance (e.g., Cederlöf, Honsson, & Sorenson, 1967). When given a positive induction about a nearby Air Force base, residents were significantly less likely to report that they were greatly inconvenienced by aircraft noise. Similarly, Jonsson and Sorenson (1967) gave subjects either a positive or a negative induction treatment by telling them that local officials were either very concerned about airport noise or that they did not consider it a problem. Manipulated attitudes toward the source again influenced evaluation of the stressor: Subjects in the positive induction condition were less likely to report that the noise could be a "great disturbance."

Fear of nearby airplane crashes seems to be the single most powerful predictor of individual annoyance in response to airport noise (Tracor, Inc., 1971). In two different samples, Leonard and Borsky (1973) found correlations between fear and annoyance of + .72 and + .62. Two surveys conducted among residents near Heathrow Airport indicated that a sizable percentage perceived a danger from nearby crashes: 42% in 1961 (Wilson, 1963) and 38% in 1967 (MIL Research, 1971). It is interesting to note that fear decreased during a time period in which there was a substantial increase in air traffic. Although the authors hypothesized that fear decreased as a result of the increase in number of respondents who had flown in commercial aircraft, it is possible that the increased exposure of residents to air traffic without accidents or crashes during the interim period was also an important factor in producing some decrease in levels of fear. Prior experience has been shown to be a determinant of response to a stressor as each subsequent episode either exacerbates stress (e.g., Glass & Singer, 1972) or facilitates coping and adaptation (Baum, Fisher, & Solomon, 1981). Such adaptation may sometimes be physiological as well as psychological. Bell (1980) discusses the consequences of prolonged exposure to heat, noting that the performance of acclimatized subjects is less affected than that of unacclimatized subjects.

An analogy may be drawn to residents of Richland, Washington, site of the oldest U.S. atomic facility, the Hanford Project, which has been in operation since 1945. Although they live on the edges of a 570-square mile nuclear park that houses 75% of the radioactive wastes in the United States, the residents of Richland express great feelings of confidence and safety (Kirk & Campbell, 1979). Richland is a one-industry town: the nuclear industry. The economic well-being of the town is inextricably linked with the Hanford Project, and this is probably the strongest determinant of the residents' overwhelmingly pro-nuclear opinions and the relative absence of stress due to the proximity of such an extensive nuclear reservation. Consistent with this, Evans and Jacobs (1981) report that employees of industries identified as major polluters are generally less concerned than most other people about the consequences of air pollution.

Perception of risk and danger. The perception of risks associated with a stressor and the nature of the threats or dangers posed by it will also mediate appraisal of the stressor. Assessment of risk appears to be influenced by certain biases in perception that may be related to cognitive limitations in information processing. Simon (1957) has considered a theory of "bounded rationality," asserting that decision makers must necessarily construct simplified models of the world to be able to deal with all of it. These models are inevitably influenced by the attitudes and characteristics of the individuals who have constructed them. They are not veridical with objective reality, and they rest upon general inferential rules, guidelines, or heuristics that simplify difficult mental calculations (e.g., Taylor & Fiske, 1978).

In situations in which evidence of a certain degree of risk or danger is not immediately available, individuals are likely to use heuristics to estimate the degree of danger. The need for certainty and confidence often leads to biases in judgment. Under some conditions, when people are able to make predictions about events (i.e., they have enough information to do so), some degree of uncertainty is desirable. In such instances, absolute certainty makes prediction obvious, meaningless, and seemingly trivial (e.g., Kaplan, 1978). However, uncertainty is aversive when predictions cannot be made with any expected accuracy, and in order to reach a decision and reduce uncertainty, people may give undue weight to dramatic instances or overestimate the reliability of data from small samples (e.g., Tversky & Kahneman, 1971, 1974). The result of such bias is often a deficit in probabilistic judgments. Thus, when Hynes and Vanmarcke (1976) asked geotechnical engineers to specify upper and lower limits for the height at which an embankment would cause a clay foundation to collapse, not one of the experts' estimates successfully enclosed the true failure height. Biases in judgment made in the absence of adequate information often lead to decisions made primarily to reduce uncertainty. Information may be distorted or simply denied, as among flood victims (Kates, 1962), some of whom denied that their area might be flooded again by believing that the flood had been a freak occurrence or by placing great emphasis on new forms of flood control.

Another heuristic relevant to risk perception is availability. People generally believe an event is more likely to occur if they can imagine it or recall examples of it. Although the availability heuristic may be useful in evaluating events that occur frequently, its application to rare events can lead to distortions in judgment. The availability bias is especially relevant to stress that may or may not accompany proximity to nuclear power plants such as Three Mile Island. Atomic bombs and the Cold War, books and movies depicting nuclear holocaust, and the anti-nuclear portion of the American public have all served to create vivid images of nuclear disaster in our minds. It has been noted that attempts to impress the public with the low probability of a reactor accident may have the reverse effect (Slovic, Lichtenstein, & Fischhoff, 1979). While a speaker may be discussing the improbability of a number of different factors that could result in a nuclear accident, the audience may be shocked by the realization that so many things could go wrong. A more mundane instance is reflected by the relatively large amounts of money that public agencies spend for aircraft safety compared to auto safety – in effect implying that a life lost in a dramatic plane crash is more valuable than one lost in a commonplace auto wreck. Other research findings support the notion that dramatic threats may be overestimated as to real danger potential and may therefore evoke stress reactions of greater magnitude (Slovic et al., 1979). Perceived risk appears to depend, in part, on how dramatic the events in question are, and response to these events seems to be based on potential for danger rather than likelihood of threat. Thus, the steady but largely unnoticed pollution of the atmosphere by industries, transportation, heating systems, and the like evokes a lower level response than it should; although the likelihood of suffering some effect of pollution is high for most people, the consequences are neither dramatic nor even apparent (cf. Evans & Jacobs, 1981). The potential danger of air pollution is probably judged to be low by many people, even though the likelihood of being affected by pollution is fairly high. Perception of risk, attitudes, and other influences on the appraisal of a stressor can help to determine whether or not an event is seen as threatening, the extent of arousal and intensity of coping, and the degree of concern and attention given to the event.

Dispositional variables. Factors related to individuals' prior experiences and predispositions are also important in mediating the effects of stressors. The existence of a "high-stress" or "high-risk" personality, for example, has been indicated by a number of studies. Grinker and Spiegel (1945) noted that only a relatively small number of air combat crews serving during World War II ever developed serious or diagnosable stress-related ailments. Some of the airmen studied had previously established neuroses that made them more susceptible to the stress of battle. This vulnerability notion has been used often in more recent research, providing an explanation for selective onset of schizophrenia (e.g., Zubin, 1976), illness (Kobasa, 1979), and other stress-related disturbances (e.g., Kasl & Cobb; 1970, 1976). One index of vulnerability in crowded situations is a person's preferences and needs with regard to interindividual distancing. People who prefer large amounts of space between themselves and others are more susceptible to the effects of spatial density than are those who can get along with less space (e.g., Aiello & Thompson, 1980).

Coping styles or behavior patterns have also been identified, and these appear to affect the ways in which events are appraised, as well as which types of coping are involved. Work on a number of these dimensions, such as repression–sensitization, arousal seeking, screening and denial, has indicated that people differing along them may interpret situations differently (e.g., Byrne, 1964; Janis, 1958; Mehrabian, 1977; Zuckerman, 1971). A study by Baum, Calesnick, Davis, and Gatchel (in press), for example, suggests that individuals who cope with overload by screening and setting priorities on demands are less susceptible to the effects of social density than are people who do not cope in this way.

Glass (1976) has described a particularly vivid instance of this kind of predisposition. Individuals who manifest a type A behavior pattern respond to stress as if it were control threatening and interpret any threats to control as stressful. Their appraisal of events is particularly sensitive to anything that might reduce their control over a situation. The time urgency, competitiveness, and hostility that accompany this response, together with the enhanced likelihood of experiencing stress and physiological concomitants of that stress, make type A's more at risk for coronary heart disease (Glass, 1976). It is tempting to speculate that this behavior pattern might make people more reactive and susceptible to stressors such as crowding or noise, of which loss of control may be a direct antecedent or cause (e.g., Baron & Rodin, 1978; Baum & Valins, 1979; Cohen, 1980).

Control. Perceived control is a powerful mediator of stress, providing a sense of being able to cope effectively, predict events, and determine what will happen. Unfortunately, data on the effects of perceived control are not available for all potential stressors. For example, little research has been done on the relationship between control and heat stress (Bell, 1980); however, the relationship between control and other stressors has been studied extensively. Glass and Singer (1972) considered the effects of perceived controllability in their studies of stress due to noise and found that predictable or controllable noise exacted smaller costs in adaptation. The perception that the noise might be accurately anticipated or even turned off if so desired facilitated adaptation with minimal aftereffects. Subsequently, Sherrod (1974) found the same relationship for stress due to crowding, and Rodin, Solomon, and Metcalf (1978) found that providing control reduced crowding stress (see Cohen, 1980; Epstein, 1981). The degree to which control operates by influencing appraisal of the stressor is more speculation than fact, however.

A study of Staub, Tursky, and Schwartz (1971) bears on this point. Subjects who were given perceived control over shocks reported less discomfort than did subjects who did not "control" the intensity or administration of the shock. This was so even though all subjects actually received the same number and intensity of shocks. The perception of control seemed to affect perception of the stressor used in that study.

Somewhat more direct evidence of control influencing appraisal of stressors comes from the growing literature on cognitive control. By providing subjects with information about a stressor prior to their exposure to it, researchers have been able to reduce the threat appraisal made when the stressor is experienced. Some studies have considered medical settings and have found that the stress of surgery or of unusual medical procedures can be reduced by providing patients with accurate expectations of what they will feel (e.g., Johnson, 1973; Johnson & Leventhal, 1974). By giving normative information about sensations to patients, researchers have provided them with "road maps" telling them what they should experience. As a result, when these sensations are experienced they will not be appraised as abnormal or frightening. Other studies have found that accurate expectations also reduce crowding stress (Langer & Saegert, 1977; Baum, Fisher, & Solomon, 1981). Inaccurate or violated expectations of crowding result in some negative response, but this appears to be quickly remedied when people realize what has happened and form new expectations (Greenberg & Baum, 1979).

On a broader level, perceived control may also be a very important prerequisite for meaningful social change. Evans and Jacobs (1981) discuss the relationship between public apathy toward air pollution abatement and the belief that individuals have little or no control over such pollution. If most of the population believe that a given stressor is beyond their control, they will be less likely to attempt ameliorative actions.

The stress response

Despite the sometimes overwhelming nature of stressors or the likelihood that they will be appraised as threatening, stress cannot be defined without reference to the response made by the organism. These physiological, cognitive, and social reactions or effects are therefore an important aspect of the stressor–stress process.

The most common measures of stress allow inferences about emotional states by assessing physiological reactivity. This has been done directly, by measuring levels of catecholamines and corticosteroids in the blood urine (e.g., Frankenhaeuser, 1975) and indirectly, by measuring systemic reactions caused by increased levels of these hormones (e.g., Ax, 1953). Thus, cardiovascular reactivity (e.g., heart rate, blood pressure), muscle potential changes, and skin conductance measures have also been used to show the effects of stress. At this level the stress response seems to be fairly nonspecific (Selye, 1976). That is, physiological arousal and related somatic changes are similar for most stressors, although Mason (1975) and others have made a strong case for the patterning of endocrine responses to different stressors. Some of the responses to psychological stress are virtually indistinguishable from those evoked by direct assault on body tissue. Recalling Selye's three-stage process, it is clear that physiological stress results in heightened secretion of adrenal steroids during the alarm reaction followed by a decline in reactivity through resistance and exhaustion. While corticosteroid secretion may be a more specific response to certain stressors (e.g., Mason, 1975), response to stress typically conforms to this pattern. Research has associated emotional distress with these same patterns of arousal (e.g., Euler, 1964; Konzett, 1975). Further, challenge, loss of control or predictability, and psychosocial stressors have been linked to increased adrenal activity (Frankenhaeuser, 1978; Glass, 1976; Konzett, Hortnagel, Hortnagel, & Winkler, 1971). Overstimulation and understimulation, defined as an overload of task and prolonged work on monotonous tasks, respectively, have also been associated with negative affect and increased secretion of epinephrine and norepinephrine (Frankenhaeuser, Nordheden, Myrsten, & Post, 1971).

These somatic consequences of stress are important for a number of reasons. First, increased catecholamine and corticosteroid secretion is associated with a wide range of other physiological responses, such as the aforementioned changes in heart rate, blood pressure, breathing, muscle potential, and other autonomic functions. Prolonged or sudden elevation of circulating catecholamines may damage body tissue, as is suggested for the pathogenesis of atherosclerosis. Catecholamines also appear to affect cognitive and emotional functioning, and elevated levels of epinephrine or norepinephrine in the blood may affect our mood and behavior.

In order to view this link more fully, it is necessary to reconsider Cannon's pioneering work on the "emergency function" of catecholamines. Cannon (1928, 1931) suggested that epinephrine has a salutary effect on adaptation; by arousing the organism, epinephrine provides a biological advantage to the organism, enabling it to respond more rapidly to danger. Thus, stress-related increases in catecholamines may facilitate adaptive behavior. In fact, studies have shown superior performance on tasks following epinephrine infusion (Frankenhaeuser, Järpe, & Mattell, 1961) and among people with higher catecholamine output in the face of challenge (e.g., Frankenhaeuser, 1971). However, arousal has also been associated with impaired performance on complex tasks (cf. Evans, 1978).

Although there may be cognitive benefits of stress, it is also evident that the simple "fight or flight" model derivable from Cannon's work is inadequate for predicting response to danger in our complex society. Aside from the "wear and tear" on our bodies generated by repeated or prolonged stress, a number of less desirable outcomes are likely when stress does not readily abate. Most of the research that finds support for facilitating aspects of stress has considered acute situations in which adjustment leads to a decrease in stress (e.g., Frankenhaeuser, 1971; Frankenhaeuser et al., 1961). The consequences of unabated stress or repeated exposure to stress as in the case of background stressors have only recently come under study. Among these consequences are decrements in ability to cope with subsequent stress, aftereffects, and, in some cases, physiological dysfunction, tissue damage, or death.

Thus, physiological responses to stress may be both specific and nonspecific and may be chronic or acute. Those responses that are short-lived, either because adaptation is achieved or because the stressor was brief, resemble Cannon's mobilization response. When frightened by a loud noise or exposed to a highly threatening but rapidly unfolding situation (e.g., we see a car heading right for us at high speed, and it speeds by, just missing us), the organism is alerted to the danger and readies itself to respond. However, when stress responses are repeated or prolonged, the alarm reaction no longer functions. If adaptation is not achieved, prolonged arousal can lead to tissue damage and diseases of exhaustion (Selye, 1956).

As we have already noted, stress can cause cognitive deficits as well as improved performance. Cognitive deficits may in turn be caused by behavioral strategies that are used for coping; for instance, the person exposed to loud noise may "tune out" or narrow his or her field of attention (e.g., Cohen, 1978; Deutsch, 1964). At this level, response may become more specific to the stressor being experienced. Behavioral aspects of the stress response may often reflect the specific causes of discomfort as the organism copes with the stressor.

To this point, most aspects of the stress response are symptoms or indicators of a response rather than consequences or end products. When an organism experiences stress, it responds. Part of this reaction is physiological, as sympathetic arousal prepares the organism for further response and increased secretion of corticosteroids facilitates use of bodily stores of energy. Part of it is psychological, as continuing appraisal of situational variables guides coping and, in some cases, directly alters perceptions of the situation. And part of this response is coping itself. In other words, the stress response is exactly that – a reaction to appraisals of stress.

When stress is chronic or repeated, however, a different kind of "effect" becomes relevant, an effect that is not part of the stress response but rather is a *consequence* of it. Chronic stress exerts wear and tear on the many organ systems involved in response, and damage, dysfunction, and/or disease may occur as stress continues. Gradual weakening of the organism as it approaches exhaustion thus may have negative consequences for it. By the same token, perpetual use of coping strategies that are adaptive in the face of stress may become maladaptive when these strategies are stereotypically applied to other aspects of one's surroundings. Psychological and physiological deficits may appear as a consequence of prolonged stress response.

Coping behavior seems to be directly related to characteristics of the source of stress. People may respond to crowding caused by a surfeit of people by withdrawing and avoiding social contacts whereas they may respond to crowding caused by inadequate amounts of space by becoming aggressive (e.g., Baum & Koman, 1976). By the same token, they may respond to job loss actively if the loss was caused by a lack of effort or ability, or may become helpless under certain conditions (e.g., Abramson, Seligman, & Teasdale, 1978). Coping with victimization appears to be specific to different levels of self-blame (e.g., Bulman & Wortman, 1977), and the type of strategy taken also seems to be related to the kind of problems confronted during exposure to a stressor.

Aftereffects, on the other hand, are not always specific to certain stressors. Defined as consequences that are experienced after exposure to a stressor has terminated, these effects fit into Selye's (1976) notion of limited adaptive energy. As exposure to stress increases, the adaptive reserves are depleted, causing aftereffects and reductions of subsequent coping ability. Evidence for the existence of poststressor effects comes from a number of sources, including research on the effects of noise (e.g., Glass & Singer, 1972; Rotton, Olszewski, Charleton, & Soler, 1978; Sherrod & Downs, 1974; Sherrod, Hage, Halpern, & Moore, 1977), crowding (Sherrod, 1974; Evans, 1979), and electric shock (Glass, Singer, Leonard, Krantz, Cohen, & Cummings, 1973). However, explanations for these effects are not as clear.

Aftereffects that have been associated with stress include decreases in cognitive functioning and reduced tolerance for frustration, aggressiveness, helplessness, decreased sensitivity to others, and withdrawal (Cohen, 1980). They also seem to be sensitive to perception of control with fewer aftereffects following experiences in which participants felt that they had control (Cohen, 1980). However, evidence for aftereffects as costs of the adaptive process is equivocal, although consideration of effort expended during adaptation may better reflect this relationship. In addition to psychic costs, aftereffects may represent persistent coping responses (Baum & Valins, 1979), the effects of restricted cue utilization or narrowing of attention (Cohen, 1978; Easterbrook, 1959), or symptoms of learned helplessness (Baum, Aiello, & Calesnick, 1978; Glass & Singer, 1972; Rodin, 1976; Rodin & Baum, 1978).

Perhaps most important among aftereffects is the simple effect stress seems to have on ability to adapt in the future. Calhoun's (1970) discussions of crowding included "refractory periods" during which organisms recover from interactions with others, and several studies have suggested that repeated or prolonged exposure to stress can reduce one's ability to cope. Support for this position has also come from studies of adjustment to life change (e.g., Dohrenwend & Dohrenwend, 1974; Holmes & Rahe, 1967). This work has suggested that there are physiological and psychological costs associated with adaptation, especially when events that require adjustment or adaptation are clustered together in time. When people must adapt to a number of changes of varying magnitude, either serially or at once, ease and success of adjustment decrease and adaptation becomes increasingly difficult. If the amount of adjustment required is large enough, it may render the individual unable to cope and will lead to severe consequences.

Illness and death are clear examples of the most severe consequences of stress. Again, the psychosocial determinants of this stress are important. The interaction of people has been viewed as an important aspect of the effects of population density. Unwanted interaction and inability to regulate contact have been implicated as causes of behavioral and physiological dysfunction among humans and animal populations (e.g., Baum & Valins, 1977; Calhoun, 1962, 1970; Christian, 1963). Population density has also been associated with health in a number of settings (see Epstein, 1981). In one study, stress associated with population density appeared to contribute to death rates (Paulus, McCain, & Cox, 1978).

Studies of stress and illness also provide evidence of negative effects of stress. Traditionally, illness has been viewed as a biological phenomenon, the result of specific physiological dysfunction or invasion by some foreign substance. However, there appear to be diseases that do not fit within a strict biomedical model. Diseases of "life-style," such as heart disease, seem to be related to patterns of coping. Hypertension, heart disease, and the like are not contagious; they do not seem to be caused by germs, microbes, or other simple infectious mechanisms. Rather, they develop over a person's life and are contributed to by a number of factors, including diet, working habits, whether or not the person smokes, and how he or she responds to stress.

Research on the relationships between stress and illness has been conducted in several settings and at different levels. Early research, for example, considered the stress of the bombings of London beginning in 1940 during World War II (e.g., Stewart & Winser, 1942), and stress associated with the German concentration camps also has been studied. Many survivors of these brutalities showed relatively permanent adjustment problems, elevated blood pressures during initial exposure and greater physical illness later, and a greater incidence of premature or sudden death than people their age who were not confined (Cohen, 1953).

More recent studies (Eliot & Buell, 1979; Reynolds, 1974; Warheit, 1974) reveal another example of stress-related illness and death. Research conducted at the space center at Cape Kennedy during the last years of this country's Apollo program considered base employees who monitored moon missions from the ground. These workers, in addition to having high-pressure jobs, were also exposed to a rather stressful paradox. Their goal was to put men on the moon, a highly rewarding end in and of itself. But they knew that once a successful mission was completed, the program would be cut back and eventually discontinued. Thus, these workers were pushed to do difficult jobs so that the United States could land men on the moon, with the ultimate payoff being unemployment. Increased rates of alcoholism and divorce were observed as pressure to complete the mission increased. More seriously, there was a spontaneous increase in sudden deaths among the relatively young workers. These deaths, presumably caused by heart failure, were nearly 50% more frequent than the average for that age group. The number of sudden deaths peaked as the space program was being phased out and, as Eliot and Buell (1979) note, "was most notable during the year when space employees were fired more often than rockets."

As mentioned earlier, there may exist a stress-prone personality that renders some people more susceptible to the consequences of stress. In the space program studies, most workers did not die, but were able to cope with the stress they experienced without such a dramatic toll. Kasl and Cobb's (1970) research on stress associated with job loss also found that only some subjects became ill, but a greater proportion were affected than one would expect based on averages for the age groups studied. Following loss of job, some subjects showed an increase in blood pressure, ulcers, and swollen joints. Some evidence of incipient diabetes and atherosclerosis was also found in blood samples of men who recently had lost their jobs.

Although these and other studies may have methodological weaknesses that have led to some questioning of these findings, the evidence does suggest some linkages between stress and physical illness. Environmental events or interpretations of them that lead to perceptions of threat or danger can generate stress responses, and prolonged exposure to such stimuli can result in physiological dysfunction or death. However, the link between stress and illness is still, for the most part, unexplained. Theories of elevated levels of circulating catecholamines may explain some cases of stress-related disorders. More likely, these theories will yield to new ones that consider additional stress-related changes (e.g., fluctuations in circulating levels of steroids) in explaining the etiology of some disease states. By considering the progression from source, transmission, and impact of stress, the potential relationships between environmental stressor variables and "effects" – illness, arousal, performance deficits, and the like – are made more apparent.

This way of organizing research on stress also clarifies appropriate strategies for determining how to study specific questions of interest. Jenkins (1979) has discussed some of the problems with the traditional two-variable (stressor–response) view of stress. In the same way that stimulus response models of behavior that include organismic variables (S-O-R) provide more complex perspectives on behavior than do simple stimulus response (S–R) perspectives, the inclusion of an adaptive capacity (Jenkins, 1979), appraisal (Lazarus, 1966), or transmission variable facilitates a more complete understanding of stress. As noted, one persistent and, for the most part, unanswered question has been why some people are susceptible to stress-related disorders and others are not. The answers to this question, we believe, may be most profitably explored by considering transmission variables. For example, prior experience may be an important factor that can be viewed as both (1) providing coping resources for future encounters with the stressor, and (2) influencing the perception and appraisal of that stressor. In general, coping resources such as skills, social support, and material, as well as appraisal variables, cultural context, and dispositional characteristics, may be responsible for different responses to identical stressors. Further investigation of such variables would delineate the relationship between characteristics of stressors and variations in response through examination of the organism's interpretations of external and internal events.

Implications for study

Our emphasis on a unified, dynamic, whole-body response has important implications for the study of stress. As we have argued elsewhere (Baum, Grunberg, & Singer, 1982), stress is best understood by simultaneously considering a number of responses at several different levels. Subjective and psychological aspects of stress, when considered with behavioral and physiological responses, become more meaningful. For example, in our research at Three Mile Island, correlations among biochemical, behavioral, and psychological measures of stress were usually significant, showing moderate degrees of association among them. Thus, those aspects of stress measured by proofreading ability, symptom reporting, threat perception, and urinary catecholamine levels appear to be part of the response pattern demonstrated by area residents. The modest level of correlations suggests that these aspects of response are overlapping but not identical and further highlights the complexity of the stress response.

Given these complexities, we must expect that different investigators may look at different aspects and combinations of these variables as their theories and predilections move them. Several points can be emphasized, however. First, the three components of stress – source variables, transmission, and response – are interactive. So, for example, recipients can modify a stressor directly (e.g., they can turn off a noise or leave a densely populated room), or they can reappraise the nature of the stressor, deciding that although dense with people, the room is neither noisy nor crowded. Second, some stressors, such as extremely high temperature, may override the recipient's use of defense mechanisms and may produce debilitating reactions despite resistance. Third, appraisal and coping mechanisms may span periods of time longer than just the application of the stressor; evaluation processes may begin well in advance, may be affected by the recipient's personal history, and may persist to influence evaluation of future stressors. Fourth, the recipient has several potential reactions to stress. Two of these, the pituitary–adrenocortical reaction and sympathetic–adrenomedullary reaction, are moderately well researched. The General Adaptation Syndrome (Selye, 1956) may include both of these reactions, as well as an unspecified number of other ones. Fifth, although many stresses are triggered by a noxious agent, it is not always possible to identify such an agent or even to specify the circumstances under which such an agent or pathogen is present. Indeed, several types of anxiety may be defined as a source of psychological stress in which no apparent agent is present.

Conclusion

The environment is the source of a number of stressors that initiate a variety of reactions. Some of these reactions are physiological and others are psychological. They range from endocrine secretion to complicated appraisals and evaluations of the sources. Transmission events such as regularity and control intervene between the source and the recipient. Few investigators attempt to study all aspects of the process simultaneously, and still fewer do so successfully. Yet many studies, which on the surface are dissimilar, can be fundamentally related to the same underlying model. We have attempted in this discussion to make those relationships explicit, at least for those studies conventionally considered to be environmental.

References

Abramson, L. Y., Seligman, M., & Teasdale, J. Learned helplessness in humans: Critique and reformulation. *Journal of Abnormal Psychology*, 1978, *87*, 49–74.

Aiello, J. R., & Thompson, D. Personal space, crowding, and spatial behavior in a cultural context. In I. Altman, A. Rappoport, & J. Wohlwill (Eds.), *Human behavior and environment* (Vol. 4). New York: Plenum, 1980.

Ax, A. R. The physiological differentiation between fear and anger in humans. *Psychosomatic Medicine*, 1953, *15*, 433–442.

Baker, G. W., & Chapman, D. W. (Eds.) *Man and society in disaster*. New York: Basic Books, 1962.

Baron, R., & Rodin, J. Personal control as a mediator of crowding. In A. Baum, J. E. Singer, & S. Valins (Eds.), *Advances in environmental psychology (Vol. 1): The urban environment*. Hillsdale, N.J.: Erlbaum, 1978.

Baum, A., Aiello, J. R., & Calesnick, L. E. Crowding and personal control: Social density and the development of learned helplessness. *Journal of Personality and Social Psychology*, 1978, *36*(9), 1000–1011.

Baum, A., Calesnick, L. E., Davis, G. E., & Gatchel, R. J. Individual differences in coping with crowding: Stimulus screening and social overload. *Journal of Personality and Social Psychology*, in press.

Baum, A., Fisher, J. D., & Solomon, S. Type of information, familiarity, and the reduction of crowding stress. *Journal of Personality and Social Psychology*, 1981, *40*, 11–23.

Baum, A., Gatchel, R., Streufert, S., Baum, C. S., Fleming, R., & Singer, J. E. *Psychological stress for alternatives of decontamination of TMI-2 reactor building atmosphere.* Washington, D.C.: U. S. Nuclear Regulatory Commission (NUREG/CR-1584), 1980.

Baum, A., & Greenberg, C. I. Waiting for a crowd: The behavioral and perceptual effects of anticipated crowding. *Journal of Personality and Social Psychology*, 1975, *32*(4), 671–679.

Baum, A., Grunberg, N. E., & Singer, J. E. *The use of psychological and neuroendocrinological measurements in the study of stress.* Unpublished manuscript, 1982.

Baum, A., & Koman, S. Differential response to anticipated crowding: Psychological effects of social and spatial density. *Journal of Personality and Social Psychology*, 1976, *34*, 526–536.

Baum, A., & Valins, S. *Architecture and social behavior: Psychological studies of social density.* Hillsdale, N.J.: Erlbaum, 1977.

Baum, A., & Valins, S. Architectural mediation of residential density and control: Crowding and the regulation of social contact. In L. Berkowitz (Ed.), *Advances in experimental social psychology* (Vol. 12). New York: Academic Press, 1979.

Bell, P. A. Physiological, comfort, performance, and social effects of heat stress. *Journal of Social Issues*, 1981, *37*, 71–94.

Bulman, R., & Wortman, C. B. Attributions of blame and coping in the "real world": Severe accident victims react to their lot. *Journal of Personality and Social Psychology*, 1977, *35*, 351–363.

Byrne, D. Repression-sensitization as a dimension of personality. In B. Mayer (Ed.), *Progress in experimental personality research* (Vol. 1). New York: Academic Press, 1964.

Calhoun, J. B. Population density and social pathology. *Scientific American*, 1962, *206*(2), 139–150.

Calhoun, J. B. Space and the strategy of life. *Ekistics*, 1970, *29*, 425–437.

Cannon, W. B. Neural organization for emotional expression. In M. L. Reymert (Ed.), *Feelings and emotions: The Wittenberg Symposium.* Worcester, Mass.: Clark University Press, 1928.

Cannon, W. B. Studies on the conditions of activity in the endocrine organs. XXVII. Evidence that the medulliadrenal secretion is not continuous. *American Journal of Physiology*, 1931, *98*, 447–452.

Cederlöf, R., Honsson, E., & Sorenson, S. On the influence of attitudes toward the source of annoyance reactions to noise: A field experiment. *Nordisk Hygiensk Tidskrift*, 1967, *48*, 46–55.

Christian, J. The pathology of overpopulation. *Military Medicine*, 1963, *128*, 571–603.

Cobb, S. Social support as a moderator of life stress. *Psychosomatic Medicine*, 1976, *38*(5), 300–314.

Cohen, E. A. *Human behavior in the concentration camp.* New York: Norton, 1953.

Cohen, S. Environmental load and the allocation of attention. In A. Baum, J. E. Singer, & S. Valins (Eds.), *Advances in environmental psychology* (Vol. 1). Hillsdale, N.J.: Erlbaum, 1978.

Cohen, S. Aftereffects of stress on human performance and social behavior: A review of research and theory. *Psychological Bulletin*, 1980, *87*, 578–604.

Cohen, S., Evans, G. W., Krantz, D., & Stokols, D. Physiological, motivational and cognitive effects of aircraft noise on children: Moving from the laboratory to the field. *American Psychologist*, 1980, *35*(3), 231–243.

Cohen, S., Krantz, D. S., Evans, G. W., & Stokols, D. Community noise and children, motivational and physiological effects. In J. V. Tobias (Ed.), *Proceedings of the Third International Congress on Noise as a Health Problem*. Washington, D.C.: American Speech and Hearing Association, 1979.

Cohen, S., & Weinstein, N. Nonauditory effects of noise on behavior and health. *Journal of Social Issues*, 1981, *37*(1), 36–70.

Coyne, J. C., & Lazarus, R. S. Cognition, stress, and coping: A transactional perspective. In I. L. Kutash & L. B. Schlesinger (Eds.), *Pressure point: Perspectives on stress and anxiety*. San Francisco: Jossey-Bass, in press.

Davis, G. E. *Attitudinal mediation of annoyance to transportation noise*. Unpublished manuscript, 1975.

Deutsch, C. P. Auditory discrimination and learning: Social factors. *The Merrill-Palmer Quarterly of Behavior and Development*, 1964, *10*, 277–296.

Dohrenwend, B. S., & Dohrenwend, B. P. (Eds.) *Stressful life events: Their nature and effects*. New York: Wiley, 1974.

Easterbrook, J. A. The effects of emotion on cue-utilization and the organization of behavior. *Psychological Review*, 1959, *66*, 183–201.

Eliot, R., & Buell, J. *Environmental and behavioral influences in the major cardiovascular disorders*. Presented at the Annual Meeting of the Academy of Behavioral Medicine Research, Snowbird, Utah, 1979.

Epstein, Y. Crowding stress and human behavior. *Journal of Social Issues*, 1981, *37*(1), 126–144.

Euler, U. S. von. Quantitation of stress by catecholamine analysis. *Clinical Pharmacological Therapy*, 1964, *5*, 398–404.

Evans, G. W. Human spatial behavior: The arousal model. In A. Baum & Y. M. Epstein (Eds.), *Human response to crowding*. Hillsdale, N.J.: Erlbaum, 1978.

Evans, G. W. Crowding and human performance. *Journal of Applied Social Psychology*, 1979, *9*, 27–46.

Evans, G. W. Introduction. *Journal of Social Issues*, 1981, *37*(1), 1–3.

Evans, G. W., & Jacobs, S. V. Air pollution and human behavior. *Journal of Social Issues*, 1981, *37*(1), 95–125.

Flynn, C. B. *Three Mile Island telephone survey: Preliminary report on procedures and findings*. U. S. Nuclear Regulatory Commission (NUREG/CR-1093), 1979.

Folkman, S., & Lazarus, R. An analysis of coping in a middle-aged community sample. *Journal of Health and Social Behavior*, 1980, *21*, 219–239.

Frankenhaeuser, M. Behavior and circulating catecholamines. *Brain Research*, 1971, *31*, 241–262.

Frankenhaeuser, M. Experimental approaches to the study of catecholamines and emotion. In L. Levi (Ed.), *Emotions: Their parameters and measurement*. New York: Raven, 1975.

Frankenhaeuser, M. *Coping with job stress: A psychobiological approach*. Reports from the Department of Psychology, University of Stockholm, 1978 (532).

Frankenhaeuser, M., & Gardell, B. Underload and overload in working life: Outline of a multidisciplinary approach. *Journal of Human Stress*, 1976, *2*(3), 35–46.

Frankenhaeuser, M., Järpe, G., & Mattell, G. Effects of intravenous infusion of adrenaline and noradrenaline on certain physiological and psychological functions. *Acta Physiologia Scandinavia*, 1961, *51*, 175–186.

Frankenhaeuser, M., Nordheden, B., Myrsten, A. L., & Post, B. Psychophysiological reactions to understimulation and overstimulation. *Acta Psychologia*, 1971, *35*, 298–308.

Fried, M. Grieving for a lost home. In A. Keiv (Ed.), *Social Psychiatry* (Vol. 1). London: Routledge & Kegan Paul, 1963.

Gentry, W. D., Foster, S., & Harvey, T. Denial as a determinant of anxiety and perceived health status in the coronary care unit. *Psychosomatic Medicine*, 1972, *34*, 39–44.

Glass, D. C. *Behavior patterns, stress, and coronary disease*. Hillsdale, N.J.: Erlbaum, 1976.

Glass, D. C. Stress, behavior patterns, and coronary disease. *American Scientist*, 1977, *65*(2), 177–187.

Glass, D. C., & Singer, J. E. *Urban stress: Experiments on noise and social stressors*. New York: Academic Press, 1972.

Glass, D. C., Singer, J. E., Leonard, H. S., Krantz, D., Cohen, S., & Cummings, H. Perceived control of aversive stimulation and the reduction of stress responses. *Journal of Personality*, 1973, *41*, 577–595.

Greenberg, C. I., & Baum, A. Compensatory response to anticipated densities. *Journal of Applied Social Psychology*, 1979, *9*, 1–12.

Greene, W. A. The psychosocial setting of development of leukemia and lymphoma. *Annals of the New York Academy of Science*, 1966, *125*, 794–801.

Grinker, R. R., & Spiegel, J. P. *Men under stress*. New York: McGraw-Hill, 1945.

Hackett, T. P., & Weisman, A. D. Reactions to the imminence of death. In G. H. Grosser, H. Wechsler, & M. Greenblatt (Eds.), *The threat of impending disaster*. Cambridge, Mass.: MIT Press, 1964, 300–311.

Hall, E. T. *The hidden dimension*. New York: Doubleday, 1966.

Harburg, E., Erfrut, J. C., Chaperi, E., Nauenstein, L. F., Schull, W. F., & Schork, M. A. Socioecological stressor areas and black-white blood pressure: Detroit. *Journal of Chronic Diseases*, 1973, *26*, 595–611.

Holmes, T. H., & Rahe, R. H. The social readjustment rating scale. *Journal of Psychosomatic Research*, 1967, *11*, 213–218.

Houts, P. S., Miller, R. W., Tokuhata, G. K., & Ham, K. S. Health-related behavioral impact of the Three Mile Island nuclear incident. Report submitted to the TMI Advisory Panel on Health Research Studies of the Pennsylvania Department of Health, Part I, April 8, 1980.

Hovland, C., & Janis, I. *Personality and persuasibility*. New Haven, Conn.: Yale University Press, 1959.

Hynes, M., & Vanmarcke, E. Reliability of embankment performances predictions. *Proceedings of the ASCE Engineering Mechanics Division Specialty Conference*. Waterloo, Canada: University of Waterloo Press, 1976.

Janis, I. *Psychological stress*. New York: Wiley, 1958.

Janis, I. Stages in the decision-making process. In R. Abelson & E. Aronson (Eds.), *Theories of cognitive consistency: A sourcebook*. Skokie, Ill.: Rand–McNally, 1968, 577–588.

Jenkins, D. C. Psychosocial modifiers of response to stress. *Journal of Human Stress*, 1979, *5*(4), 3–5.

Johnson, J. Effects of accurate expectations about sensations on the sensory and distress components of pain. *Journal of Personality and Social Psychology*, 1973, *27*, 261–275.

Johnson, J. E., & Leventhal, H. Effects of accurate expectations and behavioral instructions on reactions during a noxious medical examination. *Journal of Personality and Social Psychology*, 1974, *29*, 710–718.

Jonsson, E., & Sorenson, S. On the influence of attitudes toward the source on annoyance reactions to noise: An experimental study. *Nordisk Hygiensk Tidskrift*, 1967, *48*, 35–45.

Kahn, R. L., & French, J. R. P. Status and conflict: Two themes in the study of stress. In J. E. McGrath (Ed.), *Social and psychological factors in stress*. New York: Holt, Rinehart and Winston, 1970.

Kaplan, S. Perception of an uncertain environment. In S. Kaplan & R. Kaplan (Eds.), *Humanscapes*. North Scituate, Mass.: Duxbury Press, 1978.

Kasl, S. V., & Cobb, S. Blood pressure changes in men undergoing job loss: A preliminary report. *Psychosomatic Medicine*, 1970, *32*, 19–38.

Kates, R. W. Hazard and choice perception in flood plain management. *Research Paper 78*. Chicago: Department of Geography, University of Chicago Press, 1962.

Kirk, M., & Campbell, M. *Do I look like I want to die?* Produced for KCTS, Seattle, 1979.

Kiretz, S., & Moos, R. H. Physiological effects of social environments. *Psychosomatic Medicine*, 1974, *36*, 96–114.

Kobasa, S. C. Stressful life events, personality and health: An inquiry into hardness. *Journal of Personality and Social Psychology*, 1979, *37*(1), 1–11.

Konzett, H. *Jahre osterreichische Pharmakologie Wien Med Wochenscher*. 125 (1-2 Suppl.): 1–6, 1975.

Konzett, H., Hortnagel, H., & Winkler, H. On the urinary output of vasopressin, epinephrine and norepinephrine during different stress situations. *Psychopharmacologia*, 1971, *21*, 247–256.

Langer, E. J., & Saegert, S. Crowding and cognitive control. *Journal of Personality and Social Psychology*, 1977, *35*, 175–182.

Lazarus, R. S. *Psychological stress and the coping process*. New York: McGraw-Hill, 1966.

Lazarus, R. S., & Cohen, J. B. Environmental stress. In I. Altman & J. F. Wohlwill (Eds.), *Human behavior and environment* (Vol. 1). New York: Plenum, 1977.

Lazarus, R. S., & Launier, R. Stress-related transactions between person and environment. In L. A. Pervin & M. Lewis (Eds.), *Perspectives in interactional psychology*. New York: Plenum, 1978.

Lazarus, R. S., Opton, E. M., Norrikos, M. S., & Rankin, N. O. The principle of shortcircuiting of threat: Further evidence. *Journal of Personality*, 1965, *33*, 622–635.

Leonard, S., & Borsky, P. N. A causal model for relating noise exposure, psychosocial variables and aircraft noise annoyance. In W. Ward (Ed.), *Proceedings of the International Congress on Noise as a Public Health Problem*. Washington, D.C.: Environmental Protection Agency, 1973.

Lundberg, U. Psychophysiological aspects of performance and adjustment to stress. In H. W. Krohne & L. Laux (Eds.), *Achievement, stress, and anxiety*. Washington, D.C.: Hemisphere Press, 1979.

McGrath, J. E. *Social and psychological factors in stress*. New York: Holt, Rinehart and Winston, 1970.

Mason, J. W. A review of psychoendocrine research on the pituitary-adrenal cortical system. *Psychosomatic Medicine*, 1968, *30*, 576–607.

Mason, J. W. A historical view of the stress field. *Journal of Human Stress*, 1975, *1*, 6–12, 22–36.

Mehrabian, A. A questionnaire measure of individual differences in stimulus screening and associated differences in arousability. *Environmental Psychology and Nonverbal Behavior*, 1977, *1*, 89–103.

MIL Research. *Second survey of aircraft noise annoyance around London airport*. London: Her Majesty's Stationary Office, 1971.

Parkes, C. M. *Bereavement*. New York: International Universities Press, 1972.

Paulus, P., & Matthews, R. Crowding, attribution and task performance. *Basic and Applied Social Psychology*, 1980, *1*(1), 3–14.

Paulus, P., McCain, G., & Cox, V. Death rates, psychiatric commitments, blood pressure and perceived crowding as a function of institutional crowding. *Environmental Psychology and Nonverbal Behavior*, 1978, *3*, 107–116.

Reynolds, R. C. Community and occupational influences in stress at Cape Kennedy: Relationships to heart disease. In R. S. Eliot (Ed.), *Stress and the heart*. New York: Futura, 1974.

Rodin, J. Crowding, perceived choice and response to controllable and uncontrollable outcomes. *Journal of Experimental Social Psychology*, 1976, *12*, 564–578.

Rodin, J., & Baum, A. Crowding and helplessness: Potential consequences of density and loss of control. In A. Baum & Y. M. Epstein (Eds.), *Human response to crowding*. Hillsdale, N.J.: Erlbaum, 1978.

Rodin, J., Solomon, S., & Metcalf, J. Role of control in mediating perceptions of density. *Journal of Personality and Social Psychology*, 1978, *36*(9), 988–999.

Rose, R., Poe, R. O., & Mason, J. W. Psychological state and body size as determinants of 17-OHCS excretion. *Archives of Internal Medicine* (Chicago), 1968, May, *121*, 406–413.

Rosenstock, I. M. Why people use health services. *Millbank Memorial Fund Quarterly* (Part II), 1966, *44*, 94–124.

Rotton, J., Oszewski, D., Charleton, M., & Soler, E. Loud speech, conglomerate noise, and behavioral aftereffects. *Journal of Applied Psychology*, 1978, *63*, 360–365.

Schachter, S. *The psychology of affiliation*. Stanford, Calif.: Stanford University Press, 1959.

Schulz, R. Effects of control and predictability on the physical and psychological well-being of the institutionalized aged. *Journal of Personality and Social Psychology*, 1976, *33*, 563–573.

Selye, H. *The stress of life*. New York: McGraw-Hill, 1956/1976.

Sherrod, D. R. Crowding, perceived control and behavioral aftereffects. *Journal of Applied Social Psychology*, 1974, *4*, 171–186.

Sherrod, D. R., & Downs, R. Environmental determinants of altruism: The effects of stimulus overload and perceived control on helping. *Journal of Experimental Social Psychology*, 1974, *10*(5), 468–479.

Sherrod, D. R., Hage, J., Halpern, P. L., & Moore, B. S. Effects of personal causation and perceived control on responses to an aversive environment: The more control, the better. *Journal of Experimental Social Psychology*, 1977, *13*, 14–27.

Simon, H. A. *Models of man: Social and rational*. New York: Wiley, 1957.

Sims, J. H., & Baumann, D. D. The tornado threat: Coping styles of the north and south. In J. H. Sims & D. D. Baumann (Eds.), *Human behavior and the environment: Interactions between man and his physical world*. Chicago: Maaroufa Press, 1974.

Singer, J. E., Lundberg, U., & Frankenhaeuser, M. Stress on the train: A study of urban commuting. In A. Baum, J. E. Singer, & S. Valins (Eds.), *Advances in environmental psychology* (Vol. 1). Hillsdale, N.J.: Erlbaum, 1978.

Slovic, P., Lichtenstein, S., & Fischhoff, B. Images of disaster: Perception and acceptance of risks from nuclear risks. In G. Goodman (Ed.), *Impacts and risks of energy strategies: Their analysis and role in management*. New York: Academic Press, 1979.

Speisman, J. C., Lazarus, R. S., Mordkoff, A., & Davison, L. Experimental reduction of stress based on ego defense theory. *Journal of Abnormal and Social Psychology*, 1964, *68*, 367–380.

Staub, E., Tursky, B., & Schwartz, G. Self-control and predictability: The effects on reactions to aversive stimulation. *Journal of Personality and Social Psychology*, 1971, *18*(2), 157–162.

Stewart, D., & Winser, D. Incidence of perforated peptic ulcers during the period of heavy air raids. *Lancet*, 1942, *1*, 259–261.

Taylor, S. E., & Fiske, S. T. Salience, attention and attribution: Top of the head phenomena. In L. Berkowitz (Ed.), *Advances in experimental social psychology* (Vol. 11). New York: Academic Press, 1978.

Tracor, Inc. *Community reaction to aircraft noise* (Vol. 1). Washington, D.C.: National Aeronautics and Space Administration, NASA Report CR-1761, 1971.

Tversky, A., & Kahneman, D. Belief in the law of small numbers. *Psychological Bulletin*, 1971, *76*(2), 105–110.

Tversky, A., & Kahneman, D. Judgment under uncertainty: Heuristics and biases. *Science*, 1974, *185*, 1124–1131.

Vaillant, G. M. Northwood history of male psychologic health. *New England Journal of Medicine*, 1979, *301*(23), 1249–1254.

Warheit, G. J. Occupation: A key factor in stress at the Manned Space Center. In R. S. Eliot, *Stress and the heart*. New York: Futura, 1974.

Wilson, A. H. Noise: Final report of the committee on the problem of noise. London: Her Majesty's Stationary Office, Cmnd. 2056, 1963.

Wolf, S., & Goodell, H. *Stress and disease*, Springfield, Ill.: Thomas, 1968.

Zubin, J. Role of vulnerability in the etiology of schizophrenic episodes. In L. J. West & D. E. Flinn (Eds.), *Treatment of schizophrenia: Progress and prospects*. New York: Grune & Stratton, 1976.

Zuckerman, M. Dimensions of sensation seeking. *Journal of Consulting and Clinical Psychology*, 1971, *36*, 35–52.

2. Nonauditory effects of noise on behavior and health

Sheldon Cohen and Neil Weinstein

Noise pollution is rapidly growing as a major environmental concern. Sources of noise in communities, residential dwellings, offices, and factories are numerous. They range from the moderately intrusive sounds of our neighbors, children, pets, and televisions to the high-intensity sounds of aircraft, automobiles, trucks, and construction equipment. Although some recent federal, state, and local regulations specify permissible noise levels, noise exposure in the United States may still be growing (cf. Bragdon, 1971).

Is noise harmful to our health and well-being? Does it interfere with human performance in work settings, distort and degrade interpersonal interactions, and cause physiological disturbances? This paper provides partial answers to these questions by presenting an overview of research and theory on the effects of noise on human behavior and health. The discussion is restricted to the nonauditory effects of noise. There is no discussion of the effects of noise on hearing acuity or of the role of noise in disrupting verbal communication (see Kryter, 1970; Miller, 1974). Moreover, we generally limit ourselves to studies of noises likely to impact large numbers of people, excluding discussion of infrasonic and ultrasonic sound and of sounds loud enough to cause physical pain or vestibular disturbances (see A. Cohen, 1977; Kryter, 1970, for reviews of this literature).

Noise versus sound

Noise researchers have long made a distinction between sound and noise. Sound is changes in air pressure that are detected by the ear. These pres-

Preparation of this chapter was supported by grants from the National Science Foundation (BNS 77-08576 and BNS 79-23453) and the National Institute of Environmental Health Sciences (1 R01 ES0176401). Dr. Weinstein contributed the section on community noise annoyance. The authors are indebted to Donald Broadbent, Alex Cohen, Jerry Lukas, and Paul Knipschild for their comments on an earlier draft.

sure changes are created by wavelike motions of air molecules in response to object vibration. Frequency, the number of times per second a wave motion completes a cycle, is perceived by the listener as pitch. Variations in wave height or amplitude are determined by the amount of energy or pressure and are experienced as differences in loudness.

The intensity of sound is commonly expressed in decibels (abbreviated dB). Zero decibels is about the level of the weakest sound that can be heard by a person with very good ears in an extremely quiet environment. Fifty-five decibels is roughly equivalent to light traffic, 70 dB to a vacuum cleaner at 10 feet, 110 dB to a riveting machine, and 120 dB to a jet takeoff at 200 feet. The decibel scale is logarithmic with an increment of 3 dB reflecting a doubling of the intensity (energy) of the sound. An increment of about 10 dB is required, however, for a perceived doubling of loudness.

Most behavioral studies of sound use the A decibel scale (dBA) that is designed to closely approximate *perceived* loudness. Since people perceive high-frequency sounds as louder than low-frequency sounds of equal sound pressure, this scale assigns lesser weights to low-frequency than high-frequency sounds in calculating total sound level.

Noise is a psychological concept and is defined as sound that is unwanted by the listener because it is unpleasant, bothersome, interferes with important activities, or is believed to be physiologically harmful (Kryter, 1970). Sounds can be unwanted because of their physical properties (e.g., intensity, frequency, and intermittency) or because of their signal properties (i.e., their meaning). Unwanted effects of sound that are related to its physical properties include the masking of wanted sound, auditory fatigue and hearing damage, excessive loudness, bothersomeness, and startle (Kryter, 1970). Recent data also suggest that the meaning of a sound plays an important role in determining its effects on annoyance, performance and possibly health (Borsky, 1980; S. Cohen, 1980a; S. Cohen, Glass, & Phillips, 1979). Thus, even fairly loud sounds may sometimes be viewed as desirable, whereas relatively soft sounds can be viewed as noisy. For example, your neighbor might enjoy listening to an album of rock music at 110 dB, but you might find the same physical stimulus quite aversive, and although the sound of a couple whispering during a theater performance may be barely audible, it may also be reacted to as an intruding noise.

Noise and human performance

How does noise influence performance? Existing theory and data on the relationship between noise and performance suggest that effects depend on the kind of noise and the type of performance (Loeb, 1980). Moreover, a recent analysis suggests that accurate prediction of noise–performance relationships also requires an emphasis on the meaning of the sound and the social context of the setting for the person(s) performing in noise (cf. S. Cohen, 1980a).

It is important to note that even with the myriad of existing studies, we are unable to predict with much confidence the effects of noise on performance in a particular situation (cf. Loeb, 1980). The noise–performance literature is complex, often at least seemingly inconsistent, and subject to a number of different interpretations. While a thorough review of this literature is beyond the scope of this paper (see Broadbent, 1979; Loeb, 1980, for recent reviews), short summaries of several theoretical approaches and an overview of existing data are provided. This selective review emphasizes deleterious as opposed to positive effects of noise.

Theories

People in management or otherwise concerned with human efficiency are often interested in the possible effect of a specific source or type of noise on a particular task. While psychologists have studied the impact of high-intensity sound on a wide range of tasks, the probability is small that there is reliable evidence associating a specific noise with the task of interest. Thus, judgments of whether noise will have a deleterious effect in a setting are usually made by interpreting the situation in the context of an established theoretical framework that relates noise to task performance.

Theories about the relationship of noise and performance have undergone substantial changes in the last 25 years. In order to provide some theoretical structure to this section, we will provide short summaries of three recent approaches: those of Broadbent, Cohen, and Poulton. The descriptions of these theories are limited and the interested reader is directed to Broadbent (1971, 1978), S. Cohen (1978), and Poulton (1977, 1978, 1979) for more elaboration. The relation of existing evidence to these theories is still considered controversial.

Broadbent (1971) has argued that exposure to moderate and high-intensity noise causes an elevation in arousal. Heightened arousal, in turn, is said to lead to a narrowing of one's attention. The first inputs to be ignored are those that are irrelevant or only partially relevant to task performance. As arousal increases, attention is further restricted and task relevant cues may also be neglected. In some tasks, proficiency demands the use of only a restricted range of cues. Such tasks improve with moderate narrowing of attentional focus to the extent that competing cues are no longer noticed. In other tasks, proficiency demands the use of a wide range of cues (e.g., dual-task performance or single tasks requiring the integration of information from many sources). Any narrowing of attention during such tasks is likely to affect performance adversely. It follows that the optimal level of arousal (and thus attentional focus) varies with the complexity (number of cues required) of the task. Optimal levels of arousal for complex tasks are lower than those for simple tasks. Thus, high levels of arousal like those that are presumably elicited by laboratory noise manipulations, are usually assumed to have detrimental effects on complex but not on simple tasks.

S. Cohen (1978) similarly predicts attentional focusing will often occur under high-intensity noise but explains the focusing as a strategy commonly used to decrease the amount of information processed when one's processing capacity is overloaded by the combined demands of the stressor (the noise) and the ongoing task. Cohen also argues that the information load imposed under noise exposure is affected more by the meaning of the noise and the situation than by the intensity of the sound. Specifically, he suggests that predictability and controllability of the noise and one's expectancies about its effects are important factors to consider. S. Cohen (1980a) also emphasizes that even if one accepts Broadbent's argument that attentional focusing occurs because of heightened arousal, it is likely that the level of arousal is determined by the meaning of the noise and situation, not merely by the physical parameters of the sound.

Poulton (1978, 1979) argues that there is an increase in arousal when continuous noise is first switched on, but that the arousal gradually lessens over time. He asserts that this initial increase in arousal often results in improved performance. Poulton also suggests that reported deficits in task performance under *continuous* noise occur because of subjects' inability to hear acoustic cues (including hearing one's own internal speech) that aid performance when the task is performed in quiet. Deleterious effects of *intermittent* noise are attributed to the distraction that occurs at the onset of the noise.

Decrements in task performance that *follow* exposure to unpredictable, uncontrollable high-intensity noise (e.g., Glass & Singer, 1972) are variously attributed by these theorists to learned helplessness (Broadbent, 1978), to cognitive fatigue and consequent loss of information-processing capacity (S. Cohen, 1978), and to decreased level of arousal following the termination of the noise (Poulton, 1978).

Tasks that are unaffected by noise

Although there is little agreement on the nature of situations in which noise will affect performance, there are a number of tasks that most investigators agree will not be affected detrimentally. In a recent review, Broadbent (1979) suggests a simple rule for classifying such tasks. "Almost any task in which a person has to react only at certain definite times, receives a clear warning of the need for reaction, and receives an easily visible stimulus will show no effect in continuous loud noise" (p. 174). One category of tasks that generally fit Broadbent's rule is tests of visual functioning. Examples of visual tasks unaffected by quite intense noise levels include visual acuity for lines and discs (Krauskopf & Coleman, 1979), the ability to detect contrasts (Broussard, 1979), to judge distance, dark vision, speed of moving the eyes to a visual angle, and speed of changing focus (Stevens, 1972). The ability to make practiced and repetitive dexterous and coordinated movements is similarly unlikely to show noise-induced impairment.

For example, the squeezing of a dynamometer (Miles, 1953) and the dexterity with which nuts and bolts can be undone and retightened (Harris, 1973) are relatively unaffected by high-intensity noise. A task requiring the repetitive printing of the same sequence of letters (McBain, 1961) actually shows fewer errors during noise exposure.

Tasks affected by noise

It is well established that *novel or unusual* noise will interfere with efficiency on most tasks (cf. Broadbent, 1979). This effect occurs during the first few presentations of the noise, then disappears. Similar effects occur with cessation of noise. Hence, task interference seems to be due to a change in stimulation and may not be peculiar to intense noise.

There has also been some consistency in reports of effects of familiar noise on multiple-source tasks and vigilance tasks. These effects are thought to occur with noise levels of 95 dBA or more. They are less likely to occur under fixed–intermittent than continuous noise, and most likely to occur under unpredictable-intermittent exposure.

Multiple-source tasks require subjects to perform two tasks simultaneously or to process multiple inputs from the same task. Subjects are generally instructed that some sources (e.g., one of the two tasks in the dual-task paradigm) are more important than others. In general, the results of these studies show that noise increases the amount of effort applied to the primary task cues (or task) at the expense of the less important cues (cf. Broadbent, 1971, 1979). Examples of tasks used in these studies include the watch keeping of multiple signal lights with different probabilities of occurrence (e.g., Hamilton, 1969), simultaneous visual tasks (e.g., Hockey, 1970a, 1970b), various visual monitoring tasks with auditory secondary tasks (e.g., Boggs & Simon, 1968; Finkleman & Glass, 1970), and tasks in which subjects are instructed to memorize particular stimuli and then are asked to recall some incidental feature of the stimulus display (e.g., Hockey & Hamilton, 1970; O'Malley & Poplawsky, 1971). It should be noted that the reliability of some of these effects has been questioned (e.g., Forster & Grierson, 1978; Loeb & Jones, 1978; Smith & Broadbent, 1980).

Vigilance tasks require continuous monitoring for faint, infrequent signals. These tasks have been employed in noise studies because of their presumed similarity to certain kinds of industrial quality control tasks and to military requirements for radar monitoring. In a recent review, Broadbent (1979) concludes that vigilance performance seems to improve under relatively low levels of noise, especially varied noise. Decrements in performance occur, however, in levels of noise higher than 95 dBA under certain conditions. Task deficits are most likely to occur when (1) the signals are hard to see, (2) the situation is not one that encourages caution, i.e., one in which even the most doubted judgment should be reported, (3) the length of the watch is long, and (4) there are a number of sources from which the signal may come. The fact that the multiple-source vigilance tasks are more likely to be affected is consistent with the attentional focusing phenomenon predicted by both Broadbent and Cohen.

The most reliable finding in studies of vigilance performance under high-intensity noise seems to be that noise reduces the frequency of doubtful and uncertain judgments and increases the frequency of confident ones (Broadbent, 1979). Thus, tasks that require one to report even the least confident judgments are detrimentally affected, whereas those requiring one to report only those signals that one is absolutely sure of improve under noise.

Variability of performance

Although the average efficiency on many tasks appears to be unaffected by exposure to high-intensity noise, there is evidence that noise sometimes produces highly variable performance – moments of inefficiency interspersed with normal and compensating spurts of efficient performance. Highly variable performance in industrial settings can mean poor product reliability and can result in increased accident potential in some work settings (A. Cohen, 1979).

As pointed out earlier, performance can be disturbed by both the onset and offset of the noise. With *random–intermittent* noise, even experienced subjects seem to show recurrent momentary deteriorations of performance at noise onset and offset that are compensated for by increased efficiency between the bursts of noise (cf. Broadbent, 1979). Examples of tasks showing this variability effect include clerical tasks (e.g., Sanders, 1961), continuous serial reaction time tasks (Fisher, 1972), and mental arithmetic (Woodhead, 1964). There is also some evidence that exposure to *continuous* noise similarly results in performance variability. It seems to occur on tasks that involve tracking targets whose rate of movement is set by the subject and on some forms of serial reaction time tasks, for example, those in which lights are widely separated from the response board (cf. Broadbent, 1979; Hartley, 1973; Wilkinson, 1963). Additional studies of intrasubject variability under both intermittent and continuous noise are needed to clarify the role of noise in the distribution of effort over time.

Aftereffects of noise on human performance

Recent studies indicate that there are effects of noise on human performance that occur *after* noise exposure is terminated (see S. Cohen, 1980b, for review). For example, Glass and Singer (1972) found that in comparison with a control group not previously exposed to noise, subjects exposed to unpredictable (random–intermittent), 108 dBA, or 56 dBA noise showed less tolerance for frustration and performed more poorly on both proofreading and a competitive response (Stroop color word) task. Similar effects following exposure to unpredictable–intermittent noises (varying from 80 to 100 dBA) have been reported by a number of investigators (e.g., Rotton, Olszewski, Charleton, & Soler, 1978; Gardner, 1978). Moreover, studies of the impact of variable intensity *continuous* noise, where there are unpredictable components of the noise (e.g., aperiodic bursts of static or office noise), report similar poststimulation effects (e.g., Wohlwill, Nasar, DeJoy, & Foruzani, 1976; Sherrod, Hage, Halpern, & Moore, 1977).

It is important to note that the same poststimulation effects on performance also occur after exposure to a number of other unpredictable and uncontrollable stressors including electric shock, high density, bureaucratic stress, and cold pressor (see review by S. Cohen, 1980b). Thus, this effect is not specific to high-intensity noise. Moreover, the noise aftereffects (as well as the deleterious effects of the other stressors) can be ameliorated by providing the subject with accurate expectancies of when the stressor will begin and end (increased predictability) and/or providing the subjects with the perception that they can terminate the stressor at will (increased control). Thus, noise aftereffects are principally related to cognitive factors – predictability and controllability of the sound – rather than to acoustic parameters. Finally, S. Cohen (1980b) has noted that this research has employed a limited number of aftereffects tasks whose common characteristics are not clear. It is thus difficult to predict whether similar effects will occur on any specific task.

Field research

Industrial and office performance during noise. Results of studies on the impact of noise on performance conducted in factories and offices have produced mixed results that often are difficult to interpret (see reviews by Ahrlin & Öhrström, 1978; Broadbent, 1979; Moos, 1976). Most of these studies compare a group of workers in a noise-impacted part of a factory or office to a second group working on the same task in an area recently made quieter through some sort of noise abatement technique. A problem in many of these studies is that the mere fact that someone cared enough to introduce the intervention or to assess the effects of noise on the workers affects the morale and production of both those working in noise and in quiet. An example of this problem is reported by Broadbent and Little (1960). The same workers were moved back and forth from noise-treated (89 dB) to untreated (99 dB) parts of a plant over the course of the year. The rate of threading rolls of film onto a machine showed improvement after the noise abatement work was completed, but the improvement was equally large both during quiet and noise exposure.

A study of weavers reported over 30 years ago (Weston & Adams, 1979) uses a design that provides a better test of the hypothesis that noise deleteriously effects performance. In this case, the efficiency of weavers was examined during a 6-month period of alternative weeks of wearing and not wearing ear plugs. The looms had a sound level of 95 dB and the ear plugs attenuated the noise by 10 to 15 dB. Worker efficiency was up about 12% during the period that ear plugs were worn.

Recent reviews of field studies conducted in offices and factories (e.g., Broadbent, 1979; Moos, 1976) generally conclude that there is no conclusive evidence that noise affects the average rate of work. Broadbent (1979) points out, however, if accidents or errors caused by momentary inefficiency are important, it is likely that noise increases these hazards.

Scholastic performance during noise. Two field studies have artificially increased classroom noise levels and assessed the effects on student behavior and performance. These studies should be distinguished from those that follow in that they are the only studies of school performance during noise that randomly assign students to the noise and quiet treatments. Ward and Suedfeld (1973) broadcast traffic noise outside a large university classroom building. Less student participation and attention were observed under induced sound, compared to a no-noise control group. McCroskey and Devens (1977) similarly induced a 4-dB increase in the ambient noise level of several fifth- and sixth-grade classrooms by adding a white-noise background. Children tested in the classrooms with the additional noise showed impaired auditory discrimination, visual motor skills, and visual discrimination as compared with children tested in classrooms without the additional noise.

Several recent studies compare the scholastic achievement of children attending schools near urban airports to that of children attending schools in quieter areas. Such groups are usually matched on important variables (e.g., demographic makeup of enrollment). For example, a study contracted by a school board to support its lawsuit against the Seattle-Tacoma airport (Maser, Sorensen, & Kryter, 1978) found that children *with low aptitudes* attending noisy (in flight path) schools showed a cumulative deficit in tested achievement compared to children in quiet control schools. Differences between noise and quiet groups were not significant, however, until the 10th grade. A recent dissertation by Green (1979) reports a positive correlation between school noise level (as determined by a noise contour map) and the percentage of second- through sixth-grade children scoring 1 or more years below grade level. The effect was found after controlling for various racial and socioeconomic characteristics of the schools. Bronzaft and McCarthy (1975) similarly found that second- through fourth-grade children in classrooms on the side of a school facing train tracks performed more poorly on a reading achievement test than children in classrooms on the quiet side of the building.

In a study of the effectiveness of aircraft noise abatement, S. Cohen, Evans, Krantz, Stokols, and Kelly (1981) report that after controlling for possible socioeconomic and racial differences, third-grade children who spent the year in noise-abated classrooms had better math scores than children in nonabated rooms. A similar, although nonsignificant, pattern was found for reading scores. It should be noted that experimental studies of the effects of noise on both adults (cf. Broadbent, 1979) and children (e.g., Slater, 1968; Weinstein & Weinstein, 1979) generally suggest that intellectual tasks performance is not impaired during short-term noise exposure. Thus, although these studies are concerned with tests taken during noise, the effects may actually occur because of the cumulative effects of the noise on the learning process.

Scholastic performance outside of noise. A number of recent studies have investigated the impact of living and/or attending school in noisy conditions on task performance *outside* of the stressful environment. For example, S. Cohen, Glass, and Singer (1973) studied third- through fifth-grade children living in apartment buildings built on bridges spanning a busy expressway. When tested in a *quiet* setting, children living in noisier apartments showed greater impairment of auditory discrimination and reading ability than those living in quieter apartments. The magnitude of the correlation between noise and auditory discrimination increased with the length of residence. Race, social class variables, and hearing losses were ruled out as possible alternative explanations. Similarly, S. Cohen, Evans, Krantz, and Stokols (1980) studied third- and fourth-grade children attending school under the air corridor of a busy metropolitan airport. When tested in *quiet*, children attending noisy schools were poorer on both a simple and difficult puzzle-solving task and were more likely to "give up" on the task than their counterparts from quiet schools. Again, race, social class, and hearing damage were ruled out as possible explanations.

A recent study (Moch-Sibony, in press) comparing children from a quiet (soundproofed) elementary school in the air corridor of Orly (Paris) Airport to children from a nearby noisy (without soundproofing) school matched on socioeconomic variables found poorer auditory discrimination among children from the noisy school. There were, however, no differences between schools in reading achievement. Moch-Sibony also reported that children from the noisy school showed less tolerance for frustration than their counterparts from the quiet school.

Finally, a study of 4 1/2- to 6 1/2-year-old children from homes described by their parents as either noisy or quiet (Heft, 1979) indicates that when tested in *quiet*, children from noisy homes performed more poorly on both a matching and an incidental memory task than those from quieter homes. Analyses controlled for age, preschool experience, and income level of parents. It should be noted, however, that self-reports of noise level do not usually correlate highly with objective noise measures (cf. Kryter, 1970) and thus limit the generality of Heft's findings.

In sum, there is increasing evidence of noise effects on human performance that persist (or possibly occur only) outside of the noisy environment. It should be noted, however, that all of these studies involve *children* and all are *correlational*. One explanation for deficits in achievement scores of children attending noisy schools is that the noise interferes with the teaching–learning process, thus resulting in a cumulative and progressive deficit. For example, noise may decrease teaching time by forcing teachers to continuously pause or by making it difficult for the student and teacher to hear one another (Crook & Langdon, 1974). Other possible explanations include noise-produced influence on children's information-processing strategies (cf. S. Cohen et al., 1973, 1980; Heft, 1979), on their feelings of personal control (cf. S. Cohen et al., 1979, 1980), and on their level of arousal (S. Cohen et al., 1980).

Noise and social behavior

Although psychologists have studied the relationship between noise and human performance for over a half a century, there has been little interest in the impact of noise on interpersonal behavior until very recently. The experimental work in this area has dealt primarily with the relationship between noise and one's sensitivity to others, especially the willingness to give aid both during and immediately following noise exposure. For example, in a laboratory study, Mathews and Canon (1975) examined the effects of various noise levels on the percentage of subjects willing to help someone pick up accidentally dropped materials. Those exposed to 85-dB noise were less likely to help than those exposed to 65 dB or lower, ambient noise levels. Similar results were found in a field experiment reported in the same paper. Subjects were less likely to aid a person who had dropped a pile of books when a loud lawnmower was running than when it was quiet. Moreover, a subtle cue suggesting the legitimacy and degree of need for assistance – a cast on the victim's arm – increased helping under ambient conditions but did not affect the frequency of helping under noise.

In a study conducted in the Netherlands, Korte, Ypma, and Toppen (1975) used sound level, traffic count, pedestrian count, and the number of visible "public" buildings to specify areas that they characterized as either high or low on environmental inputs. They report that regardless of whether the area is in a city or small town, people in low-input areas were more likely to assist a lost person and to grant a street interview than people in high-input area. Page (1977) similarly reported that construction noise decreased the granting of small favors. Page also found that noise was more likely to reduce compliance to requests for verbal aid than for physical assistance.

A similar noise-induced lack of sensitivity to others is reported by Sauser, Arauz, and Chambers (1978). Subjects were asked to work on a simulated management task in 70–80-dBA office noise or in quiet (50–57 dBA). Those working in noise recommended lower starting salaries for new employees than recommended by their counterparts in quiet offices.

Other effects of noise on interpersonal behavior were found in two studies of traffic noise in natural settings. Appleyard and Lintell (1972) studied the relative effects of traffic noise on three residential streets in a San Francisco neighborhood of "moderate" income. The streets differed in the amount of traffic (light, moderate, heavy) and in associated noise levels. There was substantially more casual social interaction on the street with light traffic than on the other two. There was virtually no sidewalk activity on the street with heavy traffic. People on the noisy street also reported that the street was a rather lonely place to live, whereas those on the street with light traffic perceived their street as a rather friendly, sociable area. These patterns of social behavior may have been affected by the type of people who live on the street as well as by the level of traffic noise.

Damon (1977) studied the effects of traffic noise on a residential project in a lower income neighborhood. Noise intensities varied from low levels around the interior buildings to very high levels (averaging 80 dB during the day time) along one border exposed to heavy traffic. Residents in the noisy area were arrested more often, were less likely to take care of their entry ways, and more likely to be truant from school than their counterparts from quieter areas. Unfortunately, there were differences between the noisy and quiet areas in family size, density, and age that make the results difficult to interpret.

A study finding decreased helping *after* noise exposure has been reported by Sherrod and Downs (1974). Their subjects worked on a demanding task which was presented with a "soothing simulated seashore" background or with a distracting recording of Dixieland jazz plus a voice reading nonrelevant prose. In a third condition, subjects were exposed to the distracting recording but were told that they could terminate the distracting stimulation if they found it necessary (perceived control). After completion of the experiment, subjects were confronted by a second experimenter who asked for voluntary help in pretesting some experimental materials. Those exposed to the seashore sounds were most helpful, followed by those with perceived control over the distracting tape, with the least assistance offered by those who were exposed to the distracting tape without the option of terminating the noise. A similar study of post-noise aggression (Donnerstein & Wilson, 1976) found that angered subjects who were exposed to noise without perceived control administered more shock to a confederate than subjects with perceived control over the termination of the noise. These findings are similar to work on the aftereffects of noise on performance, discussed earlier, indicating that perceived control over the termination of the noise lessens or completely eliminates noise aftereffects.

Two other laboratory studies suggest that noise may cause people to oversimplify and distort perceptions of complex social relationships. Siegel and Steele (1979) report that subjects exposed to 92-dB random intermittent white noise are less able to discriminate between behaviors and make attributions of responsibility than those working in quiet. Similarly, Rotton et al. (1978) found that both loud (80-dBA) speech and the combination of 80-dBA noise with a difficult task reduced subject's ability to differentiate the characteristics of people occupying different roles (e.g., self, best friend) *after* the noise is terminated.

As mentioned earlier, both Broadbent's and Cohen's theoretical approaches to the effects of noise on performance suggest that unpredictable, uncontrollable high-intensity noise causes a focusing of one's attention on the most important aspects of a situation to the neglect of other cues. S. Cohen (1978; S. Cohen & Lezak, 1977) has pointed out that this restriction of attention affects the processing of less relevant *social* as well as nonsocial cues. Thus, many of the studies reviewed in the foregoing discussion can be interpreted as noise causing the subject to focus his or her attention on the most salient aspects of a situation to the neglect of subtle interpersonal cues. For example, Mathews and Canon's (1975) finding that an arm cast increased the proportion of people helping a confederate in quiet but not in noise can be interpreted as a neglect of a subtle cue (the arm cast) under noise but not under quiet.

There are alternative explanations for the decreased sensitivity to others that occurs in noise. For example, decreases in helping may be attributable to a negative affective state induced by the noise (cf. Isen, 1970; Moore, Underwood, & Rosenhan, 1973). Further research is necessary to clarify the roles of attentional and affective mechanisms in response to noise and their implications for interpersonal behavior.

Community annoyance

Excessive noise is mentioned more frequently by community residents than any other neighborhood problem (U.S. Bureau of Census, 1973). In examining the effects of community noise problems, it is important to distinguish between public complaint behavior and annoyance. Although annoyance often leads to public action, many variables may intervene. Complainants, for example, are better educated and hold higher-status jobs than noncomplainants (McKennell, 1973). This is not because people with more education and higher occupational status tend to be more annoyed, but, apparently, because such people are more likely to feel that their complaints will be listened to.

Since complaint behavior is not an accurate measure of public sentiment, most community noise research has focused on individual annoyance, assessed through interviews. A major goal of community noise surveys has been to generate response curves that indicate the degree of annoyance to be expected at different sound levels. Such curves can be used to predict noise impact and to set community standards for permissible noise exposures.

Smooth and nearly linear response curves are produced when the mean annoyance or the proportion deemed "highly annoyed" is plotted against noise levels (Alexandre, 1973; McKennell, 1973) and it is likely that these curves are relatively stable across different settings (Schultz, 1978). These data are misleading, however, because they give the impression that subjective reactions to noise are a simple function of the exposure. In fact, the physical stimulus – the sound level itself – accounts for a relatively small percentage of the variability in self-reported annoyance, usually 10 to 25% (e.g., Griffiths & Langdon, 1968; McKennell, 1963). At any particular sound level, such dose-response curves do not tell whether a given individual will be highly annoyed or unconcerned.

In attempting to explain individual differences, researchers have searched for measures of noise exposure that will correlate more closely with the subjective reports. Dozens of noise indexes are now in existence. Although some of these are more highly correlated with annoyance than others (cf. U.S. Environmental Protection Agency, 1974), it is questionable whether significant improvements in predictive accuracy can be produced by further refinement of the indices. Furthermore, the limited predictive ability of noise indices cannot be attributed to unreliable annoyance measures. The multi-item scales employed generally have quite satisfactory internal reliability (e.g., McKennell, 1963) although the stability of annoyance measures is not so clearly established (Griffiths & Delauzun, 1977; Leonard & Borsky, 1973).

Intervening variables

From many surveys it has become apparent that age, sex, income, education, and occupational status are not significantly related to annoyance (Weinstein, 1976). Attempts to relate annoyance to the personality scales of the MMPI and Rorschach Inkblot Test (Moreira & Bryan, 1972), the Eysenck Personality Inventory (Griffiths & Delauzun, 1977; Moreira & Bryan, 1972), and Cattell's 16 PF (Griffiths & Delauzun, 1977) have been inconclusive. On the other hand, several studies have demonstrated that people do differ in their general sensitivity to noise and that this attribute is responsible for part of the variability in reported annoyance (e.g., Griffiths & Delauzun, 1977; Weinstein, 1978). Among college students, greater self-reported sensitivity to noise is associated with lower intellectual ability and less confidence during interpersonal interactions (Weinstein, 1978). It has also been observed (Weinstein, 1979) that people are consistent in their tendency to be critical or uncritical about many aspects of their surroundings, including judgments of noise, privacy, air pollution, neighborhood services, and other neighborhood characteristics (cf. Broadbent, 1972; Griffiths & Delauzun, 1977). It is not yet known, however, whether this consistency in environmental judgments represents a response style – a variation in the willingness to *express* dissatisfaction – or whether highly critical people are genuinely less satisfied with their surroundings.

Much of the research on intervening variables has examined the meanings people attach to noise situations. For example, people who are afraid of airplane crashes report greater aircraft noise disturbance than people who are not. Presumably, the former interpret each passing plane as a signal of possible danger (Borsky, 1973). Other studies (e.g., Tracor, Inc., 1970) have shown that people who have a positive attitude toward the source of the noise are less annoyed than people who think the noise source serves no useful purpose or who believe that the authorities are not making a genuine effort to control the noise. A field experiment in Sweden, for instance, demonstrated that reports of annoyance by people living near an air force base were reduced by propaganda that produced a more positive attitude toward the air force (Sörensen, 1970). Similarly, laboratory studies have shown that a sound is rated as noisier if it is attributed to a teenager's hot rod than if it is attributed to a taxi (Cederlöf, Friberg, Hammarfors, Holmquist, & Kajland, 1961).

Although many beliefs are correlated with annoyance, there is no accepted theory of annoyance to bring order to the data. In some cases "annoyance" may represent fear or simply aversiveness, but many of the correlates of annoyance are predictable if one views annoyance as a mild form of anger. According to cognitive theories of emotion, anger is produced when people believe that they have been harmed and believe that the harm was both avoidable and undeserved (Brown & Herrnstein, 1975; Crosby, 1976). The harm produced in noisy situations may include threats to health and to property values, blocking of behavioral goals, or simply exposure to an aversive stimulus.

Coping and adaptation

Although many noise effects decrease rapidly in the laboratory (Glass & Singer, 1972; Kryter, 1970), community noise research provides little evidence that people adapt to noise in residential settings. Surveys find consistently that longtime neighborhood residents are at least as bothered by noise as more recent arrivals. Longitudinal studies, which avoid some of the self-selection problems inherent in the usual surveys, also find more disturbance at the end of the study period than at the beginning (Jonsson & Sörensen, 1973; Weinstein, 1978).

It is possible that the data are misleading and that people do adapt to noise. After a while, they may pay less attention to the noise and fall asleep more quickly, but their survey responses may continue to reflect their original feelings about the noise rather than their current reactions. Nevertheless, it is worth emphasizing that people appear to have much more difficulty in adjusting to noise than is commonly believed.

Some studies (e.g., Appleyard & Lintell, 1972; Grandjean, Graf, Lauber, Meier, & Müller, 1973) have described the overt actions people take to cope with noise, including such responses as changing bedrooms, planting trees, installing doublepane windows, and taking sleeping pills. There is considerably less work, however, examining cognitive coping mechanisms – attention deployment strategies, self-coaching about how not to react – that might facilitate adaptation or account for individual differences. Only attentional deployment in children has received any attention (S. Cohen et al., 1980; Heft, 1979).

New directions

There is considerable room for progress in community noise research. Investigators have not distinguished carefully between behavioral interference, emotional distress, judgments of aversiveness, or opinions about the acceptability of the noise (cf. Jonsson, Arvidsson, Berglund, & Kajland, 1973). The noise levels in many communities clearly interfere with communication and sleep, and certainly evoke strong emotional reactions. But behavioral interference does not necessarily produce an emotional response. Futhermore, noise can be aversive without producing other behavioral interruptions or emotional reactions, as when subjects are asked to rate loud noises in the laboratory.

The answers given in community surveys probably reflect a mixture in all these reactions. Even if investigators deliberately formulate questions in attempts to separate these components of dissatisfaction, respondents may be unable to make the discriminations requested. Nevertheless, a clear conception of the kinds of noise reactions that can occur should help to develop more precise models of the noise response process.

Since almost all community noise research has used a cross-sectional survey design, most conclusions about the psychological variables that influence annoyance have been based on correlational data. An association between the belief that the noise is a health threat and annoyance, for example, is generally interpreted to mean that this belief is a cause of annoyance. On the other hand, respondents may conclude that the noise is harmful *because* they find that they are upset and sleeping poorly. To classify such beliefs as *either* causes *or* effects is to oversimplify the issue. Noise appraisals are likely to influence noise reactions *and* be altered by those reactions (Alexandre, 1973). Field experiments and longitudinal studies are needed to provide a more realistic model of noise reactions. Progress in community noise research will also require less reliance on self-report measures and more direct observations of the physiological, behavioral, and interpersonal consequences of noise exposure.

Noise, mental health, and cognitive development

If noise causes annoyance and frustration, it seems plausible that prolonged exposure could cause or aggravate mental illness. Existing studies suggest the possibility of a relationship between noise and symptoms of serious mental distress, but the evidence is mixed and rather weak.

Industrial surveys, for example, report that noise exposure results in increased anxiety and emotional stress. Workers habitually exposed to high-intensity noise (usually 110 dB or above) show increased incidence of nervous complaints, nausea, headaches, instability, argumentativeness, sexual impotency, changes in general mood, and anxiety (cf. A. Cohen, 1969; Granati, Angelepi, & Lenzi, 1959; Miller, 1974). Jansen (1961) reports that workers in the noisiest parts of a steel factory have a greater frequency of social conflicts both at home and in the plant. These results are difficult to interpret, however, since the same workers are often subject to other work stresses (e.g., task demands and risks) that may precipitate or contribute to the reported symptoms.

Studies of the impact of community noise exposure on self-reported neurotic symptoms provide inconsistent evidence for a link between noise and pathology. Thus, in a recent review, McLean and Tarnopolsky (1977) report that although a number of community surveys indicate an association between noise and various symptoms – being tense and edgy (Office of Population Census and Survey, 1970), irritability (Finke, Guski, Martin, Rohrman, Schümer, & Schümer-Kohrs, 1974), nervousness, sleep difficulties, and headaches (Kokokusha, 1973) – the questions in these studies were worded in a way that seemed to invite one to blame noise for one's ailments. In a study by Grandjean (1974), where aircraft noise was not mentioned as a possible cause, there were no correlations between symptoms and exposure. A survey of general practitioners in high and low noise areas around Amsterdam's airport (Knipschild, 1976) did, however, find a high proportion of psychological and psychosomatic complaints in the high noise area. Differences in social class of the noise and quiet areas, however, provide a possible alternative explanation.

Hospital admissions

Work on community response to aircraft noise suggests a possible relationship between noise level and admission rates to community mental health facilities (cf. reviews by Arhlin & Öhrström, 1978; McLean & Tarnopolsky, 1977). Several studies relating sound level and mental hospital admissions have been conducted in the vicinity of London's Heathrow Airport. Abbey-Wickrama, a'Brook, Gattoni, and Herridge (1969; Herridge & Chir, 1972) compared the psychiatric hospital admission rates of those residing in noisy and less noisy parts of the same borough. Admission rates were higher for the noisy area; persons most at risk were older single, widowed, or separated women suffering from neurotic or organic mental illness. These results have been challenged by Chowns (1970), who argues that the noise index used was inappropriate and that noisy and less noisy (control) neighborhoods were poorly matched on demographic factors. A replication of this work (Gattoni & Tarnopolsky, 1973), using a different technique of indexing noise and carefully matching the noise and control groups on a number of socioeconomic variables, found similar but small (nonsignificant) differences between noise and quiet areas. Recent work on mental hospital admissions around Heathrow (Hand, Tarnopolsky, Barker, & Jenkins,

1980) has looked at the admission rates of several different community facilities, rather than studying the single hospital examined in the studies described. This work has resulted in mixed (different for each hospital) results.

A recent comparison of noise and control populations around Los Angeles International Airport (Meecham & Smith, 1977) indicates a marginal increase in mental hospital admissions among those living in maximum noise areas. Poor matching of quiet and noise areas on race and socioeconomic status, however, severely limits confidence in these results.

In sum, existing studies suggest that there may be a small difference between mental hospital admission rates of quiet neighborhoods and neighborhoods subjected to aircraft noise. However, the studies are all retrospective and involve differences between the admission rates of noise and quiet groups that are so small (between 0.001 and 0.003%) as to be considered by many as trivial. It should be noted, however, that admission to community mental hospitals represents only the severest cases of mental distress. It is likely that many sufferers would see their general practitioner rather than visiting a community mental health facility (e.g., Knipschild, 1976). Moreover, what may be considered a serious deviation from normality in one social class or ethnic group may be an acceptable deviation in another. Thus, depending on the background of the population, the sensitivity of these admission rates to mental distress could vary substantially. Prospective studies of community mental health that include a wider range of psychiatric care would help clarify this issue. It is also important to note that these data do not indicate whether noise causes severe mental distress in otherwise healthy individuals or whether it merely aggravates existing problems (cf. McLean & Tarnopolsky, 1977).

Cognitive development

Recent studies by Wachs and his colleagues suggest that noise in the home may interfere with normal psychological development. For example, Wachs, Uzgiris, and Hunt (1971) administered a Piagetian test of intellectual development to 102 infants between 7 and 22 months of age. There was a negative relationship between scores on the test and mothers' reports of home noise levels. Moreover, infants whose homes did not have a place where the infants could be isolated from the noise performed more poorly on the developmental test than those who had opportunities to escape. Similar effects have been found for slightly older infants although these effects may be sex specific (Wachs, 1978, 1979). It is important to note that self-reports of noise do not necessarily correlate well with objective sound levels (cf. Kryter, 1970) and that these studies are correlational and open to alternative explanations. Although not allowing any conclusions about the relationship between home noise level and psychological development, this work does suggest the necessity for further research in this area.

Noise and health

Does noise hurt the human body? Most would argue that outside of the effects of high-intensity sound on hearing (see Kryter, 1970; Miller, 1974), there is little convincing evidence for a causal link between noise and physical disorders. However, noise can alter physiological processes including the functioning of the cardiovascular, endocrine, respiratory, and digestive systems (see review by McLean & Tarnopolsky, 1977). Since such changes, if extreme, are often considered potentially hazardous to health, many feel that pathogenic effects of prolonged noise exposure are likely. Physiological changes produced by noise consist of nonspecific responses typically associated with stress reactions (Glorig, 1971; Selye, 1956). These include increases in electrodermal activity, catecholamine secretions, vasoconstriction of the peripheral blood vessels, and increases in diastolic and systolic blood pressure. Most of these reactions have been documented in laboratory studies involving short-term exposure to relatively high sound levels (cf. A. Cohen, 1977).

Do such physiological effects constitute evidence that noise is detrimental to health? The question is difficult to answer. On the one hand, there is mixed evidence that a number of physiological responses *do not* habituate to repeated exposure (cf. Jansen, 1969; McLean & Tarnopolsky, 1977) and thus could constitute the physiological bases for long-term harmful effects of noise. On the other hand, others report that habituation of these responses occurs after only short exposure to noise (e.g., Glass & Singer, 1972); thus, prolonged exposure might not necessarily produce continuous elevation of physiological processes inimical to normal bodily function. Kryter's (1970) conclusion that "the exact course and degree of adaptation of all these responses has not been very thoroughly studied" (p. 491) probably represents the state of our knowledge in this area.

Industrial studies

A recent review of the industrial noise literature (Welch, 1979) concludes that there is elevated morbidity among people who have been exposed at work to sound of 85 dBA or greater for at least 3–5 years. Moreover, the morbidity associated with exposure to relatively high intensities of sound increases with advancing age and years of employment for both men and women. Morbidity also tends to be greater under unpredictable–intermittent, impulse sound than under periodic, continuous, or relatively steady sound; and it affects those whose work involves mental concentration more than those who do mainly manual work.

Welch argues that the strongest case for industrial noise impacting health derives from the research on cardiovascular problems. He interprets the data (over 40 different studies) to indicate that long-term work under high-intensity sound is associated with at least a 60% increase in risk of cardiovascular disease. Impaired regulation of blood pressure (including hypertension) is the best documented of these effects (e.g., Parvizpoor, 1976; Pokrovskii, 1966). Other concomitants of prolonged routine exposure to intense industrial sound include cardiac morbidity (e.g., Capellini & Maroni, 1974; Raytheon Service Company, 1972), poor peripheral circulation (e.g., Jansen, 1959), and elevated cholesterol levels (e.g., Khomulo, Rodinova, & Rusinova, 1967).

Although there is an impressive amount of data suggesting that cardiovascular morbidity is greater among workers exposed to high noise levels, there are a number of reasons to be critical (or at least cautious) about Welch's conclusions. All of these studies suffer from the methodological problems associated with correlational field research and as many as half of the existing studies are either poorly designed (inadequate control groups) or do not report sufficient information to allow a critical analysis of the work (see critique in Peterson, 1979). Our confidence in the relationship between prolonged exposure to high-intensity noise and cardiovascular problems would be significantly increased if similar effects were found in prospective research. Cardiovascular response could be monitored over time in a new work group entering a particular noisy environment and compared with similar workers not so exposed (cf. A. Cohen, 1979; Peterson, 1979).

Besides cardiovascular changes, reports have linked industrial noise to a number of other health problems. The data in all of these cases are suggestive but as yet inconclusive (cf. Welch, 1979). For example, there are a number of studies reporting increased gastrointestinal complaints for noise-exposed workers. Reported problems include gastrointestinal ulcers (e.g., Kangelari, Abramovich-Polyakov, & Rudenko, 1966), chronic gastritis (e.g., Dokukina, Koberts, & Lyubomudrov, 1972), and general digestive problems (Raytheon Service Company, 1972).

Although there has been a lot of speculation about the effect of prolonged exposure to noise on resistance to infectious disease, the small number of existing studies are mixed and inconclusive (cf. Welch, 1979). Similarly, predictions about the impact of high-intensity sound on the reproductive system are virtually unstudied. An interesting investigation by Carosi and Calabro (1968) did, however, indicate that Italian families in which either husband or wife worked in a noisy job had a smaller number of sons born than nonnoise families matched for age. Factory noise has also been associated with increased reports of sore throats and laryngitis (cf. A. Cohen, 1969) and increased job-related injuries (e.g., A. Cohen, 1973, 1976). It is likely that the former are attributable to workers raising their voices in order to be heard, and the latter, to some degree, to not hearing warning signals. However, A. Cohen's (1976) finding that there are fewer accidents among workers wearing hearing protections then those without protection suggests that the masking of warning signals is not entirely responsible for increased injuries. Finally, a small number of studies suggest that prolonged exposure to high-intensity industrial noise is implicated in functional neural change, with the most convincing data suggesting impaired control of circulation (Welch, 1979).

It is also important to note that several industrial surveys failed to find a relationship between noise and ill health. For example, Finkle and Poppen (1948) report that men working in turbojet noise of 120 dB showed complete adaptation to noise. Results for renal function tests, electroencephalography, and hematological examinations were all negative. Glorig (1971) also reports no increase in cardiovascular problems, ulcers, or fatigue for those working in noisy industries.

In sum, although several years' exposure to industrial noise has been associated with a number of specific nonauditory diseases, only cardiovascular problems have received enough attention and enough consistent support to allow a convincing argument that they are noise induced. This argument is to some extent corroborated by both short-term laboratory studies of humans (see review by McLean & Tarnopolsky, 1977) and animal studies of long-term exposure (cf. Peterson, 1979) showing similar effects on the cardiovascular system. More research will be required before even tentative conclusions can be made about the relation of industrial noise to other diseases.

It should also be noted that noise may not be etiologically specific to any given disease (cf. Cassel, 1974) but may enhance susceptibility to disease in general and thus cause a wide variety of symptoms of physical and psychiatric disorder. This perspective suggests that studies of the relationship of noise to any specific disease (or even just somatic or just psychiatric diseases) may be insensitive to noise-induced effects and that a broader definition of health that encompasses both mental and physical aspects may be more productive.

Community studies

A number of recent studies have examined the effects of community noise on cardiovascular problems and physiological risk factors related to cardiovascular disease. In a series of these studies conducted in the neighborhoods adjacent to Schiphol (Amsterdam) airport, Knipschild (1977) reports that residents in areas with high levels of aircraft noise are more likely to be under medical treatment for heart trouble and hypertension, more likely (especially women) to be taking drugs for cardiovascular problems, and more likely to have high blood pressure and pathologically shaped hearts than an unexposed population. While these differences could not be explained by age, sex, smoking habits, or obesity, the noisy and quiet areas did differ in socioeconomic status. A final study, not subject to this alternative explanation, reports that increases in the purchase of cardiovascular drugs were positively correlated with the number of aircraft overflights at night.

A recent study of elementary school children in Los Angeles (S. Cohen et al., 1980) indicates that children living and attending elementary school under the air corridor to Los Angeles International Airport have higher systolic and diastolic blood pressure than matched counterparts living in quieter neighborhoods. These differences, though small in magnitude, were obtained with a conservative statistical analysis that controlled for race, grade, social class, length of residence in the neighborhood, height, and obesity. Similarly, a Russian study (Karagodina, Soldatkina, Vinokur, & Klimukhin, 1969) suggests that children (9–13 years old) in noise-impacted areas around nine airports show blood pressure abnormalities, higher lability of pulse, cardiac insufficiency, and local and general vascular changes. Unfortunately, the report does not provide any information on the nature of the quiet control population or any details of the measurement procedures.

Studies of the effects of traffic noise on cardiovascular measures are less consistent. A German study of children in the seventh through tenth grades (Karsdorf & Klappach, 1968) reports higher systolic and diastolic pressure for children from noisy schools, and a Dutch study (Knipschild & Salle, 1979) found no evidence for increased risk of cardiovascular disease in middle-aged housewives living on streets with high levels of traffic noise as compared with their neighbors living on quieter streets. Overall, like the industrial studies, the studies of community noise suggest that such noise is associated with an increased incidence of cardiovascular disease and some factors related to the risk of cardiovascular pathology. One striking aspect of these data is the evidence that children as well as adults (and possibly even more than adults) show noise-associated cardiovascular effects (cf. Cohen et al., 1979).

There are a number of other studies investigating the impact of aircraft noise on various health problems. For example, increased noise has been associated with pregnancy complications and decreases in the health and survival of newborn infants (e.g., Ando & Hattori, 1973, 1977; Edmonds, Layde, & Erickson, 1979; Jones & Tauscher, 1978; Knipschild, Meijer, & Salle, 1977). These data are somewhat inconsistent, however, and as yet inconclusive (see review by Knipschild et al., 1977). It has also been reported that increased noise levels due to aircraft overflights are associated with increased *death* rates due to strokes and cirrhosis of the liver (Meecham & Shaw, 1979), although a reanalysis of the same data, carefully controlling for the confounding effects of age, race, and sex, found no difference in the mortality rates of the airport and control areas (Frerichs, Beeman, & Coulson, 1980). Other studies report noise-associated increases in nervous and gastrointestinal diseases (Karagodina et al., 1969), consumption of sleeping pills and visits to doctors (Grandjean et al., 1973), and self-reported incidences of a variety of chronic illnesses (Cameron, Robertson, & Zaks, 1972). In isolation, this work (some of which suffers from serious methodological flaws) can only be viewed as suggestive of possible pathogenic effects of community noise exposure. Replication of these studies would greatly increase our confidence in their findings.

Conclusion

Two themes recur throughout this article and deserve some additional emphasis. The first theme has to do with the importance of psychological factors, particularly the predictability, controllability, and meaning of the noise, in mediating the relationship between noise and human response. The second theme involves the possibility that the masking of auditory communication is responsible for a number of what we have presented as nonauditory effects.

The preceding review suggests that the ability to predict and control the occurrence of the noise mediates both psychological and physiological response. Hence, unpredictable noise is more likely to disrupt performance, to lead to variable performance, to be reported as annoying, and to be linked with pathological response than predictable noise. One's perception that a noise is controllable, i.e., that it can be escaped or avoided, can eliminate post-exposure deficits in task performance and interpersonal sensitivity. Perceptions of control also play a role in reported annoyance and may be an ameliorative factor in noise-induced disease.

The respondents' perception of the role of noise in a particular context is also important in mediating the relationship between noise and human response. Noise that is perceived as disruptive of an important goal, unnecessary, representative of something that is feared or loathed, and is produced without concern for the respondent is more likely to elicit stress-related responses than noise without these characteristics. Although the strongest data for this conclusion are those collected in noise annoyance surveys, there is reason to believe that these factors are also important in predicting the impact of noise on performance and pathological response.

Although we limited this article to the discussion of nonauditory effects of noise, the masking of auditory communication provides a possible explanation for a number of reported effects, particularly the deleterious effects of noise on human performance. It is obvious that a task whose performance requires auditory communications will suffer under high-intensity noise. As mentioned earlier, Poulton (1977) has also argued that even in situations in which masking is not obvious, noise may interfere with the reception of subtle auditory feedback cues or with hearing one's own internal speech. Noise masking of parent–child and teacher–child communication may also be responsible for the poorer scholastic performance among children living and/or attending school in noisy neighborhoods and masking of supervisor–worker or worker–worker communication may be partly responsible for increased incidence of accidents for those working in noisy industrial settings. It also seems likely that decreased social interactions under noise (e.g., Appleyard & Lintell, 1972) may be wholly or partly due to one's expectancy that communication would be awkward and difficult under noisy conditions.

In sum, it is clear that the mere existence of unwanted sound, even at relatively high intensities, is often not sufficient to cause a deleterious effect of noise. Our response to any particular noise is determined to some degree by its physical properties, its meaning (including its significance), and various characteristics of the respondent. Even so, an overall view of the existing research suggests that prolonged exposure to high-intensity noise in community or work settings is often harmful to the health and behavior of large segments of the exposed populations.

References

Abbey-Wickrama, I., a'Brook, M. F., Gattoni, F. W. G., & Herridge, C. F. Mental hospital admissions and aircraft noise. *Lancet*, 1969, *2*, 1275–1277.

Ahrlin, U., & Öhrström, E. Medical effects of environmental noise on humans. *Journal of Sound and Vibration*, 1978, *59*, 79–87.

Alexandre, A. Decision criteria based on spatio-temporal comparisons of surveys of an aircraft noise. In W. D. Ward (Ed.), *Proceedings of the International Conference on Noise as a Public Health Problem* (EPA 550/9-73-008). Washington, D.C.: U.S. Government Printing Office, 1973.

Ando, Y., & Hattori, H. Statistical studies on the effects of intense noise during human fetal life. *Sound and Vibration*, 1973, *27*, 101–110.

Ando, Y., & Hattori, H. Effects of noise on human placental lactogen, (HPL) levels in maternal plasma. *British Journal of Obstetrics and Gynaecology*, 1977, *84*, 115–118.

Appleyard, D., & Lintell, M. The environmental quality of city streets: The residents' viewpoint. *Journal of the American Institute of Planners*, 1972, *38*, 84–101.

Boggs, D. H., & Simon, J. R. Differential effects of noise on tasks of varying complexity. *Journal of Applied Psychology*, 1968, *52*, 148–153.

Borsky, P. N. *A new field-laboratory methodology for assessing human response to noise* (NASA CR-221). Washington, D.C.: National Aeronautics and Space Administration, 1973.

Borsky, P. N. Research on community response to noise since 1973. In J. V. Tobias (Ed.), *The proceedings of the Third International Congress on Noise as a Public Health Problem*. Washington, D.C.: American Speech and Hearing Association, 1980.

Bragdon, C. R. *Noise pollution: The unquiet crisis*. Philadelphia: University of Pennsylvania Press, 1971.

Broadbent, D. E. *Decision and stress*. New York: Academic Press, 1971.

Broadbent, D. E. Individual differences in annoyance by noise. *Sound*, 1972, *6*, 56–61.

Broadbent, D. E. The current state of noise research: Reply to Poulton. *Psychological Bulletin*, 1978, *85*, 1052–1067.

Broadbent, D. E. Human performance and noise. In C. M. Harris (Ed.), *Handbook of noise control*. New York: McGraw-Hill, 1979.

Broadbent, D. E., & Little, F. A. J. Effects of noise reduction in a work situation. *Occupational Psychology*, 1960, *34*, 133–140.

Bronzaft, A. L., & McCarthy, D. P. The effects of elevated train noise on reading ability. *Environment and Behavior*, 1975, *7*, 517–527.

Broussard, I. G. Cited in Broadbent, D. E. Human performance and noise. In C. M. Harris (Ed.), *Handbook of noise control*. New York: McGraw-Hill, 1979.

Brown, R., & Herrnstein, R. J. *Psychology*. Boston: Little, Brown, 1975.

Cameron, P., Robertson, D., & Zaks, J. Sound pollution, noise pollution, and health: Community parameters. *Journal of Applied Psychology*, 1972, *56*, 67–74.

Capellini, A., & Maroni, M. Clinical survey on hypertension and coronary disease and their possible relations with the environment in workers of a chemical plant (Italian). *Medicina del Lavoro*, 1974, *65*, 297–305.

Carosi, L., & Calabro, F. Fertility of couples working in noisy factories. *Folia Medica*, 1968, *51*, 264–268.

Cassel, J. Psychosocial processes and "stress": Theoretical formulation. *International Journal of Health Services*, 1974, *4*, 471–482.

Cederlöf, R., Friberg, L., Hammarfors, P., Holmquist, S. E., & Kajland, A. Studier över ljudnivaer och hygieniska olägenheter av trafikbuller samt förslag till atgärder. *Nordisk Hygienisk Tidskrift*, 1961, *42*, 101–192.

Chowns, R. H. Mental-hospital admissions and aircraft noise. *Lancet*, 1970, *1*, 467.

Cohen, A. Effects of noise on psychological state. In W. Ward & J. Fricke (Eds.), *Noise as a public health hazard*. Washington, D.C.: American Speech and Hearing Association, 1969.

Cohen, A. Industrial noise and medical, absence, and accident record data on exposed workers. In W. D. Ward (Ed.), *Proceedings of the International Congress on Noise as a Public Health Problem*. Washington, D.C.: U.S. Government Printing Office, 1973.

Cohen, A. The influence of a company hearing conservation program on extra-auditory problems in workers. *Journal of Safety Research*, 1976, *8*, 146–162.

Cohen, A. Extraauditory effects on acoustic stimulation. In D. K. Lee, H. L. Falk, S. D. Murphy, & S. R. Geiger (Eds.), *Handbook of physiology: Reactions to environmental agents, Section 9*. Baltimore: Williams & Wilkins, 1977.

Cohen, A. *Remarks as discussant at symposium: Research needs with regards to the nonauditory effects of noise*. Presented at the Annual Meeting of the American Psychological Association, New York, September, 1979.

Cohen, S. Environmental load and the allocation of attention. In A. Baum, J. E. Singer, & S. Valins (Eds.), *Advances in environmental psychology, Vol. 1*. Hillsdale, N.J.: Erlbaum, 1978.

Cohen, S. Cognitive processes as determinants of environmental stress. In I. Sarason & C. Speilberger (Eds.), *Stress and anxiety, Vol. 7*. Washington, D.C.: Hemisphere Press, 1980. (a)

Cohen, S. The aftereffects of stress on human performance and social behavior: A review of research and theory. *Psychological Bulletin*, 1980, *88*, 82–108. (b)

Cohen, S., Evans, G. W., Krantz, D. S., & Stokols, D. Physiological, motivational and cognitive effects of aircraft noise on children: Moving from the laboratory to the field. *American Psychologist*, 1980, *35*, 231–243.

Cohen, S., Evans, G. W., Krantz, D. S., Stokols, D., & Kelly, S. Aircraft noise and children: Longitudinal and cross-sectional evidence on adaptation to noise and the effectiveness of noise abatement. *Journal of Personality and Social Psychology*, 1981, *40*, 331–345.

Cohen, S., Glass, D. C., & Phillips, S. Environment and health. In H. E. Freeman, S. Levine, and L. G. Reeder (Eds.), *Handbook of medical sociology*. Englewood Cliffs, N.J.: Prentice-Hall, 1979.

Cohen, S., Glass, D. C., & Singer, J. E. Apartment noise, auditory discrimination, and reading ability in children. *Journal of Experimental Social Psychology*, 1973, *9*, 407–422.

Cohen, S., & Lezak, A. Noise and inattentiveness to social cues. *Environment and Behavior*, 1977, *9*, 559–572.

Crook, M. A., & Langdon, F. J. The effects of aircraft noise in schools around London Airport. *Sound and Vibration*, 1974, *34*, 221–232.

Crosby, F. A model of egoistical relative deprivation. *Psychological Review*, 1976, *83*, 85–113.

Damon, A. The residential environment, health, and behavior: Simple research opportunities, strategies, and some findings in the Solomon Islands and Boston, Massachusetts. In L. E. Hinkle, Jr., & W. C. Loring (Eds.), *The effect of the man-made environment on health and behavior*. Atlanta: Center for Disease Control, Public Health Service, 1977.

Dokukina, G. A., Koberts, G. P., & Lyubomudrov, V. Y. On the nonspecific effect of noise and vibration (Russian). *Vrachneboe Delo*, 1972, *2*, 134–136.

Donnerstein, E., & Wilson, D. W. Effects of noise and perceived control on ongoing and subsequent aggressive behavior. *Journal of Personality and Social Psychology*, 1976, *34*, 774–781.

Edmonds, L. D., Layde, P. M., & Erickson, J. D. Airport noise and teratogenesis. *Archives of Environmental Health*, 1979, *34*, 243–247.

Finke, H. O., Guski, R., Martin, R., Rohrmann, B., Schümer, R., & Schümer-Kohrs, A. Effects of aircraft noise on man. *Proceedings of the Symposium on Noise in Transportation, Section III, paper 1*. Southampton: Institute of Sound and Vibration Research, 1974.

Finkelman, J. M., & Glass, D. C. Reappraisal of the relationship between noise and human performance by means of a subsidiary task measure. *Journal of Applied Psychology*, 1970, *54*, 211–213.

Finkle, A. L., & Poppen, J. R. Clinical effects of noise and mechanical vibrations of a turbo-jet engine on man. *Journal of Applied Physiology*, 1948, *1*, 183–204.

Fisher, S. A "distraction effect" of noise bursts. *Perception*, 1972, *1*, 223–236.

Forster, P. M., & Grierson, A. T. Noise and attentional selectivity: A reproducible phenomenon? *British Journal of Psychology*, 1978, *69*, 489–498.

Frerichs, R. R., Beeman, B. L., & Coulson, A. H. Los Angeles Airport noise and mortality-fault analysis and public policy. *American Journal of Public Health*, 1980, *70*, 357–362.

Gardner, G. T. Effects of federal human subjects regulations on data obtained in environmental stressor research. *Journal of Personality and Social Psychology*, 1978, *36*, 628–634.

Gattoni, F., & Tarnopolsky, A. Aircraft noise and psychiatric morbidity. *Psychological Medicine*, 1973, *3*, 516–520.

Glass, D. C., & Singer, J. E. *Urban stress: Experiments on noise and social stressors*. New York: Academic Press, 1972.

Glorig, A. Non-auditory effects of noise exposure. *Sound and Vibration*, 1971, *5*, 28–29.

Granati, A., Angelepi, F., & Lenzi, R. L'influenza dei rumori sul sistema nervoso. *Folia Medica*, 1959, *42*, 1313–1325.

Grandjean, E. *Sozio-psychologische Untersuchungen vor den Fluglarms*. Bern, 1974.

Grandjean, E., Graf, P., Lauber, A., Meier, H. P., & Müller, R. A survey on aircraft noise in Switzerland. In W. D. Ward (Ed.), *Proceedings of the International Congress on Noise as a Public Health Problem.* Washington, D.C.: U.S. Government Printing Office, 1973.

Green, K. B. *The effects of community noise exposure on the reading and hearing ability of Brooklyn and Queens school children.* Dissertation submitted to the Program in Environmental Health Sciences, New York University, 1979.

Griffiths, I. D., & Delauzun, F. R. Individual differences in sensitivity to traffic noise: An empirical study. *Journal of Sound and Vibration,* 1977, *55,* 93–107.

Griffiths, I. D., & Langdon, F. J. Subjective response to road traffic noise. *Journal of Sound and Vibration.* 1968, *8,* 16–32.

Hamilton, P. Selective attention in multisource monitoring tasks. *Journal of Experimental Psychology,* 1969, *82,* 34–37.

Hand, D. J., Tarnopolsky, A., Barker, S. M., & Jenkins, L. M. Relationships between psychiatric hospital admissions and aircraft noise: A new study. In J. V. Tobias (Ed.), *The Proceedings of the Third International Congress on Noise as a Public Health Problem.* Washington, D.C.: American Speech and Hearing Association, 1980.

Harris, C. S. The effects of different types of acoustic stimulation on performance. In W. D. Ward (Ed.), *Proceedings of the International Congress on Noise as a Public Health Problem.* Washington, D.C.: U.S. Environmental Protection Agency, 1973.

Hartley, L. R. Effect of prior noise or prior performance on serial reaction. *Journal of Experimental Psychology,* 1973, *101,* 255–261.

Heft, H. Background and focal environmental conditions of the home and attention in young children. *Journal of Applied Social Psychology,* 1979, *9,* 47–69.

Herridge, C. F., & Chir, B. Aircraft noise and mental hospital admissions. *Sound,* 1972, *6,* 32–36.

Hockey, G. R. J. Effect of loud noise on attentional selectivity. *Quarterly Journal of Experimental Psychology,* 1970, *22,* 28–36. (a)

Hockey, G. R. J. Signal probability and spatial location as possible bases for increased selectivity in noise. *Quarterly Journal of Experimental Psychology,* 1970, *22,* 37–42. (b)

Hockey, G. R. J., & Hamilton, P. Arousal and information selection in short-term memory. *Nature,* 1970, *226,* 866–867.

Isen, A. M. Success, failure, attention, and reaction to others: The warm glow of success. *Journal of Personality and Social Psychology,* 1970, *15,* 294–301.

Jansen, G. On the origin of functional vegetative change due to working under noise (German). *Archiv für Gewerbepathologie und Gewerbehygiene,* 1959, *17,* 238–261.

Jansen, G. Adverse effects of noise in iron and steel workers. *Stahl und Eisen,* 1961, *81,* 217–220.

Jansen, G. Effects of noise on physiological state. In W. D. Ward & J. E. Fricke (Eds.), *Noise as a public health problem.* Washington, D.C.: American Speech and Hearing Association, 1969.

Jones, F. N., & Tauscher, J. Residence under an airport landing pattern as a factor in teratism. *Archives of Environmental Health,* 1978, *33,* 10–12.

Jonsson, E., & Sorensen, S. Adaptation to community noise—A case study. *Journal of Sound and Vibration,* 1973, *26,* 571–575.

Jonsson, E., Arvidsson, O., Berglund, K., & Kajland. A. Methodological aspects of studies of community response to noise. In W. D. Ward (Ed.), *Proceedings of the*

International Conference on Noise as a Public Health Problem (EPA 550/9-73-008). Washington, D.C.: U.S. Government Printing Office, 1973.

Kangelari, S. S., Abramovich-Polyakov, D. K., & Rudenko, V. F. The effects of noise and vibration on morbidity rates (Russian) *Gigiena Truda i Professional 'nye Zabolevaniya*, 1966, *6*, 47–49.

Karagodina, I. L., Soldatkina, S. A., Vinokur, I. L., & Klimukhin. A. A. Effect of aircraft noise on the population near airports. *Hygiene and Sanitation*, 1969, *34*, 182–187.

Karsdorf, G., & Klappach, H. Einflüsse des Verkehrslärms auf Gesundheit und Leistung bei Oberschülern einer Grofzstadt. *Zeitschrift fur die Gefamte Hygiene*, 1968, *14*, 52–54.

Khomulo, L. P., Rodinova, L. P., & Rusinova, A. P. Changes in the blood lipid metabolism of man owing to the prolonged effects of industrial noise on the central nervous system (Russian). *Kardologia*, 1967, *7*, 35-38.

Knipschild, P. G. *Medische Gevolgen van Vliegtuilawaai* (doctoral thesis with English summary, pp. 127-129). Amsterdam Coronel Laboratorium, 1976.

Knipschild, P. Medical effects of aircraft noise. *International Archives of Occupational and Environmental Health*, 1977, *40*, 185-204.

Knipschild, P., Meijer, H., Salle, H. *Aircraft noise and birth weight*. Coronel Laboratory, University of Amsterdam, 1054 BW Amsterdam, The Netherlands, 1977.

Knipschild, P. & Salle, H. Road traffic noise and cardiovascular disease: A population study in the Netherlands. *International Archives of Occupational and Environmental Health*, 1979, *44*, 55–99.

Kokokusha, D. *Report on Investigation of Living Environment around Osaka International Airport*. Japan: Association for the Prevention of Aircraft Nuisance, 1973.

Korte, C., Ypma, A., & Toppen, C. Helpfulness in Dutch society as a function of urbanization and environmental input level. *Journal of Personality and Social Psychology*, 1975, *32*, 996–1003.

Krauskopf, J., & Coleman, P. D. Cited in Broadbent, D. E. Human performance and noise. In C. M. Harris (Ed.), *Handbook of noise control*. New York: McGraw-Hill, 1979.

Kryter, K. D. *The effects of noise on man*. New York: Academic Press, 1970.

Leonard, S., & Borsky, P. N. A causal model for relating noise exposure, psychological variables and aircraft noise annoyance. In W. D. Ward (Ed.), *Proceedings of the International Conference on Noise as a Public Health Problem* (EPA 550/9-73-008). Washington, D.C.: U.S. Government Printing Office, 1973.

Loeb, M. Noise and performance: Do we know more? In J. V. Tobias (Ed.), *The Proceedings of the Third International Congress on Noise as a Public Health Problem*. Washington, D.C.: American Speech and Hearing Association, 1980.

Loeb, M., & Jones, P. D. Noise exposure, monitoring, and tracking performance as a function of signal bias and task priority. *Ergonomics*, 1978, *21*, 265–279.

McBain, W. N. Noise, the "arousal hypothesis," and monotonous work. *Journal of Applied Psychology*, 1961, *45*, 309–317.

McCroskey, R. L., & Devens, J. S. *Effects of noise upon student performance in public school classrooms*. Proceedings of the Technical Program, National Noise and Vibration Control Conference. Chicago, Illinois, 1977.

McKennell, A. C. *Aircraft noise annoyance around London (Heathrow) Airport* (Central Office of Information, U.K. Government Social Survey S.S. 337). London: Her Majesty's Stationary Office, 1963.

McKennell, A. C. Psycho-social factors in aircraft noise annoyance. In W. D. Ward (Ed.), *Proceedings of the International Conference on Noise as a Public Health Problem* (EPA 550/9-73-008). Washington, D.C.: U.S. Government Printing Office, 1973.

McLean, E. K., & Tarnopolsky, A. Noise, discomfort and mental health: A review of the socio-medical implications of disturbance by noise. *Psychological Medicine,* 1977, *7,* 19–62.

Maser, A. L., Sorensen, P. H., & Kryter, K. D. *Effects of intrusive sound on classroom behavior: Data from a successful lawsuit.* Paper presented at the Annual Meeting of the Western Psychological Association, San Francisco, 1978.

Mathews, K. E., Jr., & Canon, L. K. Environmental noise level as a determinant of helping behavior. *Journal of Personality and Social Psychology,* 1975, *32,* 571–577.

Meecham, W. C., & Shaw, N. Effects of jet noise on mortality rates. *British Journal of Audiology,* 1979, *13,* 77–80.

Meecham, W. C., & Smith, H. G. Effects of jet aircraft noise on mental hospital admissions. *British Journal of Audiology,* 1977, *11,* 81–85.

Miles, W. A. *In the Benox Report.* Chicago University, 1953.

Miller, J. D. Effects of noise on people. *Journal of the Acoustical Society of America,* 1974, *56,* 729–764.

Moch-Sibony, A. Study of the effects of noise on the personality and certain psychomotor and intellectual aspects of children, after a prolonged exposure. (French). *Travail Humain,* in press.

Moore, B., Underwood, B., & Rosenhan, D. L. Affect and altruism. *Developmental Psychology,* 1973, *8,* 99–104.

Moreira, M. N., & Bryan, M. E. Noise annoyance susceptibility. *Journal of Sound and Vibration,* 1972, *21,* 449–462.

Moos, R. H. *The human context.* New York: Wiley, 1976.

Office of Population Census and Survey. *Second survey of airport noise annoyance around London (Heathrow) Airport.* London: Her Majesty's Stationary Office, 1970.

O'Malley, J. J., & Poplawsky, A. Noise induced arousal and breadth of attention. *Perceptual and motor skills,* 1971, *33,* 887–890.

Page, R. A. Noise and helping behavior. *Environment and Behavior,* 1977, *9,* 311–334.

Parvizpoor, D. Noise exposure and prevalence of high blood pressure, among weavers in Iran. *Journal of Occupational Medicine,* 1976, *18,* 730–731.

Peterson, E. A. *Some issues and investigations concerning extra auditory effects of noise.* Paper presented at annual meeting of the American Psychological Association, New York, September, 1979.

Pokrovskii, N. N. On the effect of industrial noise on the blood pressure level in workers in machine building plants (Russian). *Gigiena Truda i Professional 'nye Zabolevaniya,* 1966, *10,* 44–46.

Poulton, E. C. Continuous intense noise masks auditory feedback and inner speech. *Psychological Bulletin,* 1977, *84,* 977–1001.

Poulton, E. C. A new look at the effects of noise: A rejoinder. *Psychological Bulletin,* 1978, *85,* 1068–1079.

Poulton, E. C. Composite model for human performance in continuous noise. *Psychological Review,* 1979, *86,* 361–375.

Raytheon Service Company. *Industrial Noise and Worker Medical, Absence and Accident Records.* National Institute of Occupational Safety and Health Contract Report TRL-NIOSH RR-17, 1972.

Rotton, J., Oszewski, D., Charleton, M., & Soler, E. Loud speech, conglomerate noise, and behavioral aftereffects. *Journal of Applied Psychology*, 1978, *63*, 360–365.

Sanders, A. F. The influence of noise on two discrimination tasks. *Ergonomics*, 1961, *4*, 253–258.

Sauser, W. I., Jr., Arauz, C. G., & Chambers, R. M. Exploring the relationship between level of office noise and salary recommendations: A preliminary research note. *Journal of Management*, 1978, *4*, 57–63.

Schultz, T. J. Synthesis of social surveys on noise annoyance. *Journal of the Acoustical Society of America*, 1978, *64*, 377–405.

Selye, H. *The stress of life*. New York: McGraw-Hill, 1956.

Sherrod, D. R., & Downs, R. Environmental determinants of altruism: The effects of stimulus overload and perceived control on helping. *Journal of Experimental Social Psychology*, 1974, *10*, 468–479.

Sherrod, D. R., Hage, J. N., Halpern, P. L., & Moore, B. S. Effects of personal causation and perceived control on responses to an aversive environment: The more control, the better. *Journal of Experimental Social Psychology*. 1977, *13*, 14–27.

Siegel, J. M., & Steele, C. M. Noise level and social discrimination. *Personality and Social Psychology Bulletin*, 1979, *5*, 95–99.

Slater, B. R. Effects of noise on pupil performance. *Journal of Educational Psychology*, 1968, *59*, 239–243.

Smith, A. P., & Broadbent, D. E. The effects of noise on performance on embedded figures tasks. *Journal of Applied Psychology*, 1980, *65*, 246–248.

Sörensen, S. On the possibilities of changing the annoyance reaction to noise by changing the attitude to the source of annoyance. *Nordisk Hygienisk Tidskrift, Supplementum 1*, 1970, 1–76.

Stevens, S. S. Stability of human performance under intense noise. *Journal of Sound and Vibration*, 1972, *21*, 35–36.

Tracor, Inc. *Community reactions to airport noise, Volume I* (NASA CR-1761). Washington, D.C.: National Aeronautics and Space Administration, 1970.

U.S. Bureau of Census, *Annual housing survey: 1973 U.S. and regions: Part B, Indicators of housing and neighborhood quality*. Current Housing Report Series H-150-73-B. Washington, D.C.: U.S. Government Printing Office, 1973.

U.S. Environmental Protection Agency. *Information on levels of environmental noise requisite to protect public health and welfare with an adequate margin for safety* (EPA 550/9-74004). Washington, D.C.: U.S. Government Printing Office, 1974.

Wachs, T. D. The relationship of infants' physical environment to their Binet performance at 2-1/2 years. *International Journal of Behavioral Development*, 1978, *1*, 51–65.

Wachs, T. D. Proximal experience and early cognitive-intellectual development: The physical environment. *Merrill-Palmer Quarterly of Behavior and Development*, 1979, *25*, 3–41.

Wachs, T. D., Uzgiris, I. C., & Hunt, J. McV. Cognitive development in infants of different age levels and from different environmental backgrounds: An exploratory investigation. *Merrill-Palmer Quarterly of Behavior and Development*, 1971, *17*, 288–317.

Ward, L. M., & Suedfeld, P. Human response to highway noise. *Environmental Research*, 1973, *6*, 306–326.

Weinstein, C. S., & Weinstein, N. D. Noise and reading performance in an open space school. *Journal of Educational Research*, 1979, *72*, 210–213.

Weinstein, N. D. Human evaluations of environmental noise. In K. Craik & E. H. Zube (Eds.), *Perceiving environmental quality*. New York: Plenum, 1976.

Weinstein, N. D. Individual differences in reactions to noise: A longitudinal study in a college dormitory. *Journal of Applied Psychology*, 1978, *63*, 458–466.

Weinstein, N. D. Individual differences in critical tendencies and noise annoyance. *Journal of Sound and Vibration*, 1979, *67*, 241–248.

Welch, B. L. *Extra-auditory health effects of industrial noise: Survey of foreign literature.* Aerospace Medical Research Laboratory, Aerospace Medical Division, Air Force Systems Command, Wright-Patterson, June, 1979.

Weston, H. C., & Adams, S. *Part II, Report no. 65, Industrial Health Research Board.* London: Her Majesty's Stationary Office, 1932. Also cited in Broadbent, 1979.

Wilkinson, R. T. Interaction of noise, with knowledge of results and sleep deprivation. *Journal of Experimental Psychology*, 1963, *66*, 332–337.

Wohlwill, J. F., Naser, J. L., DeJoy, D. M., & Foruzani, H. H. Behavioral effects of a noisy environment: Task involvement versus passive exposure. *Journal of Applied Psychology*, 1976, *61*, 67–74.

Woodhead, M. M. The effect of bursts of noise on an arithmetic task. *American Journal of Psychology*, 1964, *77*, 627–633.

3. Thermal stress: Physiological, comfort, performance, and social effects of hot and cold environments

Paul A. Bell and Thomas C. Greene

Human cultures have adapted to climatic extremes ranging from frigid arctic cold to debilitating tropical heat. Even within a culture, circumstances may require that humans encounter wide variation in temperatures. There is little question about the capability of humans to tolerate thermal extremes. There is concern, however, about the cost of such tolerance, for there are demonstrable effects of exposure to abnormally high or low ambient temperatures. These effects include physiological adaptation, changes in performance, and influences on social behavior. Concern about a number of circumstances under which humans encounter these physiological and behavioral consequences of thermal stress has prompted considerable research, much of which is of interest to psychologists and others studying social issues.

First, there is concern about consequences of naturally changing temperatures, as typified by studies relating crime and violence to seasonal fluctuations in temperature. Second, industry has studied worker safety and productivity in temperature extremes, as exemplified by work near blast furnaces, on the Alaska Pipeline, or undersea. Third, military researchers are interested in the effects of moving troops rapidly from one climate to another. Finally, especially because of energy costs and shortages, researchers have become concerned about the effects of slightly uncomfortable temperatures on office and classroom performance.

Homo sapiens is biologically a tropical or subtropical species, yet human societies thrive in arctic latitudes. A number of authors (e.g., Edholm, 1978; Griffiths, 1975; Sloan, 1979) have remarked that humans often avoid severe cold by using technology (clothing, shelter) and thus show relatively little biological adaptation. In fact, Griffiths (1975) states that biological cold adaptation is somewhat academic since clothing and shelter adjustments are so common. On the other hand, social and privacy pressures against removal of clothing or the use of highly transparent shelter prevent similarly easy modes of coping with elevated ambient temperatures in many cultures. Furthermore, since technological adjustments predominate adaptation to cold stress, most behavioral research on thermal stress concentrates on heat effects. Accordingly, the present review will emphasize research on heat stress, with research on cold stress presented as it is available. Perception of temperature and physiological mechanisms involved in thermoregulation are covered first, followed by a review of the effects of thermal stress on performance. Next, research on ambient temperature and social behavior is covered, with a concluding section on theory and future research priorities.

Perception of ambient temperature and physiological mechanisms in thermoregulation

Changes in a number of physiological states, such as arousal, have marked effects on performance and other behaviors. Since thermal stress has clear effects on physiology and comfort, it is not surprising that it influences overt behavior. Consequently, it is worthwhile to examine the physiology of thermal stress, including core temperature and thermoreceptors, thermoregulation, physical disorders associated with extreme ambient temperatures, and effects on arousal, before discussing more overt behavioral effects. More detailed reviews of the physiology of heat stress may be found in Folk (1974) and Mount (1979). The physiological effects of cold and heat stress are discussed in similar detail by Edholm (1978), Itoh (1974), and Le Blanc (1975). In addition, the present discussion will note the important complicating variables of air speed, humidity, clothing, and acclimatization, which contribute to physiological reactions to, and accompanying sensations of, thermal comfort and discomfort.

Physiological effects of heat and cold are closely tied to the need to keep the core temperature of the body (i.e., internal temperature) near 37°C (98.6°F). A core temperature above 45°C (113°F) or below 25°C (77°F) leads to death. Because ambient temperature has major effects on core temperature, there is definite survival value in being able to assess ambient temperature accurately. Although all humans know they can detect cold and warmth via the skin, there is debate over the exact nature of thermoreceptors in the skin (e.g., Carlson, 1977). Most of the current evidence suggests that these nerve endings are receptive to changes in temperature rather than to absolute temperature, and they habituate rather rapidly to steady state stimuli.

Aside from these peripheral thermoreceptors, the mechanism central to thermoregulation and core temperature detection is the anterior hypothalamus. Apparently, this limbic mechanism is directly sensitive to changes in temperature, both from body fluids and from implantation of heating or cooling devices (Myers, 1974). Largely through the action of the hypothalamus, the body adapts to changes in core temperature, which is generated by body metabolism. If all is working well, enough heat is retained to keep core temperature near 37°C, and excess heat is dissipated into the environment by means of convection and radiation from the skin, evaporation of moisture from the skin and lungs, and conduction. At temperatures slightly above the ideal, the major adaptive mechanism is peripheral vasodilation, or dilation of surface blood vessels to increase the loss of heat through convection and radiation. At higher temperatures, sweating occurs to increase heat loss through evaporation, and activity level may slow to reduce heat production. More detailed analysis of these adaptive reactions to heat is given in Goldman (1978) and Rowell (1978).

Mild cooling can be tolerated with a rise in metabolic rate, but further core temperature decreases are met with physiological or behavioral reactions that either increase heat production or decrease heat loss. Methods of accelerating heat production incude increased muscular activity, shivering, and complex metabolic thermogenesis. Heat loss is reduced in body extremities through peripheral vasoconstriction that reduces blood flow (and thus loss through convection) and through behaviors such as huddling. Huddling moderates heat loss by reducing body surface area by as much as 50%. Stiffening of skin hairs (piloerection) accompanied by "goose bumps" may further reduce heat loss at the skin by trapping a thin layer of insulating air near the skin, although some authorities (Edholm, 1979) dispute the effectiveness of this mechanism in humans.

If thermoregulatory mechanisms fail to restore core temperature to normal, several physiological disorders can result (see also, Folk, 1974). In the case of heat stress, the mildest problem is heat exhaustion, characterized by faintness, nausea, vomiting, headache, and restlessness. Replacement of lost water and salt, with rest, will cure heat exhaustion in a short time. A more serious and life-threatening problem is heat stroke, characterized by confusion, staggering, headache, delirium, coma, and eventually death. In this disorder, the sweating mechanism has broken down (the absence of sweat distinguishes it from heat exhaustion) and immediate cooling, such as immersion in ice water, is necessary for survival. Another heat-related disorder can be heart attack, resulting from excessive demands on the cardiovascular system in the thermoregulatory process. In fact, it is common to find marked increases in death due to heart attacks during heat wave conditions. The analogous disorder associated with cold stress is hypothermia, or lowering of the body core temperature. As the body core temperature approaches 32°C (90°F), shivering is replaced by muscular rigidity, confusion, and eventually, loss of consciousness. If warmth is not restored, coma and death from heart attack follow below a core temperature of about 25°C (77°F) (Poulton, 1970).

Measures of arousal are very complex in the case of heat stress, partly because of the thermoregulatory mechanisms. For example, there may well be an increase in blood pressure due to an initial "startle" response to sudden extreme ambient temperatures. However, as peripheral vasodilation occurs, blood pressure usually drops. As heat stroke approaches and the heart pumps harder to move more blood to the periphery, blood pressure may rise and then fall off again as coma and death approach. Heart rate, on the other hand, may increase linearly with heat stress. Galvanic skin response will increase markedly as thermoregulatory sweating occurs. Electrophysiological arousal measured from the reticular activating system indicates relatively low arousal at a core temperature of 37°C, with arousal increasing as core temperature gets higher or lower (Griffiths, 1975; Provins, 1966). Subjectively, most people report feeling lethargic as temperatures increase beyond a comfortable range, and self-report measures of arousal indicate that arousal decreases as ambient temperature increases (Cervone, 1977). Thus, arousal is very complex in heat stress, and no single measure of arousal under heat stress is a reliable predictor of performance.

Complicating factors in thermal stress

The impact of thermal stress on an individual is not just a function of ambient temperature. Rather, the crucial factor is how well the body can maintain core temperature. Consequently, any factor that reduces the efficiency of homeothermic mechanisms will increase thermal stress, and any factor that increases this efficiency will reduce it. Among these factors are air speed, humidity, clothing, and acclimatization. Provided that air temperature is below body temperature, increases in air velocity will increase convective heat loss. If air temperature is above body temperature, the reverse process will occur (for more detailed information, see Griffiths, 1975; Mount, 1979).

High humidity reduces the efficiency of heat loss through evaporation in high ambient temperatures and increases heat loss through convection in low ambient temperatures. Attempts have been made to account for the subsequent effects of humidity on comfort by devising effective temperature scales (cf., Nevins, Rohles, Springer, & Feyerherm, 1966). For example, in terms of comfort a thermometer reading of 30°C (86°F) at 80% relative humidity is equivalent to an effective temperature of 44°C (111°F) at 0% humidity (Landsberg, 1969).

Another factor influencing heat stress is clothing, which provides varying degrees of insulation and thus retards heat loss. Insulation values are determined by measuring heat flow from a heated manikin to the outside of the clothing, either in a unit called a *clo* or a *tog* (Newburgh, 1968).

Acclimatization. A final consideration in studying physiological changes in thermal stress is acclimatization, characterized by increased physiological tolerance after continued exposure to high or low thermal environments. Acclimatization is of practical significance in such situations as work in hot mines or near blast furnaces, shifts of military forces from one climate to another, and even in space exploration (e.g., Hardy, 1964). Acclimatization to thermal environments may take several forms. Some thermal acclimatization may emerge from a genetically inherited ability to tolerate thermal extremes. Alternatively, we can acclimatize to one or more environmental factors as with changing seasons, or exhibit diminished central nervous system reactivity to a particular stimulus (habituation). Frisancho (1979) suggests that developmental changes account for acclimatization in populations native to environments characterized by thermal extremes. Most acclimatization, however, appears to be a physiological process requiring time (usually a matter of days) and is supplemented by behavioral adjustments such as clothing modifications and changes in diet (e.g., Itoh, 1974; Sloan, 1979).

For prolonged exposure to high ambient temperatures, acclimatization can be reasonably achieved in 4–7 days (Fox, 1965; Frisancho, 1979; Ingram & Mount, 1975; Lee, 1964; Leithead & Lind, 1964). Although the primary consequence of acclimatization to heat is increased sweating efficiency, the classic pattern is one of reduced discomfort, reduced heart rate, reduced body temperature, and higher volume of sweat with reduced concentration of salt. Daily exposure of an hour or so is adequate to achieve acclimatization. The better physical condition one is in, the more rapidly acclimatization is achieved (Ingram & Mount, 1975). Leithead and Lind (1964) suggest 100 minutes per day as the most economical exposure and indicate that two such daily exposures will not improve acclimatization. It is often found, moreover, that acclimatization to one hot environment at a certain level of physical exertion does not produce acclimatization to the same temperature at a higher level of physical activity, nor to a hotter environment at the same level of physical activity (Ingram & Mount, 1975). However, if an individual's body temperature is raised while not at work (through induced hyperthermia), that individual can show acclimatization to work in a hot environment (Fox, 1965; Ingram & Mount, 1975). The physiology of acclimatization is discussed in more detail in Frisancho (1979) and Ingram and Mount (1975).

Although there is some argument for genetic differences in acclimatization through natural selection, the evidence is mixed. It is suggested, for example, that the Saharan Touareg have a tall, slender body shape that maximizes surface cooling area relative to the amount of heat-producing tissue (Beighton, 1971; Sloan, 1979). However, this population also avoids heavy exercise during the hot part of the day and wears loose and porous clothing (Beighton, 1971; Sloan, 1979), so there would appear to be both genetic and behavioral factors operating in their acclimatization. It is often suggested that the melanin pigment in the skin of black Africans represents a genetic adaptation to the environment (e.g., Sloan, 1979). This pigment provides some protection from sunburn and from overexposure to ultraviolet light. More important for acclimatization to heat, the pigment increases skin temperature by increasing the absorption of heat, which promotes sweating (Sloan, 1979). However, Ladell (1964) found that acclimatized Europeans showed the same response to heat as native Africans, including initial sweating at the same rectal temperature, equivalent rates of sweating, and similar low salt content in the sweat (Sloan, 1979). On the other hand, Frisancho (1979) reports studies that do show physiological differences between acclimatized Europeans and Africans. Whatever genetic differences exist in acclimatization across populations, they do not seem to be as significant as time of exposure in accounting for differences in acclimatization. Frisancho (1979), moreover, in comparing native and nonnative populations in thermally extreme environments, suggests that developmental changes account for many differences in acclimatization. Within a population, there do seem to be individual differences in acclimatization. Wyndham (1970), for example, has found considerable variation in acclimatization among Bantu workers in hot South African gold mines. Generally, those with lower body temperatures are more tolerant of heat. High body temperature, in turn, seems to be associated with what is physiologically called low maximum oxygen intake (Sloan, 1979).

In populations that have inhabited cold regions, some increased genetic capacity for physiological adaptation seems to have been created by natural selection (Sloan, 1979). In some instances, this adaptation requires the ability to tolerate continuous exposure to moderate cold, whereas other instances illustrate relatively short exposures to more severe cold (Le Blanc & Wilber, 1975). In general, it appears that the adaptive mechanisms of groups who have lived nude or poorly clothed in cold environments differ from the short-term responses to cold (e.g., shivering) already described. Physiological responses of nonnative individuals acclimatized to a cold environment, though, may not differ substantially from natives' responses. The aborigines of central Australia and Bushmen of the Kalahari Desert both experience cold overnight temperatures, but unlike unacclimatized Europeans in the same conditions, they do not shiver and seem to sleep soundly (Le Blanc, 1975). Le Blanc (1956), though, found a similar reduction in shivering among a group of Canadian soldiers who had been acclimatized to a cold environment.

Interestingly, the rectal temperatures in the Australian aborigines and Kalahari Bushmen show more cooling than is observed in Europeans. Apparently, the fundamental adaptation is not to resist the temperature drop with shivering, but rather to allow a slight reduction in core temperature while avoiding the discomfort of shivering (Le Blanc, 1975; Edholm, 1979). Metabolic factors may also play a role in acclimatization. The Alacaluf Indians of Tierra del Fuego, for example, do not show the temperature drops of other native groups because of an elevated metabolic rate (Hammel, Elsner, Andersen, Scholander, Coon, Medina, Strozzie, Milan, & Hock, 1960, as cited in Le Blanc, 1975). Le Blanc (1975) notes that the Alacalufs exhibit a rather constant elevation in metabolism, with little observable physiological response to cold.

A somewhat different situation involves those who move from warm to cold climates. Although there is support for some acclimatization, this adaptation is less dramatic than acclimatization to heat stress (Edholm, 1979). Budd (1973) for example, found that members of an Australian Antarctic expedition who were of European heritage exhibited an increased ability to adjust to cold with nonshivering ways of generating heat. Le Blanc (1956), as described, observed the responses of a group of 10 soldiers who were transferred from southern to northern Canada in late fall, and who spent much of their time outdoors. The soldiers developed responses similar to those of the aborigines, with reduced shivering and tolerance to, rather than elimination of core temperature reduction.

A different type of adaptation involves individuals who are exposed to intermittent but severe cold. When faced with full-body cooling, Eskimos exhibit shivering and other reactions very similar to unadapted Europeans. Le Blanc (1975) suggests that this is not surprising because these individuals have succeeded in protecting themselves so effectively with shelter and clothing that they seldom are exposed to uncomfortable full-body cold. On the other hand, Eskimos are frequently exposed to severe cold on the extremities and exhibit very effective adaptation in performing fine movements despite lengthy exposure to cold air or water. Apparently, this ability results from increased blood flow to the hands. Although there is some evidence that this ability is partially genetically determined (Edholm, 1978; Le Blanc, 1975), cold acclimatization of the fingers and hands has been convincingly demonstrated for many human populations (cf. Mackworth, 1955). A classic example is provided by fishermen of the Gaspé Peninsula in Quebec who immerse their hands in cold water for hours while at work (Le Blanc, 1962; Le Blanc, Hildes, & Héroux, 1960), yet report little discomfort. Recall that one physiological response to cold is peripheral vasoconstriction. If cooling persists but remains less than severe, vasodilation subsequently occurs, rewarming the extremity. If exposure continues, so does the cycle of constriction and dilation, apparently helping to avoid frostbite (Edholm, 1978). In general, for people who are regularly exposed to the cold, initial constriction is less severe, and subsequent dilation and rewarming are more rapid and long lasting.

Thermal comfort

Many times when temperature stress is studied the manipulation of ambient temperature is designed not to produce an extreme degree of stress, but rather to produce varying degrees of discomfort. Especially for studies of heat effects on social behavior, discomfort has more theoretical relevance than does stress. Typically, thermal comfort studies expose individuals to systematically varied ambient temperatures and humidities while asking them to evaluate their feelings on the 7-point thermal comfort scale devised by Bedford (1964). The corresponding subjective judgments for the numerical values of this scale are 1 = much too cool; 2 = too cool; 3 =

comfortably cool; 4 = comfortable, or neither cool nor warm; 5 = comfortably warm; 6 = too warm; and 7 = much too warm. In general, a mean of 4.0 is achieved on the Bedford scale with an ambient temperature of 23°C (73°F), assuming still air, relative humidity between 40% and 60%, and a *clo* value of about 0.75 (trousers and a long-sleeved shirt). More detailed values for other levels of air velocity, humidity, and *clo* levels are given by Fanger (1972) and McIntyre (1973).

Rather than delimiting mean temperatures for a given level of comfort, the American Society of Heating, Refrigerating, and Air-Conditioning Engineers (ASHRAE) has endorsed the concept of a modal comfort envelope, or MCE, which allows for a range of ambient conditions that will provide comfort for most people. The upper and lower limits of the envelope with relative humidity of 45% are 27°C (80°F) and 24°C (76°F). These limits are for a relatively small *clo* value of 6 and sedentary activity (Rohles, 1973, 1974).

A number of ambient and individual difference variables have been examined to determine their influence on thermal comfort. In general, where radiant as well as convective heat contributes to the sensation of warmth, air temperature contributes slightly more to a judged Bedford scale value than does radiant temperature (Griffiths, 1975). Studies examining cultural differences (cf. Griffiths, 1975) have reported no substantial differences in cultural preferences for comfortable ambient temperatures, including comparisons among individuals living in North America, Europe, New Guinea, and Singapore. With respect to humidity, Rohles (1971) reports that for males temperature has seven times more influence on thermal sensation than does humidity, whereas for females this ratio is 9:1. Most studies report no reliable and substantial sex differences for comfort ratings (Fanger, 1972; Griffiths, 1975). Others (e.g., Hori, Mayuzumi, Tanaka, & Tsujita, 1978; Nadel, Roberts, & Wenger, 1978; Wyndham, Morrison, & Williams, 1965) suggest that because of extra skin folds, different surface area, or other factors, females are slower than males in responding to an increase in temperature (e.g., they sweat less), but they may show more physiological stress than males. Kuhlmeier, Fine, and Dukes-Dobos (1978) report that as body temperature increases, heart rate increases faster in males than females. Rohles, Woods, and Nevins (1973) suggest that differences between sexes in clothing insulation values or how tight or loose clothes are worn may account for women reporting less initial discomfort from heat.

Although it is commonly assumed that elderly people require warmer ambient temperatures for comfort than do younger individuals, little or no difference in comfortable temperatures between elderly and college-age adults have been found (Fanger, 1972; Rohles, 1969; Rohles & Johnson, 1972). Interestingly, however, data from Rohles and Johnson (1972) suggest that the elderly both report feeling warmer than college-age persons at temperatures in the 70s (°F) and prefer slightly warmer temperatures (around 2°F more) for comfort. Thus, comfort for the elderly may actually be a warmer physiological or psychological experience than for younger individuals.

Finally, it should be noted that although temperatures outside those judged to be comfortable may produce discomfort, they do not necessarily result in thermal stress. For example, McNall and Schlegel (1968) asked healthy college-age males to pedal a bicycle on a 15-minute work–15-minute rest cycle over an 8-hour period. At 80% relative humidity, ambient temperatues of 32°C (90°F), 29°C (85°F), and 27°C (80°F) for low, moderate, and high activity levels, respectively, were established as upper limits before the onset of clearly defined heat stress. Accordingly, many behavioral effects of high ambient temperatures may be a function of discomfort or adaptive mechanisms, rather than of formal heat stress.

For cold temperatures, there is some indication that the greatest degree of discomfort may be attributed to the unpleasant nature of the uncontrolled muscular activity of shivering. Marcus and Belyavin (1978), for instance, report that the onset of shivering causes an increase in discomfort. It is interesting to recall here the earlier discussion suggesting that physiological adaptation to cold may largely represent an elimination of this shivering response rather than an increased ability to maintain core body temperature. Interestingly, Marcus and Redman (1978) report that voluntary physical exercise reduces discomfort independent of any effect the activity has upon core temperature. These authors suggest that this effect is largely due to distraction from cold-induced discomfort. Conceivably, perceived control over the stress (see *Interpreting the data: Theoretical integration*) could also account for this result.

Thermal stress and performance

Heat stress

Over the past 30 or so years a number of studies have examined the effects of elevated ambient and/or core temperatures on various aspects of mental and manual performance. In previous reviews of some of this research (e.g., C. Bell, 1967; Pepler, 1963; Poulton, 1970; Provins, 1966), it has been noted that over a period of time sufficiently high ambient temperatures or core temperatures will hurt performance. A number of other studies, however, have shown that elevated temperatures can actually help performance on some tasks. Still other studies have shown patterns wherein high temperatures first help, then hurt performance, and other studies have shown exactly the reverse pattern. Why these patterns occur is open to debate. Since the mediators (arousal, attention, etc.) of the effects of heat on performance are probably also related to heat effects on social behavior, it should be worthwhile to examine the complexity of the heat–performance relationship. Accordingly, it is appropriate to review performance decrements and increments associated with heat, as well as theoretical interpretations of these relationships.

Variables that influence the effects of heat on performance

In the preceding review of physiological correlates of heat stress it was noted that a number of factors moderate heat stress. Similar factors influence the effects of heat on performance. For example, performance of unacclimatized subjects is more adversely affected by heat than is that of acclimatized subjects, and lighter clothing retards debilitating effects of heat on performance (C. Bell, 1967). Moreover, Pepler (1963) indicates that incentives and knowledge of results can forestall negative effects of heat on performance, and Provins (1966) suggests that giving subjects water can have similar moderating effects. In addition, Provins and C. Bell (1960) and C. Bell and Provins (1962) indicate that effort can compensate for performance decrements associated with heat. Studies of heat stress on performance also differ according to the type and number of tasks performed simultaneously (Wilkinson, 1969, 1974). The more complex the task and the more tasks involved, the worse the performance decrements. Studies combining heat and additional stressors such as noise or high altitudes (P. Bell, 1978; Fine & Kobrick, 1978) generally find that combinations of stressors are more debilitating than individual stressors. Finally, it should be noted that effective temperatures differ across studies, and equal dry-bulb readings may have different results if wet-bulb readings differ (e.g., Allen & Fischer, 1978).

Studies reporting performance decrements associated with heat

Most reviews of heat stress and performance begin with historic studies by Mackworth (e.g., 1961). This researcher exposed acclimatized military personnel to high ambient temperatures and found that performance deteriorated with increased heat on all tasks, including coding and decoding, visual vigilance, and a pursuitmeter task. More recent research has confirmed heat-associated performance decrements for choice reaction time (Pepler, 1959; Cervone, 1977), paired associate learning (Allen & Fischer, 1978), and tracking tasks (Azer, McNall, & Leung, 1972; Teichner & Wehrkamp, 1954). In an applied study, Link and Pepler (1970) noted that productivity of women apparel workers declined as temperature rose.

In some research subjects have performed simultaneous tasks, with the results not always being decrements on more than one task. For example, although Bursill (1958) found simultaneous tracking and signal detection decrements and Azer et al. (1972) reported central tracking and peripheral reaction time decrements associated with heat, C. Bell, Provins, and Hiorns (1964) reported more missed signals but no vigilance deficits. In addition, P. Bell (1978) reported no effects of heat on a primary pursuit motor task but found harmful effects of heat on a secondary number processing task.

Poulton (1970), citing work by Wing (1965) and Lind (1967), suggests that there are identifiable temperatures above which one can be reasonably sure that performance will deteriorate. For example, at an effective temperature of 32°C (90°F) performance on mental tasks will deteriorate after 2 hours of exposure for unacclimatized subjects. Shorter exposure times will show performance decrements at higher temperatures. For moderate physical work, 32°C (90°F) is the approximate limit for 1 hour of exposure, and for simply resting an effective temperature of 38°C (100°F) can be tolerated for 2 or more hours before physiological problems are experienced.

Performance decrements during cold stress

Exposure to cold without sufficiently protective clothing usually occurs during accidental exposure, such as with shipwreck, or during certain special circumstances in which humans must function for brief periods with lowered skin and/or body temperatures as part of arctic expeditions, military operations, or underwater activities. Often these tasks are physical in nature, and it is to these activities that most research is directed (see Fox, 1967, for a review).

Peripheral cooling effects

It is generally accepted that as the body cools, the skin of the hands and feet shows the fastest and most dramatic cooling in response to cold-induced vasoconstriction. Furthermore, fine manual tasks frequently require exposure of the hands, while the rest of the body remains comfortably insulated by bulky clothing. Not surprisingly, the most noticeably limiting factors in human ability to withstand cold are probably the effects on the extremities (Fox, 1967; Goldman, 1964; Poulton, 1970). As Fox (1967) summarizes, studies have demonstrated decreased tactile sensitivity, dexterity, and strength with exposure to low ambient temperature, particularly in windy or humid conditions. It appears that functioning remains near normal until a critical hand skin temperature (HST) is reached for the respective ability, then drops precipitously.

Although it seems clear that reduced HST affects performance, one critical area of investigation concerns differences between whole-body cooling versus cooling of the extremities alone. Several studies (cf. Gaydos, 1958; Gaydos & Dusek, 1958; Veghte, 1961) suggest that within limits, cooling of the surface of the rest of the body produces little performance decrement if the hands are kept warm. Lockhart (1966, 1968) notes that severe cooling of the rest of the body does produce some impairment even with warm hands, but less than with cooling of the hands alone. Furthermore, warming cold hands with infrared heaters may improve dexterity (Lockhart & Keiss, 1971).

Central cooling effects

There is realtively little evidence for more central effects of exposure to cold. As Poulton (1970) suggests, somewhere between loss of consciousness due to hypothermia and normal body temperature, some loss of mental capacity must occur. Poulton, Hitchings, and Brooke (1965) have reported decrements in functioning for a watchkeeping task aboard the bridge of a ship in winter weather as oral temperature fell to 35.6°C (96.2°F). No similar performance decrement was observed for similarly dressed sailors in more temperate waters. Another study found decreased ability on rotary pursuit tasks at 15°C (55°F) (Teichner & Wehrkamp, 1954). Allen and Fisher (1978) found an effect on recall of paired associate learning tasks in college students, with performance declining at low or high temperatures, but later suggested that verbal learning may not be impaired at even very low temperature under controlled humidity conditions.

Perhaps the best evidence for central effects of cold exposure comes from studies conducted upon divers in cold water. Under these conditions, heat loss by convection is much greater than in air (Edholm, 1978), so the cooling effects of total immersion are probably more severe than commonly investigated (cf. Frisancho, 1979). These studies are of practical significance, because nearly all commercial diving occurs in cold water (Bowen, 1968). Motor performance decrements created by total immersion parallel those of partial immersion or exposure to cold air (Bowen, 1968; Stang & Wiener, 1970; Vaughn & Mavor, 1972). Moreover, total cold immersion may adversely affect ability to estimate time (Baddeley, 1966), general mental coherence (Beckman, 1964; Keatinge, 1969), and tasks requiring intense attention and considerable short-term memory (Bowen, 1968). On the other hand, some studies (Stang & Wiener, 1970; Vaughn & Mavor, 1972) have not found decrements in mental functioning because of cold immersion.

Studies showing facilitated or mixed performance under thermal stress

Most studies reporting facilitating effects of high temperatures on performance also report performance decrements, although in one recent cockpit simulation study heat had no detrimental effects on two tracking tasks and strictly facilitated performance on another tracking task (Nunneley, Dowd, Myhre, Stribley, & McNee, 1979). Other studies report an *initial* stimulating effect of warmth (e.g., Poulton & Kerslake, 1965). In one such study, Provins and C. Bell (1970) found that heat initially benefited performance on a reaction time task, although this effect soon dissipated. Simultaneous vigilance performance was unaffected by temperature. Fine and Kobrick (1978) also found slightly improved performance for 3 hours of exposure to heat for several cognitive tasks, but deteriorated performance upon continued exposure (see also, Grether, 1973). Other tasks in this experiment showed strictly performance decrements associated with heat.

An interesting pattern of results has been reported by Wilkinson, Fox, Goldsmith, Hampton, and Lewis (1964) wherein performance on a math test initially improved as body temperature increased but later deteriorated. Simultaneous auditory vigilance, however, showed the reverse pattern: impairment and later improvement with increased body temperature. This pattern of slightly elevated temperatures helping performance has been found by others for tracking and classification of digits (Griffiths & Boyce, 1971), for academic performance of school children (Holmberg & Wyon, as cited by Griffiths, 1975), and for nude children (Johansson & Lofstedt, as cited by Griffiths, 1975).

For cold temperatures, Auliciems (1972) reported optimal performance on mental tasks by English school children when indoor temperatures were comfortably cool (15–17°C or 58.5–62°F). This effect may be related to the observation that children have a higher metabolic rate than adults and prefer temperatures somewhat cooler than adults. Similar results supporting cool temperature facilitation of mental tasks have not been confirmed for adults (Allen & Fischer, 1978). There is some evidence, however, that application of local cold that is not directly involved in a performance task may facilitate performance. Clark and Flaherty (1963), for instance, demonstrated enhanced performance when the nonperforming hand was cooled for a knot-tying task. Thus, despite the lack of much supporting data, it seems reasonable to expect that sudden cold may be arousing, which should facilitate performance under some circumstances. One limitation of most of the research on cold stress and performance is the short temporal parameters used in these experiments. It is unclear how cold would affect performance over more prolonged time periods.

Sometimes heat or cold is found to have no effects on performance (e.g., Dean & McGlothen, 1965), and one must suspect that the frequency of this result is higher than reported in the literature since data of this nature are probably not as likely to be published (Avery & Cross, 1978). Finally, at least one study (Colquhoun & Goldman, 1968) has also found, in a signal detection task, that high body temperature was associated with both increased correct detections and increased false reports.

Interpreting the data: theoretical integration

Why should such diverse patterns of results as those indicated above occur? Although differences in acclimatization, clothing, humidity, and the like may explain the presence of performance deterioration in some studies and the absence of such effects in others, U-shaped and inverted U-shaped performance curves as a function of heat or time of exposure cannot be so simply explained. Four possible theoretical explanations for these complex findings include body temperature, arousal, attention, and perceived control. As indicated elsewhere in this chapter, these explanations have implications for thermal effects on social behavior that will be discussed later. Moreover, they have implications for techniques that might be employed to overcome some of the negative effects of heat.

Body temperature. Early experimenters looking at heat and performance concluded that body temperature and physiology were not related to performance (e.g., Mackworth, 1961; Pepler, 1958). So complex was the relationship between any given measure of physiology and performance that these researchers believed some other mechanism or mechanisms must be involved. Provins (1966), however, believes that body temperature is important. Unfortunately, as Edholm (1978) laments, body temperature is rarely measued in most studies. Rather, experimenters prefer to report ambient temperature. Interestingly, Allnutt and Allan (1973) suggest that core and skin temperature differential may be the key. In their research, elevated core temperature was associated with faster reaction times, shortened time estimates, and more frequent movements in tracking. If core temperature remained elevated while skin temperature was cooled, however, reaction time remained good and errors were less frequent. The utility of body temperature as a mediator, though, must unfortunately await more research in which both body and skin temperatures are monitored during performance.

Arousal. Provins (1966) advocates arousal as the mediator of heat effects on performance, with body temperature as the most valid measure of arousal in heat studies. Following the Yerkes–Dodson Law, Provins (1966), Poulton (1970), Wyon (1970), and others suggest that there is an optimal arousal level for any task. This optimum is lower for complex tasks than for simple tasks. Thus, performance will suffer for any task if arousal level is on either side of the task-specific and *person-specific* optimum (see also, Wilkinson, 1969). The problem, then, is determining the level of arousal at a given point in the exposure to heat. It will be recalled from the review of physiology and heat that measures of arousal during heat stress follow complex patterns. Provins (1966) has reviewed work by Macpherson and others showing that heat exposure leads to overarousal. This may be one reason, for example, that hot or cold temperatures interfere with sleep. Provins also reviews animal studies that purport to show an initial decrease in arousal from heat exposure followed by a subsequent increase with prolonged exposure. Poulton and Kerslake (1965), moreover, suggest a slightly more complex pattern: There is an initial stimulating effect of warmth, followed by a decrease associated with the beginning of adaptation (e.g., a drop in blood pressure), which in turn is followed by an increase in arousal as the body fights to keep core temperature under control. Finally, as exhaustion and coma approach arousal again decreases. Although the arousal pattern for cold stress is less clear, there is most likely some initial stimulating effect of cold, and later decrements in arousal. According to this arousal hypothesis, then, performance measured on first contact with a thermal extreme should show facilitative effects (as in the Poulton and Kerslake study); performance at an intermediate time might show increments (as in most of the tracking and vigilance studies above); and performance in the long run should show decrements (as in the Mackworth studies). The nature of the task and complexity of response required can explain slight variations within this pattern (as in Wilkinson et al., 1964). Moreover, this pattern would suggest that intervention by reducing or increasing arousal (e.g., with air conditioning, cool water, warm drinks, breaks in the work routine, adding other stressors) may not have the desired effect if a person ends up on the wrong peak or valley of this arousal curve. Although arousal fairly well explains the effects of cold on performance, this explanation does not account for long-term facilitative effects of heat stress (as in Nunneley et al., 1979) and requires a very complex fluctuation in arousal. In fact, in studying the effects of other stressors on arousal and subsequently on performance, Broadbent (1963) suggests that some other mechanism accounts for performance effects of heat.

Attention. Pepler (1963) and others (e.g., P. Bell, 1978) suggest that narrowing of attention accounts for decrements in performance associated with heat. Especially for complex mental tasks, excessive demands may be placed on attentional capacity (cf. Broadbent, 1958; Cohen, 1978; Milgram, 1970; Poulton, 1970). Heat, cold, and other environmental stressors requiring resource expenditures for adaptation reduce the overall capacity of the organism to attend to the task at hand. Thus, the more resources required to attend to the task and to adapt to the stressor(s), the worse the performance. The first performance to suffer will be anything requiring attention to stimuli noncentral to the task (e.g., Bell, 1978; Bursill, 1958; Cohen, 1978; Easterbrook, 1959; Milgram, 1970) since priority for allocation of resources is given to primary or central stimuli. The attention model has the advantage of explaining decrements in behavior associated with combinations of stressors (Milgram, 1970). Perhaps the studies of cold effects upon divers offer just such a situation, in which the environment presents both cold stress and stress from being in an underwater environment, as suggested by Bowen (1968). The attention model also suggests that one might learn from experience to attend to more peripheral stimuli during environmental stress. Although the attention explanation has merit, it is not as effective as the arousal model in accounting for the facilitating effects of heat or cold on performance.

Perceived control. Research in the last decade on environmental stressors other than temperature has suggested that a cognitive perception of control over the environment can reduce the negative effects of environmental stressors (e.g., Baum, Singer, & Baum, Chap. 1, this volume; P. Bell, Fisher, & Loomis, 1978; Glass & Singer, 1972). This approach is sometimes incorporated into a behavior constraint model of environmental stress, which includes stages of perceived loss of control, psychological reactance (i.e., motivation to restore freedom of action), and learned helplessness. Although such a process has not typically been suggested as mediating thermal stress effects, it is quite possible that some performance decrements could be accounted for by individuals reducing efforts as if they are "giving up" in the face of uncontrollable heat or cold stress. Greene and P. Bell (1980), for example, report that subjects feel more dominated by a thermal environment of 35°C (95°F) than one of more comfortable temperatures (see also Cervone, 1977). The perceived-control notion works well with other stressors and needs to be examined as a possible mediator in thermal stress.

Integration of theoretical perspectives. No single construct appears adequate for explaining the complex effects of thermal stress on performance. Physiological adaptation, arousal, attention, and perceived control all need to be considered. As a first step, under prolonged exposure to heat, especially for physically demanding activities, performance decrements may be largely a function of physiological exhaustion, regardless of the degree of activation of the reticular system. Since all research on such heavy activity in elevated temperature conditions, including industrial (Crockford, 1967; Hill, 1967) and military (Adam, 1967) research, points in this direction, it seems unnecessary to invoke arousal or attention for such circumstances. Similarly, studies of subjects' performance while they are totally immersed in cold water may approach human physiological limits. As Vaughn and Mavor (1972) suggest, under these conditions physiological limits rather than performance decrements may be the most appropriate measures. If arousal and attention are factors, they seem to be overridden at points near physiological limits. Although one could argue that an individual is overaroused or underaroused when near the point of physical exhaustion, the conflicting measures of arousal at this point lead one to believe that physiological exhaustion per se is a more parsimonious explanation.

As a second step, there is little question that arousal is being influenced by temperature; the only questions are whether it is going up or down and whether it predicts performance. Poulton (1976) provides evidence that any number of environmental stressors, including heat, can be demonstrated to increase arousal at *some* point of exposure. Poulton and others, as cited previously, provide ample evidence that one of these points is upon initial exposure. Whether from a startle response, an orienting reflex, or the activation of initial adaptive mechanisms, it seems reasonable to conclude that initial exposure to heat or cold increases arousal. If so, this increase seems a reasonable explanation for most of the research that shows an improvement in performance upon initial exposure to heat, and for any similar potential effects of cold.

Moreover, given the physiological evidence that after prolonged exposure the body is coping with the thermal stress, it seems unlikely that arousal is decreasing at this time. Rather, considerable evidence already cited suggests that high temperatures at this point are overarousing. Certainly for complex tasks, this overarousal adequately explains at least some performance decrements.

As a third step in this theoretical integration, it also seems evident that attention is being affected during thermal stress. The research discussed indicates that peripheral information frequently suffers as the stress continues, which points to a narrowing of attention. It is conceivable, furthermore, that any initially arousing effect actually intensifies attentional processes, either in identifying the source of the stress or alternative ways of coping with it (e.g., seeking shelter, shedding or adding clothes, finding water), or if the stress is anticipated (as it usually is in both the lab and the field), in focusing available resources on the task at hand so that performance does not suffer, and giving the feeling that one is in control of the situation.

Thus, arousal, attention, and perceived control initially may complement one another in coping with heat stress. As arousal intensifies to cope with the stress, however, fewer and fewer resources are available to attend to performance tasks. At first, peripheral activities are sacrificed, then central ones. At the point of physiological exhaustion, attention no longer matters. Moreover, at any point in time, loss of perceived control might lead to increased efforts to regain control of the environment, or to resignation and reduced effort.

Ultimately, tests of these theoretical speculations will require a large factorial, longitudinal study with many variables monitored. Until such time, however, it seems reasonable to presume that physiological processes, arousal mechanisms, attention processes, and possibly even perceived control are affected by thermal stress. Still at issue, though, is whether any or all of these factors account for changes in performance.

High ambient temperatures and social behavior

During the past decade considerable research has examined whether heat stress has reliable and profound effects on social behavior. Part of this concern has stemmed from general awareness of the role of the physical environment in everyday living, part of it from concern over "heat wave" conditions and social strife, and part of it from interest in purely theoretical issues. Among the behaviors so studied are attraction, aggression, and helping behavior.

Heat and attraction

Griffitt (1970) exposed groups of college students to comfortably cool or uncomfortably hot ambient temperatures while they assessed personal comfort. In addition, following the Byrne (1971) paradigm, subjects were presented with an attitude survey ostensibly completed by a stranger, but actually completed by the experimenter to agree 25% or 75% with the subject's own attitudes (assessed previously by the experimenter). Attraction responses toward the bogus stranger were higher for similar others than for dissimilar others and were also higher in the cool condition. Griffitt and Veitch (1971) replicated these findings and also found that another factor, crowding, had additive effects, in combination with heat, to further reduce attraction. The experimenters interpreted these results in terms of the reinforcement–affect model of attraction (Byrne, 1971), which posits that attraction is a linear function of affect associated with the target.

Further research by P. Bell and Baron (1974, 1976), however, failed to find that heat reduced attraction. In this research, in addition to receiving attitudes purportedly held by a bogus stranger, subjects in a hot or cool room also received a compliment or insult from the stranger. Although heat had strong effects on measures of affect, only attitude similarity and the personal evaluations had powerful effects on attraction. So powerful were these effects, in fact, that they probably "wiped out" any negative influence of heat on attraction. In additional unpublished research, P. Bell also failed to find that heat influences attraction, suggesting that the earlier findings of a negative effect of heat on attraction are limited to some presently unspecifiable conditions. Although it is probably premature to make any reliable generalizations, it is possible that heat has a negative impact on attraction toward total strangers, but, in part due to a "shared suffering" phenomenon, has minimal effects on previously established relationships.

Heat and aggression

Most published research on heat and social behavior has examined aggression and violence. Spawned by beliefs that urban riots in the 1960s were in part attributable to heat wave conditions, this research has involved laboratory, archival, and field studies. On a relatively informal note, the United States Riot Commission (1968) observed that all but one of the riots studied in 1967 began on days when outdoor temperature was at least 27°C (80°F). Police departments have long known that high temperatures are associated with elevated crime rates, (Sells & Will, 1971; Will & Sells, 1969). Futhermore, Goranson and King (1970) plotted temperatures for several days before and after the outbreak of riots and observed that temperatures were elevated relative to a control year an average of about 3°C (6°F) 3 days before the riot outbreak. It is difficult to infer a cause–effect relationship between heat and violence from such studies, because other factors such as students' being out of school and increased daylight hours also covary with seasonal heat.

The relationship between heat and aggression in laboratory studies is complex. With rats, one study has shown that heat facilitates fighting in the presence of shock (Berry & Jack, 1971), whereas with mice, another study has indicated a decrease in fighting associated with heat (Ginsberg & Allee, 1942). In an early study with humans, Rohles (1967) placed juveniles in a heat chamber and observed increased incidents of aggressive displays. In other studies subjects have ostensibly been given the opportunity to deliver a series of electric shocks to a confederate, supposedly in order to punish the "victim" for errors in learning a list of consonant–vowel–consonant nonsense syllables, or so that physiological reactivity of the victim can be assessed under various levels of duress. In some cases the victim has an opportunity to compliment or insult the subject prior to delivery of the shocks (an anger manipulation), or a model (another confederate) administers shocks before the subject. The intensity and duration of shocks administered then become measures of aggression. (See Baron, 1977, for more discussion of this paradigm.)

In one such laboratory study, Baron (1972) found that subjects in a hot room were less aggressive than those in a cool room. This relationship was found for both angered and nonangered subjects. In another study using only angered subjects, Baron and Lawton (1972) found that although heat decreased aggression in the absence of a model, with an aggressive model present the high temperature did not reduce aggression. In a subsequent study factorially combining temperature, anger, and model presence, Baron and P. Bell (1975) found that heat decreased aggression for angered subjects but increased it for nonangered subjects. The model increased aggression independently of the other conditions. The same relationship, without a model, was found again by Baron and P. Bell (1976) using a wider range of ambient temperatures.

This complex pattern of results was explained by Baron and P. Bell (1976) in terms of negative affect. Both heat and the insult from the anger manipulation produce discomfort or negative affect (Byrne, 1971; Griffitt, 1970). The hypothesis that an inverted-U relationship exists between negative affect and aggression would then explain the previous data. That is, at moderate levels of discomfort (regardless of the source of discomfort) aggression would be facilitated, but at more severe levels of discomfort aggression would be inhibited. Thus, anger in a cool condition and the absence of anger in a hot condition might produce an intermediate level of discomfort and consequently increase aggression relative to a comfortably cool and nonangry condition. Anger combined with heat, however, would be so unpleasant as to produce lethargy or a flight response. Support for this view comes from another experiment by Baron and P. Bell (1976) in which half the subjects were given lemonade to counteract the discomforting effects of the heat. In this case, lemonade did not affect the aggressiveness of subjects in the cool condition. In the hot condition, however, lemonade mitigated the effects of heat on aggression. For nonangry subjects heat again increased aggression, but not for those subjects drinking lemonade. By decreasing subjects' negative affect, the lemonade increased aggression for angry subjects in the hot condition, but decreased it for nonangry subjects in the hot condition. It should be noted that an inverted-U relationship between arousal and aggression would also explain these results, but the difficulty of determining whether a given heat condition increases or decreases arousal has led Baron and P. Bell to favor the affect mediation interpretation.

Further support for this inverted-U relationship was offered by P. Bell and Baron (1976). In this study, subjects in a cool or hot room were presented with similar or dissimilar attitudes from the victim but also received either a compliment or an insult from the victim. Prior to ostensibly shocking the victim, the subjects indicated their level of comfort. Results indicated a distinct quadratic trend between level of comfort and level of shock. P. Bell and Baron (1977) once again found this inverted-U relationship, even with negative affect manipulated in part by low (17°C, 63°F) ambient temperatures. Using another measure of hostility, however, P. Bell (1980) found that subjects who had been insulted by an experimenter evaluated that experimenter more negatively in high than in "normal" temperatures.

In a study using archival records, Baron and Ransberger (1978) examined frequency of urban riots between 1967 and 1971 as a function of temperature. The frequency of riots increased and peaked between 27 and 29°C (81–85°F) before falling off sharply as temperature increased further. Carlsmith and Anderson (1979), however, noted that temperatures in this peak range are more frequent anyway, regardless of whether riots occur on days with these temperatures. When natural frequency of temperature was statistically controlled for, a positive linear trend appeared between temperature and riot frequency. Schwartz (1968), moreover, concluded that urban violence (coup, assassination, terrorism) was not related to climatic zone, but that revolutions since World War II were more frequent in climatically hot regions. Furthermore, across all nations, violence was less frequent in the hottest and coldest quarters of the year than in the two intermediate quarters.

Finally, Baron (1976) observed that horn honking by automobile drivers, which can be an indication of irritation or hostility, was more frequent when the temperature was above about 29°C (85°F) than when it was cooler. Heat did not elevate honking, however, for drivers in air-conditioned cars.

What can one conclude from all of these studies? As with the literature on heat and performance, it is fairly easy to draw conclusions on the effects of *very* high temperatures and aggression. If the temperature is high enough, aggression is relatively absent, either because of lethargy or flight responses, or both. At intermediate temperatures, however, the evidence is just as mixed as it is for performance. In at least some circumstances, there is a facilitating effect of heat on aggression. Exactly what these circumstances are and the parameters of contributing conditions must await further research. One must speculate, however, that opportunity, rather than a cause–effect relationship, may be most significant. Other factors, such as increased consumption of alcohol during hot weather, probably also play a role. One might expect, for example, that during a month-long heat wave, the inverted-U relationship would predict an initial decrease in violence. As individuals acclimatize, however, prolonged exposure may result in less negative reactions to the heat and thus lead to more violence. In addition, if efforts to cope with heat include persistently staying indoors, a "cabin fever" syndrome might occur in which one perceives a loss of control over the environment (see later discussion). This perceived loss of control combined with an increased probability of irritation toward those in indoor confinement and increased alcohol consumption, might result in increased domestic violence, such as spouse beating and child abuse. Future research will be needed to examine these possibilities.

Heat and helping behavior

A brief examination of the potential effects of heat on helping behavior concludes this section on high ambient temperatures and social interaction. Some research has suggested that feelings of discomfort may reduce helping behavior, whereas other research has suggested that such feelings may facilitate helping by people who want to feel better as a result of offering aid (Cialdini & Kenrick, 1976; Weyant, 1978). Accordingly, the discomfort of heat may influence helping. In one study, Page (1978) observed that after leaving a hot experimental room, subjects were less likely to volunteer to help in another study than were subjects who had been in a cool room. Cunningham (1979) found that ambient temperature correlated − .16 with helping an interviewer in a survey during the summer and + .37 during the winter. Outdoor temperature did not, however, affect the generosity of tips in an indoor restaurant. Furthermore, a recent study (Schneider, Lesko, & Garrett, 1980) found that neither high nor low temperatures reduced helping of (1) a person on crutches who dropped a book, (2) a person who dropped groceries, (3) a person who lost a contact lens, or (4) an interviewer asking for help with a survey. Some of our unpublished laboratory data, moreover, show no effects of heat on helping either during exposure to the heat or afterward.

It seems reasonable that in the Page and Cunningham studies discomfort reduced helping. In the other studies, however, the tendency for discomfort to facilitate helping may have counteracted a tendency for discomfort to inhibit helping, leading to no noticeable change in helping. Since there are so few studies available on temperature and helping, it is safer not to draw conclusions on these temperature effects. If heat does have an effect on helping, it may be so minor as to be of little practical significance. The theoretical significance of the absence or presence of heat effects on helping, however, may lie in their relation to the seemingly contradictory findings of discomfort on helping.

Cold and social behavior

Little published research addresses the effects of cold on social behavior, although three of the studies cited in the foregoing discussion on heat and social behavior did examine relatively low temperatures. P. Bell and Baron (1977) observed that temperatures of 18°C (64°F) may relate to aggression in the same inverted-U pattern described for high temperatures. With respect to helping behavior, the finding by Cunningham (1979) suggests a slight decrease in volunteering for an interview associated with low tempera-tures, but the Schneider et al. (1980) study failed to support effects of cold temperatures on helping. With so little research available, it is appropriate not to make any generalizations with respect to effects of cold temperature on social behavior.

Integration and future concerns

It is apparent that the effects of thermal stress on comfort, performance, and social behavior are complex. There seems little question that additional research is needed, especially for the moderately warm and cold tempera-ture range, before this complexity will be better understood. Nevertheless, there are some trends apparent in the extant data that are sufficient to suggest some theoretical underpinnings as well as to give direction to future research.

Theory building

As indicated earlier, there seems little doubt that temperature influences arousal. The remaining questions concern (1) the direction of that change in arousal; (2) whether such changes in arousal mediate changes in per-formance and social behavior; and (3) the direction of those performance changes. The same can be said for comfort or affect and, most likely, for attention and adaptive capacity as well. Another potential theoretical me-diator is behavior constraint (cf. P. Bell et al., 1978), wherein loss of per-ceived control over the situation and eventual learned helplessness result. Unfortunately, little research to date has studied the effects of perceived control on thermal stress. Such a model has been applied to other envi-ronmental stressors (see Baum et al., Chap. 1, this volume), and future research applying it to hot and cold environments might be fruitful (e.g., Greene & P. Bell, 1980).

Given that heat and cold influence arousal, affect, attention, and possi-bly perceived control, how do these mediators in turn account for the complex effects of heat on behavior? The answer probably includes two or more of these mediators, as any one of them does not sufficiently explain all the data. Changes in arousal (including physical exhaustion) and atten-tion and adaptive capacity, as indicated, can account for performance ef-fects of heat exposure. Affect, arousal, attention, and adaptive capacity, in turn, seem sufficient to account for the influence of heat on social behavior. Specifying the interrelationship of these mediators and their relation to cold stress must await more precise measurement. For example, until re-ticular and autonomic arousal is constantly monitored while performance and social responses are recorded, it will be impossible to provide adequate predictions of behavior from temperature-influenced arousal. This also ap-plies to the other aforementioned mediators. At present, there is probably no adequate information on the parameters of the "load" of heat or cold stress. Also, as indicated earlier, there is little if any information on the relationship of perceived control to thermal stress.

Other future research

Aside from experiments monitoring arousal and systematically varying perceived control, a number of other research directions are dictated by theoretical concerns. For one thing, the effects of heat or cold stress on multiple tasks should be more adequately explored. In most of the studies reported in this review subjects performed one or two tasks. Most often, cognitive tasks appear to suffer from thermal stress primarily when combined with other tasks. In such cases, attention decrements and reduced adaptive capacity seem the most appropriate explanations of the data. Additional research that systematically varies the cognitive demands of the task(s) would be most valuable.

Other research should look at combinations of stressors. Some stressors (noise, for example) have more specifiable effects on behavior. Combining such stressors with heat or cold might give some indication of the direction of influence thermal stress has on arousal or other mediators (see also Pepler, 1960; Wilkinson, 1969).

Still other research should explore the effects of other factors in thermal stress (humidity, wind, acclimatization, sex differences) as they influence behavior. The effects of systematic combinations of temperature, humidity, and air speed on comfort are known. Does the same level of comfort, regardless of temperature, humidity, and air speed, have the same effect on social behavior? If so, support could be offered for the affective interpretation of thermal effects on social behavior, provided of course that other mediators are experimentally controlled. More research is certainly needed on the social effects of thermal stress, especially with respect to lower temperatures.

Finally, future research should explore more ways to reduce discomfort and task decrements associated with moderately uncomfortable temperatures. As energy shortages increasingly become a permanent factor in life, higher indoor temperatures will have to be tolerated in the summer, as will lower temperatures in the winter. Future research will inevitably examine ways to maximize comfort under such conditions. Other research may well examine ways to increase feelings of warmth, even if only psychologically, for energy shortage consequences during winter months (cf., Greene & Bell, 1980).

References

Adam, J. M. Military problems of air transport and tropical service. In C. N. Davies, P. R. Davis, & F. H. Tyrer (Eds.), *The effects of abnormal physical conditions at work.* London: Livingstone, 1967.

Allen, M. A., & Fischer, G. J. Ambient temperature effects on paired associate learning. *Ergonomics*, 1978, *21*, 95–101.

Allnutt, M. F., & Allan, J. R. The effects of core temperature elevation and thermal sensation on performance. *Ergonomics*, 1973, *16*, 189–196.

Anastasi, A. *Field of applied psychology*. New York: McGraw-Hill, 1979.

Auliciems, A. Some observed relationships between atmospheric environment and mental work. *Environmental Research*, 1972, *5*, 217–240.

Avery, D. D., & Cross, H. A. *Experimental methodology in psychology*. Monterey, Calif.: Brooks/Cole, 1978.

Azer, N. Z., McNall, P. E., & Leung, H. C. Effects of heat stress on performance. *Ergonomics*, 1972, *15*, 681–691.

Baddeley, A. D. Time estimation at reduced body temperature. *American Journal of Psychology*, 1966, *79*, 475–479.

Baron, R. A. Aggression as a function of ambient temperature and prior anger arousal. *Journal of Personality and Social Psychology*, 1972, *21*, 183–189.

Baron, R. A. The reduction of human aggression: A field study of the influence of incompatible reactions. *Journal of Applied Social Psychology*, 1976, *6*, 260–274.

Baron, R. A. *Human aggression*. New York: Plenum, 1977.

Baron, R. A., & Bell, P. A. Aggression and heat: Mediating effects of prior provocation and exposure to an aggressive model. *Journal of Personality and Social Psychology*, 1975, *31*, 825–832.

Baron, R. A., & Bell, P. A. Aggression and heat: The influence of ambient temperature, negative affect, and a cooling drink on physical aggression. *Journal of Personality and Social Psychology*, 1976, *33*, 245–255.

Baron, R. A., & Lawton, S. F. Environmental influences on aggression: The facilitation of modeling effects by high ambient temperatures. *Psychonomic Science*, 1972, *26*, 80–83.

Baron, R. A., & Ransberger, V. M. Ambient temperature and the occurrence of collective violence: The "long hot summer" revisited. *Journal of Personality and Social Psychology*, 1978, *36*, 351–360.

Beckman, E. L. *A review of current concepts and practices used to control body heat loss during water immersion*. Research Report, NMRI, 1964.

Bedford, T. A., *Basic principles of ventilation and heating*. London: H. K. Lewis, 1964.

Beighton, P. Fluid balance in the Sahara. *Nature*, 1971, *233*, 275–277.

Bell, C. R. Hot environments and performance. In C. N. Davies, P. R. Davis, & F. H. Tyrer (Eds.), *The effects of abnormal physical conditions at work*. London: Livingstone, 1967.

Bell, C. R., & Provins, K. A. Effects of high temperature environmental conditions on human performance. *Journal of Occupational Medicine*, 1962, *4*, 202–211.

Bell, C. R., Provins, K. A., & Hiorns, R. F. Visual and auditory vigilance during exposure to hot and humid conditions. *Ergonomics*, 1964, *7*, 279–288.

Bell, P. A. Effects of noise and heat stress on primary and subsidiary task performance. *Human Factors*, 1978, *20*, 749–752.

Bell, P. A. Effects of heat, noise, and provocation on retaliatory evaluative behavior. *Journal of Social Psychology*, 1980, *110*, 97–110.

Bell, P. A., & Baron, R. A. Environmental influences on attraction: Effects of heat, attitude similarity, and personal evaluations. *Bulletin of the Psychonomic Society*, 1974, *4*, 479–481.

Bell, P. A., & Baron, R. A. Aggression and heat: The mediating role of negative effects. *Journal of Applied Social Psychology*, 1976, *6*, 18–30.

Bell, P. A., & Baron, R. A. Aggression and ambient temperature: The facilitating and inhibiting effects of hot and cold environments. *Bulletin of the Psychonomic Society*, 1977, *9*, 443–445.

Bell, P. A., Fisher, J. D., & Loomis, R. J. *Environmental psychology*. Philadelphia: Saunders, 1978.

Berry, R. M., & Jack, E. C. The effect of temperature upon shock-elicited aggression in rats. *Psychonomic Science*, 1971, *23*, 341–343.

Bowen, H. M. Diver performance and the effects of cold. *Human Factors*, 1968, *10*, 445–464.

Broadbent, D. E. *Perception and communication*. Oxford: Pergamon, 1958.

Broadbent, D. E. Differences and interactions between stresses. *Quarterly Journal of Experimental Psychology*, 1963, *15*, 205–211.

Budd, G. M. Australian physiological research in the Antarctic and the Subarctic, with special reference to thermal stress and acclimatization. In O. G. Edholm & E.K.E. Gunderson (Eds.), *Polar human biology*. London: Heinemann, 1973.

Bursill, A. E. The restriction of peripheral vision during exposure to hot and humid conditions. *Quarterly Journal of Experimental Psychology*, 1958, *10*, 113–129.

Byrne, D. *The attraction paradigm*. New York: Academic Press, 1971.

Carlsmith, J. M., & Anderson, C. A. Ambient temperature and the occurrence of collective violence: A new analysis. *Journal of Personality and Social Psychology*, 1979, *37*, 337–344.

Carlson, N. R. *Physiology of behavior*. Boston: Allyn & Bacon, 1977.

Cervone, J. C. *An environmental social approach to an arousal-behavior relationship*. Unpublished master's thesis, Colorado State University, Fort Collins, 1977.

Cialdini, R. B., & Kenrick, D. T. Altruism as hedonism: A social development perspective on the relationship of negative mood state and helping. *Journal of Personality and Social Psychology*, 1976, *54*, 907–914.

Clark, R. E., & Flaherty, C. F. Contralateral effects of thermal stimuli on manual performance capability. *Journal of Applied Psychology*, 1963, *18*, 769–771.

Cohen, S. Environmental load and the allocation of attention. In A. Baum & S. Valins (Eds.), *Advances in environmental research*. Hillsdale, N.J.: Erlbaum, 1978.

Colquhoun, W. P., & Goldman, F. R. The effect of raised body temperature on vigilance performance. *Ergonomics*, 1968, *11*, 48.

Crockford, G. W. Heat problems and protective clothing in iron and steel works. In C. N. Davies, P. R. Davis, & F. H. Tyrer (Eds.), *The effects of abnormal physical conditions at work*. London: E. & S. Livingstone, 1967.

Cunningham, M. R. Weather, mood, and helping behavior: Quasi experiments with the sunshine samaritan. *Journal of Personality and Social Psychology*, 1979, *37*, 1947–1956.

Dean, R. D., & McGlothen, C. L. Effects of combined heat and noise on human performance, physiology and subjective estimates of comfort and performance. *Proceedings of the Institute of Environmental Sciences 1965 Annual Technical Meeting*, 1965.

Easterbrook, J. A. The effect of emotion on cue utilization and the organization of behavior. *Psychological Review*, 1959, *66*, 183–201.

Edholm, O. G. *Man – hot and cold*. London: Arnold, 1978.

Fanger, P. O. Improvement of human comfort and resulting effects on working capacity. *Biometeorology*, 1972, *5*, 31–41.

Fine, B. J., & Kobrick, J. L. Effects of altitude and heat on complex cognitive tasks. *Human Factors*, 1978, *20*, 115–122.

Folk, C. E., Jr. *Textbook of environmental physiology.* Philadelphia: Lea & Febiger, 1974.

Fox, R. H. Heat. In O. G. Edholm & A. L. Bacharach (Eds.), *The physiology of human survival.* London: Academic Press, 1965.

Fox, W. F. Human performance in the cold. *Human Factors*, 1967, *9*, 203–220.

Frisancho, A. R. *Human adaptation.* St. Louis: Mosby, 1979.

Gaydos, H. F. Effect on complex manual performance of cooling the body while maintaining the hands at normal temperatures. *Journal of Applied Physiology*, 1958, *12*, 373–376.

Gaydos, H. F., & Dusek, E. R. Effects of localized hand cooling versus total body cooling on manual performance. *Journal of Applied Physiology*, 1958, *12*, 377–380.

Ginsberg, B., & Allee, W. C. Some effects of conditioning on social dominance and subordination in inbred strains of mice. *Physiological Zoology*, 1942, *15*, 485–506.

Glass, D. C., & Singer, J. E. *Urban stress.* New York: Academic Press, 1972.

Goldman, R. F. The Arctic soldier: Possible research solutions for his protection. In C. A. Kolb and E. M. G. Holstrom (Eds.), Review of research on military problems in cold regions. *USAF Arctic Aeromedical Laboratory Technical Documentary Report* No. 64-28, 1964.

Goldman, R. F. Prediction of human heat tolerance. In L. J. Folinsbee, J. A. Wagner, J.F. Borgia, B. L. Drinkwater, J. A. Gliner, & J. F. Bedi (Eds.), *Environmental stress: Individual human adaptations.* New York: Academic Press, 1978.

Goranson, R. E., & King, D. *Rioting and daily temperature: Analysis of the U.S. riots in 1967.* Unpublished manuscript, York University, Toronto, 1970.

Green, T. C., & Bell, P. A. Additional considerations concerning the effects of "warm" and "cool" wall colours on energy conservation. *Ergonomics*, 1980, *23*, 949–954.

Grether, W. F. Human performance at elevated environmental temperatures. *Aerospace Medicine*, 1973, *44*, 747–755.

Griffiths, I. D. The thermal environment. In D. C. Canter (Ed.), *Environmental interaction: Psychological approaches to our physical surroundings.* New York: International Universities Press, 1975.

Griffiths, I. D., & Boyce, P. R. Performance and thermal comfort. *Ergonomics*, 1971, *14*, 457–468.

Griffitt, W. Environmental effects on interpersonal affective behavior: Ambient effective temperature and attraction. *Journal of Personality and Social Psychology*, 1970, *15*, 240–244.

Griffitt, W., & Veitch, R. Hot and crowded: Influences of population density and temperature on interpersonal affective behavior. *Journal of Personality and Social Psychology*, 1971, *17*, 92–98.

Hammel, H. T. Terrestrial animals in cold: Recent studies of primitive man. In D. B. Dill, E. F. Adolph, and C. G. Wilber (Eds.), *Handbook of physiology* (Pt. 4). Washington, D.C.: American Physiological Society, 1964.

Hardy, J. D. Temperature problems in space travel. In J. D. Hardy (Ed.), *Physiological problems in space exploration.* Springfield, Ill.: Thomas, 1964.

Hill, J. W. Applied problems of hot work in the glass industry. In C. N. Davies, P. R. Davis, & F. H. Tyrer (Eds.), *The effects of abnormal physical conditions at work.* London: E. & S. Livingstone, 1967.

Hori, S., Mayuzumi, M., Tanaka, N., & Tsujita, J. Oxygen intake of men and women during exercise and recovery in a hot environment and a comfortable environment. In L. J. Folinsbee, J. A. Wagner, J. F. Borgia, B. L. Drinkwater, J. A. Gliner, & J. F. Bedi (Eds.), *Environmental stress: Individual human adaptations*. New York: Academic Press, 1978.

Ingram, D. L., & Mount, L. E. *Man and animals in hot environments*. New York: Springer-Verlag, 1975.

Itoh, S. *Physiology of cold-adapted man*. Sapporo: Hokkaido University School of Medicine, 1974.

Keatinge, W. R. *Survival in cold water*. Oxford: Blackwell Scientific Publications, 1969.

Kuhlmeier, K. V., Fine, P. R., & Dukes-Dobos, F. N. Heart rate—Rectal temperature relationships during prolonged work: Males and females compared. In L. J. Folinsbee, J.A. Wagner, J. F. Borgia, B. L. Drinkwater, J.A. Gliner, & J. F. Bedi (Eds.), *Environmental stress: Individual human adaptations*. New York: Academic Press, 1978.

Ladell, W. S. Terrestrial animals in humid heat: Man. In A. B. Dill, E. F. Adolph, & C. G. Wilber (Eds.), *Handbook of physiology* (Sect. 4). Washington, D. C.: American Physiological Society, 1964.

Landsberg, H. E. *Weather and health*. New York: Doubleday, 1969.

Le Blanc, J. Impairment of manual dexterity in the cold. *Journal of Applied Physiology*, 1956, *9*, 62–64.

Le Blanc, J. Local adaptation to cold of Gaspé fishermen. *Journal of Applied Physiology*, 1962, *17*, 950–952.

Le Blanc, J. *Man in the cold*. Springfield, Ill.: Thomas, 1975.

Le Blanc, J., Hildes, J. A., & Héroux, O. Tolerance of Gaspé fishermen to cold water. *Journal of Applied Physiology*, 1960, *15*, 1031–1034.

Lee, D. H. K. Terrestrial animals in dry heat: Man in the desert. In D. B. Dill, E. G. Adolph, & C. C. Wilber (Eds.), *Handbook of physiology*. Washington, D.C.: The American Physiological Society, 1964.

Leithead, C. S., & Lind, A. R. *Heat stress and heat disorders*. London: Cassell, 1964.

Lind, A. R. Man's intolerance to extreme heat. In C. N. Davies, P. R. Davis, & F. H. Tyrer (Eds.), *The effects of abnormal physical conditions at work*. London: E. & S. Livingstone, 1967.

Link, J. M., & Pepler, R. D. Associated fluctuations in daily temperature, productivity and absenteeism. *ASHRAE Transactions*, 1970, *76* (Pt. 2), 326–337.

Lockhart, J. M. Effects of body and hand cooling on complex manual performance. *Journal of Applied Psychology*, 1966, *50*, 57–59.

Lockhart, J. M. Extreme body cooling and psychomotor performance. *Ergonomics*, 1968, *11*, 249–260.

Lockhart, J. M., & Keiss, H. O. Auxiliary heating of the hands during cold exposure and manual performance. *Human Factors*, 1971, *13*, 457–465.

Mackworth, N. H. Cold acclimatization and finger numbness. *Proceedings of the Royal Society*, 1955, *143*, 392–407.

Mackworth, N. H. Researches on the measurement of human performance. In H. W. Sinaiki (Ed.), *Selected papers on human factors in the design and use of control systems*. New York: Dover, 1961.

Marcus, P., & Belyavin, A. Thermal sensation during experimental hypothermia. *Physiology and Behavior*, 1978, *21*, 909–914.

Marcus, P., & Redman, P. Effect of exercise on thermal comfort during hypothermia. *Physiology and Behavior*, 1978, *22*, 831–835.

McIntyre, D. A. A guide to thermal comfort. *Applied Ergonomics*, 1973, *4*, 66–72.

McNall, P. E., & Schlegel, J. C. Practical thermal environmental limits for young adult males working in hot, humid environments. *ASHRAE Transactions*, 1968, *74* (Pt. 2), 225–235.

Milgram, S. The experience of living in cities. *Science*, 1970, *167*, 1461–1468.

Mount, L. E. *Adaptation to thermal environment*. Baltimore: University Park Press, 1979.

Myers, R. D. *Handbook of drug and chemical stimulation of the brain*. New York: Van Nostrand, 1974.

Nadel, E. R., Roberts, M. F., & Wenger, C. B. Thermoregulatory adaptations to heat and exercise: Comparative responses of men and women. In L. J. Folinsbee, J. A. Wagner, J. F. Borgia, B. L. Drinkwater, J. A. Gliner, & J. F. Bedi (Eds.), *Environmental stress: Individual human adaptations*. New York: Academic Press, 1978.

Nevins, R. G., Rohles, F. H., Springer, W., & Feyerherm, A. M. A temperature-humidity chart for thermal comfort of seated persons. *ASHRAE Transactions*, 1966, *72*, 283–291.

Newburgh, L. H. *Physiology of human heat regulation and the science of clothing*. New York: Hafner, 1968.

Nunneley, S. A., Dowd, P. J., Myhre, L. G., Stribley, R. F., & McNee, R. C. Tracking-task performance during heat stress simulating cockpit conditions in high-performance aircraft. *Ergonomics*, 1979, *22*, 549–555.

Page, R. A. *Environmental influences on prosocial behavior: The effect of temperature*. Paper presented at the meeting of the Midwestern Psychological Association, Chicago, May 1978.

Pepler, R. D. Warmth and performance: An investigation in the tropics. *Ergonomics*, 1958, *2*, 63–68.

Pepler, R. D. Warmth and lack of sleep: Accuracy or activity reduced. *Journal of Comparative and Physiological Psychology*, 1959, *52*, 446–450.

Pepler, R. D. Warmth, glare, and a background of quiet speech: A comparison of their effects on performance. *Ergonomics*, 1960, *3*, 68–73.

Pepler, R. D. Performance and well-being in heat. In J. Hardy (Ed.), *Temperature: Its measurement and control in science and industry*, 3, Pt. 3. New York: Van Nostrand Reinhold, 1963.

Poulton, E. C. *The environment and human efficiency*. Springfield, Ill.: Thomas, 1970.

Poulton, E. C. Arousing environmental stress can improve performance, whatever people say. *Aviation Space and Environmental Medicine*, 1976, *47*, 1193–1204.

Poulton, E. C., Hitchings, N. B., and Brooke, R. B. Effect of cold and rain upon the vigilance of lookouts. *Ergonomics*, 1965, *8*, 163–168.

Poulton, E. C., & Kerslake, D. McK. Initial stimulating effect of warmth upon perceptual efficiency. *Aerospace Medicine*, 1965, *36*, 29–32.

Provins, K. A. Environmental heat, body temperature, and behavior: An hypothesis. *Australian Journal of Psychology*, 1966, *18*, 118–129.

Provins, K., & Bell, C. R. The effects of heat on human performance. *Proceedings of the Second International Bioclimatic Congress*. Oxford: Pergamon Press, 1960.

Provins, K. A., & Bell, C. R. Effects of heat stress on the performance of two tasks running concurrently. *Journal of Experimental Psychology*, 1970, *85*, 40–44.

Rohles, F. H. Environmental psychology: A bucket of worms. *Psychology Today*, 1967, *1*, 54–63.

Rohles, F. H. Preference for the thermal environment by the elderly. *Human Factors*, 1969, *11*, 37–41.

Rohles, F. H. Thermal sensations of sedentary man in moderate temperatures. *Human Factors*, 1971, *13*, 553–560.

Rohles, F. H. The revised modal comfort envelope. *ASHRAE Transactions*, 1973, *79* (Pt. 2), 52–59.

Rohles, F. H. The modal comfort envelope and its use in current standards. *Human Factors*, 1974, *16*, 314–322.

Rohles, F. H., & Johnson, M. A. Thermal comfort in the elderly. *ASHRAE Transactions*, 1972, *78*, 131–137.

Rohles, F. H., Woods, J. E., & Nevins, R. G. The influence of clothing and temperature on sedentary comfort. *ASHRAE Transactions*, 1973, *79* (Pt. 2), 71–80.

Rowell, L. B. Human adjustments and adaptations to heat stress—where and how? In L. J. Folinsbee, J. A. Wagner, J. F. Borgia, B. L. Drinkwater, J. A. Gliner, & J. F. Bedi (Eds.), *Environmental stress: Individual human adaptations*. New York: Academic Press, 1978.

Schneider, F. W., Lesko, W. A., & Garrett, W. A. Helping behavior in hot, comfortable, and cold temperatures. *Environment and Behavior*, 1980, *12*, 231–240.

Scholander, P. F., Hammel, H. T., Hart, J. S., Le Messurler, D. H., & Steen, J. Cold adaptation in Australian aborigines. *Journal of Applied Physiology*, 1958, *13*, 211–218.

Schwartz, D. C. On the ecology of political violence: "The long hot summer" as a hypothesis. *American Behavioral Scientist*, 1968, July-August, 24–28.

Sells, S. B., & Will, D. P. *Accidents, police incidents, and weather: A further study of the city of Fort Worth, Texas, 1968*. Technical Report No. 15, Group Psychology Branch, Office of Naval Research and Institute of Behavioral Research, Texas Christian University, Fort Worth, 1971.

Sloan, A. W. *Man in extreme environments*. Springfield, Ill.: Thomas, 1979.

Stang, P. R., & Wiener, E. L. Diver performance in cold water. *Human Factors*, 1970, *12*, 391–399.

Teichner, W. H., & Wehrkamp, P. F. Visual motor performance as a function of short-duration ambient temperature. *Journal of Experimental Psychology*, 1954, *47*, 447–450.

United States Riot Commission. *Report of the National Advisory Commission on Civil Disorders*. New York: Bantam, 1968.

Vaughn, W. S. Jr., & Mavor, H. S. Diver performance in controlling a wet submersible during four-hour exposures to cold water. *Human Factors*, 1972, *14*, 173–180.

Veghte, J. H. Human physiological response to extremity and body cooling. *USAF Arctic Aeromedical Laboratory Technical Report* No. 61-26, 1961.

Weyant, J. M. Effects of mood states, costs, and benefits on helping. *Journal of Personality and Social Psychology*, 1978, *36*, 1169–1176.

Wilkinson, R. T. Some factors influencing the effect of environmental stressors upon performance. *Psychological Bulletin*, 1969, *72*, 260–272.

Wilkinson, R. T. Individual differences in response to the environment. *Ergonomics*, 1974, *17*, 745–756.

Wilkinson, R. T., Fox, R. H., Goldsmith, R., Hampton, I. F. G., & Lewis, H. E. Psychological and physiological responses to raised body temperature. *Journal of Applied Physiology*, 1964, *19*, 287–291.

Will, D. P., & Sells, S. B. *Prediction of police incidents and accidents by meteorological variables*. Technical Report No. 14, Group Psychology Branch, Office of Naval Research and Institute of Behavioral Research, Texas Christian University, Fort Worth, 1969.

Wing, J. F. Upper thermal tolerance limits for unimpaired mental performance. *Aerospace Medicine*, 1965, *36*, 960–964.

Wyndham, C. H. Adaptation to heat and cold. In D. H. K. Lee & D. Minard (Eds.), *Physiology, environment, and man*. New York: Academic Press, 1970.

Wyndham, C. H., Morrison, J. F., & Williams, C. G. Heat reaction of male and female caucasians. *Journal of Applied Physiology*, 1965, *20*, 357–364.

Wyon, D. P. Studies of children under imposed noise and heat stress. *Ergonomics*, 1970, *13*, 598–612.

4.   Air pollution and human behavior

Gary W. Evans and Stephen V. Jacobs

In 1976, 43 major cities comprising over half the total U.S. population had unhealthy air quality (President's Council on Environmental Quality, 1978). Direct negative impacts on real estate and agriculture run in the tens of billions in the U.S. alone (Stern, 1977). Furthermore, Lave and Seskin (1970), focusing on respiratory-related epidemiological studies, have derived a lower bound estimate of $200 million yearly savings in U.S. health costs if air quality were improved 50%. This estimate may be low, since other reasonable disease links such as cardiovascular disorders were not given full coverage, and since the impacts of major air pollution disasters, which in the past have been linked to excess mortality and morbidity, were not included (cf. Goldsmith & Friberg, 1977), and since potential psychological costs, as developed in this paper, were not calculated.

Below we offer an overview of the effects of air pollution on human health and then discuss in detail affective reactions and behavioral effects of air pollution. Although the role of human behavior in air pollution is considerable, research has emphasized the technical, economic, and physical health aspects of the problem. Human behaviors such as energy use or choice of transportation mode directly affect the production of air pollution. Less directly, our attitudes and political and economic decisions about environmental protection also affect pollution levels.

Air pollution also affects human behavior. Directly, pollution affects the amount of time we spend outdoors and the extent of our physical activity. Residential location and migration decisions may also be made in part on the basis of pollution levels. Air pollution also affects recreation patterns, task performance, and interpersonal relationships. The subject of this chap-

Preparation of this chapter was partially supported by the Southern California Edison Company-(B-2058902, J-1909902)-and the Focused Research Program on Stress, University of California, Irvine. We thank Mary Barker, Steven Horvath, Joseph E. McGrath, and James Rotton for critical comments on earlier drafts.

ter is the various ways in which human behavior effects and is affected by air pollution.

Health and physiology

Research on the health effects of air pollution in humans has been conducted both in laboratory settings and in situ where aggregate correlations between pollutant levels and disease rates are obtained. The major constituents of ambient air pollution include photochemical oxidants (smog), carbon monoxide, nitrogen oxides, sulfur oxides, and particulates. Toxicological and epidemiological findings on each of these major pollutants are summarized below, followed by a critique of these studies.

Health effects of specific agents

Photochemical oxidants. Photochemical oxidants are produced by photosynthetic processes involving hydrocarbon and nitrogen oxide emissions from internal combustion. The major toxic component of oxidants is ozone. Toxicological studies indicate that low-level, ambient-range exposures of humans to ozone cause eye irritation, mouth dryness, and substernal soreness. Some sophisticated psychophysical scaling procedures have been utilized by psychologists in measuring eye irritation from smog. M. Jones (1972), for example, using an ascending series method of limits has established very stable correlations, in the .70 to .80 range, between particular components of smog (e.g., formaldehyde) and absolute occular pain thresholds. Levels of .5 parts per million (ppm) cause more severe reactions including nausea, headache, anorexia, pulmonary edema, and reduction in pulmonary capacity. Animal studies suggest additional outcomes with more chronic, high-level exposures that include severe respiratory disorder, reduced host resistance to infection, premature aging, biochemical alteration of hemoglobin (lipid peroxidation) that reflects shifts in reactivity to oxidant challenge, cardiovascular distress, and possibly carcinogenic effects (Coffin & Stokinger, 1977; National Academy of Sciences, 1977). Epidemiological findings suggest small but significant associations between ozone levels and respiratory-related hospital admissions and respiratory infection rates, but moderate associations between those levels and aggravation of preexisting respiratory diseases, respiratory discomfort, and eye irritation (Goldsmith & Friberg, 1977; National Academy of Sciences, 1977).

Sulfur oxides. The principal source of ambient sulfur oxides is the combustion of fossil fuels. Human toxicological exposures to sulfur oxides within ambient range generally produce irritation of upper respiratory passages, reduced mucosillary clearance, and reduced pulmonary functioning. Animal studies with greater exposures also find pulmonary and nasal lesions, pulmonary edema, bronchitis and pneumonia, pulmonary cancer, and more severe pulmonary disorder (Coffin & Stokinger, 1977). Epidemiological studies suggest associations with upper respiratory tract infections, possibly bronchitis and asthma, aggravation of preexisting respiratory diseases, and decrements in pulmonary function (Goldsmith & Friberg, 1977).

Nitrogen oxides. Nitrogen oxides, which are ubiquitous in air, are also produced by fossil fuel combustion in motor vehicles and electrical power production. A few human toxicological studies have demonstrated reduced pulmonary functioning, reduced host resistance to disease, diminished weight gain, general bronchial inflammation, and lipid peroxidation of hemoglobin (Coffin & Stokinger, 1977; National Academy of Sciences, 1977). Epidemiological studies have found associations with increased respiratory illness but no strong data on disease rates (Goldsmith & Friberg, 1977; National Academy of Sciences, 1977).

Carbon monoxide. Carbon monoxide resulting from incomplete combustion is emitted primarily from motor vehicles and cigarette smoking. Human toxicological studies indicate that headache, dizziness, and nausea are related to oxygen deprivation. Volunteers with angina pectoris also report faster onset of pain when exposed to carbon monoxide. Animal studies with higher dosages find additional symptoms including alteration of cortical cellular structure, altered heart beat, vascular diseases, impaired liver function, fetal growth retardation, and increased perinatal mortality (Coffin & Stokinger, 1977; National Academy of Sciences, 1977). Epidemiological studies have related carbon monoxide exposure to low birth weight, increased perinatal mortality, increased distress in patients with cardiovascular disease, and possible occurrence of cardiovascular disease. Some of the negative effects of cigarette smoking are generally linked to carbon monoxide exposure. Among these effects are changes in arterial blood vessels, accelerated atherosclerosis, fetal and neonatal asphyxiation, and reduced birth weight (Goldsmith & Friberg, 1977; National Academy of Sciences, 1977).

Particulates. Particulates can absorb various chemicals including carcinogens and increase their penetration and longevity in the lungs. Particulates also condense water and other vapors and augment effects of gaseous pollutants like sulfur oxides. The major particulates of concern are asbestos, lead, mercury, and several other heavy metals and halogens. Toxicological effects from asbestos include pulmonary lesions and carcinoma, and mesothelial tissue damage; from lead, gastrointestinal cramping, anemia, and impaired neural functioning; and from mercury, neural dysfunction, upper respiratory inflammation, and thyroid disturbance. Asbestos has also been linked to pulmonary cancer, and lead poisoning may affect retardation and possibly hyperactivity in children (Coffin & Stokinger, 1977; Goldsmith & Friberg, 1977).

Critical analysis

Although toxicological studies of air pollution and human health provide rigorous controls over extraneous variables such as other pollutants and weather conditions, plus ensuring random assignment of subjects, several deficiencies in this approach are apparent. First, the toxic substances are different. In situ air pollutants covary and are known to have synergistic effects and to interact with meteorological factors such as humidity. Sulfur dioxide, for example, has considerably more pronounced health effects in the presence of ozone and high humidity (Coffin & Stokinger, 1977). Second, dosage parameters differ considerably between toxicological and ambient conditions. Experimental studies often expose subjects to doses greater than or equivalent to ambient doses for short periods of time, without gradual exposure buildup time. Under ambient conditions, pollutants fluctuate daily and seasonally and are experienced for longer periods of time. The importance of temporal patterns of exposure is evidenced by research showing that animals and possibly humans adapt to air pollutants, building up tolerance with sustained exposure (Coffin & Stokinger, 1977).

Epidemiological studies of air pollution suffer from several logical and conceptual shortcomings. First, many of these studies rely largely on catastrophic indexes of health such as mortality or disease. Researchers should also explore discomfort, irritability, and potentially more serious mental health outcomes such as depression and anxiety. Given the established effects of oxidants and carbon monoxide on eye discomfort, headaches, and respiratory discomfort, it is reasonable to conjecture that chronic discomfort could lead to more serious mental health consequences. Furthermore, quite apart from their direct impacts on the human organism, pollutants such as nitrogen dioxide might also contribute to depression because they can substantially reduce visibility. A recent preliminary study has explored simple correlations among several pollution indexes and admissions to a psychiatric hospital in St. Louis (Strahilevitz, Strahilevitz, & Miller, 1979). Daily carbon monoxide levels correlated positively (.25) for all admissions, and nitrogen dioxide levels correlated positively (.22, .20) for admissions of alcoholics and organic brain syndrome patients.

A second limitation of most epidemiological studies of air pollution is their focus on direct, unmediated health effects. As considerable medical and psychological research shows (Baum, Singer, & Baum, Chap. 1, this volume), the effects of many environmental stressors on human health and behavior are mediated by several personal and environmental factors. One pertinent mediator of air pollution effects is the extent of an individual's previous experience with a pollutant. As discussed in more detail later, individuals chronically exposed to a pollutant are less reactive to the pollutant and cope with its effects differently than individuals newly exposed. Another relevant personal mediator between air pollution and its health effects could be the recent occurrence of other stressful life experiences such as job loss or physical illness. Just as epidemiologists treat persons with preexisting respiratory diseases as more at risk to air pollutants, we can explore whether individuals with preexisting psychological difficulties/risk are also more susceptible to negative health effects from pollutants. Given that stressors reduce host resistance to biological pathogens (Dubos, 1965), stress may also affect reactivity to environmental pollutants. Other variables that are potential mediators between air pollution and health and are as yet largely unexplored, include individual appraisals of threat and coping resources with respect to air pollution, and perceived control over exposure to and reactions to pollutants.

The remaining criticisms of epidemiological studies of air pollution and human health are largely methodological. Most epidemiological studies correlate aggregate health level indicators with ambient pollutant fluctuations. Unfortunately, under most circumstances this approach precludes inferences about individual-level effects (the ecological fallacy). In addition, numerous other variables, such as other pollutants and meteorological events, covary with a specific pollutant under study. Furthermore, in the case of mental health outcomes many other important factors such as high unemployment may also correlate with higher levels of air pollutants. Third, extent of exposure is typically inferred from residential location, yet daily exposure is substantially modified by transportation and occupational exposure, and by construction properties of the habitat. Finally, the use of one-shot, correlational designs ignores temporal variables and has serious internal validity problems. For example, by examining simultaneous correlations between a pollutant and a health outcome, one assumes that health effects are immediate, whereas many toxicological studies show that many health effects are delayed (Coffin & Stokinger, 1977). The application of more sophisticated, quasi-experimental approaches, such as cross-lagged panel designs and time series analysis, would greatly diminish many of the methodological shortcomings common in epidemiological studies of air pollution and human health.

Human behavior

The dearth of conceptually integrated, empirical investigations of personal responses to air pollution is regrettable, given the interplay between pollution and behavior and the legal mandates for incorporating such information in policy decisions concerning air pollution control and standards (Craik & Zube, 1976). Behavioral responses to air pollution can be conceptually organized in a number of ways. Loveridge (1971) suggests that there are four types of personal responses to air pollution: psychological, social, economic, and political. Psychological responses refer to attitudes about the influence of air pollution on the individual and on the human condition. Social responses include the influence of air pollution on an individual's life-style. Loveridge suggests that an individual can ignore the presence of air pollution, tolerate its effects, or change his or her social habits. For example, air pollution may affect a person's choice of, and satisfaction with, his or her place of residence, job, and recreational activities.

Economic responses refer to corrective actions through the marketplace. Loveridge distinguishes between avoiding the effects of air pollution (e.g., purchasing air filter equipment) and treating its effects (e.g., purchasing pollution-related medication). Finally, political responses refer to an individual's knowledge, attitudes, and policy opinions about air pollution and its control.

We have borrowed a social–psychological model derived from attitude–behavior theory as an alternative framework for organizing the air pollution and human behavior literature. What is generally referred to as an attitude, the predisposition to respond to some class of stimuli, includes three distinct, interrelated response components: a cognitive component, an affective component (which is the more recent and restricted definition of "attitude"), and a conative component (Bagozzi & Burnkrant, 1979; Fishbein & Ajzen, 1975; Rosenberg & Hovland, 1960). In this review the cognitive component will refer to *knowledge and beliefs* about air pollution. Since such a focus presupposes an awareness of existence of air pollution, awareness will also be discussed in this section. The affective components will refer to *feelings and emotions* regarding air pollution. Both attitudes and concern will be included here. Finally, the conative component will refer to both *overt behavioral responses* to air pollution, and verbal reports of *intentions to act* in some manner regarding air pollution

By considering research on public responses to air pollution in these terms, some important observations may be made. For instance, some studies have found a weak relationship between cognitive awareness of air pollution and an affective concern about it (Swan, 1970; Wall 1974). Similarly, other studies have demonstarted a weak realtionship between concern and certain criterion behaviors (for instance, propensity to complain) regarding air pollution (e.g., Jacoby, 1972).

Cognitive responses to air pollution

Much of the research assessing responses to air pollution has attempted to document the level of public awareness and concern (Rankin, 1969). Knowledge and beliefs about air pollution have received somewhat less attention. To date, however, there has been little systematic use of these terms. For instance, Rankin (1969) discusses data on both awareness of air pollution (from such questions as: "Is there ever air pollution in the area in which you live?") and awareness of the air pollution *problem* (from such questions as: "Do you feel that air pollution is a problem in your area?"). In this review, the former is considered to be addressing a cognitive parameter whereas the latter is viewed as addressing an affective parameter. Similar distinctions will be made throughout this review.

Awareness. Although the actual proportion of "aware" respondents ranges among studies from about 65% to 95%, public awareness of air pollution in this country has generally increased in the past two decades. The few investigations that have been undertaken in other countries have also documented a relatively high level of awareness in polluted areas (e.g., studies in Chotanagpur, India, by Bladen & Karan, 1976; and studies in Ljubljana, Yugoslavia; Budapest, Hungary; and Sheffield, United Kingdom, by Kromm, Probald, & Wall, 1973).

One major reason for variation among studies in the proportion of "aware" persons may be the phrasing of questionnaire items. As one might expect, proportion aware is higher when air pollution is directly probed (e.g., "Is there air pollution in this area at any time during the year?") than when it is not (e.g., "Please list the five most serious problems in your community."). When similar questionnaire items have been employed, the proportion of respondents who are aware of air pollution has tended to be fairly consistent across studies. Both Medalia (1964) and Creer, Gray, and Treshow (1970), for example, employed the same direct probe and found that approximately 80% of respondents were aware that there was air pollution in their area at some time during the year.

At least two factors have been shown to influence public awareness of air pollution: the nature of air pollution and publicity about it (Auliciems & Burton, 1971; Barker, 1976; Smith, Schueneman, & Zeidberg, 1964). Barker (1976) has noted that awareness of air pollution varies according to its type, amount, frequency, and source. She has suggested six cues that individuals use to detect the presence of air pollution. They include dust, odor, discoloration and damage to property, respiratory irritation, eye irritation, and poor visibility. Findings suggest that the strongest physical stimuli influencing awareness of air pollution are particulates, soiling of buildings and household objects by dustfall, and reduced visibility caused by haze. Awareness of air pollution obviously depends heavily upon visual perception. This finding takes on particular significance because many toxic gaseous pollutants cannot be seen.

Engineers and other physical scientists have conducted extensive research on the physical constituents of air pollution that influence visibility and judgments of air quality. Human judgments of visibility, for example, depend primarily on color contrast and acuity (Malm, Leiker, & Molenar, 1980; Noll, Mueller, & Imada, 1968). Physical-based models of perceived air quality indicate that human appraisals are influenced primarily by visibility, amount of particulates, and to a lesser extent by photochemical oxidants and sulfur oxides (Flacshbart & Phillips, 1980). There is considerable need for research on perceptual aspects of air quality. With few exceptions, existing research has been limited to the physical constituents of air as well as to visibility. One reason why existing models of perceived air quality are limited is that they lack consideration of important psychological processes such as adaptation, perceived control, and other individual factors.

Determining the relative importance of direct experience with air pollution compared to the influence of mass media and publicity campaigns remains problematic. DeGroot (1967) and Smith et al. (1964) maintain that direct perceptual experience probably accounts for more air pollution awareness than does mass media information, whereas Auliciems and Burton (1971) claim the opposite. Consideration of air pollution characteristics and detection cues designated by Barker may clarify this issue. For instance, some areas may be polluted with invisible gaseous pollutants that may not be directly experienced until extremely high levels are reached. The public may consequently rely more heavily upon the media to gauge the extent of air pollution in such situations.

Awareness of air pollution is mediated by a number of variables including location (Rankin, 1969), time of day and seasonal variation (Barker, 1976), and socioeconomic status (Swan, 1970). Lower SES groups tend to report less awareness of air pollution. Both DeGroot (1967) and Rankin (1969) point out that people consistently perceive their immediate communities to have less air pollution than other surrounding areas. This phenomenon may be a consequence of dissonance reduction; one diminishes or denies the amount of air pollution in an area where he or she lives. Of related interest, the association between perceived severity of air pollution and actual levels of photochemical oxidants is substantially higher for individuals with low overall neighborhood satisfaction (Hohm, 1976). Hohm also found that individuals most concerned with air pollution in their neighborhood planned to move out of the area within the next year.

Knowledge and beliefs. Somewhat less attention has been devoted to the study of knowledge and beliefs about air pollution. Knowledge is the factual information an individual possesses about air pollution; beliefs refer to what and how a person thinks about air pollution, regardless of the factual validity of his or her perceptions. Since most people possess very little factual information about air pollution (Buckout, 1972), most of these studies have dealt with public beliefs about air pollution. Medalia (1964) asked residents near a malodorous wood pulp mill, "What do you think the words 'air pollution' mean to most people in this area?" Respondents defined air pollution in terms of its effects, mentioning malodors, low visibility and nose/throat irritation. Crowe (1968) also found that most respondents define air pollution in terms of particular effects or suspected causes and very few respondents define air pollution by composition.

A few studies have investigated public beliefs about causes of air pollution (DeGroot, Loring, Rihm, Samuels, & Winkelstein, 1966; Johnson, Allegre, Burhrman, Miller, Sheldon, & Rosen, 1972; Schusky, 1966; Simon, 1971; Stanford Workshop on Air Pollution, 1970). In general, there is consensus regarding transportation and industry as major sources of air pollution.

Some investigators have also explored variables that mediate knowledge and beliefs about air pollution. Crowe (1968) observed that the propensity of respondents to define air pollution in causal terms tended to increase with education. Residence, length of residence, and sex were not significant factors in defining air pollution. Additionally, although no SES differences were apparent, Swan (1970) found that whites were more knowledgeable about air pollution than blacks. Less concern for and awareness of air pollution in racial minorities may be due to nonwhites' having more social hazards (e.g., poverty) to deal with, which takes priority and attention over environmental concerns.

Experts define air pollution more in terms of causal factors, noting the presence of motor vehicle traffic or industrial sources, whereas laypersons generally describe either visual characteristics (e.g., soot, hazy sky) or health effects (e.g., respiratory discomfort) (Barker, 1976; Hummel, Loomis, & Herbert, 1975). Barker has also found few differences among various experts in defining or rating the seriousness of air pollution. Advanced students in medicine, law, engineering, economics, and geography did differ, however, in knowledge of air pollution and descriptions of the roles of specialists in managing air pollution problems. Economists, for example, knew the least about air pollution and narrowly construed the role of air pollution management in economic areas (Barker, 1974).

Additional literature on knowledge and beliefs about air pollution has dealt with its control and amelioration. These findings are discussed later in the section on perceived control.

Affective responses to air pollution

A preponderance of the literature on public response to air pollution has understandably focused on how people evaluate or react emotionally to air pollution. For our purposes, any investigation that directly or indirectly asks if air pollution is good or bad, or has positive or negative aspects, is measuring attitudes.

Similar to the data on awareness of air pollution, the pattern of public attitudes about air pollution varies with the measurement technique employed. Few people spontaneously express concern (even in highly polluted areas), although a much larger proportion of respondents indicate their concern when asked directly (Smith et al., 1964; Swan, 1972). For example, when Smith et al. (1964) asked over 3,000 residents of Nashville, Tennessee, a city with serious air pollution problems, if Nashville was a healthy place to live, 85% responded affirmatively and less than 3% spontaneously mentioned concern about air pollution. Approximately 23% of respondents acknowledged concern about the air pollution problem when asked directly.

Some studies directly investigating concern have measured perceived seriousness of the air pollution problem. McEvoy (1972) found that the proportion of U.S. citizens evaluating air pollution as a very serious problem increased from 10% to 25% between 1965 and 1968. Rankin (1969) also found that about 90% of respondents considered air pollution at least somewhat serious. On the other hand, more recent studies have noted a general decline from 1970 to 1976 in public support for pollution control and environmental protection in general (Dunlap, Van Liere, & Dillman, 1979).

Dillman and Christenson (1972) have argued that the *value* held regarding pollution control efforts relative to other primary forms of government expenditure is a better predictor of public acceptance of pollution control measures than are mere expressions of concern. They found that expressed concern about pollution increased with pollution levels, but that the public value of pollution control did not increase. Consistent with this line of inquiry, a number of investigations have asked respondents to compare air pollution to other social problems (Crowe, 1968; DeGroot, 1967; Johnson et al., 1972; Molotch & Follet, 1971). Depending on the characteristics of the subjects or the study sites, air pollution is usually acknowledged by respondents as one of the five most serious social problems. Other important social problems include unemployment, juvenile delinquency, inflation, and so on. Additionally, various civic leaders rank air pollution sixth out of 11 urban problems (Miller, 1972). It should be noted that, relative to other social problems, air pollution may not be considered as serious in poorer, less developed countries. For instance, Bladen and Karan (1976) found that although residents of industrialized areas of India are aware of air pollution, they show little concern about it.

Concern about air pollution, as with awareness, is influenced primarily by two factors: direct exposure to air pollution and publicity through the media. Barker (1976) has noted that there is a positive relationship between concern about air pollution and some physical measures of air quality. A positive relationship has been found, for example, between particulate concentration and annoyance, dissatisfaction, concern, and nuisance ratings. Several other studies have demonstrated positive correlations (ranging from .30 to .82) between the perceived seriousness of air pollution and actual air quality (physical components) in a given area (DeGroot et al., 1966; Jacoby, 1972; Johnston & Hay, 1974; Schusky, 1966; Smith et al., 1964; Wall, 1973). It should be noted that in almost all of these studies air quality levels are based on particulates, smoke, dustfall, or some other visually discernible pollutant. It is quite possible that a much weaker relationship exists between concern and pollution levels when less visible gases are used as air quality criteria. In areas where there are high concentrations of air pollutants that are not typically visible, mass media communications may be an important factor in public awareness and concern about air pollution.

Although communications about environmental issues generally parallel increases in public concern about environmental issues (Lipsey, 1977; McEvoy, 1972), few studies have specifically investigated the impact of the media on public responses to air pollution. On the other hand, Wall (1974) found that publicity about civic efforts to reduce coal soot in England apparently induced public complacency about remaining air quality problems. Murch (1971) also noted that media typically emphasize national pollution problems and have little coverage of local environmental issues. He hypothesized that this trend might explain the tendency of the public to view pollution as a greater problem in the nation or general area in comparison to their own neighborhood.

Numerous personal variables are correlated with attitudes about air pollution. Concern is positively related to socioeconomic status (Hohm, 1976; Jacoby, 1972; Smith et al., 1964; Van Arsdol, Sabagh, & Alexander, 1964), degree of urbanness (Jacoby, 1972), and respiratory impairments (Barker, 1976). Age is negatively associated with concern (Creer et al., 1970; McEvoy, 1972), females are more concerned than males (McEvoy, 1972; Smith et al., 1964), and whites tend to be more concerned than nonwhites (Hohm, 1976; Jacoby, 1972). Length of exposure to air pollution as a mediating variable is discussed in the adaptation section.

Creer et al. (1970) conducted a particularly significant study examining the relationship between economic dependence on a primary pollution source and concern. They found a strong inverse relationship between level of concern about air pollution and economic dependence upon the pollution source. Whereas only 19% of respondents employed by the company responsible for the pollution source were seriously bothered by air pollution, over 80% of persons not employed by that company were bothered.

Conative responses to air pollution

Much of the work on conative components of public responses to air pollution has focused on individuals' intentions to perform future or hypothetical acts. The literature on behavioral intentions related to control of air pollution is presented in the section on control.

With the exception of research on the effects of air pollution on performance, extremely few studies have investigated overt behavior. Furthermore, many of these studies rely on self-report measures.

Outdoor activities. Little is known about how exposure to air pollution affects the day-to-day behavior or life-styles of individuals. Rivlin (personal communication to Baron, Byrne, & Griffitt, 1974, p. 526) studied use patterns of New York City parks using a behavioral mapping technique. She found no curtailment of outdoor activities on high-pollution days. Chapko and Solomon (1976) found a weak but significant inverse relationship between carbon monoxide, as well as oxidant levels, and attendance at outdoor recreational sites. Peterson (1975) also found moderate curtailment of recreation behavior in the Los Angeles Basin under heavy photochemical smog conditions. One interesting implication of all these studies is the consistent finding that there is remarkably little reduction in outdoor activities on high pollution days. Perhaps public health officials have not provided citizens with adequate information about the hazards of exercise when air pollution levels increase.

Social behavior. Unfortunately, only a few studies have examined social responses to air pollution. Rotton, Barry, Frey, and Soler (1978) found that malodors actually increased liking for attitudinally similar strangers but had no effect on attraction for dissimilar strangers. A second study measured whether this paradoxical odor effect was caused by empathy for the other individual's exposure to the bad odor. When the stranger was clearly not exposed to the pollutant, odor significantly reduced attraction for both attitudinally similar and dissimilar strangers. Odor also produced more negative overall mood state and negative ratings of the laboratory setting. Negative ratings of paintings and photographs are also increased by odor in a laboratory setting (Rotton, Yoshikawa, Francis, & Hoyler, 1978). J. Jones (1978) also found that nonsmokers feel more irritable, anxious, and fatigued in close contact with cigarette smoke. Apparently, shared distress is not operative when the stranger is producing the pollutant. Bleda and Bleda (1978) similarly found that individuals sitting on a public bench are more likely to leave and leave faster when their personal space is invaded by a smoking adult rather than a nonsmoking adult. On the other hand, some recent research suggests that under varying task performance conditions, the effects of cigarette smoke on nonsmokers may be more complex (Stone, Breidenbach, & Heimstra, 1979). Under low-motivation task performance conditions, but not under high-motivation conditions, smoke causes greater annoyance in comparison to a no-smoke control.

Since air pollution can apparently cause increased irritability and reduced attraction under some conditions, aggression may also be affected. Jones and Bogat (1978) reported that exposure to cigarette smoking increased feelings of aggression in nonsmokers. Furthermore, some research on weather and altruism has noted small but significant correlations between some air pollutants and helping behavior. Cunningham (1979) reported less willingness to fill out a questionnaire with heightened sulfur dioxide levels. Stronger effects of temperature and degree of sunshine on altruism, however, were not partialled out from the air pollution index. Rotton, Frey, Barry, Milligan, and Fitzpatrick (1979) found a more complex, curvilinear relationship between malodor and aggression. When in moderately bad-smelling air, persons chose to shock a confederate more, but when subjected to extremely unpleasant odor, shocking levels were as low as in clear (ambient) air, control conditions.

Since air quality is related to negative affect and interpersonal behaviors, researchers have recently hypothesized that air pollution may affect mental health and social pathology.

As discussed, Strahilevitz et al. (1979) reported some positive, simple correlations between air pollution and psychiatric admissions in St. Louis.

Two large epidemiological surveys are currently underway in the United States that explore in some detail how air pollution and mental health are associated.

In the first of these studies, 6,000 randomly selected residents of the Los Angeles metropolitan area are being interviewed in 12 panel waves, over a 3-year period. Standardized measures of depression, hostility, anxiety, general psychological health, and use of physical and mental health facilities are recorded. In addition, detailed control data are collected on stressful life events, social support, illness-reporting biases, and basic sociodemographic data.

At this time no data are available, but the two principle hypotheses under examination are (1) persons who have recently moved into the Los Angeles area will be most susceptible to the negative health effects of smog because they have not adapted to the poor air quality of the region, and (2) individuals experiencing a high level of stressful life events will be most vulnerable to negative health effects of smog.

The second study has recently been completed by James Rotton and colleagues (Rotton & Frey, 1981). They have found that high photochemical oxidants are linked to several measures of social pathology recorded by calls received at police and fire stations in Dayton, Ohio, over a 2-year period. Photochemical oxidants were significantly correlated with domestic disturbances, obscene phone calls, and psychiatric cases. Note that the latter result converges with Strahilevitz's data.

These recent studies are also important in that they use sophisticated, quasi-experimental techniques for causally modeling the impacts of an environmental variable, air quality, on human health and well-being. The first study by Evans and colleagues and Rotton and Frey's research carefully control for major, competing hypotheses as well as cope with problems of autocorrelation.

All of the foregoing studies on air pollution and social behavior illustrate several facets of the stressor–behavior relation. First, there is evidence of indirect, behavioral impacts of air pollution. Effects are not limited simply to physiological insult. Second, these indirect effects are complex. Air pollution seems to depress mood, which in turn has complex behavioral ramifications. As these few preliminary studies of air pollution and mental health suggest, there may be a vast area of largely unresearched problems in need of careful exploration by behavioral scientists.

Complaints. Several studies have focused on propensity to lodge complaints about air pollution (e.g., Auliciems & Burton, 1971; Jacoby, 1972; Kromm et al., 1973; Rankin, 1969). Rankin's (1969) study exemplifies this literature. While approximately 25% of those interviewed felt like complaining about air pollution at some time, only 5% of respondents actually did so. These findings are consistent with DeGroot et al.'s (1966) data. Low complaint rates may stem from lack of knowledge about the problem. This view is supported to some extent by Swan's (1970) data, which shows that lower SES persons are less aware, less concerned, and less likely to complain about air pollution.

Rankin's (1969) analysis, of the reasons why those persons who felt like complaining did not, provides some insight into the nature of what is regarded by some to be a problem of public apathy. About a third of the respondents who felt like complaining about air pollution in their community did not do so either because they did not know where to complain or because they felt they had no opportunity to complain. Even more interesting is the fact that almost one-half of the respondents did not complain because they believed that complaining would not do any good. Investigations by Auliciems and Burton (1971) and Kromm et al. (1973) also find that most respondents doubt the efficacy of complaining to authorities. Upon evaluation of his findings, Rankin (1969) concluded that "the average citizen while recognizing the [air pollution] problem, was unfamiliar with what could be done, or what has been done, and appeared apathetic or pessimistic regarding his own role and the likelihood of control" (p. 569). This concept of public control, either real or perceived, over air pollution may be crucial in understanding public responses to air pollution.

Human task performance

With the exception of carbon monoxide, few studies have examined the effects of air pollutants on human task performance and work capacity. Soviet researchers report that low-level exposures to gaseous pollutants such as nitrogen dioxide and sulfur dioxide affect human sensory processes, impairing darkness adaptation and brightness sensitivity (Izmerov, 1971). Decrements in human reflexes also occur, as well as increased desynchronization of alpha rhythms. All of these effects are noted at levels below human detectability and prior to clinical signs of discomfort or physiological damage.

Just a few studies have examined the impacts of photochemical oxidants on human performance. Lagerwerff (1963) found that 3-hour exposures to moderate levels of ozone significantly decreased nocturnal visual acuity, caused slight, extraoccular motor imbalance, and increased peripheral vision. No effects were noted for photopic visual acuity, stereopsis, or color vision. Nearly all subjects complained of eye irritation, which is commonly caused by photochemical oxidant exposure. Simple reaction time, submaximal work performance (Holland, Benson, Bush, Rich, & Holland, 1968), and intelligence scores (Hore & Gibson, 1968) are all unaffected by short exposures to moderate levels of photochemical oxidants. On the other hand, fluctuations in ambient-level oxidants have been associated with slower cross-country running times in high school athletes (Wayne, Wehrle, & Carroll, 1967) as well as more automobile accidents in the Los Angeles air basin (Ury, 1968).

Although there is considerable literature on the effects of carbon monoxide on human performance, very few consistent lines of evidence are apparent. In this section we highlight the major behavioral findings, note conflicts, and suggest explanations for the inconsistencies in the literature. Because of space limitations we primarily cite an excellent review paper on this topic (National Academy of Sciences, 1977) and discuss only more recent papers or exemplary studies in depth. The performance research can be divided into five subtopics: sensory effects, attention, sensorimotor coordination, memory and problem solving, and work capacity.

Sensory effects

Absolute and relative brightness thresholds may increase under carbon monoxide exposure. Several conflicting studies, however, find moderate to no effects (National Academy of Sciences, 1977). Similar mixed results have been reported for time estimation and time discrimination studies. Beard and Grandstaff (1970), for example, presented subjects with a 1-second tone and then asked them to determine whether a second tone was of the same or different duration. They found significant decrements at 50 ppm of carbon monoxide, as well as a function related to magnitude of dose up to 250 ppm. A similar pattern of results was noted for reproductions of a 30-second tone. They also report several studies that found defects in brightness and visual acuity with carbon monoxide inhalation. O'Donnell and colleagues (O'Donnell, Mikulka, Heinig, & Theodore, 1971), plus other researchers, however, using similar dosages, found no effects of carbon monoxide on brightness thresholds or time duration estimation.

One reason for these conflicting data is that many carbon monoxide studies do not monitor actual COHb levels, which directly indicate the amount of binding of carbon monoxide to hemoglobin. Different laboratory procedures, as well as individual differences among subjects, affect the relationship of carbon monoxide to COHb in human blood. A second explanation for inconsistent results lies in the amount of stimulation provided in various laboratory settings. When subjects are isolated, given few rest breaks, and generally placed under low stimulation conditions, carbon monoxide effects are more pronounced.

Attention

In general, vigilance studies find decrements from carbon monoxide ingestion under low sensory or social stimulation conditions (e.g., subject isolated in a soundproof booth) and/or when tasks are prolonged (National Academy of Sciences, 1977). These effects, plus physiological evidence for decreased reticular activity with prolonged carbon monoxide exposure (O'Donnell et al., 1971), suggest that reduced physiological activation may explain some performance decrements due to carbon monoxide. Less than optimal arousal produced by a combination of a low stimulation setting, prolonged tasks that are repetitive, and carbon monoxide may reduce reticular activity sufficiently to produce task deficits. Horvath, Dahms, and O'Hanlon (1971), for example, found negative effects of carbon monoxide on a vigilance task only under normal conditions; during an alert period when subjects responded to both target and background signals for a short time period, no deficits were found.

Individual difference variables influence the relation between carbon monoxide and human performance. For example, Ramsey (1970) measured the effects of ambient carbon monoxide during rush-hour traffic on simple reaction time for subjects who were healthy versus those who had respiratory problems. Immediately after a 90-minute rush hour exposure, the respiratory problem group slowed 8.6% and the normals slowed 6.8% in comparison to controls. Other reaction-time studies have found conflicting results (National Academy of Sciences, 1977) and are difficult to interpret because many do not adequately describe task parameters such as stimulus intensity or intertrial intervals that affect reaction time performance.

Sensorimotor coordination

Sensorimotor studies generally examine manual coordination and tracking or simulate automobile conditions. Coordination and tracking studies generally have found few effects of carbon monoxide (National Academy of Sciences, 1977), but recently Putz (1979) has shown manual tracking errors under substantial task-load conditions. Under a high-frequency tracking task with required responses to a peripheral stimulus, reliable tracking errors were found for prolonged exposure to 70 ppm carbon monoxide. Under less complex task conditions where attentional capacity was not approached, little or no task deficit occurred. Lack of carbon monoxide effects on sensorimotor performance in other studies may have been due to task demand variables. Research on air pollution and human performance, like other environmental stressors such as noise, needs to explore a wider range of task parameters such as dual tasks, high-speed signal tasks, and aftereffect measures. Only when the limits of human performance capacities are approached do we typically see immediate task decrements from the levels of environmental stressors that are typically used in experiments.

Epidemiological studies generally find little association between ambient carbon monoxide levels and traffic accidents, but some related psychomotor skills under simulated driving conditions are adversely affected by low-level carbon monoxide exposure. Rummo and Sarlanis (1974), for example, tested subjects in a driving simulator after the subjects had breathed either filtered air or 880 ppm carbon monoxide, which raised COHb to 7%. Reaction time increased for adjustments in the speed of a lead car that the driver followed, but no effects were found in overall ability to maintain a safe, constant distance from the lead car, reaction time to respond to a dashboard signal, or maintenance of lateral position on the road.

Although it is premature to draw any firm conclusions about driving ability and carbon monoxide effects, the sensorimotor and vigilance data suggest that performance decrements are more likely to occur in the presence of carbon monoxide under conditions of highly monotonous driving, or when extreme task demands are placed on drivers.

Memory and problem solving

Lewis, Baddeley, Banham, and Lovitt (1970) documented deficits in sentence comprehension, addition, and vigilance under exposure to automobile exhaust, although the effects of carbon monoxide were not isolated. Recall of nonsense syllables, repeating digits in reverse order, and performing various problem-solving tasks such as serial addition are also disrupted by exposure to moderate levels of carbon monoxide. On the other hand, location memory for dots on a matrix, simple arithmetic problems, analogies, decoding, and letter recognition are typically not disrupted by similar moderate dosages (National Academy of Sciences, 1977).

The problem-solving data are mixed, but there is some consistent evidence that short-term memory is disrupted by carbon monoxide. Unfortunately, researchers examining the effects of toxics like carbon monoxide generally have not carefully selected performance tasks with consideration of information-processing demands. Additional research on the effects of carbon monoxide on human performance should carefully consider to what extent attention, short-term memory, and long-term memory processes are involved in particular tasks.

Work capacity

There is general agreement that maximal aerobic capacity is reduced by low-level carbon monoxide exposures, but submaximal capacity (30–75% maximum) is generally unaffected (Gliner, Raven, Horvath, Drinkwater, & Sutton, 1975; National Academy of Sciences, 1977). These conclusions apply only to healthy young adult males and are probably conservative for older or less healthy persons. As an example of a work performance study, Gliner et al. (1975) required healthy young male adults to walk on a treadmill for 4 hours at 35% of their maximum aerobic capacity. This level of performance can readily be sustained for up to 8 hours. Carbon monoxide increased heart rate but had no other effects on several measures of physiological stress including cardiac output and blood pressure. These same researchers in other studies, however, have found interference with performance and physiological stress when near-maximum work capacity was required during carbon monoxide ingestion.

Summary and critique

Given the marked inconsistencies noted in the human performance literature, it is difficult to draw definitive conclusions about the effects of air
pollution on human performance. Task decrements are most reliably found
when subjects are exposed to carbon monoxide at moderate levels while
working under low stimulation conditions on tasks that demand alert vigilance. Prolonged, boring tasks, or tasks that place considerable processing
demands on attention, are prime candidates for task decrements due to
exposures to carbon monoxide. It is reasonable to conjecture that some
similar patterns may exist for other pollutants, such as photochemical oxidants, that also affect the oxygen-carrying capacity of the blood.

Air pollution and human performance is an area ripe for the application
of psychological stress perspectives. Future research must examine task
variables such as complexity and aftereffects more carefully. Individual
differences in stressor appraisal and perceived control over pollutants may
also function as important mediators of responses to air pollutants, as in
the case with other stressors (Baum, Singer, & Baum, Chap. 1, this volume). More sensitivity to subject sampling is also needed. Over 90% of the
performance studies have relied on healthy, young adult males.

Theoretical development is sorely needed as well. The parallels between
some of the carbon monoxide task effects and underarousal data have been
noted. Another potentially fruitful line of inquiry may be conceptual work
on hypoxia from high-altitude research. Many of the major gaseous pollutants reduce oxygen supply to the brain and thus may have some effects
similar to oxygen deprivation.

Mediating variables

As we have noted, there are a number of personality, geographic, and
demographic variables that may be related to behavioral responses to air
pollution, including age, sex, socioeconomic status, education, race, culture, employment orientation, degree of urbanness, and residential location. Unfortunately, few of these variables have been systematically and
unambiguously studied in the research reviewed here. Consequently, numerous questions remain unanswered, such as: What groups of people,
under what types of conditions, are most vulnerable to psychological costs
of air pollution, and what groups of people are most likely to pursue
pollution abatement activities? The study of such issues requires the investigation of these personality, demographic, and geographic variables within
some organized conceptual framework that takes into account some psychological mediating processes. Two such mediating variables seem to be
of particular importance in understanding public responses to air pollution: perceived controllability of the air pollution problem and adaptation
to air pollution.

Perceived controllability of air pollution

In addition to the multitude of serious competing social problems and the technical nature of air pollution, one important factor in the public's apathy about controlling air pollution seems to be the widely held belief that one cannot do anything to reduce air pollution (Barker, 1976; Loveridge 1971; Swan, 1972). Probably the most informative investigation of the topic is by Rankin (1969), who measured perceived control over air pollution by asking, "Do you think it is possible around here for air pollution to be greatly reduced?" Between 64.5% and 92.9% of interviewees responded affirmatively, depending upon the specific community. Rankin also found that 95% of respondents felt that it was "a good thing to do something about air pollution. . . ." However, in a national poll taken in the same year that Rankin published his results, 53% of the sample felt it was either not possible to control atmospheric pollution, or that they simply did not know if it could be controlled (Swan, 1972).

Although the majority of Rankin's subjects acknowledged that air pollution could and should be reduced, substantially fewer demonstrated awareness or knowledge of existing attempts to control air pollution. The general level of public information was low in all communities. Sixty-six percent to 90% of respondents were completely unaware of existing air pollution control activities at any level, local, state, or federal, and very few knew any factual information about air pollution control.

Creer and his associates (Creer et al., 1970) found that a respondent's perception of the control effort of a major air pollution source was related to the economic dependence of the respondent upon the source. Employees of the pollution source rated their company's control efforts to be substantially greater than did nonemployees. Although the authors interpret this finding as evidence for their cognitive dissonance hypothesis (i.e., that employees attempted to resolve the dissonance resulting from working for a major air polluter by overestimating their company's abatement efforts), these findings could reflect differential levels of knowledge about control efforts. Employees may, in fact, have been more aware of the source's actual efforts toward the reduction of air pollution.

Rankin (1969) also found that approximately one-fourth of respondents expected that no attempt would be made in the future to control air pollution in their area and that pollution levels would worsen in the subsequent half decade. One explanation of this phenomenon may be that the public, having been told for so long of the capabilities of science and technology, are reacting negatively to unfulfilled expectations. As considerable research has demonstrated (Glass & Singer, 1972), continuous experiences of lack of control over environmental events often lead to learned helplessness wherein individuals are unable to act instrumentally, even when obvious control responses are available. Recently, Rotton and colleagues examined the effects of perceived control over pollution on frustration tolerance (Rotton,

Yoshikawa, & Kaplan, 1979), utilizing the Glass and Singer (1972) aftereffects paradigm. Odor condition significantly interacted with a control manipulation, such that when individuals could not avoid exposure to a malodor, odor significantly increased frustration. Frustration was measured by persistence on impossible puzzles after the exposure condition (see Glass & Singer, 1972, for more procedural details).

Research on air pollution control has examined the burden of responsibility to reduce air pollution. Over 90% of Schusky's (1966) subjects thought that some government agencies should "do something" about air pollution. A number of studies have found that between 50% and 75% of respondents state a willingness to pay increased taxes to reduce air pollution (McEvoy, 1972; Rankin, 1969; Schusky, 1966; Stanford Workshop on Air Pollution, 1970). The amount of tax increase considered in these studies, however, has either gone undetermined or has been nominal (i.e., $1.00 or $5.00). McEvoy (1972) also noted that income, education, and concern over the environment are important factors in willingness to pay for air pollution control.

Additional tactics for air pollution abatement suggested by the public include new legislation, better law enforcement procedure, mass transportation and reduction of private auto use, auto exhaust emission control, stopping construction of smog-producing power plants, and shutting down plants and factories that fail to meet air quality standards (Johnson et al., 1972; McEvoy, 1972; Simon, 1971; Stanford Workshop on Air Pollution, 1970). It is interesting to note that, with the exception of reduced private auto use, the burden of responsibility concerning these alternatives rests with government authorities.

Another research approach to air pollution and control has investigated the relationship between the desirability of air pollution control and awareness (Dillman & Christenson, 1972) and perceived seriousness (Hohm, 1976; Medalia, 1964; Rankin, 1969) of the problem. In order to investigate the potential for public action with respect to air pollution, Medalia asked respondents the multiple-choice question, "What do you think is the most important thing people should do about air pollution where it exists?" His four response alternatives included: "Put their minds on their work instead of imagined or minor annoyances" (emotional withdrawal); "Try to get more information on the subject" (situation defining or redefining); "Support the efforts which industry is making to eliminate air pollution" (passive situation altering); and "Ask their elected officials for effective controls on air pollution" (active situation altering). Medalia found that persons showing high concern over air pollution are three times as likely to recommend the alternative of asking for effective controls (active situation altering) as are respondents in the low-concern category. The latter are five times as likely to favor situation defining or withdrawal actions. Individuals who view air pollution as a more serious community problem also report that they make greater personal sacrifices to help reduce air pollution. These behaviors include greater use of mass transportation and maintaining their cars in good mechanical condition (Hohm, 1976). Finally, Rankin (1969) found a positive relationship between perceived seriousness of air pollution and belief in the possibility of air pollution control. Individuals who felt the least control over air pollution also rated it as relatively benign.

Levels of awareness of air pollution are also positively related to desired pollution control (Dillman & Christenson, 1972). Respondents highly aware of air pollution place a high value on pollution control even at low pollution levels, whereas those with low awareness place a low value on pollution control, even at high levels of air pollution.

In general, there are a number of factors that must be considered in discussing the perception of air pollution as controllable. These include the possibility and probability of controlling air pollution at both the societal and individual level, beliefs about the existence and efficacy of past, present, and future abatement efforts, the attribution of responsibility for control efforts, knowledge of strategies for controlling air pollution, and beliefs about the costs involved in such strategies. Little is presently known about the relative importance of these factors in responses to air pollution; this issue should be given high priority in future investigations.

Adaptation

Human beings' enormous adaptive capacities will probably enable us to accommodate drastic environmental deterioration, but at severe costs in quality of life and with altered human values (Dubos, 1965). Although there is a literature on the buildup of physiological tolerance to air pollutants, there are only a couple of studies on behavioral adaptation to air pollution. Physiological studies indicate that both animals and human beings may become less reactive to gaseous pollutants with continuous, low-level exposures. For example, physiological adjustments in biochemical reactivity to oxidant challenge caused by smog have been noted in long-term residents of the Los Angeles air basin in comparison to northern Canadians (Hackney, Linn, Karuza, Buckley, Law, Bates, Hazucha, Pengelly, & Silverman, 1977). Altered mucosillary activity in industrial workers occupationally exposed to sulfur dioxide has also been found (Dubos, 1965).

Psychological adaptation can be viewed as a form of coping with environmental stressors (Lazarus & Cohen, 1978). Employing Lazarus's model of coping with stressors, adaptation can assume two basic modes: active attempts to change the impact of a stressor by moderating exposure (instrumental coping), or palliative coping, where one emotionally adjusts by reducing the perceived threat of a stressor through intrapsychic mechanisms such as denial or diminution of the negative aspects of a pollutant. A related form of adaptation is habituation or desensitization, where continuous exposure to a stimulus changes the individual's frame of reference in assessment and awareness of the stimulus dimension.

Wohlwill (1974) applied this adaptation-level perspective to environmental pollutants, finding that previous residents of a highly polluted area rated their current medium-sized city as less polluted than did previous residents of a low-pollution area. Lipsey (1977), on the other hand, has theorized that continued exposure to pollutants exacerbates rather than habituates response sensitivity because the longer people have to live with poor air quality, the more frustrated and threatened they will become. Partial support for Lipsey's hypothesis is found in a study of air pollution attitudes by Medalia (1964). He found that both awareness and negative attitudes toward a foul-smelling paper mill were greater the longer people had lived in the mill town. Unfortunately, long-term residents lived in the town prior to construction of the mill, whereas newer migrants had never experienced pre-mill air quality. Furthermore, although newer residents chose to live in the town with knowledge of the poor air quality, long-term residents did not have that choice.

Recently, Evans, Jacobs, and Frager (in press) examined psychological adaptation to photochemical smog by comparing two groups of residents who had recently moved to a high oxident area in the Los Angeles air basin. One group had previously lived in high-smog areas for at least 5 years. A second group had previously lived in low air pollution areas. Groups were matched on age, gender, health, and socioeconomic status, and none smoked. All groups were tested under ambient, high-smog conditions. At the time of recruitment for the study, subjects did not know the purpose of the study.

Results provided evidence for adaptation on three sets of measures. First, newcomers to smog reported greater respiratory health symptoms on a standardized checklist and rated smog as a more serious problem on an open-ended probe as well as a direct inquiry. Second, newcomers and long-term residents differed in their perceptual responses to photographic slides of low levels of smog. Employing a signal detection paradigm, we found that the new migrants and long-term residents of the Los Angeles air basin did not differ in visual detection abilities. However, substantial differences exist in response bias. For a given low level of smog, the long-term residents are significantly less likely to report that smog is present in the scene. See Evans et al. (in press) for more detail on the signal detection procedure.

Finally, the two groups had different patterns of coping with smog. Long-term residents frequently exhibited denial, upgraded their relative health vulnerability to smog in comparison to other healthy young adults, and greatly exaggerated their perceived, as opposed to actual, knowledge about smog. Newcomers, on the other hand, more actively sought out information about smog and were more optimistic about using mass transportation to reduce smog. Furthermore, newcomers who also were high on an internal locus-of-control measure were the only group who altered their daily behavior in response to smog. Newcomers who were high on an internal locus of control, in comparison to long-term residents and to newcomers high on external locus of control, spent more time indoors and curtailed outdoor physical activity in the presence of high smog conditions.

Both the Evans et al. (1979) findings and the Wohlwill (1974) research, plus the physiological adaptation data, point to the importance of adaptation as one process mediating the effects of air pollution on human behavior. Individuals chronically exposed to air pollutants respond differently to air pollution than others only recently exposed.

Conclusions

Human behavior is linked to air pollution both as a causal factor and as an effect. Individual decisions affect air quality, for example, in choosing whether to use mass transportation or to support certain environmental protection policies. Air quality in turn affects our health, interpersonal behaviors, mood, attitude, task performance, outdoor activities and possibly residential choice. Most social science research on air pollution has emphasized individual attitudes toward and awareness of air quality. Unfortunately this literature is generally atheoretical and lacks sophisticated methodology. Few studies have constructed scaled response formats, used cross-sectional or longitudinal designs, or produced more than simple, percentage breakdowns of response categories. In addition, reliability and validity data are almost entirely absent in the air pollution survey literature. Recent methodological work in Sweden (Berglund, Berglund, Jonsson, & Lindvall, 1977) is promising in this regard. Individual judgments of annoyance from industrial air pollution can be reliably scaled by Thurstone category scaling methods.

Research on health has overconcentrated on drastic, physical outcomes like mortality or disease. There is a need to examine mental health outcomes that may relate to air quality, such as discomfort, irritability, depression, and anxiety. Researchers should also examine the influence of mediating variables on the pollutant–health relationship. Reasonable mediators to examine are adaptation, perceived control, threat appraisal, and other stressful life experiences. Furthermore, we recommend using more sophisticated, quasi-experimental designs, such as cross-lagged panel and time series designs, to strengthen the internal validity of the epidemiological research on air pollution.

Behavioral studies have focused primarily on the effects of carbon monoxide on human task performance. Human performance research needs to expand on several dimensions. First, tasks must be chosen more carefully on the basis of prior conceptualization. Task complexity, temporal parameters of task and pollutant exposure, and task relationship to information-processing constructs are important areas to consider. Some research on other overt behaviors, such as interpersonal relationships and outdoor behaviors, has been initiated; the early data suggest that the influence of air quality on such behaviors is quite complex.

There is little theoretical basis in most of the air pollution/social science literature. Some conceptual issues that warrant further research include the roles of adaptation, control, and media information in shaping attitudes toward and awareness of air pollution; and examining air pollution from a psychological stress perspective, including such issues as cognitive appraisal, coping, and adaptation.

Social scientists can expand on our knowledge of air pollution and human behavior. In particular, they can introduce the complexities of psychological, mediating factors such as perceived control, perceived threat, and adaptation that influence human responses to air pollution. Furthermore, on the dependent variable side, social scientists can institute broader, multiple measurement strategies that include indexes of mental health, irritation, and dissatisfaction. There is great need for more involvement of social scientists in research on air pollution and other environmental problems.

References

Auliciems, A., & Burton, I. Air pollution in Toronto. In W. R. D. Sewell & I. Burton (Eds.), *Perceptions and attitudes in resources management*. Ottawa: Information Canada, 1971.

Bagozzi, R. P., & Burnkrant, R. E. Attitude organization and the attitude-behavior relationship. *Journal of Personality and Social Psychology*, 1979, *37*, 913–929.

Barker, M. L. Information and complexity: The conceptualization of air pollution by specialized groups. *Environment and Behavior*, 1974, *6*, 346–377.

Barker, M. L. Planning for environmental indices: Observer appraisals of air quality. In K. H. Craik & E. H. Zube (Eds.), *Perceiving environmental quality*. New York: Plenum, 1976.

Baron, R. A., Byrne, D., & Griffitt, W. *Social psychology: Understanding human interactions*. Boston: Allyn & Bacon, 1974.

Beard, R., & Grandstaff, N. Carbon monoxide exposure and cerebral function. *Annals of New York Academy of Sciences*, 1970, *174*, 385–395.

Berglund, B., Berglund, U., Jonsson, E., & Lindvall, T. On the scaling of annoyance due to environmental factors. *Environmental Psychology and Nonverbal Behavior*, 1977, *2*, 83–92.

Bladen, W. A., & Karan, P. P. Perception of air pollution in a developing country. *Journal of the Air Pollution Control Association*, 1976, *26*, 139–141.

Bleda, P., & Bleda, E. Effects of sex and smoking on reactions to spatial invasion at a shopping mall. *The Journal of Social Psychology*, 1978, *104*, 311–312.

Buckout, R. Pollution and the psychologist: A call to action. In J. F. Wohlwill & D. H. Carson (Eds.), *Environment and the social sciences: Perspectives and applications*. Washington, D.C.: American Psychological Association, 1972.

Chapko, M. K., & Solomon, H. Air pollution and recreational behavior. *Journal of Social Psychology*, 1976, *100*, 149–150.

Coffin, D., & Stokinger, H. Biological effects of air pollutants. In A. C. Stern (Ed.), *Air pollution* (3rd ed., Vol. 3). New York: Academic Press, 1977.

Craik, K. H., & Zube, E. H. *Perceiving environmental quality.* New York: Plenum, 1976.

Creer, R. N., Gray, R. M., & Treshow, M. Differential responses to air pollution as an environmental health problem. *Journal of the Air Pollution Control Association,* 1970, *20,* 814–818.

Crowe, J. M. Towards a 'definitional model' of public perceptions of air pollution. *Journal of the Air Pollution Control Association,* 1968, *18,* 154–158.

Cunningham, M. Weather, mood, and helping behavior: Quasi-experiments with the sunshine samaritan. *Journal of Personality and Social Psychology,* 1979, *37,* 1947–1956.

DeGroot, I. Trends in public attitudes toward air pollution. *Journal of the Air Pollution Control Association,* 1967, *17,* 679–681.

DeGroot, I., Loring, W., Rihm, A., Samuels, S. W., & Winkelstein, W. People and air pollution: A study of attitudes in Buffalo, New York. *Journal of the Air Pollution Control Association,* 1966, *16,* 245–247.

Dillman, D. A., & Christenson, J. A. The public value for pollution control. In W. R. Burch, N. H. Cheek, Jr., & L. Taylor (Eds.), *Social behavior, national resources, and the environment.* New York: Harper & Row, 1972.

Dubos, R. *Man adapting.* New Haven, Conn.: Yale University Press, 1965.

Dunlap, R., Van Liere, K., & Dillman, D. Evidence of decline in public concern with environmental quality: A reply. *Rural Sociology,* 1979, *44,* 204–212.

Evans, G. W., Jacobs, S. V., & Frager, N. B. Behavioral responses to air pollution. In A. Baum & J. Singer (Eds.), *Advances in Environmental Psychology.* Hillsdale, N.J.: Erlbaum, in press.

Fishbein, M., & Ajzen, I. *Belief, attitude, intention, and behavior: An introduction to theory and research.* Reading, Mass.: Addison-Wesley, 1975.

Flacshbart, P., & Phillips, S. An index and model of human responses to air quality. *Journal of the Air Pollution Control Association,* 1980, *30,* 759–768.

Glass, D. C., & Singer, J. E. *Urban stress.* New York: Academic Press, 1972.

Gliner, J., Raven, P., Horvath, S., Drinkwater, B., & Sutton, J. Man's physiological response to long term work during thermal and pollutant stress. *Journal of Applied Physiology,* 1975, *39,* 628–632.

Goldsmith, J., & Friberg, L. Effects of air pollution on human health. In A. C. Stern (Ed.), *Air pollution* (3rd ed., Vol. 3). New York: Academic Press, 1977.

Hackney, J., Linn, W., Karuza, S., Buckley, R., Law, D., Bates, D., Hazucha, M., Pengelly, L., & Silverman, F. Effects of ozone exposure in Canadians and Southern Californians. *Archives of Environmental Health,* 1977, *32,* 110–116.

Hohm, C. A. human ecological approach to the reality and perception of air pollution. *Pacific Sociological Review,* 1976, *19,* 21–44.

Holland, G. J., Benson, D., Bush, A., Rich, G., & Holland, R. Air pollution simulation and human performance. *American Journal of Public Health,* 1968, *58,* 1684–1690.

Hore, T., & Gibson, D. Ozone, exposure and intelligence tests. *Archives of Environmental Health,* 1968, *17,* 77–91.

Horvath, S., Dahms, T., & O'Hanlon, J. Carbon monoxide and human vigilance. *Archives of Environmental Health,* 1971, *23,* 343–347.

Hummel, C., Loomis, R., & Herbert, J. *Effects of city labels and cue utilization on air pollution judgments*. Working Papers in Environmental-Social Psychology, No. 1, Department of Psychology, Colorado State University, 1975.

Izmerov, N. Establishment of air quality standards. *Archives of Environmental Health*, 1971, *22*, 711–719.

Jacoby, L. R. *Perception of air, noise and water pollution in Detroit*. (Michigan Geographical, Publication No. 7) Ann Arbor, Mich.: Department of Geography, The University of Michigan, 1972.

Johnson, D. L., Allegre, R., Burhrman, E., Miller, S., Sheldon, M., & Rosen, A. Air pollution: Public attitudes and public action. *American Behavioral Scientist*, 1972, *15*, 533–566.

Johnston, R. J., & Hay, J. E. Spatial variations in awareness of air pollution distributions. *Quarterly Journal of Environmental Studies*, 1974, *6*, 131–136.

Jones, J. W. Adverse emotional reactions of nonsmokers to secondary cigarette smoke. *Environmental Psychology and Nonverbal Behavior*, 1978, *3*, 125–127.

Jones, J. W., & Bogat, G. A. Air pollution and human aggression. *Psychological Reports*, 1978, *43*, 721–722.

Jones, M. Pain thresholds for smog components. In J. F. Wohlwill & D. H. Carson (Eds.), *Environment and the social sciences: Perspectives and applications*. Washington, D.C.: American Psychological Association, 1972.

Kromm, D. E., Probald, F., & Wall, G. An international comparison of response to air pollution. *Journal of Environmental Management*, 1973, *1*, 363–375.

Lagerwerff, J. Prolonged ozone inhalation and its effects on visual parameters. *Aerospace Medicine*, 1963, *34*, 471–481.

Lave, L., & Seskin, E. Air pollution and human health. *Science*, 1970, *169*, 723–733.

Lazarus, R., & Cohen, J. Environmental stress. In I. Altman & J. Wohlwill (Eds.), *Human behavior and environment* (Vol. 2). New York: Plenum, 1978.

Lewis, J., Baddeley, K., Banham, K., & Lovitt, D. Traffic pollution and mental efficiency. *Nature*, 1970, *225*, 95–97.

Lipsey, M. W. Attitudes toward the environment and pollution. In S. Oskamp (Ed.), *Attitudes and opinions*. Englewood Cliffs, N.J.: Prentice-Hall, 1977.

Loveridge, R. O. Political science and air pollution: A review and assessment of the literature. In P. B. Downing (Ed.), *Air pollution and the social sciences: Formulating and implementing control programs*. New York: Praeger, 1971.

McEvoy, J. The American concern with environment. In W. R. Burch, Jr., N. H. Cheek, Jr., & L. Taylor (Eds.), *Social behavior, natural resources, and the environment*. New York: Harper & Row, 1972.

Malm, W., Leiker, K., & Molenar, J. Human perception of visual air quality. *Journal of the Air Pollution Control Association*, 1980 *30*, 122–131.

Medalia, N. Z. Air pollution as a socio-environmental health problem: A survey report. *Journal of Health and Human Behavior*, 1964, *5*, 154–165.

Miller, D. C. The allocation of priorities to urban and environmental problems by powerful leaders and organizations. In W. R. Burch, Jr., N. H. Cheek, Jr., & L. Taylor (Eds.), *Social behavior, natural resources, and the environment*. New York: Harper & Row, 1972.

Molotch, H., & Follet, R. C. Air pollution as a problem for sociological research. In P. B. Downing (Ed.), *Air pollution and the social sciences*. New York: Praeger, 1971.

Murch, A. W. Public concern for environmental pollution. *Public Opinion Quarterly*, 1971, *35*, 100–106.

National Academy of Sciences, *Medical and biological effects of environmental pollutants*. Washington, D.C.: National Academy of Sciences, 1977.

Noll, K., Mueller, P., & Imada, M. Visibility and aerosol concentration in urban air. *Atmospheric Environment*, 1968, *2*, 465–475.

O'Donnell, R., Mikulka, P., Heinig, P., & Theodore, J. Low level carbon monoxide exposure and human psychomotor performance. *Journal of Applied Toxicology and Pharmacology*, 1971, *18*, 593–602.

Peterson, R. L. *Air pollution and attendance in recreation behavior settings in the Los Angeles Basin*. Chicago, IL: American Psychological Association, 1975.

Putz, J. The effects of carbon monoxide on dual-task performance. *Human Factors*, 1979, *21*, 13–24.

President's Council on Environmental Quality, Environmental Protection Agency. Washington, D.C.: U.S. Government Printing Office, 1978.

Ramsey, J. Oxygen reduction and reaction time in hypoxic and normal drivers. *Archives of Environmental Health*, 1970, *20*, 597–601.

Rankin, R. E. Air pollution control and public apathy. *Journal of the Air Pollution Control Association*, 1969, *19*, 565–569.

Rosenberg, M. J., & Hovland, C. I. Cognitive, affective and behavioral components of attitudes. In M. J. Rosenberg, C. I. Hovland, W. J. McGuire, R. P. Abelson, & J. W. Brehm (Eds.), *Attitude organization and change: An analysis of consistency among attitude components*. New Haven, Conn.: Yale University Press, 1960.

Rotton, J., Barry, T., Frey, J., & Soler, E. Air pollution and interpersonal attraction. *Journal of Applied Social Psychology*, 1978, *8*, 57–71.

Rotton, J., & Frey, J. *Weather, air pollution, and social pathology: First approximations*. Unpublished manuscript. Florida International University, 1981.

Rotton, J., Frey, J., Barry, T., Milligan, M., & Fitzpatrick, M. The air pollution experience and interpersonal aggression. *Journal of Applied Social Psychology*, 1979, *9*, 397–412.

Rotton, J., Yoshikawa, J., Francis, J., & Hoyler, R. *Urban atmosphere: Evaluative effects of malodorous air pollution*. Atlanta, Ga.: Southeastern Psychological Association, 1978.

Rotton, J., Yoshikawa, J., & Kaplan, F. *Perceived control, malodorous air pollution and behavioral aftereffects*. New Orleans, La.: Southeastern Psychological Association, 1979.

Rummo, N., & Sarlanis, K. The effect of carbon monoxide on several measures of vigilance in a simulated driving task. *Journal of Safety Research*, 1974, *6*, 126–130.

Schusky, J. Public awareness and concern with air pollution in the St. Louis Metropolitan Area. *Journal of the Air Pollution Control Association*, 1966, *16*, 72–76.

Simon, R. J. Public attitudes toward population and pollution. *Public Opinion Quarterly*, 1971, *35*, 94–99.

Smith, W. S., Schueneman, J. J., & Zeidberg, L. D. Public reaction to air pollution in Nashville, Tennessee. *Journal of the Air Pollution Control Association*, 1964, *14*, 418–423.

Stanford Workshop on Air Pollution. The public and air pollution. In *Air pollution in the San Francisco Bay area*. Stanford, 1970.

Stern, A. C. *Air pollution* (3rd ed.), Vol. 3. New York: Academic Press, 1977.

Stone, J., Breidenbach, S., & Heimstra, N. Annoyance response of nonsmokers to cigarette smoke. *Perceptual and Motor Skills*, 1979, *49*, 907–916.

Strahilevitz, M., Strahilevitz, A., & Miller, J. Air pollutants and the admission rate of psychiatric patients. *American Journal of Psychiatry*, 1979, *136*, 205–207.

Swan, J. A. Response to air pollution: A study of attitudes and coping strategies of high school youths. *Environment and Behavior*, 1970, *2*, 127–152.

Swan, J. A. Public response to air pollution. In J. F. Wohlwill & D. H. Carson (Eds.), *Environment and the social sciences*. Washington, D.C.: American Psychological Association, 1972.

Ury, H. Photochemical air pollution and automobile accidents in Los Angeles: An investigation of oxidant and accidents, 1963 and 1965. *Archives of Environmental Health*, 1968, *17*, 334–342.

Van Arsdol, M. D., Jr., Sabagh, G., & Alexander, F. Reality and the perception of environmental hazards. *Journal of Health and Human Behavior*, 1964, *5*, 38–42.

Wall, G. Public response to air pollution in South Yorkshire, England. *Environment and Behavior*, 1973, *5*, 219–248.

Wall, G. Public response to air pollution in Sheffield, England. *International Journal of Environmental Studies*, 1974, *5*, 259–270.

Wayne, W., Wehrle, P., & Carroll, R. Oxidant air pollution and athletic performance. *Journal of American Medical Association*, 1967, *199*, 901–904.

Wohlwill, J. F. Human response to levels of environmental stimulation. *Human Ecology*, 1974, *2*, 127–147.

5. Crowding stress and human behavior

Yakov M. Epstein

During the 1970s, well over 200 studies examined some aspect of crowding. A number of monographs dealing with various aspects of crowding have also recently appeared (cf. Aiello & Baum, 1979; Altman, 1975; Baum & Epstein, 1978; Baum & Valins, 1977; Esser & Greenbie, 1978; Freedman, 1975). This chapter emphasizes the need to think of crowding as a *group* phenomenon. In this vein, it highlights the role of group orientation in explaining the results of studies of crowding. In addition to group-level issues, individual attempts to cope with the problems of crowding also need to be considered in accounting for the effects of crowding. This paper utilizes the concept of perceived control as a salient person-level concept. The literature on crowding is organized into two settings – residential and laboratory. Residential studies are further grouped into studies of family, dormitory, and prison settings. The roles of group orientation, and of perceived control, are considered as processes accounting for the results of studies in each of these settings. The paper ends with a discussion of some shortcomings in current theorizing about crowding-related phenomena and describes some directions for future research.

A model of crowding

In any setting, crowded or uncrowded, occupants must manage the environment in order to achieve their goals. For example, most people clear their desks before attempting serious writing. In so doing, they provide a work space needed to accomplish their goal. When other persons become a part of the individual's environment, he or she must coordinate his or her need for resources, activities, level of interpersonal interaction, and spatial location with theirs. As the number of people populating an individual's environment increases, the task of managing and coordinating that environment increasingly drains attention ordinarily available for goal attainment. Further, each individual has a unique set of goals that he or she wishes to attain in a given setting. Assuming that at any one time the goal of any particular individual may be incompatible with the goal of another person, increasing the number of occupants increases the number of potentially conflicting goals. At the very least, this presents a problem in coordination. In addition, it may make some individual goals impossible to attain.

When an environment becomes crowded resources may become scarce; activities of one person may interfere with the activities of another person; unavoidable interpersonal interaction may distract the individual or may create group maintenance behaviors that prevent the individual from attaining his or her personal goals; violations of spatial norms may increase arousal and discomfort.

When individual goal attainment is thwarted in one or more of these manners, the individual may feel threatened. Under conditions of perceived threat, the individual attempts to cope by using behaviors he or she has learned that are compatible with the norms of the culture in which he or she lives.

Several factors are involved in the attempt to cope. The first is the individual's appraisal of the severity of the threat to goal attainment posed by the high-density environment. The second is the goal structure of the group occupying the high-density environment. The group occupying a high-density environment may have a cooperative or a competitive goal structure. The third factor is the set of internal resources that the individual has available for coping with the problems caused by the high-density environment.

If the potentially thwarted goals are important to the individual, if the threat is appraised as severe, if the individual cannot induce other occupants to engage in behaviors that will facilitate his or her goal attainment, and if an alternate path to the goal that does not require coordinated activities with others is unavailable, then the individual may perceive that he or she lacks control over his or her environment. If she or he cannot escape from this environment and find an alternative environment in which her or his goals can be attained, she or he will experience stress as a concomitant of the perceived lack of control.

This model suggests that high density *alone* does not lead to stress reactions – a conclusion amply demonstrated by the program of research of Freedman and his colleagues (Freedman, 1975). Yet the layperson holds a naive model, which posits that high density may be the cause of his or her inability to attain desired goals in the setting. Thus, when the occupant labels a setting as crowded, she or he is attributing the problems experienced to the presence of others. The likelihood that the person will attribute outcomes to the presence of others depends upon cues in the environment, situational norms, and his or her social learning history. Additionally, the act of attributing problems to the "crowdedness" of the environment has important consequences. For example, it may reduce the likelihood that the individual will attribute malevolent intentions to the behaviors of others that block her or his goal attainment. If a stranger presses against you in a crowded bus, you are less likely to consider him or her a pervert than if the same act occurred on a bus with only two other occupants.

For the scientist, on the other hand, the question is not whether high density has major negative consequences but rather under what conditions such negative consequences are likely to occur. The model suggested provides a basic outline for specifying the conditions under which we may expect high density to have such negative effects. Let us examine the literature to see how well the model explains the data.

Before turning to such an examination, it is important to note that the nature of the setting specifies to some degree which goals are important to the person and the relationship between group members. Therefore, the literature will be organized as a function of the major types of settings that have been investigated.

Research on crowding has focused mainly on two settings: residential settings and laboratory settings. Some additional research has investigated the effects of crowding in public settings whereas a very small number of studies have investigated crowding in classrooms. We will review studies of residential and laboratory settings as the bulk of the research has been conducted in these settings. We begin with studies of residential crowding.

Residential crowding

Three types of residential settings have been studied: family dwellings, dormitories (either in college or noncollege environments), and prisons. Given the model proposed, high density can be expected to produce different types of results in these settings. Family dwellings house families – that is, groups of people who are normatively expected to be cooperatively interdependent. Further, alternate paths outside the home can be used to obtain many of the important goals in the home. For example, if the home is too congested to permit TV viewing, the neighborhood bar or a friend's home can provide an alternative. Further, given their cooperative orientation and the obligations owed and sanctions available to family members, the possibility of inducing other family members to engage in behaviors that will facilitate the individual's goal attainment is relatively high. We can speculate that this is even more the case for adult family members than for children, since adults are, for the most part, better able to induce children to enact desired behaviors than vice versa. This observation suggests that youngsters should be more adversely affected by crowding than adults, a conclusion reached by Evans in his review of developmental aspects of crowding (Evans, 1978). The cooperative interdependence and high level of inducibility in families should prevent a feeling of loss of control, thereby minimizing the negative effects of crowding.

Two types of strategies have been used to investigate the effects of crowding in family dwellings. Prior to 1970, the method of ecological correlation was the typical mode of investigation. This method is described in detail elsewhere, and its serious shortcomings are described in Epstein and Baum (1978). Despite the drawbacks of this approach, however, one can, to some degree, generalize about the findings drawn from this literature. In general, it fails to provide clear evidence that crowding causes major ill effects. Measures such as juvenile delinquency, crime, mortality, and the like fail to show clear and consistent relationships with crowding (see Freedman, 1975, for a summary of this literature). In addition, one study of this genre that adequately controlled for the major statistical artifacts generally found in these studies found essentially no evidence of pathology associated with high density (Freedman, Heshka, & Levy, 1975). It is interesting to note that the single exception in this study was the relationship between density and psychiatric hospitalizations: Higher density was associated with increased rates of psychiatric hospitalization. We can speculate that the mentally ill, being constrained by their individual needs, are less likely to cooperate with other family members (cf. Johnson & Matross, 1977). One strategy for dealing with this problem is to hospitalize these individuals.

The second type of study utilized interviews with residents. Two large-scale interview studies of residents living under conditions of high density have been reported in the literature. The first, and perhaps most dramatic, study was conducted in Hong Kong by Mitchell (1971). The average occupant shared a 400-square-foot dwelling with 10 or more persons. This averages out to 40 or less square feet per person, which is less than half of the 85 square feet per person considered a minimum in households in which all of the occupants are normally healthy (see Committee on the Hygiene of Housing, American Public Health Association, 1950). In many cases, the dwelling was shared by two unrelated families. Despite these conditions, Mitchell found no evidence of deficits in emotional health related to density. Of greater interest, in light of the coping formulation suggested previously, are Mitchell's data on the presence of an unrelated family within the household and the floor level on which the household was located. Mitchell finds that these two factors combine in an interactive way to produce greater levels of emotional illness. Persons living on the sixth floor and above in households containing two or more unrelated families showed the greatest degree of emotional illness and the highest levels of hostility. Additionally, the presence of an unrelated family increases the likelihood of stressful interactions when persons are trying to coordinate activities under conditions of resource scarcity. Although Mitchell does not say so, we can speculate that the ability to adopt cooperative strategies to cope with these demands is reduced by the presence of two groups rather than a single related one. Floor level affects the occupants' ability to monitor the activities of their children and to escape from the problems of the household. Those living on a lower floor of a walk-up can retreat to the sidewalks to find a respite from the heat, congestion, and arguments in the household. Those living on higher floors are less likely to take advantage of this alternative. In terms of behavioral control, they have less of a choice in their exposure to the noxious aspects of overcrowding.

Booth (1976) assessed both objective measures of density and subjective measures of perceived crowding in Toronto. He found no important differences related to varying levels of density. One finding that is of interest, however, is that men who grew up in crowded households were less likely to experience stress-related diseases under conditions of high density than men who grew up in less crowded households. This study suggests that individual difference variables related to prior experience are important contributors to experiencing problems posed by residential crowding. However, this study did not attempt to shed light on what coping mechanisms are involved.

Finally, in a study of smaller scope, Rohe (1978) examined reactions to a stratified sample of residents of State College, Pennsylvania, to dwellings differing in density. Density had little direct effect on behavior. However, Rohe reports that in competitively structured dwellings, reports of interpersonal stress were highly correlated with persons per room. The effect was significantly weaker in cooperatively structured homes.

Three field experiments have been performed assessing the effects of crowding on children. Rodin (1976) and McConohay and Rodin (1976) studied the social behavior of lower class children. Crowded lower class children showed higher levels of learned helplessness and competed even when competitive behavior minimized their own rewards. Shapiro (1974) studied the effects of crowding and socioeconomic status on motor task behavior of Israeli children. Crowding predicted poor task performance among lower class boys, but it had no effect on lower class girls or on middle class children of either sex. These three studies present a contrast of sorts to the pattern of results previously discussed. In accordance with the model presented earlier, we can speculate about several variables that may be contributing to these differences. We noted that the ability to induce others to act in ways that facilitate one's own goal attainment is important. We can conjecture that children have less ability to induce family members to facilitate their goal attainment than adults have. This would be consistent with the findings of more negative effects observed among children than among adults. Second, lower class households have greater scarcity than middle class households. Increasing scarcity heightens the probability of competitive behavior (cf. Deutsch, 1973). Thus, lower class children may be at greater risk than middle class children regarding negative effects of crowding. Finally, crowding seemed to have little effect on children in Hong Kong, whereas it has some effects on children in American and Israeli cultures. We can speculate that differing cultural norms may mediate the effects of high density for children.

We now turn to an examination of the effects of dormitory crowding. Unlike the situation faced by families, who are normatively expected to maintain a high degree of cooperation, we may consider the basic orientation of dormitory residents as individualistic. As Deutsch (1973) has demonstrated, however, individualistic orientations are unstable and are likely to become either cooperative or competitive depending upon important features of the social situation. One such feature is resource scarcity. Ordinarily, scarce resources increase the likelihood of competitive behavior. However, it is possible to create a social structure that will minimize competition in the face of scarce resources and, under unusual circumstances, may even promote cooperation. Thus, the effects of crowding on the social behavior of dormitory residents should be quite variable – at times reflecting the adverse effects of competitive orientations while at other times responding to the positive effects of a cooperative orientation.

In terms of control, dormitories also provide a more variable environment than do family dwellings on the one hand, or prisons, on the other. Young people live in dormitories because they have chosen to be a part of a particular social world. Thus, they exercise some voluntary control over the choice of a place to live. But for many students, roommates are assigned, resources are limited, and their ability to exert decisional control over the allocation of those resources that are available is lower than the control available to adults in family residences. Some youths may treat such circumstances as a desirable challenge, thereby avoiding feelings of loss of control over the environment. Others may find their goals thwarted, thereby experiencing low levels of environmental control.

In an early study, MacDonald and Oden (1973) demonstrated that youths living in crowded dormitory-style accommodations, but having a high degree of perceived control and a strongly cooperative orientation, showed positive effects. Five married couples, all Peace Corps volunteers, volunteered to share an unpartitioned 30 by 30-foot room for 12 weeks of training. They made this choice so as to experience some of the hardships that they expected during their Peace Corps assignment. They were compared to Peace Corps volunteer couples who lived in hotel accommodations. The crowded couples not only failed to show adverse effects but showed enhanced marital relationships, were chosen as socioemotional leaders by other volunteers, and regretted leaving their living accommodations more than those living in hotel accommodations. The authors' description makes it clear that these couples developed a high degree of cooperation with each other and with their spouses while dealing with adversity. Further, they had volunteered to enter the setting, saw it as a challenge and as part of their training. Thus, they experienced a high degree of decisional control over their environment. Under such circumstances, it would seem that crowding can lead to positive rather than negative effects.

In an interesting program of research, Baum, Valins, and their colleagues investigated the effects of dormitory architecture on social behavior. In some of their studies, they compared groups of students living in traditional double-loaded long-corridor dormitories with students living in suite-style accommodations. In other studies, long-corridor dormitory residents were compared with residents of short-corridor dormitories. All residents had equivalent square footage of living space available to them. However, long-corridor residents were more likely to encounter unwanted social interaction than were short-corridor or suite residents. The investigators suggest that excessive unwanted social interaction decreases feelings of control over the environment. Additionally, we can speculate that the desire to avoid interaction with others minimizes the possibility of cooperation, a condition requiring coordinated efforts with others. Indeed, these investigators found that long-corridor residents felt more helpless and acted more competitively than did students living in accommodations of a different architectural variety (Baum, Aiello, & Calesnick, 1978; Baum & Gatchell, 1980; Baum & Valins, 1977). In addition, such students perceived a high degree of crowding and experienced greater overall stress than did their counterparts (Baum & Valins, 1977). Two other sets of investigators have found similar effects (Stokols & Resnick, 1975; Zuckerman, Schmitz, & Yosha, 1977).

In a program of research conducted at Rutgers University, students living two to a room were compared with students who were tripled in traditional double-loaded corridor dormitory rooms intended for two-person occupancy. Tripled students were more disappointed and stressed than doubled students. These results were especially severe for tripled women who, in an attempt to make a homelike environment, spent significantly more time and invested more in their rooms than did men. Crowded men escaped to alternate locations (Karlin, Epstein, & Aiello, 1978). Both tripled men and tripled women, however, showed equivalent reductions in grade point averages when crowded. This effect disappeared in subsequent years, however, when they no longer lived in high-density environments (Karlin, Rosen, & Epstein, 1979). Clearly, these tripled students all experienced goal blockage as a result of resource scarcity. Among other things, dormitory rooms were unavailable for adequate studying. Hence, grades suffered. Faced with this situation, men pursued their goals in alternate settings. Women, on the other hand, wanted to create a homelike environment in their rooms. To do so, they needed to coordinate activities with their roommates. Lacking specialized training, they were unable to accomplish this difficult task given the problems created by resource scarcity. Attempts by these women to form cooperative groups failed. Instead, coalitions emerged, and by the end of the semester, all of the tripled women disbanded their threesomes in favor of alternate living arrangements. Men, on the other hand, did not form coalitions and continued to live as threesomes (Karlin et al., 1978).

Baron, Mandel, Adams, and Griffen (1976) also investigated the effects of tripled living conditions among college dormitory residents. Consistent with the formulation advanced in the foregoing discussion, these investigators found evidence indicating that tripled students perceived less control over their environment.

In addition to studies in college dormitories, studies of dormitory living have been conducted with naval personnel. Dean, Pugh, and Gunderson (1975) found that crowding had few effects. Smith and Haythorn (1972), using a simulated undersea laboratory, also found few main effects attributable to crowding. However, crowding interacted with other factors to produce important effects on social behavior. For example, when crowded groups consisted of men whose personalities were incompatible with one another, men withdrew from social interaction to a greater extent than less crowded men whose personalities were incompatible. However, crowded men with compatible personalities spent more time together in recreational activities than noncrowded compatible individuals.

Thus, in general, crowded dormitory living, as predicted, has widely variable effects that may be understood in light of the perceived control and interpersonal orientation of residents.

In family residences, adults have a high degree of control and usually cooperate with one another. Dormitory residents, who are usually young adults, generally experience less control over their environment and tend to be less cooperatively oriented. We now turn to a discussion of the results of studies conducted in prisons, where inmates have very little control and are likely to be competitively oriented toward one another. Under these conditions, we would expect crowding to lead to more negative effects than it would in family residences or in college dormitories.

McCain, Cox, and Paulus (1976) found that prisoners sharing a dormitory cell with others had higher numbers of illness complaints than those housed in single cells. Persons living in single cells have more control over their environment than persons sharing a cell with others. Apparently, this modicum of added control in a rather uncontrollable environment influences the amount of stress experienced. D'Atri (1975) compared blood pressure of inmates living in dormitory-type cells with those housed in single cells. Consistent with the McCain et al. (1976) findings and the control formulation suggested, he found that both systolic and diastolic blood pressure was higher for inmates sharing a cell. Paulus, McCain, and Cox (1978) used archival data to examine the relationship between crowding in prisons and various measures of pathology. They found that the more crowded the prisons were, the higher were the death rates, the number of psychiatric commitments, and inmates' blood pressure. Cox, Paulus, McCain, and Schkade (1979) found a positive correlation between level of density and palmar sweat for prisoners in a Texas county jail. In sum, as expected under a formulation highlighting the central role of control and cooperation in adverse reactions to crowding, studies conducted in prison environments where prisoners have very little control show consistent evidence of adverse effects.

Thus, if one organizes the literature on residential crowding in terms of the degree of cooperation and control available to residents, the findings present a fairly clear picture. The lower the degree of cooperation and control, the more adverse the effects.

Crowding in laboratory settings

Studies of the effects of crowding in residential environments have clear implications for policy decisions. A large number of studies, however, have been conducted in laboratory settings in which crowding is usually engendered by placing a relatively large number of people in a relatively small room for short periods of time. Unlike residential environments, crowding is not usually engendered in laboratories by creating a scarcity of resources or a reduction in desired levels of privacy. Rather, normative expectations about appropriate interaction distances between strangers are violated. Thus, at first glance there is little resemblance between crowded homes and crowded laboratory rooms. Some investigators have argued that findings from laboratories are therefore of little use for understanding crowding in the "real world" (Baldassare & Fisher, 1976). However, in our view the basic psychological processes responsible for the effects of crowding in residences – that is, degree of control over an environmental stressor and group orientation for dealing with this stressor – should also be the critical variables determining the effects of crowding in the laboratory. Below, we will briefly review studies of crowding that have been conducted in laboratory settings.

Studies of laboratory crowding vary in the degree to which they subject participants to violations of expectations about appropriate social behavior among strangers. At one extreme, subjects are so closely spaced that they are forced to touch one another and are unable to avoid eye contact with one another. Under these circumstances, subjects almost universally show stress reactions. Stress reactions have been demonstrated physiologically by increases in skin conductance level (Aiello, DeRisi, Epstein, & Karlin, 1977; Aiello, Epstein, & Karlin, 1975; Epstein, Teitelbaum, Karlin, Katz, & Aiello, 1979; Nicosia, Hyman, Karlin, Epstein, & Aiello, 1979) and in cardiac function (Epstein, Lehrer, & Woolfolk, 1978; Karlin, Katz, Epstein, & Woolfolk, 1979). In the latter study, the stressful effects of crowding persisted after three weekly exposures to crowding. Similar effects have been found on task measures (Aiello et al., 1977; Epstein & Karlin, 1975). In addition, crowded subjects show lower tolerance for frustration (Nicosia et al., 1979) and report more negative mood, greater discomfort, and more symptoms of physiological arousal than their noncrowded counterparts (Aiello et al., 1977; Epstein & Karlin, 1975; Epstein et al., 1979; Epstein et al., 1978; Nicosia et al., 1979). If this level of social inappropriateness is reduced by eliminating bodily contact or eye contact at close range, the stressful effects of crowding tend to be lessened (Epstein et al., 1978; Freedman, 1975; Freedman, Klevansky, & Ehrlich, 1971; Kutner, 1973; Nicosia et al., 1979; Paulus, Annis, Seta, Schkade, & Matthews, 1976). Epstein et al. (1978) report that crowded subjects report less control over the environment than do noncrowded subjects. This is consistent with observations of increased defensive posturing (Epstein & Karlin, 1975; Epstein et al., 1978; Evans, 1979) during crowding and even prior to crowding but following the anticipation of future crowding (Baum & Greenberg, 1975). When subjects are given a means to control this otherwise uncontrollable situation, stress reactions are ameliorated. Sherrod (1974) provided crowded subjects with a button, which, if pressed, would signal the experimenter to remove them from the crowded environment. Although subjects did not, in fact, press the button, the sense of control that it offered reduced adverse reactions to crowding.

In addition, a number of studies have shown that the social orientation of the group mediates reactions to crowding. For example, in situations that require the formation of an achievement-oriented team, males more easily form cooperative groups than do females. Under such circumstances, crowded males become even more cooperative and crowded females less cooperative than their noncrowded counterparts (Marshall & Heslin, 1975). Alternately, in situations requiring a high degree of socioemotional group maintenance, women are more likely to band together cooperatively than are men. Under these circumstances, it has been found that crowded females become more cooperative and crowded males more competitive than their noncrowded counterparts (Epstein & Karlin, 1975). Following an extensive program of research, Freedman (1975) has concluded that high density intensifies the prevailing social orientation among group members. The results cited are consistent with his formulation.

Thus, the effects of laboratory crowding, like those of residential crowding, are ameliorated when subjects perceive a high degree of control. In addition, the social effects of crowding, such as mood and liking for others, are largely determined by the interpersonal orientation of the group.

This review has focused on crowding in residential settings and in the experimental laboratory. Research conducted in public settings such as supermarkets (Langer & Saegert, 1977), department stores (Saegert, McIntosh, & West, 1975), or city streets (Heshka & Pylypuk, 1975) also suggests that crowding may be stressful, and that strategies that afford control to the crowded individual help to alleviate this stress. We turn now to a consideration of the unique features of crowding stress and some of the ways in which it differs from other stressors discussed in this volume.

Crowding and other stressors

This volume focuses on the effects of several environmental stressors. I would like to briefly highlight an important difference between crowding stress and some of the other environmental stressors discussed. My argument follows from the analysis presented in this chapter and hinges on the fact that crowding, in contrast to stressors such as heat, noise, and air pollution, is of necessity a *group* phenomenon.

It is certainly true that spatial restriction is an important component of crowding. Yet, if an individual were to be placed alone in an extremely small and confined environment, he or she would be cramped, but not crowded. To be crowded, one must share an environment with others. The problems created by crowding are problems arising from difficulties in interaction and the coordination of activities with others.

Let me amplify this point by considering one set of findings discussed in this review. I have reported the findings of Baum and Valins (1977), which demonstrate the stressful consequences of being subjected to unwanted interactions with others. The problem is one of inadequate coordination of activities with others. Individuals are expected to talk with others when they do not wish to do so. The problem is amenable to solution if members of the group could discuss their difficulties, examine the prevailing norms, and determine whether they wish to substitute a different set of norms more appropriate to the situation. Baum and Valins show that suite architecture promotes a different form of group organization, which minimizes these problems of coordination. One concomitant of this differing architecture is that it creates meaningful small groups for those living in suites while organizing residents of corridor dormitories into dyads, cliques, and collectives of hallmates. The differential effects of corridor and suite architecture can then be traced to the differing properties of meaningful intact groups compared with loosely organized collectivities. Suitemates have obligations to one another comparable to the obligations that family members have to one another. They learn to coordinate their activities with each other and have a basis for inducing others in their suite to cooperate so as to facilitate their goal attainment.

Because crowding is a social phenomenon and the salient causes of the problem are other individuals, we can speculate that many of the important consequences of crowding will be social. If others in the home prevent the individual from achieving privacy, for example, they may be seen as the source of the individual's frustration, and it is quite likely that they may become the objects of his or her response to frustration. We can speculate that this should not be the case for noise, heat, or air pollution. The problems created by noise, heat, or air pollution may sometimes be attributable to the behavior of other persons, but oftentimes they can be attributed to more impersonal agents. Moreover, of those times when noise, heat, and air pollution are blamed on the behavior of others, it is probably the case that in a large proportion of the instances, the others responsible are not linked to the individual in a close relationship.

From the foregoing discussion, it follows that the problems created by crowding are more likely to be ameliorated by concerted group action than are the problems arising from noise, heat, or air pollution. In residences, persons living together must learn to communicate in ways that will allow them to indicate how the behavior of the other person may be interfering with their own goal attainment. Methods of interpersonal negotiation and persuasion can then be used to change behaviors that are causing problems. For example, in families living in quarters with insufficient space for studying and watching TV or listening to music simultaneously, rules for cooperatively scheduling these activities can help to ameliorate these problems. I am assuming that some of the internal stress and tension that the crowded individual experiences may arise from failures to communicate with other group members about the problems that their behaviors are creating for that person. Airing these grievances and successfully inducing others to take corrective action is one way to reduce stress. It is also likely to induce the belief that one has some control over the environment.

This analysis has concentrated on the problems created by crowding in residences. I believe that chances of reducing the stressful effects of crowding in mass transportation or in public settings are smaller, because the problems are attributable to others who are not cooperatively linked to the individual. Hence, the task of inducing these individuals to coordinate their activities to facilitate joint goal attainment is more difficult and is more comparable to the difficulties encountered in attempting to induce strangers making noise or polluting the environment to desist from these activities.

Future directions

Research on crowding has done little to examine the processes that persons use to cope with the problems created by crowding. It would be extremely enlightening, for example, to conduct case studies of families living under conditions of high density who, nevertheless, manage to adapt successfully. This presupposes that we have adequate measures of good versus poor adaptation. Assuming that we can identify persons who adapt successfully, can we discover what it is that they do? Studying the process of adaptation requires a longitudinal approach. We also need to learn how experience with crowded conditions over a long period of time influences the appraisal of the problem and how it changes behavior. Several studies have begun to use this approach (cf. Baron et al., 1976; Baum & Gatchel, 1980; Karlin et al., 1978; Karlin et al., 1979). More such longitudinal research is needed.

In accordance with the theme presented in this chapter, another fruitful direction for crowding research would be to explore how group phenomena affect the crowding experience (Stokols, 1972). How do variables such as status within a group, the organization of the group, the group's norms of cooperativeness or competitiveness, or social roles influence reactions to crowding? A beginning has been made by Baum, Harpin, and Valins (1975). More is needed.

There is a paucity of research on crowding in work settings and class-rooms. With respect to the latter, there have been numerous studies relating class size to pupil achievement, and these have reported contradictory findings. In a thorough review of that literature, Blake (1954) summarized the results of several hundred studies by noting a slight majority showing better achievement in smaller classes. But none of these studies examined the processes that occur in crowded, as opposed to uncrowded, classrooms. It would be useful to know, for example, how teachers allocate their attention, what differences there are in planned activities, and whether there is a greater disparity in the attention teachers pay to poor versus good students, as crowding increases.

Relatively little crowding research has focused on individual and cross-cultural differences. For example, there is some research (see Evans, 1978, for a summary) indicating that young children are more adversely affected by crowding than older persons. But this does not hold across cultures. While crowding may have negative effects on youngsters in Western cultures, children in the Kung society do not suffer ill effects (Draper, 1974). Although studies of crowded residential living in Chicago show that the higher the density the greater the pathology (cf. Galle, Gove, & McPherson, 1972), a study in the Netherlands (Levy & Herzog, 1974) shows the reverse relationship, whereas a study of residential crowding in Hong Kong – perhaps as crowded a residential setting as can be found anywhere – revealed no overall adverse effects of high-density living (Mitchell, 1971). Studies conducted in laboratory settings indicate that variables such as personal space preferences (cf. Aiello et al., 1977) or locus of control (cf. Schopler, McCallum, & Rusbult, 1977) may mediate reactions to crowding. We would hope that one important direction in which future research on the effects of crowding can move is toward an Actor by Setting by Process model of the sort advocated by Altman (1976) in his discussion of the fruitful integration of environmental and social psychology. Perhaps the ideas offered in this chapter will encourage such directions.

References

Aiello, J., & Baum, A. (Eds.). *Residential Crowding and Design*. New York: Plenum, 1979.

Aiello, J. R., DeRisi, D. T., Epstein, Y. M., & Karlin, R. A. Crowding and the role of interpersonal distance preference. *Sociometry*, 1977, 40, 271–282.

Aiello, J. R., Epstein, Y. M., & Karlin, R. A. Effects of crowding on electrodermal activity. *Sociological Symposium*, 1975, 14, 43–57.

Altman, I. *The environment and social behavior: Privacy, territoriality, crowding and personal space*. Monterey, Calif.: Brooks/Cole, 1975.

Altman, I. Environmental psychology and social psychology. *Personality and Social Psychology Bulletin*, 1976, 2, 96–113.

Baldassare, M., & Fisher, C. The relevance of crowding experiments to urban studies. In D. Stokols (Ed.), *Psychological Perspectives on Environment and Behavior*. New York: Plenum, 1976.

Baron, R. M., Mandel, D. G., Adams, C. A., & Griffen, L. M. Effects of social density in university residential environments. *Journal of Personality and Social Psychology*, 1976, *34*, 434–446.

Baum, A., Aiello, J., & Calesnick, L. Crowding and personal control: Social density and the development of learned helplessness. *Journal of Personality and Social Psychology*, 1978, *36*, 1000–1011.

Baum, A., & Epstein, Y. (Eds.), *Human Response to Crowding*. Hillsdale, N.J.: Erlbaum, 1978.

Baum, A., & Gatchel, R. *Cognitive determinants of reaction to uncontrollable events: Development of reactance and learned helplessness*. Unpublished manuscript, Uniformed Services University of the Health Sciences, 1980.

Baum, A., & Greenberg, C. Waiting for a crowd: The behavioral and perceptual effects of anticipated crowding. *Journal of Personality and Social Psychology*, 1975, *32*, 671–679.

Baum, A., Harpin, R., & Valins, S. The role of group phenomena in the experience of crowding. *Environment and Behavior*, 1975, *7*, 185–198.

Baum, A., & Valins, S. *Architecture and social behavior: Psychological studies of social density*. Hillsdale, N.J.: Erlbaum, 1977.

Blake, H. *Class size: A summary of selected studies in elementary and secondary schools*. Unpublished doctoral thesis, Teachers College, Columbia University, 1954.

Booth, A. *Urban crowding and its consequences*. New York: Praeger, 1976.

Committee on the Hygiene of Housing, American Public Health Association, *Planning the home for occupancy: Standards for healthful housing series*. Chicago: Public Administration Service, 1950.

Cox, V. C., Paulus, P. B., McCain, G., & Schkade, J. K. Field research on the effects of crowding in prisons and on off-shore drilling platforms. In J. R. Aiello & A. Baum (Eds.), *Residential crowding and design*. New York: Plenum, 1979.

D'Atri, D. A. Psychophysiological responses to crowding. *Environment and Behavior*, 1975, *7*, 237–250.

Dean, L. M., Pugh, W. M., & Gunderson, E. K. Spatial and perceptual components of crowding: Effects on health and satisfaction. *Environment and Behavior*, 1975, *7*, 225–236.

Deutsch, M. *The resolution of conflict*. New Haven, Conn.: Yale University Press, 1973.

Draper, D. Crowding among hunter-gatherers: The Kung Bushmen. *Science*, 1974, *182*, 301–303.

Epstein, Y. M., & Baum, A. Crowding: Methods of study. In A. Baum & Y. M. Epstein (Eds.), *Human response to crowding*. Hillsdale, N.J.: Erlbaum, 1978.

Epstein, Y. M., & Karlin, R. A. Effects of acute experimental crowding. *Journal of Applied Psychology*, 1975, *5*, 34–53.

Epstein, Y. M., Lehrer, P., & Woolfolk, R. L. *Physiological, cognitive and behavioral effects of repeated exposure to crowding*. Unpublished manuscript, Rutgers University, 1978.

Epstein, Y., Teitelbaum, R., Karlin, R., Katz, S., & Aiello, J. *An assessment of the effectiveness of two tactics to reduce arousal in mass transit settings*. Unpublished manuscript, Rutgers University, 1979.

Esser, A., & Greenbie, B. (Eds.). *Design for communality and privacy*. New York: Plenum, 1978.

Evans, G. W. Crowding and the developmental process. In A. Baum & Y. Epstein (Eds.), *Human response to crowding*. Hillsdale, N.J.: Erlbaum, 1978.

Evans, G. W. Behavioral and physiological consequences of crowding in humans. *Journal of Applied Social Psychology*, 1979, *9*, 27–46.

Freedman, J. *Crowding and behavior*. San Francisco: Freeman, 1975.

Freedman, J. L., Heshka, S., & Levy, A. Population density and pathology: Is there a relationship? *Journal of Experimental Social Psychology*, 1975, *11*, 539–552.

Freedman, J., Klevansky, S., & Ehrlich, P. The effect of crowding on human task performance. *Journal of Applied Social Psychology*, 1971, *1*, 7–25.

Galle, O., Gove, W., & McPherson, J. Population density and pathology: What are the relations for man? *Science*, 1972, *176*, 23–30.

Heshka, S., & Pylypuk, A. *Human crowding and adrenocortical activity*. Paper presented at meeting of the Canadian Psychological Association, Quebec, Canada, June 1975.

Johnson, D., & Matross, R. Interpersonal influence in psychotherapy: A social psychological view. In A. Gurman & A. Razin (Eds.), *Effective psychotherapy: A handbook of research*. Elmsford, N.Y.: Pergamon, 1977, 395–432.

Karlin, R. A., Epstein, Y. M., & Aiello, J. R. Strategies for the investigation of crowding. In A. Esser & B. Greenbie (Eds.), *Design for community and privacy*. New York: Plenum, 1978.

Karlin, R. A., Katz, S., Epstein, Y. M., & Woolfolk, R. L. The use of therapeutic interventions to reduce crowding related arousal: A preliminary investigation. *Environmental Psychology and Nonverbal Behavior*, 1979, *3*, 219–227.

Karlin, R. A., Rosen, L., & Epstein, Y. M. Three into two doesn't go: A follow-up on the effects of overcrowded dormitory rooms. *Personality and Social Psychology Bulletin*, 1979, *5*, 391–395.

Kutner, D. H., Jr. Overcrowding: Human responses to density and visual exposure. *Human Relations*, 1973, *26*, 31–50.

Langer, E. J., & Saegert, S. Crowding and cognitive control. *Journal of Personality and Social Psychology*, 1977, *35*, 175–182.

Levy, L., & Herzog, A. Effects of population density and crowding on health and social adaptation in the Netherlands. *Journal of Health and Social Behavior*, 1974, *15*, 228–240.

McCain, G., Cox, V. C., & Paulus, P. B. The relationship between illness, complaints and degree of crowding in a prison environment. *Environment and Behavior*, 1976, *8*, 283–290.

McConahay, J., & Rodin, J. *Interactions of long and short term density on task performance*. Unpublished manuscript, Yale University, 1976.

MacDonald, W. S., & Oden, C. W., Jr. Effects of extreme crowding on the performance of five married couples during twelve weeks of intensive training. *Proceedings of 81st Annual Convention of the American Psychological Association*, 1973, *8*, 209–210.

Marshall, J., & Heslin, R. Boys and girls together: Sexual composition and the effect of density and group size on cohesiveness. *Journal of Personality and Social Psychology*, 1975, *31*, 952–961.

Mitchell, R. E. Some implications of high density housing. *American Sociological Review*, 1971, *36*, 18–29.

Nicosia, G., Hyman, D., Karlin, R. A., Epstein, Y. M., & Aiello, J. R. Effects of bodily contact on reactions to crowding. *Journal of Applied Social Psychology*, 1979, *9*, 508–523.

Paulus, P., Annis, A. B., Seta, J. J., Schkade, J. K., & Matthews, R. W. Density does affect task performance. *Journal of Personality and Social Psychology*, 1976, *34*, 248–253.

Paulus, P., McCain, G., & Cox, V. Death rates, psychiatric commitments, blood pressure and perceived crowding as a function of institutional crowding. *Environmental Psychology and Nonverbal Behavior*, 1978, *3*, 998–999.

Rodin, J. Density, perceived choice and responses to controllable and uncontrollable outcomes. *Journal of Experimental Social Psychology*, 1976, *12*, 546–578.

Rohe, W. *Effects of mediating variables on response to density in residential settings*. Paper presented at the American Psychological Association Meeting, Toronto, 1978.

Saegert, S., McIntosh, E., & West, S. Two studies of crowding in urban public spaces. *Environment and Behavior*, 1975, *7*, 159–184.

Scholper, J., McCallum, R., & Rusbult, C. *Behavioral interference and internality-externality as determinants of subject crowding*. Unpublished paper, University of North Carolina, 1977.

Shapiro, A. H. Effects of family density and mothers' education on preschoolers' motor skills. *Perceptual and Motor Skills*, 1974, *38*, 79–86.

Sherrod, D. R. Crowding, perceived control and behavioral after-effects. *Journal of Applied Social Psychology*, 1974, *4*, 171–186.

Smith, S., & Haythorn, W. Effects of compatability, crowding, group size, and leadership seniority on stress, anxiety, hostility and annoyance in isolated groups. *Journal of Personality and Social Psychology*, 1972, *22*, 67–79.

Stokols, D. On the distinction between density and crowding: Some implications for future research. *Psychological Review*, 1972, *79*, 275–277.

Stokols, D., & Resnick, S. *The generalization of residential crowding experiences to nonresidential settings*. Paper presented at the Annual Meeting of the Environmental Design Research Association, Lawrence, Kansas, 1975.

Zuckerman, M., Schmitz, M., & Yosha, A. Effects of crowding in a student environment. *Journal of Applied Social Psychology*, 1977, *7*, 67–72.

Part II

Ambient stress and the designed environment

Craig Zimring introduces this section with a novel perspective on architecture and behavior, utilizing the concept of dysfunction between basic human needs and goals and environmental supports and constraints. While most research on design has used atheoretical postoccupancy evaluations of user satisfaction, Zimring demonstrates how the stress concept can be used to derive some preliminary theoretical models of behavior in the designed environment. In particular, he illustrates how human needs for socialization and geographic orientation can be influenced by architecture.

Each of the four chapters on individual settings shows how the concept of person–environment fit can be a useful heuristic for understanding dysfunction in environmental design. Sally Ann Shumaker and Janet Reizenstein emphasize the vulnerability of hospital patients and illustrate how their relative powerlessness in the hospital social structure is reinforced by hospital architecture. These authors call our attention to the critical interplay between organizational factors and physical design in institutional settings. Sherry Ahrentzen and her colleagues argue that the paucity of definitive research trends in the school design and behavior literature is a result of insufficient appreciation of individual differences in children's environmental needs. Ahrentzen develops a taxonomy of physical features of the classroom that interact with individual needs for control, stimulation, and order, as well as various personality factors.

In the fourth chapter of this section, Jean Wineman deals with the office environment and integrates ergonomic research with office studies of air quality and temperature, lighting, and privacy. She notes the overreliance on self-report data in the field of occupational stress and suggests several additional measures of stress in the workplace worthy of future study. Finally, she discusses how various social parameters such as social interaction, symbolic identification, and personal control, both in and out of the office setting, can influence worker satisfaction with office design.

Finally, in Chapter 10, Ralph Taylor tackles the difficult problem of how to define neighborhood and offers a taxonomy of direct and indirect neighborhood design impacts that influence human health and well-being. He discusses neighborhood-level, block-level, and individual-level impacts on a host of outcome variables including crime and social control, incivilities, health, migration, and neighborhood satisfaction.

Each of the chapters in this section demonstrates the ways in which physical design can inhibit the satisfaction of important, individual needs and goals. Stress is viewed as a result of design–behavior dysfunction. The authors offer design guidelines to reduce environmental barriers to human satisfaction and well-being.

6. The built environment as a source of psychological stress: Impacts of buildings and cities on satisfaction and behavior

Craig Zimring

For many of us, the built environment is no more conspicuous than the surrounding air. Like air, the built environment intrudes on our consciousness only when it causes particular harm, discomfort, pleasure, or awe. Despite our lack of awareness, however, there is growing evidence that the designed environment may produce stress, both directly and indirectly. The purpose of this chapter is to explore several ways in which the designed environment interacts with important behavioral processes and to consider these interactions from the perspective of stresses imposed on the individual.

The *designed environment* and *stress* are complex issues, and a great variety of definitions and operational approaches have appeared in the literature. The designed environment is conceived here as a social–physical system in which physical elements interact in complex ways with social structure and with individual goals and needs. In general, however, I will address those physical aspects of the environment that can be manipulated by an architect: spatial arrangement, circulation system design, and site planning.

This chapter will primarily consider *psychological* stress, that is, situations in which psychological variables affect an individual's interpretation of a situation and his or her stress reactions and coping responses. For example, if a visitor to Boston searches for a famous building, such as the new Quincy Market, and is unsuccessful, stress may result because the traveler's goal is blocked. The amount of stress, however, is linked with the importance of the goal. This is actually quite a complex situation. The visitor brings a number of characteristics to the situation: previous experience with Boston, ability to cope by reading maps or asking directions, need to feel oriented, and so forth. Also, the designed environment helps or hinders. In this case, Boston has a complex, irregular street pattern, yet Quincy Market is centrally located. Finally, situational factors affect the interpretation of the situation by the visitor, for example, whether he or she has to be at the Market at a fixed time.

In Chapter 1 of this volume, Baum, Singer, and Baum suggest that potentially stressful situations can be understood by analyzing three components: stressors, transmission variables, and recipients of stress. With regard to Boston, the complex city is the stressor, the situational factors are the transmission variables (i.e., they serve as mediators, helping the recipient to decide whether the situation is stressful), and the traveler is the recipient of the stress.

Following the model proposed by Baum and his colleagues (and similar models proposed by other stress researchers), this chapter will be based on two general suppositions. First, stress results from a dynamic process in which people attempt to achieve a fit between their needs and goals and what the environment provides. This process is dynamic because an individual's needs are highly variable over time and vary widely from person to person; environments vary widely as well.

Moreover, the perceptions people have of situations are variable, as are their available coping responses. As a result, this chapter will examine the *processes* for resolving "misfits," rather than simply considering misfits as static situations.

Both overt and intrapersonal coping strategies may be used to resolve a misfit. In the example of finding Quincy Market, the visitor may try to resolve the misfit by actively trying to control the situation by asking directions, or he or she may decide that finding the market is not so important after all. Similarly, an office worker who is sharing an office with a loud co-worker may control the situation by asking the person to be quiet or by leaving the office for a quieter place. The office worker may also decide that quiet is not necessary. Either strategy allows the misfit to be reduced, although the short-term and long-term costs of coping strategies may differ.

A second supposition is that transmission variables must be considered when examining psychological stress caused by designed environments. In an office setting, status, perceived control, and other qualities serve as transmission variables: They are influences on the individual's appraisal of a situation that help to determine whether a situation is stressful.

Although not the main focus of this chapter, the designed environment may also provide direct physiological stressors. A poor ventilating system may contribute to physiological stress caused by air pollution; machine noise may create negative auditory and nonauditory impacts; poor design may contribute to high temperatures within a building and lead to accompanying decrements in performance. Although physical stressors are also affected by transmission variables such as the individual's perception of control, the sheer physiological impact of these stressors sometimes overwhelms the individual's coping resources.

In the two major sections that follow, "Regulation of social interaction," and "Environmental knowing: Wayfinding and orientation," I examine several ways in which the designed environment may cause stress to the individual. These stresses occur both because the design of the environment may directly or indirectly block important goals of users and also because the design may limit coping strategies for resolving the blockage.

Regulation of social interaction

As this chapter is being written, dramatic and poignant events are unfolding. The New Mexico State Penitentiary has been overrun by its inmates, and 10 people have died. This incident – like the uprising at Attica – is being blamed at least in part on the dense, crowded conditions in the prison (Andelman, 1980). The high rise Pruitt–Igoe public housing complex in St. Louis, hailed in the 1950s as a prototypic design, was recently dynamited by the city, in part because its design was thought to contribute to alienation, anomie, and crime (Rainwater, 1972).

In addition to these highly publicized examples, the research literature has documented many other situations in which design dysfunction has interacted with psychosocial goals to produce negative outcomes for users (e.g., Baum & Valins, 1977; Paulus, McCain, & Cox, 1978).

These outcomes may be understood from the perspective of the stresses experienced by building users: They represent instances in which design thwarted goals for intimate interaction, for social networks, and perhaps most important, for control over the time and place for social interactions. When this thwarting occurs, and when no efficient coping strategies are provided, serious psychological and social consequences may result, including anxiety, depression, anomie, and asocial acts such as acting out, and crime (see Epstein, Chap. 5, this volume, for a review).

Several writers have suggested that the interactions of users and the designed environment may be organized through the concept of hierarchy of space (e.g., Altman, 1975; Reizenstein, 1980). Psychosocial needs, and the spaces that serve them, may be considered as concentric areas. The outermost area is public space; in physical terms this is the street, the plaza, and the shopping mall, for example. Public space supports anonymous, impersonal contact. The innermost area is private space; this is the bathroom, the bedroom, and so forth. These spaces support solitude and intimate interactions.

There are different sets of needs at these levels, and not fulfilling them brings different types of consequences. At the public level, people have a need for social networks and for a sense of mutual caring and protection; when these networks break down, crime and vandalism may result. At the private level, individuals need solitude for self-reflection and intimate conversations to create and maintain personal relationships. When these needs are frustrated, intrapersonal costs may result: withdrawal, depression, illness.

Semipublic space: Strategies for increasing social networks

The number and quality of one's friendships are good predictors of one's overall satisfaction (Craik & Zube, 1976). When friendships are absent, an individual may feel depressed and unconstrained by other social norms. In addition, a cohesive social network can moderate the effects of other environmental stressors such as crowding or family difficulty (see Epstein, Chap. 5, this volume). Two strategies have been proposed for increasing social networks: proximity and defensible space modifications.

First, research suggests that the proximity of residences affects patterns of friendship and neighborly interactions. Several studies have found that the incidence of apartment- and house-dwellers' friendships is proportional to the distance between residences; residents knew most of their nearby neighbors, but knew few of their neighbors who lived further away (Lawton, 1980; Michelson, 1976). However, the effect is due not to distance per se, but rather to physical arrangements that encouraged frequent casual face-to-face contacts. For example, Festinger and his colleagues found that apartment residents on the second floor knew first-floor residents who lived on their path out of the building and with whom they interacted frequently, but they did not know other first-floor residents (Festinger, Schachter, & Back, 1950).

The effect of such contact on friendship is apparently mediated by the perceived homogeneity of residents, by their need for friendship (Michelson, 1976; Roscow, 1967), and by the extent to which they trust their neighbors (Saegert, 1977). Most of the earlier studies examined groups such as veterans or young executives who were highly similar to each other and who had few friends (e.g., Festinger et al., 1950). When housing patterns brought into contact people who saw each other as similar, and who needed friends, friendships developed. Recent studies examining more heterogeneous groups have found that proximity alone is a poor predictor of friendship or interaction with one's neighbors (Roscow, 1967; Tomeh, 1969; Zeisel & Griffin, 1975).

As a second strategy, Newman (1973, 1975) argues that crime is a symptom of stress caused by designs that destroy social networks and that crime can be reduced by appropriate design of semipublic spaces. By employing designs that clearly indicate who has responsibility for spaces, Newman suggests that residents can be encouraged to feel a sense of belonging and mutual support and will care for their space and challenge intruders. He proposes that "defensible space" may be created by: (a) providing for natural surveillance through physical designs that allow users to overlook common space (e.g., kitchen windows that overlook apartment lobbies) and hence be aware of intruders; (b) establishing territoriality and a sense of proprietorship by providing symbolic markers such as paving differences or low walls; and (c) creating symbolic identification by improving the appearance of subsidized housing and instilling pride in residents.

Newman's proposals are based on his analyses of public housing in St. Louis and New York City. He found, for example, that two neighboring apartment complexes in Brooklyn had similar residents, yet one had a much higher crime rate. The complex with the higher crime rate was a tall slab building with multiple entrances and many apartments per floor; the building with the lower crime rate was a low rise that clustered apartments around separate entrances. He suggested that the difference in crime rates was due to the clearly marked semipublic space in the low-rise development. Because relatively few families adjoined the corridors, residents recognized who belonged and were encouraged to challenge outsiders (Newman, 1973). Newman has recently produced explicit architectural guidelines for defensible space incorporating natural surveillance, territoriality, and symbolic identification. He suggests that his principles can be applied both to remodeling older buildings and to designing new ones (Newman, 1975).

There has been considerable criticism of Newman's work and evidence. Early critics argued that he happened to pick settings that supported his ideas and that nearby apartment complexes would not have done so. It was argued that there exist complexes with high crime rates that embody his defensible space principles and complexes with low crime rates that were not "defensible" in design (Hillier, 1973; Patterson, 1977).

A recent quasi-experimental evaluation of Newman's work challenges several of his suggestions (Kohn, Franck, & Fox, 1975). Kohn and his colleagues studied modifications Newman made at two public townhouse developments in New York City: Closen Point and Markham. Newman renovated the developments by: (a) providing more attractive, less institutional lighting; (b) adding fencing to create individual front yards and to create private backyards and semiprivate play areas; and (c) adding front curbing to create individual front yards and to create widened sidewalks for children's play.

Kohn et al. (1975) assessed these design renovations by using several before-and-after measures such as surveying residents to determine their attitudes toward the design and their perceptions of safety; observing residents' activities in public spaces; assessing vandalism and upkeep on the sites; and examining records showing location of crime. Although the findings were complex, after the renovations it was found that residents were more active in outside spaces and that generally the perception of safety improved. Crimes, and especially serious crimes, decreased in frequency and the peak crime period moved from evening to afternoon, suggesting that juveniles were responsible for many of the postrenovation crimes. However, at Closen Point, vandalism actually increased after renovation, yet some fragile features such as streetlights were not broken. At least in the Kohn et al. (1975) study, defensible space modifications increased use of the outdoors and perceptions of safety and seemed to reduce crime, but the findings were somewhat equivocal. In addition, it is difficult to separate the effects of greater pride caused by a more attractive environment from the subtler psychological effects predicted by Newman (e.g., a sense of proprietorship caused by symbolic markers).

In sum, some studies have shown that proximity and defensible space modifications reduce stress because they encourage social networks and hence reduce the asocial behavior that is linked to lack of a network. In addition, stress may be reduced as fear of crime is reduced. However, proximity seems to encourage networks only in situations where residents perceive neighbors to be similar to themselves. Furthermore, defensible space modifications may relieve fear of crime, but not crime itself. It remains for these two research questions to be combined within a single investigation.

Semipublic space: Impacts of activity nodes

A major component of day-to-day social interaction is casual, low-involvement social interaction. In personal contact, this may be the offhand comments that help maintain or establish friendships. In business, it may involve the communication of partially formed ideas. Although no quantitative analysis of these sorts of interactions has been made, their value and importance for the individual are well recognized (e.g., Goffman, 1959). It is becoming clear that one way environmental designs may produce stress in users is by making casual interactions difficult and personally costly.

Bechtel (1977) has suggested that informal contacts may be encouraged by activity nodes where people naturally come into contact with each other in the course of their daily activities. These spaces – often the building foyer or the area outside the washroom or drinking fountain – allow informal social contact and enable business and recreation to be carried on in a low-keyed, casual manner. In his studies of Alaskan army bases, Bechtel (1977) found that the residents' satisfaction with the base was at least partially dependent on the existence of an activity node. In a study of shared spaces in housing for the elderly, Howell, Epp, Reizenstein, and Albright (1976) found that the most used lounges frequently were on main circulation paths and near the entrance, and that more distant lounges were seldom used. The authors suggest that this occurred at least in part because the social commitment involved in the distant lounges was much greater. If, after seeing who was in a lounge, a resident did not want to interact, disengagement was easy in the lounges on circulation paths: A resident could simply pretend he or she was just passing by.

Bechtel (1977) proposed several principles distinguishing effective activity nodes: (a) They are centrally located and equally accessible to all persons in the community; (b) much traffic passes by them (this can be achieved by locating well-used and necessary functions nearby); (c) they have few visual boundaries, allowing people to see and be seen.

An important aspect of activity nodes is who the occupants can see. Archea (1977) suggested that people situate themselves in semipublic space as a function of how many other people they can see (their visual access) and how many people can see them (their visual exposure). Most people choose areas of high access and low exposure, such as the periphery of a room. However, people who are engaged in activities meant to be seen, such as public speaking, choose areas of high exposure. In Archea's terms, an effective activity node would be one that offered a wide range of access and exposure. Similarly, stress may result when the environment does not allow a user to fill his or her need for access or exposure.

Semiprivate space: Impacts of design on activity boundaries

The designed environment is important in creating boundaries between potentially conflicting activities. For example, outside walls and doors prevent unknown or undesirable people from entering our homes or offices, and interior walls and doors provide privacy and prevent conflicting activities from interfering with each other. However, when activities do overlap, and when mutually exclusive activities interfere with each other, stress may develop when important goals are thwarted. For example, behavior constraint investigations of crowding have found that such interference may result in negative affect, in heightened physiological stress, and in decreased task performance (Epstein, Chap. 5, this volume). Settings where many simultaneous activities occur are particularly conducive to stress of this sort. In hospitals, open schools, and open-plan offices, for example, the overlap may prevent the goals of participants from being met.

In a rehabilitation hospital, Le Compte and Willems (1970; cited in Bechtel, 1977) found that conflicting activities such as skill training and counseling were planned for a large open space. Boundaries between the activities were inadequate, however, and the activities interfered with each other. As a result, residents erected their own temporary walls to separate areas. Similar boundary-related problems were seen by Knight, Weitzer, and Zimring (1978) in their study of an institution for the developmentally disabled (also see Zimring, Weitzer, & Knight, in press). Prior to renovations, large dayhalls were expected to provide for multiple activities, including rough-and-tumble play, instruction, and quiet conversation. Because all of these activities occurred simultaneously, none were successfully undertaken, with the result that little play, little instruction, and little conversation occurred. After the institution was renovated and separate spaces were provided, these activities took place more frequently. A major reason for this was that the new design provided clear, distinct boundaries that allowed separation of activities.

Boundary control problems have also proved particularly difficult in open-plan schools (Evans & Lovell, 1979) and open-plan landscaped offices (see Wineman, Chap. 9, this volume). In both settings, the openness of the spaces has been touted as making them flexible and easy to change. However, user-oriented evaluations of both settings have shown that activities frequently overlap. For example, a science area may overlap with a reading area, play may interfere with quiet reading, and so on. The competing activities create overload and block goals of students and teachers (Evans & Lovell, 1979). In fact, this boundary control problem has seriously limited the growth of open-plan design in schools. In open-plan offices, there has been consistent dissatisfaction with the lack of auditory privacy. Office workers often sense they are being overheard and are particularly concerned with confidentiality (e.g., Wineman, Chap. 9, this volume).

Private space: Social impacts of floorplan design

Several studies have assessed the importance of the number of people occupying bedrooms in institutional settings, and of overall floorplan design. In general, these studies have found that when users are provided with well-defined private space, such as private rooms in institutions, the users tend to be more social and less withdrawn (Zimring et al., in press). Providing fully enclosed private space with lockable doors gives users a sense of control and allows them to hold intimate conversations; it also allows users to retreat when needed, and encourages residents to challenge unwanted intruders. Lack of private space encourages more aggressive boundary-control behaviors in public, as well as withdrawal to limit interaction.

Zimring and co-workers (Knight et al., 1978; Zimring et al., in press) studied staff and residents before and after interior institutional renovations. Before renovations, the state school was a traditional institutional style with large, barren, hard-surface dayhalls and sleeping wards. After renovations, the school provided several somewhat improved living arrangements including a suite-type design, with several two-to-four-person bedrooms surrounding a central lounge; a corridor design, with single and double bedrooms flanking double-loaded corridors; and modular units in which 4.5-ft. (1.36-m) partitions were used to separate the existing dayhalls and sleeping wards.

When comparing these new arrangements with the unrenovated condition, it was found that the suite and corridor designs – but not the modular design – had significant effects on the social behavior of residents. In the suite and corridor design, residents were less withdrawn, more alert, interacted more with other residents, and used their own space more. These changes were seen despite the very low functional ability of the residents. The corridor design had the largest impacts on residents' behavior, despite the fact that this design was viewed by architects and administrators as less homelike and more institutional than the suite design. Interviews and participant observation revealed that, despite its institutional appearance, the corridor design had the greatest impact because it allowed the residents the opportunity to control their social interaction and their ambient environment (light, heat, noise); residents could reduce or encourage social interactions and could regulate direct physical stressors.

Specifically, the corridor design offered effective individual mechanical controls and a clearly marked hierarchy of spaces. Each room had its own light switch that could be manipulated and a door that could be closed. In addition, single and double rooms opened onto a hallway separated by a fire door from the main activity core. This fire door helped define semiprivate space and helped insure that "ownership" of each area was clear. In contrast, the suite design, although more visually attractive, had rooms shared by two to four people that opened directly onto semipublic lounges, and activity in the lounges spilled over into the rooms. It was hard to limit interaction, to predict when one could sleep or awaken, or to engage in quiet activity. In sum, the corridor design helped reduce social stress because it gave a wider choice of spaces that were better defined as to ownership and that helped reduce direct, physical stress by means of improved mechanical controls.

A second research program examined similar designs in college dormitories. Baum and Valins (1977) examined several freshman dormitories at the State University of New York at Stony Brook and at Trinity College. At Stony Brook, freshmen were randomly assigned by the housing office to one of two different room arrangements: (a) rooms located on double-loaded corridors with 36 residents sharing a common lounge and bathroom; or (b) suites where six students shared a lounge and bathroom. Baum and Valins observed and interviewed the students living in the two types of dorm and had them participate in several experimental studies.

Despite having comparable floor area per person, residents felt more crowded and behaved differently in the experimental long-corridor settings than did the residents in suites. Specifically, when asked to place small figures in a scale model room until it "felt crowded," corridor residents placed fewer figures than did suite residents. When placed in a stressful situation (waiting for a dentist) corridor residents reacted more negatively to the presence of other people. When placed in a situation that allowed a choice between cooperation or competition, corridor residents chose competition, and suite residents chose cooperation. In a comparable study at Trinity College, Baum and Valins compared long and short corridors and found similar results (Baum & Valins, 1977).

Baum and Valins attributed the differences between the designs to the amount of control each offered. The suite and short-corridor arrangements provided semiprivate spaces (lounges and hallways) that served only a small number of people. In these, residents could better predict who they were going to encounter in lounges and semipublic space. Hence, the results obtained by Baum and Valins were similar to those of Knight et al. (1978) and Zimring et al. (in press): When the jurisdiction over space was clear, residents would actively adjust social interaction to fit their needs, and stress due to uncertainty and to inappropriate levels of interaction was reduced.

Several other studies have shown similar effects of room type. Proshansky, Ittleson, and Rivlin (1970) found that institutionalized psychiatric patients interacted more frequently when they were given private rooms. Holahan and Saegert (1973) found similar effects with developmentally disabled people. DeLong (1970) found comparable effects with geriatric patients. In an extensive study of prisons, Paulus et al. (1978) compared prisoners living in different facilities such as large, open dormitories, single cells, double cells, dormitories separated by partitions, and other living arrangements. Although the results are complex, prison records indicated that inmates living in dormitories and double cells generally exhibited more effects of stress than inmates in single cells, including increased disciplinary incidents, increased sick calls, increased complaints, and higher mortality rates among men over 45.

Links to stress

The design of the environment affects social interaction by making regulation of interaction easier or more difficult. Social interaction, or the lack of it, serves a variety of functions for the individual (cf. Altman, 1975). As a result, environments that make control of interaction difficult may have a range of consequences. For example, we use social interaction to ask others to quiet down, or for a range of services, to get us material items, food, safety, and so on. If there is no one to ask, or if awkwardness or unfamiliarity makes asking difficult, these important goals may be thwarted and psychological stress may result. Frustration of these needs also has specific physical costs independent of stress; for example, we may perform poorly if a competing task interferes with our work, or we may be tired if a noisy neighbor keeps us awake.

Social interaction also serves more fundamental instrumental psychological functions. Altman (1975) proposed that interaction occurs in part because it provides important information about oneself. Social-comparison theory (Festinger, 1954) and theories of privacy (e.g., Altman, 1975) suggest that people need to evaluate themselves, others, and situations and that the style and content of the interactions we have with others foster these comparisons. If a designed setting interacts with the social system to promote unpleasant, pathological interactions, such as in prisons, healthy self-evaluation becomes difficult. Even less drastic situations such as large, double-loaded corridors in college dormitories may generate serious problems for the occupants by making them less satisfied, more anxious, and less cooperative (e.g., Baum & Valins, 1977).

The designed environment may affect the dynamic regulation of the fit between what the individual needs and what the environment provides. Needs for interaction vary from person to person and from minute to minute. Although little research has examined individual differences in this area, several studies have found that personality characteristics such as arousal seeking (Mehrabian, 1977) may predict needs for interaction. In addition, some vulnerable or low-power groups have a poorer repertoire of coping skills because of their background or social role, and hence the environment may have stronger impacts on them. For example, the preceding discussion pointed to important environmental impacts for developmentally disabled people (Knight et al., 1978), college students (Baum & Valins, 1977), prisoners (Paulus et al., 1978), older people (De Long, 1970), and others.

If built environments are not to be stress inducing, they must allow participants to change their type and level of interaction to suit their needs. Also, the effectiveness of this process has implications for continued satisfaction of needs and hence the potential for creating the nonstress costs already described; for example, although we may at times enjoy loud music, when we want to go to sleep we may need to limit the interaction involved with a neighbor's noisy party to avoid being tired the next day.

The designed environment can also affect the individual's perception of personal control. Baron and Rodin (1978) have recently proposed that control is, in fact, a central concept mediating one's social experience and that problems of crowding and undue solitude can be considered failures of control. Although it is difficult to pick a single dominant concept, considerable evidence from a variety of research literatures indicates the importance of control (cf. Baron & Rodin, 1978; Seligman, 1975; Strickland, 1977). When an individual feels in control, he or she may be happier in general, may perform better, and may be less bothered by crowding and other stressors. The designed environment may provide the opportunity to control the social environment by providing a well-differentiated hierarchy of spaces that allows both choice over different spaces and control over interaction in a given space.

However, it may be hazardous to reify control. Some of the negative effects apparently due to lack of control may actually be due to the nonstress costs of unachieved specific goals rather than to deficiencies in control per se.

Implications for design

The relationship between stress and social interaction has several implications for the environmental designer. Environmental designs that increase the predictability of interactions make those interactions easier to control and hence reduce stress (Barnes, 1980; Sherrod & Cohen, 1978). Predictability may be increased in two ways. First, if the number of potential users of a space is reduced, it becomes easier to predict who will be encountered. Second, the design of a space may interact with the social system to make the outcome of interactions more predictable. For example, symbols of ownership may make a challenge to an intruder more potent. A private room in an institution may never need to be locked because it so clearly belongs to its occupant.

The designer can encourage both choice and overt physical control by providing hierarchies of space and by other mechanisms. This hierarchy can be established both symbolically, such as with paving changes, color changes, and so on, and less subtly, by providing doors, walls, and other physical barriers. Choice of marking depends on the situation. People with poor social skills or in a dire situation such as a prison, may require physical separations; more sophisticated people in a less dire situation, such as a restaurant, may need only symbolic markers. In the same vein, Evans (1979) reviewed research in human spatial behavior and found that crowding stress may be reduced by increasing room volume, decreasing brightness, and often, by providing partitions.

Overt physical control can be enhanced by providing mechanical controls for each space or user. Rather than having central controls for entire buildings or floors, users can manipulate their own heat, light, and so forth. Similarly, manipulatable spaces, in which users can move furniture, change wall coverings, and move partitions, allow users to mold the spaces to fit their instrumental needs and encourage a sense of ownership.

Environmental knowing: Wayfinding and spatial orientation

A second major way in which the designed environment may influence stress is by affecting wayfinding and spatial orientation. Every day, all of us must find our way to work, shopping, and recreation – to destinations in cities and to destinations in buildings. Our competence in finding our way may have instrumental consequences; if we miss an airplane or an important appointment, we may pay a monetary or personal penalty. However, the skill with which we find our way also has important psychological consequences. Increasing evidence suggests that we make important self-assessments based on our performance in wayfinding and spatial orientation (cf. Lynch, 1960; Weisman, 1979). This section will consider both anecdotal and systematic evidence of the costs of poor wayfinding and orientation skills and will examine several strategies for wayfinding and orientation. I then will devote somewhat more attention to the mediator between environmental form and wayfinding that has been most thoroughly studied: environmental cognition. Finally, links between environmental form and stress will be considered. For the purpose of this section, wayfinding will be defined as the actual behaviors people employ in finding important locations in the environment. Orientation is the ability to relate one's location to other features in the environment (i.e., to know one's location in relation to cardinal directions, or to home, to work, etc.).

According to a recent newspaper article, entitled "Travellers go crazy in big Dallas–Fort Worth Airport," incidents of psychiatric disturbance at that airport are increasing, and many of these are linked to spatial disorientation. For example, it was reported that a college professor with no previous psychiatric problems suddenly started gibbering mathematical equations and tearing off his clothes when he became lost (Kilday, 1979). The literature abounds with other anecdotal accounts of less dramatic, yet nonetheless important, impacts of becoming disoriented or lost in the designed environment. In an evaluation of Boston City Hall, for example, Berkeley (1973) asserts that both visitors and regular users frequently became disoriented, and goes on to suggest that it might "make people angry, hostile toward government" (p. 73). Similarly, in an evaluation of the Arts and Architectural Building at the University of Illinois Chicago Circle campus, it has been asserted that the circulation pattern "seriously upsets the orientation of everybody who uses the building.... The first reaction among people who pride themselves on their space perception is 'indignation'" (Dixon, 1968, p. 35).

The French Radio and Television Building in Paris provides a similar scenario (Sivadon, 1970). The building is designed on a circular plan that provides only limited visual access to one's destination. In addition, the building has no perpendicular axes to provide a frame of reference. Sivadon reports that even when he became lost purposely within the building, he was able to "recapture the anxiety of being lost" (p. 416). Other authors have reported that users were displeased and even panicked when they became lost in academic buildings (McKean, 1972), in subways (Bronzaft, Dobrow, & O'Hanlon, 1976), and in hospitals and psychiatric institutions (Izumi, 1970; Spivak, 1967). Lynch (1960) points out that, "the very word 'lost' in our language means more than simple geographical uncertainty; it carries overtones of utter disaster" (p. 4).

Some limited empirical work has supported these anecdotal accounts. In a study of blind pedestrians, Peake and Leonard (1971) compared relative heart rates of subjects orienting to simple and complex routes. They found that the heart rates of blind travelers were significantly elevated when negotiating complex routes in shopping areas. However, pilot data from a study by Zimring (1979) of blind travelers negotiating simple and complex routes within buildings did not support these results, perhaps because the complex route used in the Zimring experiment was less complicated than the Peak and Leonard route. However, blind travelers reported more anxiety on complex routes. In a study of wayfinding by sighted users in Manchester (England) City Hall, Best (1970) found that some 40% of participants became lost on a complex test route ("lost" was defined as significant "deviation from the most efficient route") and that a high percentage of users reported disorientation and discomfort. Similarly, in a study of academic buildings, Weisman (1979) found that in one setting, 25% of users were often or always lost.

A recent study by Wener and Kaminoff (1980) of directional signs in a federal prison lobby shows further links between disorientation and stress. The experimenters asked visitors to rate their stress on dimensions such as comfort, crowding, confusion, and anger. The experimenters added directional signs and again surveyed the users. They found that with the addition of the signs, the visitors reported significantly less stress on several dimensions, such as increased comfort, decreased crowding, less confusion, and less anger.

In addition to these short-term costs, there is some evidence that disorientation results in serious long-term problems. When a population of older people moves into new housing, the death rate temporarily soars, an effect apparently at least partially due to disorientation (Pastalan, 1973). An orientation program involving three visits to the new facility increased the chances that patients would survive the trauma of the move (Pastalan, 1973). An ongoing research program (Hunt, n.d., cited in Weisman, 1979) uses video and model buildings to familiarize residents with their new environments. Results are not yet available.

In exploring the role of the designed environment in wayfinding and orientation, it is useful to consider alternative behavioral strategies for wayfinding. Weisman (1979) argues that several increasingly complex strategies may be used. At the simplest level, a person may actually see his or her destination. In that case, no more complex mechanism needs to be used. At a somewhat more complex level, a person may follow a sequential path to his or her destination, moving from point to point. Although this strategy may work well, especially if the choice points are well marked, a sequential strategy lacks flexibility. The traveler knows only a particular route and lacks a holistic understanding of the environment; he or she may not be able to take shortcuts when necessary. Finally, a person may use an integrated mental representation of the environment. This representation, or "cognitive map," permits shortcuts and deviations from the route and may be expanded with additional information.

Research on cognitive representations

Much research has been devoted to understanding cognitive representations (for recent reviews see Evans, in press; Moore, 1979). Despite burgeoning research in environmental cognition, relatively little attention has been devoted to the important links between (a) environmental form and cognitive representations; (b) cognitive representations and actual wayfinding and orientation behaviors; and (c) environmental form, wayfinding, and orientation. The bulk of the research has been directed instead at understanding individual differences in the cognitive representation of settings. Nonetheless, it is useful to consider the available research on these three interrelationships.

Some of the early work in environmental cognition addressed the connections between environmental form and environmental representation. This has primarily taken place on an urban scale rather than within buildings. In a seminal work, Lynch (1960) used a variety of interview techniques to assess residents' representations of Jersey City, Boston, and Los Angeles. For example, he asked people to sketch maps of the cities on paper, to give verbal descriptions of routes they took, and to name prominent features of the cities. When he prepared composite maps, Lynch found that people tend to organize their cities in terms of five elements:

memorable *landmarks, paths* people follow, *nodes* where paths cross, distinct *edges* of neighborhoods or physical areas, and socially or physically defined *districts*. However, Lynch and many later investigators have found that cognitive representations are not literal cartographic representations (cf. Evans, in press). Rather, they are schematic and idiosyncratic images that are highly dependent on the individual's abilities, age, and experience. Lynch's work has been replicated in a wide range of cities, including, for example, Idaho Falls, New York, Ciudad Guyana and Paris. These studies have generally confirmed the importance of Lynch's five elements and have especially emphasized the importance of well-defined paths and distinctive landmarks (for a review, see Evans, 1980; Moore, 1979).

Recent work with simulations has also confirmed the importance of paths and landmarks. Tzamir (1975; cited in Evans, in press) manipulated a scale model to vary the similarity of path distances and the angle of path intersections. Confirming Lynch, it was found that regular, in contrast to irregular, models produced sketch maps with fewer distortions. Similarly, Zannaras (1976) asked subjects to trace routes on city maps and on models and had them rate the importance of environmental features for wayfinding. She found that the most preferred cues were traffic features and land use cues, such as the predominant building type. In field research, Devlin (1976) provided an interesting example of a city lacking in landmarks; she found that Idaho Falls was difficult to represent because of a paucity of distinctive features. Within buildings, several studies have confirmed the importance of landmarks for children's memory of their classroom layout (Acredolo, Pick, & Olsen, 1975; Siegel & Schadler, 1977).

In one of the few studies aimed at ascertaining the important characteristics of environmental features, Appleyard (1969) explored the factors that made buildings memorable landmarks and found that buildings were remembered because of two general aspects: (a) social concerns such as social–cultural significance and high use; and (b) physical characteristics such as relative height difference and visibility from roadways. Of these two aspects, the environmental qualities (i.e., distinctiveness of design and visibility) were relatively less important than the social–cultural qualities. Appleyard's findings have been replicated under experimental conditions (Pezdek & Evans, 1979).

Although little recent research has been concerned with the second link (between cognitive representation and wayfinding behavior), a recent study of wayfinding in buildings provides a tentative understanding of this relationship. Weisman (1979) had judges rate the legibility of abstract floorplans of academic buildings and found that these ratings were a good predictor of the building users' self-reported incidences of getting lost, suggesting that users become disoriented in buildings where the overall circulation pattern is confusing and hard to image. (Weisman, 1979, also provides a particularly clear discussion of the general issues involved in wayfinding in buildings.)

The final link – the direct link between environmental form and wayfinding – has also received only limited attention. On an urban scale, Lynch (1960) proposed that a city with appropriate physical elements (distinctive landmarks, paths, nodes, districts, and edges) will produce an accurate mental representation, and suggested that such a city will encourage effective wayfinding. As a consultant involved in the design of the new town, Cuidad Guyana, Appleyard (1976) used Lynch's elements and has found anecdotal evidence that wayfinding is facilitated. Also, wayfinding manuals for armed services personnel (Boring, 1945) and for scouts (Gatty, 1958) emphasize the importance of memorable landmarks.

At the building level, somewhat more has been accomplished. Weisman (1979) suggested that wayfinding in buildings is affected by four design elements: (a) perceptual access, which is the degree to which the user can actually see interim or ultimate destinations; (b) visual differentiation, which is the visual distinctiveness and personal and community significance of design features, and the congruence between distinctiveness and significance; (c) signs and "especially those that define next decisions" (p. 68); and (d) legibility, which is defined as "geometrical relationships that are more adequately perceived and remembered" (p. 69). Weisman found that users' self-reported wayfinding behavior was predicted by plan configuration and by one aspect of architectural differentiation. Evans, Fellows, Zorn, and Doty (1980) color coded an academic building. They found that with color coding, users actually found their way more effectively, could point more accurately to landmarks, and could better recognize and recall building floorplans.

Links between environment, representation, and wayfinding have special importance for the visually impaired. In terms of the strategies for wayfinding presented at the beginning of this section (direct visual access, sequential wayfinding, and cognitive mapping) the first and simplest is not available to the visually impaired; because they cannot see their destination, they must use more complex strategies as soon as their goal is beyond arm's length. Moreover, the psychological and personal costs of getting lost are high. The visually impaired do not have the multiple, visual information-gathering strategies that the sighted have to recover their orientation when they are lost. As a result, the visually impaired report great anxiety about becoming lost (Kidwell & Greer, 1973) and have shown elevated stress (Peake & Leonard, 1971).

Although the role of cognitive representations in wayfinding and orientation for the visually impaired has been recognized by rehabilitation specialists (e.g., Hill & Ponder, 1976), there has been little empirical research on the topic. In terms of the environment–representation link, Zimring (1979) found that routes in buildings that were more complex (defined as being composed of more route segments and forming an irregular pattern) were more difficult to represent using verbal descriptions and tactual maps. Casey (1978) found that his subjects tended to simplify the environment in their representations by straightening curved lines, for example. Despite the emphasis that rehabilitation programs place upon cognitive mapping, I am unaware of empirical studies that have linked representations to wayfinding behavior for the visually impaired.

Finally, there is one research paradigm that has linked environmental form to wayfinding: maze learning. A typical task is for a blind person to be led along two sides of a geometric figure, such as a triangle, and then be told to find the origin (e.g., Juurmaa, 1970). The data indicate that people who have experienced sight perform better than the congenitally blind when paths have a simple visual referent such as a right triangle. However, the congenitally blind may have an advantage with more complex amorphous figures (Juurmaa, 1970). In addition, interview studies with blind travelers have shown that in orienting in real environments, they use a very wide range of auditory, tactual, and olfactory landmarks, including, for example, traffic sounds, running water, pavement changes, and odors from cafeterias (Hill & Ponder, 1976; Zimring, 1979).

Links between environmental form and stress

Although most studies exploring cognitive representations have not explicitly considered stress, several studies (already reviewed in more depth) have linked poor wayfinding and disorientation to stress. For example, people lost in cities and buildings have shown considerable anxiety (e.g., Evans, 1980; Weisman, 1979). Similarly, when traversing complex routes, visually impaired people have shown both anxiety and physiological stress (Peake & Leonard, 1971; Zimring, 1979). Older people have shown a higher death rate when moved to a new setting; this rate has been reduced when they were oriented to the new setting prior to the move (Pastalan, 1973).

A clearer picture emerges if the various links between environmental form, wayfinding, and stress are merged. All other things equal, environmental forms that encourage acquisition of accurate cognitive representations (and hence effective wayfinding) reduce stress. Conversely, forms that discourage accurate representations increase stress.

The link between cognitive representation and stress is two-way. When cognitive representations are ineffective and wayfinding suffers, both nonstress instrumental costs and stresses may occur. Instrumental costs result when we cannot find an important building or office; we may miss a key meeting and suffer the consequences. Several examples of stress are presented in the beginning of this section; spatial orientation is a need for many people, and when this orientation is lost they become anxious and panicky.

However, stress also affects the formation of cognitive representations. Several studies have shown, for example, that while experiencing crowding stress, people are less able to form an accurate cognitive map of their environment (Langer & Saegert, 1977; Love & Saegert, 1978).

Implications for design

The research literature has offered some limited help to designers at two levels of environmental organization. At the general scale, several researchers have found that overall regularity contributes to cognitive representations and wayfinding (Evans, 1980; Weisman, 1979). However, theorists have cautioned that regular forms must be differentiated and have areas of special significance to be memorable (Evans et al., 1980; Moore, 1979). Also, several researchers have suggested that well-defined districts and neighborhoods aid orientation to cities (Evans, 1980), and architecturally differentiated subareas aid orientation to buildings (Weisman, 1979).

At the more specific level, the research suggests that landmarks should be clearly visible and distinctive in height, use of materials, color, or other physical characteristics (Appleyard, 1969; Weisman, 1979). For the visually impaired, and perhaps for sighted people as well, redundant use of cues is important (Zimring, 1979). For example, the warmth and light of an intense lamp may provide a partially sighted person with both a visual landmark and a heat landmark.

In addition, several studies suggest that environmental cues such as signs are helpful because they help organize the input of environmental information (Love & Saegert, 1978). Any environment has too much information to encode, and the information-processing capacity of a user can be expanded through organization (Neisser, 1976).

Much evidence also suggests that the social and cultural significance of landmarks cannot be ignored (Moore, 1979). Often-used places are likely to be remembered, as are places that have special meaning for the observer. These symbols can be deliberately manipulated by designers and, in fact, the current postmodern movement in architecture advocates a return to the conscious use of symbolism (Jencks, 1978).

Additional stressors

The scope of this chapter does not allow a full discussion of all sources of stress in the designed environment, but two additional areas deserve at least brief discussion: comfort and ergonomic fit, and aesthetics and symbolism.

Comfort and ergonomic fit

Considerable research has been devoted to studying the fit between the immediate physical setting and the tasks that must be accomplished within it. Much of this work has gone on in work settings where researchers are concerned with improving factory or office design to enhance worker satisfaction and productivity. The bulk of the work has been based on self-reports by workers, although illness complaints, absenteeism, and other measures also have been examined (see Wineman, Chap. 9, this volume, for a review of environmental stressors in office settings). A number of researchers have examined the relationship of work flow to physical organization. For example, Brookes and Kaplan (1972) found that office workers reported that poorly considered "adjacencies and layout" were major sources of dissatisfaction. In addition, other sources of discomfort in work settings include lighting that produces glare or is of an unusual color or inadequate intensity; lack of exterior view; poor air quality caused by inadequate ventilation; and high noise levels (Wineman, Chap. 9, this volume).

The introduction of new technologies has also produced stress-related problems. For example, recent research has documented a number of problems among video display terminal operators. A combination of poor physical designs, such as inadequate lighting and flickering displays, and high-pressure, rigid job conditions contributes to a number of stress symptoms such as high incidence of occupational cervicobrachial syndrome, eyestrain, anxiety, depression, and fatigue (Wineman, Chap. 9, this volume).

Physical comfort and ergonomic fit have also been studied in settings other than workplaces, although this approach is much less common in other settings. For example, in their review of school settings, Ahrentzen and her colleagues (Ahrentzen, Jue, Skorpanich, & Evans, Chap. 8, this volume) report that there has been little research on the impacts of lighting, heat, or noise in school settings. The research that has been accomplished suggests that these dimensions have little effect on task performance, yet probably do affect comfort. A possible explanation for the apparent lack of effect on task performance is that most researchers have chosen simple tasks such as arithmetic or proofreading. Laboratory studies with adults have often found effects of stressors only on complex conceptual tasks. Moreover, laboratory research with adults and some school setting studies have discovered effects of stressors only after the stress experience has ended, suggesting that participants may be able to adequately cope with high noise, poor lighting, or heat during exposure but that such coping results in fatigue and an eventual decrease in task performance.

The effort to make designed settings accessible to the physically disabled is also an effort to produce a good fit between the environment and the requirements of a task. It is stressful if a person confined to a wheelchair tries to travel and is thwarted by steps or curbs; the traveler must cope by changing the route, bringing an able-bodied helper, or giving up entirely. In an interview and observational study of an apartment complex for quadriplegic adults, Reizenstein and Ostrander (in press) found that many of the residents' problems and satisfactions rested with the "details" of their apartment design: whether countertops were an appropriate height for use by those in a wheelchair, whether adequate call-buttons were provided for emergencies, whether stoves could be used by people with limited strength and dexterity, and so on. An apparent hierarchy of needs operated with this group: When daily tasks of eating, sleeping, and toileting were adequately supported, residents then could be concerned with aesthetics.

In summary, research in designed settings of physical comfort and ergonomic fit is still at a rudimentary stage. Because studies rely primarily on self-report, few unequivocal statements about stress and inadequate ergonomic parameters can be made. Some specific situations, such as the use of poorly designed video display terminals, clearly lead to stress, but in general there have been conflicting findings about the effects of moderate levels of stressors. In an effort to resolve this confusion, several researchers have begun to examine more specific aspects of person–environment fit, such as individual differences (Ahrentzen et al., Chap. 8, this volume) and specific requirements of particular jobs (Wineman, Chap. 9, this volume).

Aesthetics and symbolism

A few researchers have recently speculated on the relationship of aesthetics and symbolism to stress. Although there can be little argument that these aspects of the design of the environment are important, little evidence has so far accrued about their impacts on stress. Nonetheless, some intriguing possibilities have emerged.

In a review of research on stress to patients in medical settings, Shumaker and Reizenstein (Chap. 7, this volume) suggest that hospitals intentionally or unintentionally provide patients a large number of symbols about their role vis-à-vis the doctors, about the sterility and lack of hominess of the setting, about the quality of the hospital in comparison with other hospitals, and so on. This could evoke stress, with the outcomes dependent on mediating variables such as the patients' perceived or actual control in a situation and their past experiences with hospitals.

In an ongoing series of studies attempting to link housing designs with crime rates, Newman (1973, 1975, 1981) proposes that the image housing provides (in his terms "symbolic identification") strongly influences the pride of residents and their subsequent caretaking of the property. According to Newman, public housing is particularly susceptible to poor symbolic identification; poorly designed, low-cost construction may label residents as poor and worthless and may draw vandals to the site, whereas better construction may produce proprietary activities and better self-image. Positive physical symbols Newman discusses include windows with frames, individual front yards, individual (as opposed to uniform) building facades, and attractive lighting systems. (See Taylor, Chap. 10, this volume, for a fuller discussion of the relationship of crime to building and neighborhood design.)

The research on symbolism is at best suggestive and intriguing and supports a need for careful, expanded and more rigorous investigations. This research comes at a propitious time in the history of architecture. For the past 50 years, modern architecture has been dominated by the "less is more" philosophy of architects such as Mies Van der Rohe and other followers of the Bauhaus school of design; sleek glass-walled examples of their design can be seen in the downtown skyscrapers of every major city. The design of these buildings attempted to purify and simplify the structures and to eschew symbols. (Although, of course, these massive structures were consciously symbolic of corporate wealth and power.) Recently, however, "post-modern" architects have consciously incorporated symbols under the banner "less is a bore" (Jencks, 1978). The current deliberate use of symbols by architects makes the study of aesthetics and symbolism particularly relevant.

Methodological issues

Although studies of stress and the designed environment are increasing in both quality and frequency, they are still affected by serious methodological problems. These can be considered in two general categories: sampling and research design, and conceptualization of independent and dependent measures.

Sampling and research design

The nature of research on designed environments requires that investigations be concerned with a wide range of sampling issues. As with all behavioral research, sampling of subjects is a critical issue. In this regard, designed-environment research often has more in common with program evaluation than with experimental social science. Like program evaluation, much designed-environment research takes place in field settings where the researcher has relatively little control and often may not be able to randomly assign participants to settings or to randomly choose participants for the study. For example, studies of the impact of design on crime are frequently contaminated because building users have selected their setting. In such situations it becomes difficult to separate the effects of the environment from the effects of self-selection (Taylor, Chap. 10, this volume). A few studies have used quasi-experimental designs with nonrandom comparison groups, but such efforts are rare (see Ahrentzen, Chap. 8, this volume, for a discussion of the use of comparison groups in school-setting research and Cook & Campbell, 1979, for an in-depth review of quasi-experimental designs).

Sampling of *settings* is also critical in this research area. For example, with some exceptions, studies of hospitals have focused on one or a few hospitals (Shumaker & Reizenstein, Chap. 7, this volume); studies of offices concentrate on one or a few offices (Wineman, Chap. 9, this volume); and studies of schools have examined a similarly small number (Ahrentzen et al., Chap. 8, this volume). When studying a built environment the setting itself often becomes the unit of analysis; a study of stress in a single setting effectively becomes a study with a sample of one. Taylor (Chap. 10, this volume) suggests that this sampling issue may be even more critical with neighborhood-scale research; a study of 10 neighborhoods with 100 subjects in each neighborhood actually has an sample size of 10 rather than 1,000 if the neighborhood is the appropriate level of analysis.

Sampling of *historical time* is also critical. A number of recent researchers have adopted an open-systems approach similar to the person–environment fit model proposed in this chapter (e.g., Ahrentzen et al., Chap. 8, this volume; Shumaker & Reizenstein, Chap. 7, this volume; Wineman, Chap. 9, this volume). This approach suggests that the individual interacting with the environment can be conceived of as an open system that is affected by past experience, situational factors, individual needs, and so on. Such an approach allows greater specificity in understanding stress effects in that it explicitly labels variability that would have been lumped into the error term in a more normative approach. However, the open-systems approach requires a view of person–environment fit that is very changeable. Because the system is affected by so many factors, it will change as individuals and organizations change. For example, personal control has been shown to be an important mediator in many settings and concurrently is an important concept in popular society: Books on assertiveness and personal control dominate the best-seller lists. The importance of personal control in mediating stress may diminish as society changes. Few studies of stress have spanned historical time, and hence we have been unable to discover the impact of historical processes on stress.

In fact, few longitudinal stress studies of any time span have been attempted. Even if one ignores historical change, it is difficult to ignore the shorter-term temporal changes in a setting: seasonal cycles, daily cycles, and so on. Most stress studies have been cross sectional, examining a setting over a very short time period.

Conceptualization of independent and dependent measures

A persistent problem with stress studies is that relevant independent variables are poorly conceptualized. For example, in their discussion of school settings Ahrentzen et al. (Chap. 8, this volume) point out that that studies of open-plan schools have been particularly plagued by this problem. "Open-plan" schools have often been contrasted with "traditional" schools without carefully considering the differences between the two styles. Open-plan schools are usually physically open but may also have an "open" teaching philosophy. Also, open-plan schools vary on their degree of openness of either type. Recent efforts have been made to develop "openness scales" (Ahrentzen et al., Chap. 8, this volume). Similar problems exist in other settings: In office research, for example, similar vagueness affects comparisons of landscaped and traditional offices (Wineman, Chap. 9, this volume). In terms of dependent measures, the literature has depended heavily on self-reports of satisfaction and stress rather than on direct observation or other behavioral measures. Although some studies have noted the impacts of designed environments on "hard" measures such as inmate death rates (e.g., Paulus et al., 1978), most have relied on survey results of satisfaction with settings such as neighborhoods (e.g., Taylor, Chap. 10, this volume) or offices (Wineman, Chap. 9, this volume).

Many of these problems stem from a common problem: lack of theory. Because the origins of much of this work have been in applied disciplines such as planning, architecture, and industrial psychology, an atheoretical tradition has developed. Broadly defined qualities of environments, such as whether offices are open-plan or traditional, are linked to broadly de-fined stress measures such as questionnaire assessments of satisfaction with the workplace. However, no well-defined links have been proposed. One important role of theory is to specify the linkages between independent and dependent variables. The person–environment fit model presented earlier in this chapter begins to suggest some of these linkages. For exam-ple, it would suggest generally that open-plan offices may be stressful because they do not allow the setting to be adjusted to fit the workers' changing needs for privacy and that offices that do allow this adjustment would be less stressful. In a specific office, an examination of available coping strategies and individual needs should allow more specific predic-tions about stress responses. A few other theories, such as Archea's theory of access and exposure (Archea, 1978), propose specific, measurable as-pects of the designed environment that can be linked to specific behaviors. (For example, Archea proposes that most people in a public space will spend time where they can easily see other people yet where others ob-serve them less easily, such as around the periphery of a room.) Nonethe-less, theory is poorly developed in designed environment research.

Directions for future research

There is a notable lack of empirical research focusing on the behavioral effects of the designed environment (cf. Stokols, 1978). The present review has identified topics that warrant priority research planning.

The role of the designed environment in the regulation of social interaction

Several tentative relationships have been proposed in the present chapter, but there are few empirical studies, and even these have rarely used quasi-experimental, much less experimental, research designs. Much more re-search is needed using differences in environmental designs as independent variables. It would be useful to understand what design-related coping strategies people use to regulate interactions, in various settings such as homes, prisons, offices, and public spaces, and to understand how these strategies relate to the social organization of the setting. Similarly, research on particular strategies used to regulate social interaction by different subcultural groups (e.g., Blacks, Hispanics, the wealthy, the poor) would be useful.

The role of the physical environment in cognitive mapping, wayfinding, and orientation

Although little research has carefully explored these links, several lines of inquiry deserve attention. For example, in a setting that is changed naturally or experimentally, what changes occur in environmental representations and in processes of acquiring representations? Or, if representations are altered through training or other manipulations, what effects are seen on actual wayfinding and orientation behaviors? Or, if the environment is changed, what changes result in the process of wayfinding and spatial orientation? Most studies have used self-reports of wayfinding. Studies using observations of behavior are crucial. In addition, the hypothesized elements of cognitive maps need to be further explored. For example, what are the critical physical elements of landmarks, paths, nodes, districts, edges? Important methodological issues also need to be resolved: Do various measures of cognitive representations (e.g., sketch maps, interviews, photograph recall) tap the same underlying structure? What are the levels of reliability and validity of these measures?

The role of stress in the relation between cognitive representations and environmental form

Only a few studies have explicitly linked cognitive representations and stress. Many questions still need to be resolved. For example, what stresses or instrumental costs in fact occur with different environmental forms (e.g., with an "imagible" or "unimagible" environment)? And how does elevated stress affect cognitive representations (cf. Langer & Saegert, 1977)? Research on these and related questions is vital to our understanding of how features of the designed environment both affect and are affected by stress.

The role of individual differences in predicting the stress effects of design

Although research has shown that vulnerable groups such as the elderly and institutionalized populations are sensitive to design dysfunction, the importance of other individual difference factors (e.g., age, income level, cultural group) in predicting impacts of design is unclear.

References

Acredolo, L.P., Pick, H.L., & Olsen, M. Environmental differentiation and familiarity as determinants of children's memory for spatial location. *Developmental Psychology*, 1975, *11*, 495–501.

Altman, I. *The environment and social behavior*, Monterey, Calif.: Brooks/Cole, 1975.

Andelman, D.L. 10 reported killed after inmates seize New Mexico prison. *The New York Times*, February 3, 1980, *CXXIX* (44,482), 1, 19.

Appleyard, D.A. Why buildings are known. *Environment and Behavior*, 1969, *1*, 131–156.

Appleyard, D.A. *Planning a pluralist city: Conflicting realities in Ciudad Guyana*. Cambridge, Mass.: MIT Press, 1976

Archea, J. The place of architectural factors in behavioral theories of privacy. *Journal of Social Issues*, 1977, *33*, 116–138.

Barnes, R.D. Perceived freedom and control and the built environment. In J. Harvey (Ed.), *Cognition, social behavior and the designed environment*. Hillsdale, N.J.: Erlbaum, 1980.

Baron, R., & Rodin, J. Personal control as a mediator of crowding. In A. Baum, J.E. Singer, & S. Valins (Eds.), *Advances in environmental psychology (Vol. 1): The urban environment*. Hillsdale, N.J.: Erlbaum, 1978.

Baum, A., & Valins, S. *Architecture and social behavior: Psychological studies of social density*. Hillsdale, N.J.: Erlbaum, 1977.

Berkeley, E.P. More than you want to know about the Boston City Hall. *Architecture Plus*, 1973, February, 72–77.

Best, G.A. Direction-finding in large buildings. In D. Canter (Ed.), *Architectural Psychology*. London: RIBA Publications, 1970.

Bechtel, R. *Enclosing behavior*. Stroudsburg, Pa.: Dowden, Hutchinson & Ross, 1977.

Boring, E.G. (Ed.), *Psychology for the armed services*. Washington, D.C.: Infantry Journal, 1945.

Bronzaft, A., Dobrow, S., & O'Hanlon, T. Spatial orientation in a subway system. *Environment and Behavior*, 1976, *8*, 575–594.

Brooks, M., & Kaplan, A. Office environments: Space planning and effective behavior. *Human Factors*, 1972, *14*, 373–391.

Casey, S.M. Cognitive mapping by the blind. *Journal of Visual Impairment and Blindness*, 1978, October, 297–301.

Cook, T., & Campbell, D. Quasi-experimentation: Design and analysis for field settings. Skokie, Ill.: Rand McNally, 1979.

Craik, K., & Zube, E.H. *Perceived environmental quality indicators*. New York: Plenum, 1976.

DeLong, A. The micro-spatial structure of the older person: Some implications of planning the social and spatial environment. In L.A. Pastalan & D.H. Carson (Eds.), *Spatial behavior of older people*. Ann Arbor, Mich.: University of Michigan Press, 1970.

Devlin, A. The "small town" cognitive map: Adjusting to a new environment. In G. Moore & R. Goledge (Eds.), *Environmental knowing: Theories, research and methods*. Stroudsburg, Pa.: Dowden, Hutchinson & Ross, 1976.

Dixon, J.M. Campus city revisited. *Architectural Forum*, 1968, *129*, 28–43.

Evans, G.W. Design implications of spatial research. In J. Aiello & A. Baum (Eds.), *Residential crowding and design*. Hillsdale, N.J.: Erlbaum, 1979.

Evans, G.W. Environmental cognition. *Psychological Bulletin*, 1980, *88*, 259–287.

Evans, G.W., Fellows, J., Zorn, M., & Doty, K. Cognitive mapping and architecture. *Journal of Applied Psychology*, 1980, *65*, 474–478.

Evans, G.W., & Lovell, B. Design modifications in an open-plan school. *Journal of Educational Psychology*, 1979, *71*, 41–49.

Festinger, L. A. A theory of social comparison processes. *Human Relations*, 1954, *7*, 117–140.

Festinger, L., Schacter, S., & Back, K. *Social pressures in informal groups*. Stanford, Calif.: Stanford University Press, 1950.

Gatty, H. *Nature is your guide: How to find your way on land and sea*. New York: Dutton, 1958.

Glass, D.C. *Behavior patterns, stress, and coronary disease*. Hillsdale, N.J.: LEA, 1976.

Goffman, E. *Presentation of self in everyday life*. New York: Doubleday, 1959.

Hill, E., & Ponder, P. *Orientation and mobility techniques*. New York: American Foundation for the Blind, 1976.

Hillier, W. In defense of space. *Royal Institute of British Architects Journal*, 1973, November, 539–544.

Holahan, C.J., & Saegert, S. Behavioral and attitudinal effects of large-scale variation in the physical environment of psychiatric wards. *Journal of Abnormal Psychology*, 1973, *82*, 459–462.

Howell, S., Epp, G., Reizenstein, J.E., & Albright, C. *Shared spaces in housing for the elderly*. Boston: MIT Department of Architecture, 1976.

Izumi, K. Psychosocial phenomena and building design. In H. Proshansky, W. Ittleson, & L. Rivlin (Eds.), *Environmental psychology: Man and his physical setting*. New York: Holt, Rinehart and Winston, 1970.

Jencks, C. *The language of post-modern architecture*. New York: McGraw-Hill, 1978.

Juurmaa, J. On the accuracy of obstacle detection by the blind. *New Outlook for the Blind*, 1970, *64*, 378–391.

Kidwell, A.M., & Greer, P.S. *Sites perception and the nonvisual experience: Designing and manufacturing mobility maps*. New York: American Foundation for the Blind, 1973.

Kilday, P. Travellers go crazy in big Dallas-Forth Worth airport. *Associated Press News Service*, July 8, 1979.

Knight, R.C., Weitzer, W.H., & Zimring, C.M. *Opportunity for control and the built environment: The ELEMR Project*. Amherst, Mass.: University of Massachusetts, Environmental Institute, 1978.

Knight, R.C., Zimring, C.M., & Kent, M.J. Normalization as a social-physical system. In M.J. Bednar (Ed.), *Barrier-free environments*. Stroudsburg, Pa.: Dowden, Hutchinson, & Ross, 1977.

Kobasa, S.C. Stressful life events, personality, and health: An inquiry into hardness. *Journal of Personality and Social Psychology*, 1978, *37*, 1–11.

Kohn, I., Franck, K., & Fox, A.S. *Defensible space modifications in rowhouse communities*. National Science Foundation Report, 1975.

Langer, E., & Saegert, S. Crowding and cognitive control. *Journal of Personality and Social Psychology*, 1977, *35*, 175–182.

Lawton, M. P. *Environment and aging*. Monterey, Calif.: Brooks/Cole, 1980.

Love, K. D. & Saegert, S. *Crowding and cognitive limits: Capacity or strategy?* Paper presented at the Annual Convention of the American Psychological Association, Toronto, August 1978.

Lynch, K. *The image of the city*. Cambridge, Mass.: MIT Press, 1960.

McKean, J. University of Essex: Case study. *Architects Journal*, 1972, *156*, 645–667.

Mehrabian, A. A questionnaire measure of individual differences in stimulus screening and associated differences in arousability. *Environmental Psychology and Nonverbal Behavior*, 1977, *1*, 89–103.

Michelson, W. *Man and his urban environment*. Reading, Mass.: Addison-Wesley, 1976.

Moore, G.T. Knowing about environmental knowing: The current state of theory and research on environmental cognition. *Environment and Behavior*, 1979, *11*, 33–70.

Neisser, U. *Cognition and reality*. San Francisco: W. H. Freeman, 1976.

Newman, O. *Defensible space*. New York: Macmillan, 1973.

Newman, O. *Design guidelines for creating defensible space*. Washington, D.C.: U.S. Government Printing Office, 1975.

Newman, O. *Community of interest*. New York: Anchor Books, 1981.

Pastalan, L. Involuntary environmental location: Death and survival. In W.F.E. Preiser (Ed.), *Environmental design research* (Vol. 2). Stroudsburg, Pa.: Dowden, Hutchinson & Ross, 1973.

Patterson, A.H. Methodological developments in environment-behavior research. In D. Stokols (Ed.), *Perspectives on environment and behavior: Theory, research, and applications*. New York: Plenum, 1977.

Paulus, P.B., McCain, G., & Cox, V.C. Death rates, psychiatric commitments, blood pressure and perceived crowding as a function of institutional crowding. *Environmental Psychology and Nonverbal Behavior*, 1978, *3*, 107–116.

Peake, P., & Leonard, J.A. The use of heart rate as an index of stress in blind pedestrians. *Ergonomics*, 1971, *14*, 189–204.

Pezdek, K., & Evans, G.W. Visual and verbal memory for objects and their spatial location. *Journal of Experimental Psychology: Human Learning and Memory*, 1979, *5*, 360–373.

Proshansky, H.M., Ittleson, W.H., & Rivlin, L.G. Freedom of choice and behavior in a physical setting. In H.M. Proshansky, W.H. Ittleson, & L.G. Rivlin (Eds.), *Environmental psychology: People and their physical settings*. New York: Holt, Rinehart and Winston, 1970.

Rainwater, L. Fear and the house-as-haven in the lower class. In R. Gutman (Ed.), *People and buildings*. New York: Basic Books, 1972.

Reizenstein, J. E. Personal communication, March 6, 1980.

Reizenstein, J. E., and Ostrander, E. Design for independence: A condensed post-occupancy evaluation of housing for the severely disabled. *Environment and Behavior*, in press.

Roscow, I. *Social integration of the aged*. New York: Free Press, 1967.

Saegert, S. High-density environments: Their personal and social consequences. In A. Baum & Y. Epstein (Eds.), *Human responses to crowding*. Hillsdale, N.J.: Erlbaum, 1977.

Seligman, M. *Helplessness: On depression, development and death*. San Francisco: Freeman, 1975.

Sherrod, D., & Cohen, S. Density, personal control and design. In S. Kaplan & R. Kaplan (Eds.), *Humanscapes: Environments for people*. North Scituate, Mass.: Duxbury, 1978.

Siegel, A.W., & Schadler, M. Young children's cognitive maps of their classroom. *Child Development*, 1977, *48*, 388–394.

Sivadon, P. Space as experienced: Therapeutic implications. In H. Proshansky, W. Ittleson, & L. Rivlin (Eds.), *Environmental psychology*. New York: Holt, Rinehart and Winston, 1970.

Spivak, M. Sensory distortions in tunnels and corridors. *Hospital and Community Psychiatry*, 1967, *18*, 24–30.

Stokols, D. Environmental psychology. *Annual Review of Psychology*, 1978, *29*, 253–295.

Strickland, B.R. Internal-external control of reinforcement. In T. Blass (Ed.), *Personality and social behaviors*. Hillsdale, N.J.: Erlbaum, 1977.

Tomeh, A. K. Empirical considerations on the problem of social integration. *Sociological Inquiry*, 1969, *39*, 65–76.

Tzamir, Y. The impact of spatial regularity and irregularity on cognitive mapping. *Technical report, center for urban and regional studies*. Technion-Israel Institute of Technology, Haifa, Israel, 1975.

Weisman, G. *A study in architectural legibility*. Unpublished doctoral dissertation, University of Michigan, 1979.

Wener, R. E. & Kaminoff, R. D. *Improving environmental information: Effects of signs on perceived crowding and behavior*. Submitted for publication, 1980.

Zannaras, G. The relation between cognitive structure and urban form. In G. T. Moore & R. G. Golledge (Eds.), *Environmental knowing*. Stroudsburg, Pa.: Dowden, Hutchinson & Ross, 1976.

Zeisel, J., & Griffin, M. *Charlesview housing: A diagnostic evaluation*. Cambridge, Mass.: Architectural Research Office, Graduate School of Design, Harvard University, 1975.

Zimring, C. M. *Cognitive mapping and the blind*. Paper presented in Workshop on Cognitive Mapping and the Built Environment. Environmental Design Research Association Annual Meeting, Buffalo, N.Y., May 1979.

Zimring, C. M., Weitzer, W., & Knight, R.C. Opportunity for control and the designed environment: The case of an institution for the developmentally disabled. In A. Baum & J. Singer (Eds.), *Advances in environmental psychology* (Vol. 4). Hillsdale, N.J.: LEA, in press.

7. Environmental factors affecting inpatient stress in acute care hospitals

Sally Ann Shumaker
and Janet E. Reizenstein

In 1821, there were only three general hospitals in the United States (Vogel, 1980). Hospitalization was rare and, for the most part, medical care was the family's responsibility. Although individuals might be diagnosed in the strange surroundings of a physician's office, their actual treatment and convalescence took place within the familiar environment of their own homes, with family members temporarily adopting the roles of nurses and caretakers.

In less than 100 years, however, this profile of health care changed dramatically. Control over the spread of infectious diseases within hospitals, the development of comprehensive health insurance plans, and the emerging view of medicine as a science combined to bring about the rapid evolution of the modern general hospital. By 1920, there were over 6,000 hospitals in the United States (Vogel, 1980). Technological advances in the treatment of diseases, coupled with increasing specialization among physicians, fostered the continued growth of hospitals and hospitalization, so that in the year 1977, 37 million patients were admitted to over 7,000 hospitals in this country (Taylor, 1979).

Of all health-care workers in the United States, 65% are employed in hospitals (Knowles, 1979), and hospitals remain the fastest growing component of the health care system (Anderson & Anderson, 1979). In spite of a current trend toward outpatient care (cf. American Hospital Association, 1979), "hospitals are now a common and normal aspect of the management of many different health conditions" (Taylor, 1979, p. 157), and many

A portion of Sally Ann Shumaker's work on the chapter was prepared while she was supported by an NIMH grant on Social and Personality Factors in Health awarded to the Department of Psychology at the University of California, Los Angeles. The authors would like to thank the following people for their comments on earlier drafts on the chapter: Irwin Altman, Arlene Brownell, Gary Evans, Myron Grant, Philip Hammond, Richard Olsen, Ronald Peterson, Daniel Stokols, Ralph Taylor, Polly Welch, and John Zeisel.

people in the United States are hospitalized at least once during their lives.

In 1963, Sommer and DeWar wrote a short descriptive paper on the possible effects a hospital's physical environment may have on patients, identifying environmental attributes that potentially inhibit patient recovery. In summing up, however, they state that there is a severe "lack of studies showing how the physical environment of the hospital affects the condition of the patient" (Sommer & DeWar, 1963, p. 339).

Since 1963, a number of excellent articles and books have appeared in which the effects of the *social* environment on both hospitalized and nonhospitalized sick people are examined (Krantz, Glass, Contrada, & Miller, 1981; Moos, 1977; Stone, Cohen, & Adler, 1979; Taylor, 1979; Wortman & Dunkel-Shetter, 1979). Few researchers in this area, however, consider the effects of the *physical* environment, or the joint effects of the physical and social environments, on patients. The architectural literature on human behavior and hospital design is similarly limited to nonempirical and descriptive "show and tell" articles (Reizenstein, 1981).

Because the theoretical and empirical literature that is directly relevant to the hospital environment and inpatient stress is so limited, for this chapter we rely on research that is only tangentially related to the topic, or in some cases, on no research at all. That is, based on research conducted in nonhospital settings on nonpatient populations, we present probable relationships between the hospital's physical environment and patient stress. We view this chapter, therefore, as a kind of "research prospectus." By generating a number of hypotheses we hope to reopen the door to the issues that Sommer and DeWar first discussed in 1963, and encourage others to recognize the potential impact of the physical environment on the health and well-being of patients, as well as the potential of this environment to facilitate, rather than inhibit, recovery.

Although we recognize that hospital environments can be stressful for *all* user groups, we limit our discussion to *patients*, because their being ill and their high dependency on others and lack of familiarity with the medical environment make them the *most* vulnerable user group in hospitals (Lipowski, 1970; Moos, 1979; Sommer & DeWar, 1963). Also, they are the user group that has received the least attention in terms of the impact of the hospital environment on their health and well-being.

We further limit our presentation to acute care medical settings. Research on the effects of the environment in medical settings has dealt primarily with patients in nonacute care settings, such as psychiatric hospitals (Goffman, 1961; Good & Hurtig, 1978). This emphasis of research on nonacute care hospitals probably stems from recognition by psychiatrists of the sociophysical environment as a potentially "therapeutic milieu"; the long stay of patients in psychiatric hospitals, allowing for the study of environmental effects over time; and the limited control that psychiatric patients have over what happens to them (Reizenstein, 1981). We emphasize acute care settings because they are important environments in which many people spend time at some point in their lives.

Our emphasis is on the way that patients' transactions (Stokols & Shumaker, 1981; Stokols, 1979) with the hospital environment can influence the amount of stress in their lives, and thwart or enhance their ability to cope effectively with the stress. In order to understand the multiple sources of stress that impinge on hospitalized patients as well as the potential for design interventions, it is helpful to have some general understanding of the "typical" hospital setting. Therefore, we begin with a brief description of the hospital milieu. We discuss the organization of hospitals and the image of the hospital patient and patient role. We also describe the physical settings that patients use in a "typical" general hospital, the design priorities for different user groups, and how decisions concerning design are made.

We then present a model of stress and coping that emphasizes the effects of the physical environment on people, and we apply this model to the hospitalized patient, considering the multiple sources of stress that affect acute care patients at the time of their entry into hospitals. We examine how their being under stress might influence their *wayfinding* ability, *physical comfort*, and perceptions of *control* in terms of privacy and personal territory within the hospital setting. In addition, we discuss the *symbolic meaning* of the hospital environment and include suggestions for design interventions that could foster better coping and less stress for patients.

The hospital milieu

Hospital organization

In general, hospitals can be stressful environments for everyone who uses them, due, in part, to the nature of the organization. That is, a short-term general hospital[1] is a large, complex setting in which the major function is to provide services to a patient population with diverse needs. Within most hospitals the division of labor is extensive and is coupled with a high degree of interdependence among staff members; no individual can work independently of another in a hospital environment (Georgopoulos & Mann, 1979).

In order to meet patient needs efficiently within this system of high employee interdependency, most hospitals have evolved into very traditional and formal organizations. The management structure of general hospitals usually involves three separate lines of authority in which no individual portion of the system exercises ultimate authority. Internally, hospitals

---

[1] Short-term general hospitals are defined as ones in which more than 50% of the patients remain for less than 30 days. Such hospitals represent the modal type of medical care center in the United States (VerSteeg & Croog, 1979).

have a parallel power structure made up of administrators trained in hospital management, and physicians. Both groups exercise their power throughout the hospital system (Georgopoulos & Mann, 1979; VerSteeg & Croog, 1979). Externally, the administration of general hospitals is influenced by the communities in which they exist. In recent years, outside agencies and laypeople, representing the needs and wishes of their constituencies within a community, are increasing their control over hospital functions (American Hospital Association, 1979; VerSteeg & Croog, 1979).

Status differences among hospital employees are rigidly maintained and strictly hierarchical (Georgopoulos & Mann, 1979; VerSteeg & Croog, 1979). There are several "discrete occupational groups" within hospitals, each representing different levels within the hierarchy and each maintaining separate values and associations. Job mobility, as well as informal communication across groups, is difficult (Ver Steeg & Croog, 1979). Channels of communication among occupation groups are formal and usually flow downward. Physicians and nurses, who hold two of the most important roles in relation to the hospitalized patient, exemplify the status differences and independence of occupation groups within the hospital.

Physicians hold one of the highest status roles in American society (Mechanic, 1979) and within hospitals, where they form one component of the triadic system of management, they have a great deal of authority and power. In sharp contrast, the status of nurses is much lower than that of physicians,[2] both within and external to the hospital (Reeder & Mauksch, 1979).

Generally, the complex management structure and formalized status differences within general hospitals facilitate good patient care. The triadic system of management is designed to assure that patient needs are well represented and understood through the involvement of outside agencies and physicians, while the organization is operated efficiently by people who are trained in administration. The status hierarchy and formalized system of roles and communication facilitate the kind of precision necessary when a number of people occupy distinct roles and must work together smoothly and efficiently. For example, in a complicated surgical procedure or a crisis in an intensive care unit, the smooth orchestration of the functions among hospital personnel is of paramount importance. With a formal system of rules and authority, there is no ambiguity as to a particular person's job or the fact that the physician directs the proceedings and holds ultimate responsibility for outcomes. Katz (in press) presents an interesting example of this intricate system in action in her detailed account of the "ritual" of an operation.

---

[2] Whereas physicians are predominantly white and male, nursing is a profession "inextricably interwoven with the history of women [and] . . . the ethic of service combined with the traditional Judeo-Christian view of women as inferior and subservient to men has provided a double edged sword under which the female providers of nursing services have labored for centuries" (Reeder & Mauksch, 1979, p. 209).

Unfortunately, such organization has some negative consequences. It is not surprising that the three-pronged system of authority in hospitals is often unwieldy, creates problems in management, and produces conflicts and tensions among hospital staff. For example, nurses work under the direction of both the administrative and professional (i.e., physicians) prongs of the triad. This dualism can lead to "inconsistent orders, overlapping responsibilities, and inadequate coordination among activities" (VerSteeg & Croog, 1979).

The high status of physicians vis-à-vis nurses[3] also inhibits the open flow of information concerning patient needs. For example, as managers of patient care, nurses are expected to implement, without question, the physicians' directions for patient treatment. Often, however, nurses have more direct contact with patients than do physicians, and by following patients on a day-to-day basis, they may develop a better and more personal understanding of a patient's needs than the attending physician. Yet, the formal structure of the hospital and the status differences between physicians and nurses require that nurses offer suggestions regarding patient treatment in a "surreptitious," rather than direct, manner (Reeder & Mauksch, 1979).

Thus, for the average nurse, hospitals can be very stressful environments. Competing demands coupled with a great deal of responsibility and little power create a tense situation for them. This stress is partly responsible for high job attrition among nurses (Reeder & Mauksch, 1979), which, in turn, has been shown to negatively affect patient recovery rates (VerSteeg & Croog, 1979).

The "ultimate responsibility" that physicians have also "takes a toll." Burnout, depression, and drug abuse are not uncommon problems among physicians, and each affects the mental and technical competence of the "stressed health provider." Impairment in judgment can lead to poor decisions regarding patient treatment and care (Cartwright, 1979).

---

[3] Another example of the negative effects of severe status differences between physicians and nurses has to do with the control of infectious diseases within hospitals. Approximately 5% of today's hospitalized patients contract infectious diseases *while they are in hospitals* (Raven & Haley, 1980). In an attempt to curtail this problem, infectious surveillance and control programs (ISCP) have been implemented in hospitals throughout the United States. These programs are operated by a number of hospital personnel including a registered nurse who holds the role of infection control practitioner. In a nationwide study aimed at understanding the role of social influence on the operation of ISCPs, Raven and Haley found that nurses were often unwilling to speak to physicians, directly or indirectly, when the physicians violated procedures for controlling infectious diseases. Furthermore, when physicians ordered nurses to perform tasks that violated infectious disease control practices (e.g., transferring an infectious patient out of an isolation unit) a large proportion of nurses (39.3%) said they would comply with the physician's orders. Ironically, Raven and Haley (1980) determined that physicians are the most frequent violators of the procedures for infectious disease control.

The role of hospital patient

There is no such thing as a "typical" hospital patient. Almost all people in this country are hospitalized at one or more times during their lives. Although people represent diverse backgrounds and life-styles, when they become patients they are expected to shed their personal identities and become part of a homogeneous group with well-defined role demands (Gallagher, 1979; Haan, 1979; Parsons, 1979). As noted by Lorber (1979), "Inpatient care imposes on patients a role characterized by submission to professional authority, enforced cooperation, and depersonalized status" (p. 203).

Parsons (1979) presents one of the most thorough and influential analyses of the role of the sick person in this society. According to Parsons, this role has four specific features: an incapacity for which the individual "cannot be held responsible"; legitimate exemption from normal roles; an obligation to "try and get well"; and an obligation to "seek competent help" and cooperate fully with health care professionals.

Parsons' limited model of the sick role (Gallagher, 1979; Haan, 1979; Lipowski, 1970) captures two essential elements: total reliance on medical professionals to provide care, and cooperation that has developed into willing forfeiture of responsibility and control over one's own body (Bloom & Wilson, 1979; Lorber, 1979; Tagliacozzo & Mauksch, 1979; Taylor, 1979).

The medical establishment strongly reinforces this dependency of the sick individual (Knowles, 1979). To facilitate patient manageability and compliance, doctors and nurses often promote a sense of depersonalization among patients (Janis & Rodin, 1979; Lorber, 1979). For example, patients are treated as "clinical entities" and professionals focus on the disease rather than the whole person.[4]

Manageable or "good" patients do not disrupt the routine or "disturb the rhythm" of the hospital system (Rosengren & DeVault, 1963). "Bad" patients deviate, in some way, from the established routine. Patients are labeled "bad" for a number of reasons, including complaining about their illnesses, disagreeing with health staff about their treatment protocols, demanding more information about their condition than the doctors and nurses have provided, and, in general, attempting to gain "too much" control over their own health care[5] (Lorber, 1979; Rosengren & DeVault, 1963; Taylor, 1979).

Being labeled a bad or deviant patient has several possible consequences. It is not unusual for this label to be indicated on a patient's chart and, thereafter, influence his or her treatment and credibility among the hospi-

---

[4] Depersonalization may serve as a coping strategy for the health professional who must deal with suffering and death on a daily basis.

[5] The first definition given for patient in Webster's *New World Dictionary* is, "bearing or enduring pain, trouble, etc., without complaining or losing self-control" (Guralnik, 1978, p. 1,041).

tal staff. The bad patient is more likely to be neglected and receive less care than a good patient (Lorber, 1979).

Considering the pressures for compliance and the consequences of non-compliance, it is not surprising that the majority of hospitalized people are good patients (Taylor, 1979). In a study of hospitalized patients, Tagliacozzo and Mauksch (1979) found that most patients feel they should be cooperative and respectful and not demand too much of the hospital staff. They felt that expressions of feelings were inappropriate, and they had difficulty describing the *rights* of patients (Tagliacozzo & Mauksch, 1979). Many people feel guilty if they impose on the time of the staff. Few say that it is appropriate for them to demand the services for which they are paying.

The consequences of accepting the role of good patient may be as deleterious as being labeled "bad." For one thing, people "mute their natural propensity to cope on their own behalf" (Haan, 1979, p. 116); that is, by giving up control, patients also relinquish participation in their own health care and recovery. Taylor (1979) suggests that the good patient's loss of control may produce a state of helplessness and feelings of depression in some patients (Fiore, 1979; Seligman, 1975; Tagliacozzo & Mauksch, 1979; Wortman & Brehm, 1975). Helplessness, in turn, can inhibit recovery (Seligman, 1975; Taylor, 1979).

The physical environment

General hospitals vary considerably in their physical design and layout, and within a particular hospital there is an enormous array of types of space. We can classify the types of space with which patients come into contact into three broad categories: *public spaces, diagnostic and treatment areas,* and *inpatient units.*

Public spaces include hospital entry drives and parking structures and lots; main lobbies or reception and waiting areas; admitting departments; gift shops, newsstands, or other shops; chapels; libraries; amphitheaters; cafeterias; snack bars, vending machines or other food services; corridors; elevators and circulation spaces; cashiers; pharmacies; barber and beauty shops; outdoor spaces; restrooms; and telephone stands.

Diagnostic and treatment areas include waiting areas, dressing rooms, restrooms, and procedure (examination and treatment) rooms in different hospital departments (e.g., emergency, diagnostic, radiology, and pulmonary medicine). In addition, some departments, such as Physical Medicine and Rehabilitation, may require special types of space such as those for occupational therapy (e.g., a woodworking shop) or those for physical therapy (e.g., a gym).

Inpatient units have a variety of patient-related spaces, including patient rooms; patient bathrooms (either adjoining the patient room or separate); patient lounges; visitor waiting areas; corridors and circulation space; and examination and treatment rooms. Furthermore, nursing spaces, such as the nursing station, may have an impact on the patient. (For example, noise from the nurses' station may bother patients whose rooms are in close proximity.)

Thus, patients may come into contact with a variety of settings within a hospital. The diversity of patient-related hospital settings in combination with broad variations in patient needs creates an extremely complex task for decision makers involved in hospital design.

Little research has focused on how decisions are made about space allocation in organizations, and hospitals are no exception to this (Reizenstein, in press). It is known, at least in Australia, that hospital design decision makers do not use available research (Heath & Green, 1976).

In addition, the people who act as decision makers in hospitals vary among hospitals. Some hospitals have in-house design offices, and others contract design work. In some hospitals an administrator or facility manager is in charge of all facilities decisions, whereas others have space committees or allow departments to be responsible for their own space. The locus of design decision making may vary with the type and scale of design decisions to be made. For example, in some states Certificates of Need are required for construction projects over a certain dollar figure. Administration approval may be needed for renovation, whereas a department itself may be able to decide about furnishings.

Adding to this confusion is the fact that design decisions in many hospitals appear to be incremental, rather than reflections of long-range planning. One reason for this incremental growth relates to the symbolic importance of space. In some hospitals it is customary to redesign an entire department when a new chairperson is hired and, in fact, spatial resources may be used by the hospital as part of its recruiting strategy. This "design for the individual" approach may not be consistent with the long-range plan. Therefore, even though hospital design flexibility is often espoused, it may fall short of being implemented.

Regardless of *how* hospital design decisions are made, an important factor in this process is that space in hospitals is scarce and valuable. Few hospitals are able to simultaneously satisfy the spatial needs of patients, visitors, physicians, nurses, medical support staff, administrative personnel, and nonmedical staff. There are at least two types of spatial conflict among hospital user groups: those that occur over whose *claim to the space* should take precedence; and those that stem from whose *requirement for the design* of a particular space should prevail.

Conflicts over claims to space are quite common in hospitals. Department chairs may wage battles over the physical *size* of their departments (e.g., Should Diagnostic Radiology have more square feet than Surgery?), or they may plan their strategy for claiming a particular spatial *location* (e.g., EEGs need to be done in a quiet section of the hospital). These same issues may arise *within* a given department (How big is Dr. W's office? Is it located next to a window?). Conflict over claims to space may also take place when a particular space is "up for grabs," as in the case of a room on a patient floor. Physicians may request the space for teaching, consulting, or meeting; medical, nursing, or allied health students may claim the space for studying or lockers; visitors may desire more waiting space or a sleeping area; and nurses may say they need a lounge. It is unlikely that the view of patients will be expressed directly as they are a highly transient user group and their role is inherently passive.

Conflict may also arise over the *design* of a particular hospital space. Location of patient rooms in relation to nursing stations and the nature of the view between rooms and the hallway are difficult issues to resolve as patients and nursing preferences often conflict. Nurses tend to prefer easy viewing and access to patient rooms, but patients may prefer not to be seen from the corridor, unless they so choose (cf. Reizenstein & Grant, 1981a, Jaco, 1979).

There are almost no data on how hospital design decisions are made or on how priorities among user groups are determined. It appears, however, that research does *not* play a major role in design decisions (Heath & Green, 1976). Rather, the process is highly individualized, by hospital and based on the particular organization and power structure within a given hospital. We know that patients are a highly transient population and, therefore, do not normally act as a cohesive force. Furthermore, they do not perceive themselves as having "rights" within a hospital. Thus, it is unlikely that patients directly influence the design decision-making process of hospitals.[6]

This last point has major implications for any design-related intervention that is proposed as a means for making medical settings more congruent with patient needs. Given the complex organization of hospitals, as well as the perceived role of patients vis-à-vis other hospital user groups, only those intervention strategies consistent with the needs of other hospital user groups (especially high status groups) are likely to be implemented. We return to this point in our discussion of environmental sources of stress for patients in hospitals. Before we present these issues, however, we would like to provide a brief explanation of the concept of stress.

A transactional model of stress

This chapter focuses on ways in which the designed environment in medical settings may be stressful for hospital patients. Because we will extensively discuss specific design-related stressors, as well as available coping

---

[6] One exception to the usual hospital practice of not enabling patients to influence design decision making is occurring during the planning stage for the University of Michigan replacement hospital, a tertiary care teaching and research center that will be completed in 1986. A research and advocacy project has been underway since late 1980 to uncover patient and visitor hospital design needs and preferences, and to use this information to influence the design and planning process.

strategies, we would like to define our terms and discuss how patients fit into an overall model of stress. For an excellent review of the stress and coping literature, we direct the reader to Chapter 1 of this book.

As noted by Baum, Singer, and Baum in Chapter 1, the concept of stress has been invoked in a number of situations and settings. Definitions of stress therefore are quite varied. For our purposes, stress is *any* demand or threat that seriously challenges the adaptive ability of an individual (Lazarus, 1966; Lazarus & Launier, 1978; Selye, 1973). The degree of threat that occurs with any potential source of stress depends on how people interpret the source (their "primary appraisal"; Lazarus, 1966), as well as how they assess their ability to meet the demands of the potential stress (their "secondary appraisal"; Lazarus, 1966). The interpretations made by an individual regarding a particular stressor depend on the total context within which the event occurs. The context includes aspects of the physical, social, and psychological environment of the individual (motives, attitudes, past experiences, etc.) and the transactions that occur among these three elements (cf. Stokols & Shumaker, 1981). The individual's interpretation of an event will also be influenced by his or her style of perceiving the available information (Jacobs & Langer, 1981).

A stressful event can be responded to in a variety of ways. These *coping* strategies may be categorically defined as behavioral, physiological, and cognitive responses and employed singularly or in any combination. The effectiveness of a coping strategy depends on the context within which the stress occurs, including the capacity of the individual to effect the strategy.

Long-term exposure to a particular source of stress can delete the physical and psychological resources of an individual (Selye, 1973). Although the data linking stress with the *onset* of physical illness are limited (Andrews & Tennant, 1978; Rabkin & Struening, 1976), there is strong evidence that stress can precipitate relapse or complications in people who are already ill (Andrews & Tennant, 1978; Sklar & Anisman, 1981). For example, in an excellent review of the research on stress and cancer, Sklar and Anisman (1981) conclude that although there is no evidence to suggest that stress *causes* cancer, there are a number of studies to support the conclusion that stress can negatively influence the *process* of cancer.

In effect, stress results in compensatory biological changes to deal with the demands placed on the organism...the directed mobilization of resources or the potential exhaustion of resources render the organism less capable of efficiently contending with malignant cells. Given the relation among neurochemical, hormonal and immune systems, disruption in any of these processes could ostensibly increase the probability of cancer cell proliferation (pp. 395–396).

Thus, the absence of stress is of particular importance for hospitalized patients as it can directly influence their recovery.

Hospitalized patients are also vulnerable because fewer coping resources are available to them. As noted by Folkman, Schaefer, and Lazarus (1966),

"If a person is frail, sick, tired or otherwise debilitated, there is less energy to expend on coping" (p. 29). A patient's coping resources are also limited by the dependency inherent in his or her role, and by the fact that he or she is in an unfamiliar environment and cannot easily call upon coping strategies that have been useful in the past (e.g., the emotional comforting of a close friend or the security evoked by one's "home" territory) (cf. Searles, 1979).

Hospitals are tense and stressful for all users. Patients enter hospital settings in a vulnerable state, and *any* stressors they encounter that go beyond their illness can threaten them by diverting their physiological and psychological mechanisms from their own recovery.

In the following pages we discuss a number of design features in medical settings that can turn what is already a nonoptimal setting into an extremely stressful one. In addition, we provide specific strategies or interventions that can be implemented by patients, hospital staff, hospital designers, and/or hospital management to make the medical milieu more congruent with patient needs. Finally, we feel that good hospital design can go beyond merely limiting patient stress. Good design can facilitate patient coping strategies by providing optimal settings for these strategies to occur (e.g., by providing privacy for emotional release and social support and by providing opportunities for patients to personalize an area). Therefore, our suggestions are geared toward creating environments that act as total systems in the treatment and recovery process.[7]

Environmental factors affecting patient stress

What are the needs of hospitalized patients and how does the environment of a general hospital respond to these needs? In order to address these questions we present the experience of hospitalization from the perspective of the patient,[8] focusing on four factors in which transactions with the social and physical environments have important consequences for the patient's level of stress and effectiveness in coping. These factors include *wayfinding, physical comfort, control*[9] over privacy and personal territory, and the *symbolic meaning* of the hospital environment (Steele, 1973).

---

[7] An underlying assumption we make throughout this chapter is that it is in the best interest of the hospital and the patient to reduce the length of time of inpatient care by facilitating the recovery process.

[8] We recognize that there is no typical patient and that people's needs and resources within hospitals will differ substantially. However, we feel that the four areas of patient and hospital transactions we examine are relevant to the majority of hospitalized people in varying degrees. The degree of relevance to a particular patient depends upon the type and seriousness of illness, the patient's experience with hospital environments, and the more general cultural differences among patients.

[9] All of the issues we discuss relate in some way to the patient's degree of control over the hospital environment. These particular areas, however, depend more on the patients actually *exercising* rather than experiencing control in the hospital setting.

Before discussing these points, however, we consider how *most* people feel at the time they are admitted to a general hospital, since this influences all of their own transactions with the hospital environment that follow admission.

The entry status of patients

Sources of stress

Most people are stressed and vulnerable from the moment of their admission to a general hospital. This initial stress has a number of sources. Physical illness itself is a life crisis in which an individual's equilibrium is disrupted and his or her normal coping resources are threatened (Cohen & Lazarus, 1979; Janis & Rodin, 1979; Lipowski, 1970; Moos & Tsu, 1977).

Hospitalization adds to the stress of being sick. First, it implies that one's illness is too serious to be treated at home or in a physician's office[10] (Kornfeld, 1977). Second, through direct or vicarious experiences, most individuals learn to regard hospitals as unpleasant and frightening environments, associated with suffering and death (Brown, 1961; Taylor, 1979).

Perhaps the most stressful aspect of hospitalization is the total disruption it causes in an individual's life. Often with little warning, people go from a familiar and safe environment to a foreign one. Their relations with family, friends, and co-workers are abruptly altered or terminated, and there are no guarantees that they will be able to smoothly reenter these familiar social settings in the future (Cohen & Lazarus, 1979). Patients are temporarily disconnected from the safety, comfort, and security of their own home territory (Sommer & DeWar, 1963). While in a state of stress and anxiety, they are expected to adjust to an unknown environment in which almost everything is new and alien to them. The physical design of hospitals, medical jargon, and the functions of most medical equipment, though routine and commonplace to hospital staff, are all unfamiliar and threatening to most patients (Brown, 1961; Fiore, 1979; Kornfeld, 1977; Moos & Tsu, 1977).

Adjustment to the new setting of a hospital is made more difficult by the vulnerability of patients and the norms of the sick role. Whereas healthy people are able to attenuate the impact of their environments by leaving or changing them, sick people must accept the hospital environment as it is. They have neither the control nor the ability to alter unpleasant or dissatisfactory settings (Kornfeld, 1977; Moos, 1977; Sommer & DeWar, 1963).

---

[10] Actually, people may be hospitalized for a number of routine diagnostic and treatment procedures that do not correspond to the seriousness of their condition (Taylor, 1979). Hospitalization is necessitated by the fact that sophisticated equipment, and physicians with certain specializations, are located in hospitals, and the economics associated with the growth of general hospitals make inpatient care more fiscally sound.

Coping with entry-level stress

A number of things can be done to make the patient's entry into the hospital system less threatening and stressful. Since a large portion of the entering patient's stress is induced by the strangeness of the hospital environment, strategies that would acquaint an individual with the hospital environment, prior to hospitalization, should reduce this source of stress.

Field trips to medical settings, designed for school children, would help change a strange environment into a normal setting that serves multiple functions for many people. For the person who is about to be admitted to a hospital, films or brochures describing portions of the hospital setting relevant to incoming patients could be useful. Pastalan (1980) has found that similar techniques used in relocating the elderly decrease the negative impact of relocation. In addition, pamphlets that depict and explain the equipment to be used on the patient, the major medical terms that will be applied, and the normal hospital routine that he or she will be a part of would all help to reduce some of the anxiety derived from entry into a strange, new environment.

The severe discontinuity between a patient's home and the hospital is an unnecessary component of hospitalization. The current trends toward a decrease in the length of hospitalization, birthing centers, and hospices are, in part, responses to this problem. Even when hospitalization is necessary, there are ways to decrease the impact of this discontinuity in environments. By promoting the personalization of the patient's hospital space and encouraging and facilitating visits from family and friends, the hospital system can attenuate, rather than reinforce, the impact of an unfamiliar setting.[11] We return to these issues of social support from families and friends, and the benefits of personalization, in a later section.

Wayfinding

Wayfinding is "the actual behavior people employ in finding important locations in the environment" (Zimring, 1981, p. 159). It is a skill that is particularly relevant to the patient who occupies an unfamiliar setting and is there because of a threat to his or her physical well-being.

Although this discussion focuses primarily on the interior of hospitals, wayfinding is often a big problem for patients outside the hospital. Finding the hospital itself, locating a parking space, proceeding to an entrance and admissions can raise stress levels even before patients come in the front door. After patients reach the hospital's admitting department, they

---

[11] If one views the general hospital as a "total environment" then the introduction of outsiders (e.g., visitors, families) is a perturbation in a semiclosed system. It may be that hospital personnel run hospitals in this way and will resent the interference of outsiders. If this is true, we are suggesting a break with this view and an opening of the system.

may need to make their way to X ray or to the laboratory for various tests before they get settled into their rooms. Once they have undergone the major treatment or surgery that necessitated their hospitalization, patients often become bored and need to get away from the confining space of their rooms. For example, they may wish to visit the gift shop, the floor lounge, the cafeteria, or the main lobby during the course of their stay. In their study of inpatients at The University of Michigan Hospital, a tertiary care teaching and research center, Reizenstein and Grant (1981b) found that 68% of the patients walked to more than one destination during the course of their stay, and the three most popular destinations were the cafeteria, floor waiting areas, and the gift shop.

Patients are also indirectly affected by the wayfinding needs of their visitors. Time with friends and family is a crucial component of the sick person's recovery process (cf. Stewart, 1980). Therefore, it is very important for visitors to be able to easily locate a patient's room and to spend their time with the patient rather than in negotiating a hospital maze.

Sources of stress

Wayfinding in hospitals is often one of the first sources of stress directly related to the environment that patients and visitors mention. Wayfinding problems in hospitals stem from characteristics of patients, the social milieu of hospitals, and the designed environment.

As noted earlier, patients are usually under stress when they are admitted to the hospital, and this can impair their ability to process the information provided by the environment (Broadbent, 1971; Evans, 1980). This nonattention to environmental cues is particularly debilitating as most people are unfamiliar with the hospital environment; an average new patient cannot rely on habits or past learning for guidance through the hospital setting, making the detection of environmental cues even more difficult (cf. Saegert, 1978).

Other characteristics of patients influence their hospital wayfinding ability, including their vision, height, education, attention to signs versus other cues, and their "sense of direction." Poor vision due to improper correction, aging, or medication can result in an inability to see signs or other visual wayfinding cues. Cataracts and medication may impede wayfinding by causing a sensitivity to the glare sometimes present on signs. Since the hospital admission of elderly people, who are more likely to have visual impairments, is three times higher than that of younger people, these issues are of considerable importance to patients (American Hospital Association, 1979).

A patient's height can also be a factor in his or her ability to see signs. Signs are often posted at the eye level of a standing average-sized adult. In addition to the obvious differences in height between short and tall adults, children and people in wheelchairs need to be considered in the "short" user group.

Education, or the ability to read and understand hospital signs influences the patient's wayfinding ability. For example, if "Otorhinolaryngology" were replaced by "Ear, Nose, and Throat," it would simplify directions for most people. In some parts of the country, the particular language used in signs is also important. The many non-English-speaking people in the United States are unable to read the signs posted in most hospitals.

Two additional patient characteristics relate to hospital wayfinding. Some people simply tend not to read or follow signs, but rather rely on other types of cues. For example, in their videotape study of a hospital entry drive, Reizenstein and Grant (1981c) found that approximately 25% of the respondents ignored signs telling them that a parking deck entrance was straight ahead, and instead said they would use the parking deck entrance that they could *see*. Finally, some people have a well-developed sense of direction, or cognitive map (Evans, 1980), whereas others do not. The former are more able to find their way around a hospital, with or without good signage, than are the latter.

As already noted, hospital personnel work in a stressful setting with high demands. They do not have the time to repeatedly pause to help confused patients or visitors find their way. If staff do take the time to help patients locate a particular place within the environment, it is highly probable that their verbal directions will add to the patient's confusion. Very few people are skilled in providing clear, concise directions. A well-intentioned staff person is likely to present directions to a lost patient quickly and with an idiosyncratic cuing system that reflects the staff member's personal cognitive maps of the hospital.

Wayfinding problems in hospitals may also be due to the nature of the environment itself. Hospitals are large and they often have been added to over the years. Such incremental growth can result in long distances for patients to travel, since sequential patient functions that are related to one another may not be located in close proximity. Incremental growth may also result in inconsistent or visually different signage systems throughout the hospital that further confuse patients (Weisman, 1981).

Wayfinding in hospitals is probably most influenced by design features of the setting; these include the relationship of spaces, signage and graphics, color coding, lines on the floor or walls, and redundant cuing. Placing spaces that are functionally related to one another in close proximity aids in wayfinding by reducing the distance a patient must learn to negotiate – a wayfinding aid that is often lost when hospitals expand.

Signage and graphics are design features people rely on most as wayfinding aids (see Figure 7.1). The size, location, language, surface, colors, contrast, and size of lettering can all contribute to or detract from a sign's legibility. In an attempt to improve legibility, many hospitals have made use of "supergraphics," numbers or letters that take up the full height of the wall. Unfortunately, the unusual features of supergraphics may have exactly the opposite of the desired effect for patients who may not recognize them as

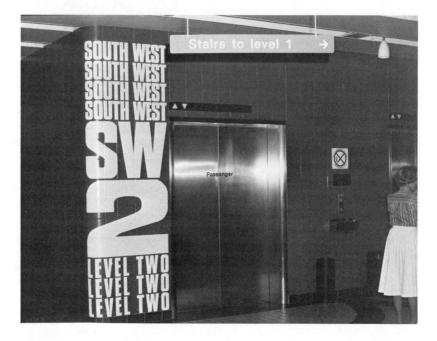

Figure 7.1. Some hospitals use large and repeating graphics to orient patients, visitors, and staff.

wayfinding cues. In addition, some of the more elaborate designs present a figure–ground problem in which patients have difficulty discerning whether the letters or the spaces between letters are the message (Devlin, 1980; Reizenstein & Grant, 1981e).

Color coding of floors is another design device often employed in an effort to encourage ease of wayfinding. Patients and visitors, however, may not notice the differences in color schemes or remember color codes for particular floors. Thus, the efficacy of color coding probably varies with building size and degree of color differentiation required. For example, color coding has been shown to facilitate wayfinding in small, self-contained office buildings (Evans, Fellows, Zorn, & Doty, 1980).

Colored lines on the floor or on the walls are becoming a familiar feature of many large institutions, including hospitals. They serve to lead patients to a specific destination (e.g., "Follow the red line to X ray"). One problem this device presents is that there is no way to have separate colored lines between *all* possible hospital destinations. Another problem concerns the location of these lines. As more hospitals install carpeting in their corridors, space for lines is lost. Lines on walls may conflict with signs, artwork, doorways, or other design features. Finally, although hospital staff may agree that the colored-line system is effective in leading patients, visitors, and new staff to their desired destinations, some users express annoyance at "being treated like a child" when directed to follow the lines (Reizenstein and Grant, 1981e). For these patients, a line system may increase their feelings of dependence within the hospital.

In contrast, some users appear to prefer the simplicity of this system and the fact that they can mindlessly flow through the hospital. For example, in a study by Shumaker and Shapiro (1981), the highly stressed parents of children with cancer remarked on how comforting and easy it was for them to follow the "footprints" on the floor of a children's hospital to each of the diagnostic and treatment facilities they needed to find for their children. It may be that people under very high levels of stress appreciate simplistic cuing systems in unfamiliar settings, while low stressed patients or those familiar with the hospital may resent simple cuing. No data directly support this hypothesis, however.

Redundant cuing (Pastalan, Mautz, & Merrill, 1973) is the use of more than one environmental cue to tell patients where they are, and it can also be a support for wayfinding. For example, color coding and graphics can simultaneously give the message that this is the (red) fourth floor. Another form of redundant cuing is designing spaces that have uses easily recognizable by patients. In contrast, a lack of overlap in design and function can be very confusing. For example, Zimring (personal communication) found that many patients who were in the cashier's department of a hospital *continued to look for it* because it was designed to look like a residential living room.

Problems in finding one's way can cause stress. When people are already upset by their illness and the disruption in their lives brought about by hospitalization, not being able to find their way or read signs that are too small, too large, too bright, or too dull can cause anxiety, frustration, anger, and confusion. These, in turn, may result in feelings of helplessness as well as raised blood pressure, headaches, increased physical exertion (e.g., having to walk longer distances), and fatigue. All of these consequences can negatively affect the patient's recovery.

From the hospital administration's perspective, wayfinding problems for patients can result in their being late or missing appointments, or in having to take up the time of staff in order to get directions. Therefore, it would appear to be in the best interest of the hospital management, as well as patients, to make wayfinding as simple and easy as possible for patients.

Coping with wayfinding problems

Patients have few strategies available to them for coping with wayfinding problems. They may expect wayfinding problems to be part of the hospital life and *accept* the status quo. This passive strategy is positive only if patients can organize their time in hospitals assuming that they may get lost and that reaching their destination will take longer than usual. This approach to wayfinding makes being lost normative, rather than a sign of patient helplessness, and makes wayfinding difficulties less threatening and stress producing. Few people, however, are able to respond to irritations in their environment so placidly, though most patients probably do try to ignore wayfinding problems in hospitals.

It is unlikely that patients would use the more active strategies available to them such as complaining about the system, no longer using the particular hospital, or demanding design changes. As noted earlier, patients do not operate as a cohesive group and they would probably not want to risk their "good patient" status by provoking hospital personnel. Lost and frustrated patients might cope reactively by defacing hospital property in some way.

Design strategies that can be initiated to facilitate patient wayfinding have been alluded to in earlier paragraphs. For example, related functions located in close proximity, and clear signs with understandable language and legible lettering may ease wayfinding. Where possible, signs with pictures, rather than simply descriptive terms, can help patients who cannot read English. Also, signs placed at all decision points within the hospital with lighting that illuminates rather than glares, and redundant cuing all may help lost patients.

Management strategies can also help patients cope with wayfinding problems. Hospital administrators can strive to locate related functions near each other, use consistent signage systems throughout the hospital complex, and distribute a set of clear maps for patients and visitors. In addition, they can post maps throughout the hospital (complete with "You are here" arrows). Information desks, at all public entrances, including emergency, would further reduce the wayfinding problems of visitors. Finally, some people are only able to make their way in a hospital by following a human guide. Administrators can consider hiring guides or organizing volunteers for this purpose.

Physical comfort

Most patients are suffering from various physical discomforts that can be easily exacerbated by seemingly minor failings in the designed environment. However, hospital designers sensitive to this problem can provide features that optimize patient comfort, enabling patients to be better able to relax and thereby enhance their own recovery process. Some aspects of the physical environment that can influence patient comfort are (1) noise; (2) temperature and humidity; (3) lighting; (4) manipulation of switches, buttons, furnishings, or equipment; (5) body positioning; and (6) odors.

Sources of stress

Noise. This can be a source of stress caused by several characteristics of hospitals and the people in them. Patients are often highly sensitive to hospital sounds due to pain, the nature of their illness, or simply the fact that they spend most of their time lying in bed with little or no control over the sounds to which they are exposed. (For a detailed discussion of the concept of noise and its relationship to stress, we refer the reader to Chapter 2 of this volume.) In addition, the sources of many hospital sounds are unfamiliar to patients (doctors and nurses talking in hallways or equipment being rolled by patients' rooms). This can add to patients' stress by driving home the fact that they are in a strange place. Sounds that can be categorized, like the moans or crying of other patients, may be frightening. Finally, the cacophony of confusing and competing sounds that occurs simultaneously in hospitals can add to the irritation and stress experienced by patients.

Some hospitals have particular noise problems because of the number of hard surfaces in the environment (Sommer, 1974); others with carpeting are enthusiastic about its sound-attenuating characteristics (Simmons, Reizenstein, & Grant, 1982). Finally, and perhaps most important, noise is often a problem in hospitals because of the lack of awareness on the part of staff, visitors, and even other patients of the need for quiet. Staff who talk directly outside a patient's room without first shutting the door, visitors who talk noisily to one patient in a double room while the other patient tries to sleep, and patients in multibed rooms who keep their televisions loud despite the wishes of roommates are all demonstrating their lack of sensitivity to the needs of others and are guilty of aggravating the problems.

Temperature. The inability of patients to match ambient temperature to their personal preferences can be, at the very least, a source of irritation and discomfort. If the ambient temperature is highly incongruent with the needs and preferences of a particular patient, it will act as another source of stress for that individual. (For a detailed discussion of the relationship between climate and stress, we refer the reader to Chapter 3 of this volume.)

Some hospitals, due to their age or energy consciousness, have antiquated or nonexistent climate control systems. For example, one notable midwestern teaching hospital does not have air conditioning in the majority of its inpatient rooms. Other hospitals have systems that are programmed to go on and off according to the calendar, rather than the weather. With one of these systems, an April or September heat wave may cause great patient (and staff) suffering. Some hospitals have temperature problems due to orientation of patient rooms, for example, due south or due west. Patients in some of these rooms may complain that they are too hot, and patients in other rooms complain that they are too cold.

Another reason for patients' physical discomfort is the lack of individual temperature controls. Patients are often forced to go along with the temperature perceived as optimal by the institution as a whole, when their illness or personal preference might call for higher or lower temperatures. For example, patients who are immobile and therefore have reduced body temperatures, or patients with fevers, may need more heat than hospital staff or more mobile patients.

Finally, although modern heating, ventilation, and air conditioning (HVAC) systems can be effective when they work as designed, they inevitably break down. Unfortunately, in newer hospitals, as in other modern buildings, windows cannot be opened and discomfort is widespread until a broken system is repaired.

Lighting conditions. Poor lighting can cause patient discomfort either because it is insufficient for proper illumination, or because it is too bright or glaring. Often lighting is a problem in hospital settings because there is little understanding about the types and optimal placement of lighting fixtures and bulbs (Lighting for health care facilities, 1978a, b). Improper selection of types of lighting fixtures and bulbs and a less than carefully designed lighting system can leave some areas in shadow while others seem "overlit."

Lighting problems, particularly glare, are also the result of design features that are planned separately, rather than as interactive systems. For example, hospital corridors are notorious for being highly polished. This is important for cleanliness and for the hospital's image as a sterile environment. However, there are usually rows of fluorescent lights on ceilings above these shiny floors that are reflected in the floors and create a large amount of glare (Spivack, 1967).

Windows need to be considered in the design of lighting systems. When located at the ends of hallways, windows are excellent as orientation aids and often provide valued views to the outside – a "contact" with the world that is important for people who are hospitalized a long time. Unfortunately, windows can also be extremely bright when compared with corridor walls and thus can be almost blinding to some patients (especially the elderly).

Window coverings are a potential lighting problem. Effective coverings block out glaring sun while allowing light into what would otherwise be a dark space.

Finally, optimal lighting may vary among user groups of the same setting. Even if the hospital designer masters the "mechanics" of lighting, priorities among user groups must be considered. For example, the lighting needed by nurses and technicians to adequately perform their tasks may be much brighter than that required by a patient who is reading or resting.

Manipulation. A patient's ability to manipulate (move or operate) various furnishings and equipment is essential to his or her physical comfort in the hospital. Manipulation can be a problem for patients both because of the type of furnishings and equipment used and the location of these things within a particular setting.

Patient beds were once manipulable (cranked) only by nurses or by someone other than the patient. Today, however, most hospitals use electric beds that the patient can control, but other types of furnishings and equipment may not be as easy for patients to operate. Many overbed tables still need to be hand cranked, which many patients cannot do.

The location of furnishings and equipment can also be a problem for patients. In some hospital rooms, the light switches are on a headwall behind the patient, making the operation of these switches impossible for all but the most adroit person. Telephones are often placed on the bedside table, too far for the patient to reach.

Aggravations induced by an environment that is difficult to manage are perhaps minor when considered individually. However, they are imbedded in a setting that has the potential to promote multiple sources of stress for patients. In addition, the inability of patients to manipulate their setting in these simple and very basic ways can enhance their image of themselves as dependent and helpless. For example, relying on a nurse to turn on a light or adjust a table reinforces the patient's self-image as a dependent, passive individual. Furthermore, assertive patients may take up a great deal of nurses' or aides' time by demanding that the environment be manipulated for them to meet their needs.

Bodily comfort. The ways in which patients are forced to position their bodies by the design and location of furnishings can be a source of discomfort and stress. For example, a chair may not give proper back support, may cut off circulation at the thighs, or may be angled in such a way that patients have difficulty standing up. Televisions, which are often placed near ceilings in the patients' rooms, may be difficult to view and some patients may not be able to find a comfortable position in which to watch them.

Sensitivity on the part of designers to the body positions that the design and location of furnishings impose on patients could eliminate another source of patient frustration and stress. Although the irritation of improper body positioning may appear minor, within the total context of hospitalization it adds to all the other irritations faced by hospitalized people. Furthermore, it is one problem within a complex social and physical environment that has simple and easily implemented solutions.

Odors. Within hospitals unpleasant odors can be very disturbing to the patient population. In hospitals where smoking is allowed, many non-smoking patients complain about smoke and cigarette smells (Reizenstein and Grant, 1981d). Odors that are indigenous to hospital settings, such as vomitus, urine, and disinfectant, are often offensive. In addition, odors may be a problem because of surfaces that retain them, such as carpeting and fabrics (Simmons, Reizenstein, & Grant, 1982).

The degree to which odors are problematic depends for the most part on the type of ventilation system used and housekeeping procedures. Where ventilation is inadequate, odors can be very upsetting for patients who are "locked into" an unpleasant setting.

Patient activities related to physical comfort

The diverse activities in which patients engage relate to environmental design as well as to the social and behavioral characteristics of medical care. In cases where an activity, design features, and the social system are congruent, stress will probably not result. However, when these are not congruent with one another, patients are likely to experience stress (Stokols, 1979; Willems, 1976). For the following discussion of patient activities that relate to physical comfort, we focus on three major types of spaces used by patients: public spaces, patients' rooms, and patients' bathrooms.

Patients in public spaces of a hospital, such as corridors, the main lobby, or the cafeteria, come into contact with more people than when in their rooms. Depending on the patients' needs and preferences, this added stimulation may be positive or negative. Attributes of the designed environment in public spaces can affect the patients' comfort. For example, carts and heels may resound noisily on the hard surface floor. Also, lights may shine in patients' eyes as they lie on the gurney. Patients may find it difficult to maneuver their intravenous pole along the hallway, and they often have difficulty finding comfortable seating in outdoor areas (see Figure 7.2).

Patients' rooms have fewer potentially overwhelming stimuli. However, since this is where patients spend the most time, even minor mismatches between the physical environment and behavior can become major annoyances. Some patient activities that occur in the room include viewing, reading, sleeping, lying in bed, receiving care, talking, and sitting.

"Viewing" includes watching television, looking outside, and watching visitors or other patients and the hallway. The features of physical comfort that are most relevant to viewing include lighting, manipulation, and body positioning. Watching television serves as a good example of how the environment can be managed to facilitate patient comfort in terms of viewing.

For people who are forced to spend most of their time in one setting, watching television comfortably can take on major importance. Television provides a primary diversion, and it is also a familiar form of entertainment for most Americans. Thus, it provides a link with the patient's "prior life." In addition, it may be the primary diversion available for patients who are nonambulatory and unable to read.

Both natural and artificial lighting must be properly chosen and positioned for the TV to be easily seen by patients. Poor lighting can result in

Figure 7.2. Outdoor seating design is important for patient and visitor comfort, as is the design of indoor seating. Seating with backs and shade is particularly important for elderly and frail users.

eyestrain or headaches from light glaring on the screen. Patients also need to be able to easily manipulate controls to the television. And, as noted earlier, the television should be placed within a room so that patients can position themselves comfortably for viewing.

The aspects of physical comfort that relate to reading, sleeping, lying in bed, receiving care, and talking include lighting, sound, manipulation, and body positioning. For reading, patients need a light that can illuminate reading material without glare. Ideally, the light should illuminate only the reading material so that a patient's roommate is able to sleep or talk undisturbed. The patient must be able to manipulate the switch and adjust the light's intensity and position to meet his or her particular needs. For sleeping, some patients need to block out natural and/or artificial light. The type of window coverings and a patient's ability to close the door or have it closed will affect his or her physical comfort for this activity. The type of bed a patient is in and the patient's ability to manipulate it will affect his or her bodily comfort for reading and sleeping.

Sounds from the hallway or from the roommate's TV or visitors can all disturb a patient trying to rest, read, carry on a conversation, or listen to a physician. Thus, sounds play a role in a patient's physical comfort during these activities.

For those patients who spend a great deal of their time sitting either in bed or in chairs, body positioning is the most important aspect of physical comfort. Therefore, beds and chairs that give proper support and allow for alternative seating positions contribute to patient comfort.

Patient activities in the *bathroom* include using the toilet, shower, and sink, and personal grooming. Physical comfort during these activities primarily relates to body positioning, manipulation of fixtures, and lighting. When people are forced to perform personal hygiene behaviors, considered to be very private, in settings that do not meet their privacy needs they experience discomfort and, if possible, they will alter the situation to be more congruent with their needs (Shumaker, 1979, 1980). Because hospitalized patients are for the most part unable to alter the settings they use, the design strategy that should be implemented in these setting is one that allows most patients to meet their personal hygiene needs in private (without the assistance of hospital personnel). This design strategy minimizes patient discomfort and allows patients to retain their sense of effectance and self-esteem.

In order to use a toilet comfortably, patients must be able to sit and rise easily. The height of the toilet and type of grab rails will play an important role. Even such a seemingly small detail as the placement of the toilet paper dispenser can be quite important.

In the shower, patients may need to sit, in which case a fold-down seat is desirable. They need to be able to see, reach, and manipulate the shower controls from either a standing or seated position. Lighting and type and distance of controls are important here. The patient should be able to reach a towel while inside the shower area, and the floor should have a nonslip surface.

Using the sink and mirror for various personal grooming activities such as brushing teeth, shaving, putting on makeup, and drying one's hair involves the same dimensions of physical comfort, including lighting, manipulation, and body positioning. Lighting over the sink and mirror can aid the patient in carrying out a specific activity and can also be important for the patient's morale. For example, lighting that makes patients' skin tones appear blue-gray or yellow may make them feel badly about themselves. The type of faucet knobs used and the location of electrical outlets will affect a patient's ability to manipulate things around the sink, and the location of the mirrors will determine how patients have to sit or stand in order to get a good view. For example, mirrors that are too high or too low may cause patients to stretch or slump uncomfortably.

Individual characteristics related to physical comfort

Although many characteristics of individuals relate to their physical comfort in hospitals, we focus on the following: mobility, age, illness, and preferences. Patients differ in their *mobility*, ranging from those who are unable to move around without tha aid of an electric wheelchair to those who may have slight difficulty walking or grasping. Hospitals need to be even more attuned to "barrier-free" design than other building types since more of their users are likely to be either permanently or temporarily disabled.

Patients also differ in *age* from one another. Considering only the extremes of the age spectrum, both pediatric and geriatric patients have special environmental needs due to physical and psychological aspects of the developmental process. For example, elderly patients may benefit from design suited to limited mobility, sensitivity to glare, and frequent opportunities for resting.

The particular *illness* patients are experiencing will affect their physical comfort while they are hospitalized. For example, certain illnesses or medications can render patients particularly sensitive to noise, light, or heat. Finally, individual tastes and *preferences* contribute to any one patient's physical comfort while in the hospital. These include such preferences as cigarette smoking, room temperature, noise levels, and social interaction.

Coping strategies

Although it is possible that patients and staff can make adjustments to accommodate poor hospital design, such adjustments may be impractical and/or too costly. For example, in areas where quiet is needed, staff can reduce their speaking volume. However, staff cannot constantly monitor their own behavior in the stressful environment of a hospital. And, more important, they have no control over such things as the hard surfaces that increase the level of unwanted sounds. Therefore, the critical sources of intervention for better physical comfort come from the design and management of the hospital environment.

There are a number of ways in which the designed environment can contribute to the physical comfort of the hospital patient. We have presented most of these strategies in our discussion of the problem. To summarize these points: in order to reduce noise problems, sound-attenuating surfaces need to be provided wherever possible. In terms of temperature-related problems, the way in which buildings are oriented can affect solar heat gain or thermal loss, and provisions can be made to compensate for these effects. In addition, designers should try to provide individual temperature controls in patient rooms and have HVAC systems that operate according to individual controls, rather than the calendar.

Whenever possible, hospitals need to utilize a lighting designer in order to be fully sensitive to the enormous number of possible combinations of light fixtures, bulbs, and specific positions. In addition, they should strive to eliminate glare, provide appropriate lighting for specific tasks, and consider more subdued lighting for conversation areas.

In terms of the problems that relate to manipulation, hospital designers can choose furnishings and equipment easily controlled by the patient. For example, patient discomfort can be reduced by locating controls for lights, TV, and nurse call on either side of the bed rail so these can be used by right- or left-handed (or injured) patients without their resorting to awkward or uncomfortable bodily contortions.

For optimal body positioning, design decision makers could select furniture that is comfortable to sit or lie on for a long period of time. Also, they need to be aware of the special needs of some patients. For example, some patients will require cushioned chair arms and chairs to facilitate easy rising.

Finally, in order to minimize offensive odors in the hospital, the design decision makers need to try to select surfaces that do not retain odors. Also, they should provide a good overall ventilation system and use special ventilation systems in areas where people will be smoking (e.g., cafeteria, lobby, and waiting areas).

Management policies and practices can work with medical care and environmental design features to contribute to the patient's physical comfort while in the hospital. For example, management can support the use of sound-attenuating materials and encourage staff to keep noise levels low.

If the lighting design system is a good one, management can ensure that lighting replacements are made with those originally specified. If the lighting design is poor they can investigate hiring a specialist and redoing the system.

In order to combat patient problems that relate to manipulation and body positioning, management can provide patients with information about the various furnishings and pieces of equipment in their rooms. This might be done over a special closed-circuit channel on the television. In addition, they can encourage the purchasing of furnishings and equipment that patients can manipulate themselves, since this will both lessen patient stress and save staff time. Finally, they can provide the additional staff needed to assist patients when designs and furnishings are nonoptimal.

To reduce the effects of unpleasant odors, hospital management can strongly encourage the quick cleanup of spills. In addition, they can make special efforts to provide separate smoking and nonsmoking areas whenever possible. Finally, patient preferences regarding smoking should be considered when assigning individuals to two-person rooms.

Summary on physical comfort

When the designed environment is severely incongruent with patients' needs, they may experience stress from noise, glare, heat or cold, offensive smells, overexertion, fatigue, headaches, loss of sleep, or injury (falls, stretching too far). This stress may manifest itself behaviorally through feelings of anger, frustration, and passivity or helplessness and depression. Thus, it is in the patients' best interest for hospital managers to provide as comfortable an environment as possible for them. Also, by promoting a designed environment that both meets patients' needs *and* is controlled by patients, hospital staff are freed from the time-consuming tasks of arranging the patients' environments.

We have suggested several design interventions that could reduce the potential of "designed discomfort" for the patient population. Although some of these strategies may not be financially feasible for most hospitals to implement in toto, they do provide a *direction and focus* for hospital design decision makers. That is, as equipment is replaced, rooms refurbished, and hospital additions built, these design strategies can be implemented over time.

Furthermore, our suggestions can sensitize hospital management to areas and settings in which designs are least congruent with patient needs. If redesign is not possible, hiring additional staff or volunteers who can assist patients in these settings would help to reduce patients' stress.

Control over privacy and personal territory

The concept of control is very popular in the theoretical and empirical literature in the fields of health and the environment (cf. Janis & Rodin, 1979; Stewart, 1980; Taylor, 1979). In general, researchers argue that noncontrol is stressful in and of itself and that it increases the impact of other sources of stress such as noise (Cohen & Weinstein, Chap. 2, this volume) and crowding (Epstein, Chap. 5, this volume). There are several problems, however, in the way control has been operationalized in the literature (see Averill, 1973; Avis, 1979; Thompson, 1981, for reviews of this issue). Definitions of control are frequently ambiguous, and related terms such as *predictability, choice, responsibility*, and *access to information* are used interchangeably with control. In spite of these weaknesses in the concept, several researchers have demonstrated that access to "control" reduces the amount of stress people experience in otherwise stressful situations (Fuller, Endress, & Johnson, 1978; Houston, 1972; Krantz & Schultz, 1979; Mills & Krantz, 1979; Rodin & Langer, 1977; Vernon & Bigelow, 1974).

Perceptions of control are relevant to hospitalized patients in several ways. Patients' involvement in their own diagnostic and treatment processes influences recovery rates and stress levels (Taylor, 1979; Thompson, 1981).[12] As we have noted previously, the ability of patients to "find their

---

[12] There is an extensive literature in social and health psychology on perceived control as it relates to the patient's access to information regarding the diagnostic and treatment process, participation in the treatment process, and compliance with the treatment regimen. In general, researchers in this area argue that greater patient control enhances compliance and decreases the stress that accompanies diagnosis and treatment (Janis & Rodin, 1979; Stewart, 1980; Taylor, 1979; Thompson, 1981). Although this literature is relevant to hospitalized patients and the amount of stress they experience, we do not review it in this chapter. Our

own way" and manipulate their physical environment is critical to their sense of efficacy and decreases the chance of their feeling helpless and depressed. In a similar way, patients' perceptions of control relate to their ability to monitor *privacy* levels and to personalize their *territory* within the hospital environment.

Privacy

Altman (1975) argues that the availability of desired levels of privacy is critical to an individual's health and well-being. Privacy can serve many functions for people, including control over personal information; an opportunity for self-disclosure and intimacy; respite from social role demands; an opportunity to rest; and an opportunity to practice new roles and self-images (Altman, 1975; Shumaker, 1979; Westin, 1967; Wolfe & Laufer, 1974). For the hospitalized patient these functions become critical.

By definition of their role, patients give up a great deal of control over their normal day-to-day lives. They are away from home and family, away from work, and have taken on what is often a new and powerless role. They are likely to be physically uncomfortable and worried about their own condition. Within this stressful context, patients must expose their bodies to a myriad of strangers and may feel that there is little in their experience as a patient that they can control. The "normal" aspects of personal privacy are continually violated for patients. Thus, visual and acoustical privacy can be very important to many patients as a way of reinforcing their sense of themselves as persons rather than as "things" to be poked, prodded, and tested.

In addition, control over interaction with friends and family can be important to hospitalized patients. A number of researchers have demonstrated the significance of social support as a major coping strategy for the stressed individual (Brownell, 1981; Cobb, 1976; Cohen & McKay, in press; Kaplan, Cassel, & Gore, 1977; Shaefer, Coyne, & Lazarus, in press). For patients who feel it is inappropriate to discuss their emotions and needs with hospital staff (Lorber, 1979), accessibility to friends and family is very important. Furthermore, it is very important for patients to have a private space available to them where they can openly discuss their needs and feelings with the people who care the most about them.

Through staff behavior, design, and economics, hospital settings limit patient privacy and thereby increase levels of stress. Due to their need to "get the job done" and sometimes to a learned insensitivity to patient

focus is on the physical environment and interventions that involve physical design features of the environment. We refer readers who are interested in this topic to the aforementioned references. In addition, Stone, Cohen, and Adler (1979), Jaco (1979), and DiMatteo and Freedman (1979) all contain several articles that relate to this topic. Shapiro and Shapiro (1979) provide an interesting argument on the potential negative consequences of too much responsibility on the patient population.

needs, medical and nursing staff do not always respect a patient's need for visual or acoustical privacy, or for a patient's need to regulate social interaction. The cubicle curtain that does not fully enclose the bed, the head of a bed lined up with the door, or visitor chairs that do not fit comfortably next to the bed are design features that limit a patient's degree of control over social contact and may be stressful. Furthermore, there may be competition among user groups for optimal designs. For example, in an early study on hospital design, Trites, Galbraith, Sturdevant, and Leckart (1970) found that the open, radially designed nursing stations were preferred by nurses to the more traditional corridor design. However, in an extensive follow-up study, Jaco (1979) found that patients in radially designed areas complained about the lack of privacy that accompanies this more open design feature. Thus, though the radial design is congruent with nurses' needs for easy access and monitoring of patients, it may be incompatible with the privacy needs of patients.

There are many reasons why patients may want privacy. Talking is one activity for which most people prefer acoustical privacy. Whether talking on the phone or talking with a visitor or with medical or nursing staff in their room, patients may not feel really free to say how they feel or what the hospital stay is like with a roommate listening.

If a patient goes to a lounge, control over social contact may still be problematic. A lounge with bright, uniform lighting in which all the seats are lined up against one wall (see Figure 7.3) may work against patients and visitors who would like to talk intimately (Evans & Howard, 1973; Sommer, 1969).

There may be times when the patient would prefer not to interact but is unable to shut out social interaction. The roommate who does not want to listen to a phone conversation or visit, but who has no way to "turn off" the sound, or the patient who does not want to be looked at through an interior window to a corridor may suffer stress from his or her inability to regulate privacy.

At least two individual characteristics bear on the stress a patient may experience with regard to privacy: the nature and severity of the illness as well as a patient's response to illness, and a patient's typical pattern of privacy needs. Individuals' usual patterns of social contact may affect their desired patterns as patients (cf. Marshall, 1972). Some individuals are used to a great deal of control over the amount of privacy they have, whereas others have limited experience with privacy. The degree to which the hospital environment is congruent with an individual's "pre–hospital" environment will affect the level of stress experienced as a result of the inadequate privacy within hospitals.

There are a number of design features that can affect patients' perceived privacy. In public spaces social contact is affected by seating and telephones. For example, chairs that can be moved around allow patients to make clusters as well as visually and acoustically separate themselves from oth-

Figure 7.3. Modular seating like this is not liked by some users because it puts people with their backs to each other and at an awkward angle for conversations.

ers according to their needs. The telephone location (e.g., in the middle of a waiting area versus in a nook along a corridor) and type of enclosure (e.g., booth, semi-enclosed, or not enclosed) will also affect perceived visual and acoustical privacy (Holohan & Slaikeu, 1977). The remarks of one patient in a study by Reizenstein and Grant (1981d) relate to this issue:

I think that it would be a good idea to have phone booths or phone rooms so that patients could have a private place to talk to their friends and relatives. I have seen and heard so many people be forced to discuss private upsetting matters on the telephone in front of many other people and be obviously uncomfortable doing so.

In the patient's room and bathroom, there are also design features that relate to the patient's control over his or her privacy. The number of patients in a room is one very important factor influencing the degree of privacy experienced by those in the room. Other features affecting privacy include the presence of an interior window to the corridor, the relation of the head of the bed to the doorway, the relation of the bathroom to the hallway, and the presence of visual screening devices (e.g., cubicle curtain) and acoustical screening devices (e.g., white noise machines) (Figure 7.4).

The coping strategies available to patients who have inadequate control over their privacy within hospitals are severely limited. However, the social milieu of the hospital can foster greater privacy for patients. Hospital

Figure 7.4. Visual screening operable by the patient between beds and between room and corridor is important if the patient is to have control over social contact and privacy.

staff can be more responsive to privacy needs by using curtains around patient beds when examining patients and by lowering their voices when discussing the patients' illness with them. In addition, the staff can try to see patients during the times when patients are not with their families and friends. Although design cannot work alone to provide patients with control over privacy, it can play an important role. As we have emphasized before, *patient control of privacy should be a design principle.*

In public spaces, hospital designers can select seating that is movable, and they should try to arrange seats so that conversation can take place among small groups (Holohan, 1979; Sommer, 1969). Also, designers can provide seats that are separated spatially. Finally, phones can be selected that provide the greatest amount of acoustical privacy.

Management can enhance patient privacy by encouraging staff to respect privacy. In addition, housekeeping staff can be instructed to keep seating groups as they were designed or rearranged by users and not to line them up in orderly rows. Finally, by implementing liberal visiting hours for friends and families, management can help promote the social support so important to a patient's coping.

There are several obstacles to our suggestions for interventions that would enhance the patients' perceptions of privacy. Visual and acoustical screening devices are costly, and the needs of user groups may conflict. For example, the easy visibility of patients by nurses conflicts with the patients' needs for privacy (Jaco, 1979). Flexibility in design and movable furniture can be a constant source of irritation for housekeeping staff who are trying to efficiently clean and order their environment. Finally, traffic and disruptions from the visits of friends and relatives may disrupt the rhythm of the hospital's routine. Hospital staff are overloaded and they rely heavily on this rhythm to meet all the demands placed on them.

In spite of these obstacles, we feel that privacy and the related issues we have discussed are critical to patient recovery. Privacy provides patients with coping strategies (i.e., access to social support and perceptions of control) that can reduce their stress and assist in their recovery, and its absence can increase the stress experienced from other sources and make the individual feel dependent and helpless. Furthermore, the research on perceived control demonstrates the importance of control and self-efficacy to recovery and health. Therefore, we consider the cost–benefit trade-off to be balanced in favor of the interventions we propose.

Personal territory

Altman (1970) defines territoriality as "the mutually exclusive use of areas and objects by persons or groups." Edney (1974, 1976) argues that territory provides people with security and stimulation and can enhance their personal identities. The security available in one's own territory allows greater freedom of action. That is, people feel more comfortable pursuing a broader range of behaviors when they are in their "own land" (Altman, 1970, 1975; Edney, 1976; Taylor, 1978).

Altman (1975) classifies territories into three distinct groups that lie on a continuum from high to low control. These are *primary* territories, where people exercise complete area control (e.g., one's own home); *secondary* territories, or areas that are semipublic (e.g., a front lawn or porch); and *public* territories (e.g., a bus seat or library table).

People often use "territorial markers" to define public and secondary areas as temporarily belonging to them. For example, Sommer (1970) found that students place books and personal belongings on library tables to "mark" the space as theirs. Furthermore, as the availability of primary territories decreases for an individual, he or she is more likely to use territorial markers (Mathis & Bakeman, 1978). Thus, the personalization of an area is a strategy that people can use to alter a public or semipublic area into one that feels more like one's own space.

Hospitalized patients leave the comfort and security of their homes (primary territories) and enter an unfamiliar setting in which the classification of territory is ambiguous. Although they are assigned to their "own rooms," patients have no choice in the furnishings of the room and only limited control over who enters the room or when a person enters it. In addition, patients are expected to perform behaviors in this environment that they have heretofore usually confined to their own primary territories (e.g., sleeping and resting, discussing personal issues with friends, and grooming).

This discontinuity between home and hospital can be a source of stress for many patients (Sommer & DeWar, 1963). At a time of great vulnerability, patients are surrounded by strange equipment and people; there is nothing inherent in a hospital setting that promotes a sense of self-identity or the security that one derives from being among familiar people *and* objects (Brown, 1961; Kornfeld, 1977). In fact, as noted earlier, much of a hospital's social and physical milieu depersonalizes patients by treating them as homogeneous entities within diagnostic categories.

Several strategies can be implemented by patients, hospital staff, designers, and management that will allow patients to develop a space of their own within the hospital environment. All of these strategies can be subsumed under the general concept of personalization (Edney & Uhlig, 1977). That is, allowing patients to personalize their setting enables them to establish their own territory within a hospital and thereby decreases the negative impact of the discontinuity that occurs between home and hospital.

The hospital design decision maker is critical to the personalization of space by patients. Hospitals can provide areas within patient rooms that are designed specifically for personalization (e.g., a bulletin board viewable from a patient's bed, a locker for clothes with shelves for grooming materials, and a table within easy reach of a patient). Hospital management can encourage the medical staff to respect the individuality of patients, and the housekeeping staff can be instructed to leave the patients' arrangements as they find them.

There are a number of obstacles to promoting patient personalization of areas within hospitals. Space in hospitals is a valued commodity and the inclusion of lockers and tables for each patient reduces the amount of space available for other needs. These items can be costly and would most likely be considered low priorities when competing with such things as a new piece of technical equipment.

Highly personalized space can disrupt the rhythm of the medical staff. In addition to minimizing costs, a major reason for conformity in spatial design within hospitals is to help staff routinize the many tasks they must accomplish. If staff have to constantly reorient themselves to each patient's room, their efficiency may decline significantly. Similarly, the housekeeping staff may have difficulty accomplishing their job when areas within the hospital vary considerably and patient rooms are "cluttered" with personal belongings. Finally, personal objects may be stolen.

Patient personalization increases a sense of security and self-identity. It not only reduces the stress that may occur from being in a completely foreign environment, but it can also *promote* other coping strategies for the patient. For example, patients are more likely to relax and rest comfortably in their "own place." For these reasons it is important for hospital designers and management to seek a compromise between the efficiency needs of the medical staff and the territorial needs of the patients. For example, clutter can be minimized by good functional designs, and personalization can be limited to small areas within the immediate vicinity of the patients' beds. Locks on patient's cabinets can minimize the risk of thefts.

Symbolic meaning

In addition to its impact on patients' wayfinding abilities, physical comfort, privacy, and territory, the physical environment of hospitals also serves a *symbolic function* (Craik & Appleyard, 1980; Rapaport, 1977). Hospital design contributes to patients' *image of the hospital* and to their *image of themselves as patients*. The symbolic meaning conveyed by hospitals serves to tie together many of the design issues addressed throughout this chapter.

Hospital images can be thought of along a continuum, with "residential" at one end and "institutional" at the other. "Residential image" refers to a "warm and friendly" atmosphere, or it may be perceived as "too loose" or "unprofessional." On the other hand, "institutional image" connotes "cold, depersonalized" treatment, but also "competent, professional" care. Hospitals face a difficult problem with regard to the image their environmental design projects as many patients desire a competent, professional setting, but resent the depersonalized implications of such designs.

The symbolic meaning of patients' status may also be reflected by the physical setting. The environment can give "messages" that the patient is powerful or powerless and/or that patients play an active or passive role in their own care. Design can reflect the idea that a patient's needs are natural, anticipated, and important or that these needs are deviant and unimportant.

There are individual differences regarding how patients "read" environmental messages. The amount and nature of patients' hospital experiences influence how they perceive a particular hospital setting. Individuals also differ in the degree to which they perceive environmental messages. Some people are very sensitive, whereas others are virtually oblivious. For example, physically handicapped people may see "barriers" in the environment where able-bodied people do not. These may be read not only as physical barriers, but also symbolic messages: "Handicapped people: Keep Out!"

Environmental design can cause stress with regard to symbolic meaning in at least two situations. The first is when an environment conveys a *negative message* to the user; for example, "You are not important." The second can be thought of as *unfulfilled environmental expectations* such as when an environment looks good, but functions poorly. We discuss the stress-causing hospital designs that relate to symbolic meanings in three settings: public spaces, the patient's room, and the patient's bathroom.

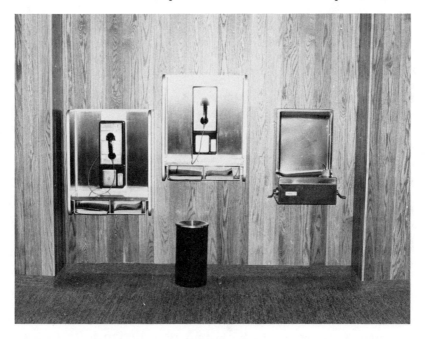

Figure 7.5. The location of hospital amenities such as telephones and water fountains can be symbolically, as well as functionally important. Here, the message to physically handicapped people is, "We've designed for your needs, too."

The size of *public spaces* in the hospital "tells" the user about the hospital's feeling about the importance of various functions. A tiny waiting area "says" that visitors are not important enough to be provided for or that patients should stay in their rooms and not wander around the hospital. The location of public spaces also has symbolic meaning. For example, in one hospital a patient complained that the patient library was in a place where no one could find it. He resented the symbolism: the hospital believed TV to be more important for patients than books (Reizenstein & Grant, 1981d).

Wayfinding can be a major problem in hospitals. Not only will patients and others have difficulty and take more time in getting to their destinations, but they may also become angry at the symbolic meaning of a bad signage system or confusing layout. Since many patients and visitors are first-time users and thus unfamiliar with the hospital, getting lost reinforces their sense of deviance or of not belonging. Ultimately, the symbolic message accompanying confusing environments is that no one in the hospital cared enough to ensure that people can find their way around.

Special features of public spaces convey symbolic messages. Rest rooms, telephones, water fountains, and vending machines that are located in close proximity to public areas show recognition of basic human needs (Figure 7.5). When these are not present, the user may feel forgotten and unimportant in the eyes of the hospital. Amenities such as plants, music, special lighting, and fountains may communicate meanings to users, and these messages may be interpreted differently by different users. For example, some may see a lobby with large comfortable chairs, soft lighting, and plants as a comfort to visitors under stress; on the other hand, staff may resent the fact that the lobby is so nice, while their lounges are somewhat bare.

Design of the *patient room* can communicate symbolic meaning to patients. In rooms occupied by more than one patient, layout and visual and acoustical screening symbolize the hospital's view of the importance of patient privacy and territoriality. The often used "privacy" curtain is an example of a design feature that operates symbolically rather than functionally. Although it does usually prevent one patient from viewing another, it does not prevent one patient from hearing conversations between the other patient and physicians, nurses, or visitors.[13] The symbolic message may be that one gives up a large measure of personal privacy when one is hospitalized.

Patient's territory is a symbolic issue in a multibed room. Proximity to the window, the bathroom, the door, or closet can loom as important, if unstated, concerns. The fact that many layouts do not allow all occupants of the room equal access to these important design features may lead to feelings of differential treatment.

Display and storage areas are potential sources of design-related stress for hospital patients. Often, there is not enough display space or it is located where patients cannot see it. For example, in one hospital, the only available display space was on the ledge of the interior window. If patients had the window curtain drawn, so as to avoid visual connection with the hallway, they also lost their view of their own flowers and cards (Reizenstein & Grant, 1981e). Often, there is insufficient storage space to accommodate patient belongings, and patients use their overbed tables for storage purposes. Reizenstein and Grant (1981e) found that nurses consider this use of the overbed table to be a problem and that patient belongings often "get in the way."

Furnishings in the patient's room can contribute to symbolic meaning. For example, visitor chairs that are uncomfortable to sit in for long periods of time can give the message to patients and visitors that the latter "do not belong here." Equipment in the patient room is a potential source of symbolic stress. Light switches, nurse call buttons, or telephones that cannot be reached easily from the bed may "tell" patients that they should not have control, that the proper patient role is a passive one. Another symbolic message given off by equipment or furnishings that cannot be manipulated by patients is that they are "less important" than the equipment.

---

[13] A parallel problem exists in the design of open offices where modular systems are used to visually divide space, yet sound is not blocked (cf. Sundstrom, Burr, & Kamp, 1980).

For example, with a ceiling-mounted television that is difficult for patients to watch comfortably the message is that *they* should be the ones to move around, rather than the television.

Design features in the patient bathroom can be sources of symbolic stress. Handicapped inaccessibility is one factor of bathroom design that not only may not allow a patient to use the bathroom independently, but which may also communicate to the patient a sense that the hospital does not recognize the need to provide design support for their physical limitations. An example of unfulfilled environmental expectations is bathrooms with grab rails only on one side. That is, for the patient who needs support on his or her right side, a grab rail on the left can be useless and, therefore, frustrating and frightening (due to fear of falling).

Many patient bathrooms fall short with regard to providing *storage space* for personal toilet articles. This can be quite frustrating to patients as there is often not an abundance of storage space for toiletries in the patient room, and if they are not ambulatory, most patients would prefer not to carry toilet articles from bed to bathroom.

Many of the design coping strategies for reducing symbolically induced stress in hospital settings have been discussed in earlier sections of this chapter. However, one important strategy may have as much to do with the *design process* as with *design products*. That is, designers need to have a clear understanding of the *desired* symbolic meanings. This may involve some work on values clarification with various design decision makers in the hospital. *We support design that symbolizes the hospital as a professional, highly competent institution in which the patient has as much control over the physical environment as possible.*

There are also management coping strategies for reducing symbolically induced stress. First, management must be aware that the physical environment communicates symbolic messages, and they should decide what kind of image they would like the hospital to project. Promoting an image of the hospital as a competent institution, and of patients as having some control over their environment, may provide payoffs in terms of attracting more patients and reducing patient stress and increasing recovery rates, and in reducing staff time consumed by various patient requests for aid.

Summary

The general hospital is an environment in which competing demands on staff, as well as conflicts over the limited space that is available combine to produce stress and tension for hospital user groups. Hospitalized patients are particularly vulnerable in this stressful milieu because of their low status among hospital user groups, their adoption of the sick role, which is inherently dependent and passive, and the concentrated period of time they must remain within the environment. In addition, the coping resources of inpatients are limited by a depletion in energy brought about by their illness, and by the fact that they are in an unfamiliar environment and cannot easily call upon the coping strategies that have been useful to them in the past.

In this chapter we present aspects of the physical environment of hospitals that may increase the amount of stress experienced by inpatients, and we discuss ways in which these potential stressors might be reduced. In addition, we suggest ways in which the designed environment of a general hospital can facilitate patient coping. Our focus has been on four issues: wayfinding, physical comfort, control of privacy and personal territory, and the symbolic meaning of the environment. Our conclusions regarding each of these issues are summarized as follows.

Wayfinding, or the manner in which people find important locations in an environment, is a difficult task for most people in the maze of large general hospitals, and it is particularly difficult for the hospitalized patient whose status and entry-level stress may inhibit recognition of wayfinding cues. We suggest several design strategies that can turn an environment that is difficult to negotiate into a highly legible one. These strategies include the use of clear, legible signage systems that are consistent throughout the hospital; locating areas with related functions in close proximity to one another to reduce the distance patients must travel; distributing clear maps for patients and visitors, as well as posting maps throughout the complex; placing information desks at all public entrances; and providing guides to assist patients who are unable to negotiate the hospital on their own.

There are a number of design-related aspects of the hospital's environment that directly impinge upon patients' *physical comfort*. Noise levels, variations in temperatures, unpleasant odors, poor lighting, and the inability of patients to adequately manipulate their environment or comfortably position themselves within it can all influence the amount of discomfort patients experience during their hospital stay.

We suggest several design interventions that can reduce the "designed discomfort" for the patient population, including the use of sound-attenuating surfaces (e.g., carpeting) wherever possible; provision of individual temperature controls within patient's rooms as well as functioning HVAC systems; utilization of lighting designers who are sensitive to the enormous number of combinations of light fixtures and positioning, and who can work to eliminate glare and provide sufficient lighting for specific tasks; the use of furnishings and equipment that can be controlled by the patient, and the selection of furniture that is comfortable for long periods of time; and minimization of offensive odors by selecting surfaces that do not retain odors and by providing good ventilation systems throughout the hospital.

Privacy and personal territory are features of the hospital environment that are almost nonexistent for hospitalized patients. However, the availability of both privacy and personal territory can enhance patient recovery by providing opportunities for social support from friends and family, a sense of personal control in a setting in which patient control is severely limited, and security that comes from having a small space defined as one's own.

We suggest that patient control of privacy be a design principle of the hospital design decision maker. In public spaces, seating can be movable and seating groups separated spatially. Telephones can be designed and located to provide maximum acoustical privacy. In patient's rooms, privacy curtains should be available and under the control of patients. Also, they should be used by hospital staff when they are examining a patient or discussing his or her condition. In terms of personal territory, the hospital could provide areas within patient's rooms that are designed specifically for personalization (e.g., bulletin boards near patients' beds and lockers for personal belongings).

Finally, the design of the hospital's physical environment serves a *symbolic* function. That is, it tells patients how they are viewed in terms of their needs vis-à-vis the needs of other user groups within the hospital. We discuss several ways in which designs may be interpreted by patients, and we suggest that hospital designers should recognize the values they want to convey. Optimally, a hospital design should symbolize the hospital as a professional, competent institution in which patients are given the opportunity to control, as much as they are able, their own treatment and recovery process.

Our suggestions focus on the needs of patients within a very complex setting in which needs among user groups often conflict. In addition, several of our proposals are costly to hospitals in the short run. Given the high price of medical care in the United States, it would be easy for hospital designers to relegate these suggestions to a low position within the total context of design needs. However, we feel that by improving the environment of hospitalized patients, hospital management will experience several long-term benefits. More patients will be attracted to a hospital that is designed with their needs in mind, patient stress will be reduced, and valuable staff time that is now consumed by patients' requests for assistance can be focused on the tasks for which health professionals were trained. This will reduce the stress experienced by health professionals and may, in turn, reduce the high attrition rates among nurses and technicians within medical settings.

References

Altman, I. *The environment and social behavior: Privacy, personal space, territory and crowding.* Monterey, Calif.: Brooks/Cole, 1975.

Altman, I. Territorial behavior in humans: An analysis of the concept. In L. Pastalan & Carson (Eds.), *Spatial behavior in older people.* Ann Arbor, Mich.: The University of Michigan Press/Wayne State University Press, 1970.

American Hospital Association. *Environmental assessment of the hospital industry,* 1979.

Anderson, R., & Anderson, O. W. Trends in the use of health services. In H.E. Freeman, S. Levine, & L. G. Reeder (Eds.), *Handbook of medical sociology*. Engelwood Cliffs, N.J.: Prentice-Hall, 1979.

Andrews, G., & Tennant, C. Being upset and becoming ill: An appraisal of the relation between life events and physical illness. *Medical Journal of Australia*, 1978, *1*, 324–327.

Averill, J.R. Personal control over aversive stimuli and its relationship to stress. *Psychological Bulletin*, 1973, *80*, 286–303.

Avis, N. *An analysis of beneficial (and not so beneficial) effects of control-enhancing strategies*. Unpublished manuscript, The University of Michigan, 1979.

Bloom, S.W., & Wilson, R.W. Patient-practitioner relationships. In H.E. Freeman, S. Levine, & L.G. Reeder (Eds.), *Handbook of medical sociology*. Englewood Cliffs, N.J.: Prentice-Hall, 1979.

Broadbent, D. *Decisions and stress*. New York: Academic Press, 1971.

Brown, E.L. *Newer dimensions of patient care: The use of the physical and social environment of the general hospital for therapeutic purposes*. New York: Russell Sage Foundation, 1961.

Brownell, A. *Emotional and tangible social support as moderators of the stress-health relationship: A test of the specificity model*. Unpublished dissertation, The University of California, Irvine, 1981.

Cartwright, L.K. Sources and effects of stress in health careers. In G.C. Stone, F. Cohen, & N.E. Adler (Eds.), *Health Psychology*. San Francisco: Jossey-Bass, 1979.

Cobb, S. Social support as a moderator of life stress. *Psychosomatic Medicine*, 1976, *38*, 300–314.

Cohen, F., & Lazarus, R.S. Coping with the stresses of illness. In G.C. Stone, F. Cohen, & N.E. Adler (Eds.), *Health Psychology*, San Francisco: Jossey-Bass, 1979.

Cohen, S., & McKay, G. Social support, stress and the buffering hypothesis: An empirical review and theoretical analysis. In A. Baum, J.E. Singer, & S.E. Taylor (Eds.), *Handbook of psychology and health* (Vol. 4). Hillsdale, N.J.: Erlbaum, in press.

Craik, K.H., & Appleyard, D. Streets of San Francisco: Brunswik's lens model applied to urban inference and assessment. *Journal of Social Issues*, 1980, *36*, 72–85.

Devlin, A. S. Housing for the elderly: cognitive considerations. *Environment and Behavior*, 1980, *12*, 451–466.

DiMatteo, M.R., & Freedman, H.S. (Eds.), Interpersonal relations in health care. *Journal of Social Issues*, 1979, *35* (whole issue).

DiMatteo, M.R., & Freedman, H.S. A social-psychological analysis of physician-patient rapport: Toward a science of the art of medicine. *Journal of Social Issues*, 1979, *35*, 12–33.

Edney, J.J. Human territoriality. *Psychological Bulletin*, 1974, *81*, 959–975.

Edney, J.J. Human territories: Comment on functional properties. *Environment and Behavior*, 1976, *8*.

Edney, J.J., & Uhlig, S.R. Individual and small group territories. *Small Group Behavior*, 1977, *8*, 457–468.

Evans, G. Environmental cognition. *Psychological Bulletin*, 1980, *88*, 219–287.

Evans, G., Fellows, J., Zorn, M., & Doty, K. Cognitive mapping and architecture. *Journal of Applied Psychology*, 1980, *65*, 474–478.

Evans, G., & Howard, R.B. Personal space. *Psychological Bulletin*, 1973, *80*, 334–344.

Fiore, N. Fighting cancer: One patient's perspective. *The New England Journal of Medicine*, February 8, 1979, 284–289.

Folkman, S., Schaefer, C., & Lazarus, R. Cognitive processes as mediators of stress and coping. In V. Hamilton & D. M. Warburton (Eds.), *Human stress and cognition: An information-processing approach*. London: Wiley, 1979.

Freedman, H.S., & DiMatteo, M.R. Health care as an interpersonal process. *Journal of Social Issues*, 1979, *35*, 1–11.

Fuller, S., Endress, M., & Johnson, J. The effects of cognition and behavioral control on coping with an aversive health examination. *Journal of Human Stress*, 1978, 18–25.

Gallagher, E. Lines of reconstruction and extension in the Parsonian sociology of illness. In E.G. Jaco (Ed.), *Patients, physicians, and illness: A sourcebook in behavioral science and health* (3rd ed.). New York: Free Press, 1979.

Georgopoulos, B.S., & Mann, F.C. The hospital as an organization. In E.G. Jaco (Ed.), *Patients, physicians, and illness: A sourcebook in behavioral science and health* (3rd ed.). New York: Free Press, 1979.

Goffman, I. *Asylum*. New York: Doubleday, 1961.

Good, L.R., & Hurtig, W.E. Evaluation: A mental health facility, its users and context. *American Institute of Architecture Journal*, 1978, *67*, 38–41.

Guralnik, D.B. (Ed.), *Webster's New World Dictionary of the American Language* (2nd ed.). World Publishing Company, 1978.

Haan, N. Psychosocial meanings of unfavorable medical forecasts. In G.C. Stone, F. Cohen, & N.E. Adler (Eds.), *Health Psychology*. San Francisco: Jossey-Bass, 1979.

Heath, M., & Green, J.R.B. *Information usage in health facilities planning and design: The state of the art*. Kensington, New South Wales, Australia, University of New South Wales, School of Health Administration, 1976.

Holohan, C. Redesigning physical environments to enhance social interactions. In R.F. Muñoz, L.R. Snowden, & J.G. Kelly (Eds.), *Social and psychological research in community settings*. San Francisco: Jossey-Bass, 1979.

Holohan, C.T., & Slaikeu, K.A. Effects of contrasting degrees of privacy on client self-disclosure in a counseling setting. *Journal of Counseling Psychology*, 1977, *24*, 55–59.

Houston, B.K. Control over stress, locus of control, and response to stress. *Journal of Personality and Social Psychology*, 1972, *21*, 249–255.

Jaco, E.G. Ecological aspects of hospital patient care: An experimental study. In E.G. Jaco (Ed.), *Patients, physicians, and illness: A sourcebook in behavioral science and health* (3rd ed.). New York: Free Press, 1979.

Jacobs, S., & Langer, E. *Implications of the mindfulness-mindlessness distinction for health-related stress*. Paper presented at the annual convention of the American Psychological Association, Los Angeles, 1981.

Janis, I., & Rodin, J. Attribution, control and decision-making: Social psychology and health care. In G.C. Stone, F. Cohen, & N.E. Adler (Eds.), *Health Psychology*. San Francisco: Jossey-Bass, 1979.

Kaplan, B.H., Cassel, J.C., & Gore, S. Social support and health. *Medical Care*, 1977, *15*, 47–58.

Katz, P. Ritual in the operating room. *Ethnology*, in press.

Knowles, J.H. Doing better and feeling worse: Health in the United States. In E.G. Jaco (Ed.), *Patients, physicians, and illness: A sourcebook in behavioral science and health* (3rd ed.). New York: Free Press, 1979.

Kornfeld, D.S. The hospital environment: Its impact on the patient. In R. Moos (Ed.), *Coping with physical illness*. New York: Plenum, 1977.

Krantz, D.S., Glass, D.C., Contrada, R., & Miller, N.E. *Behavior and health*. New York: Social Science Research Council, 1981.

Krantz, D.S., & Schultz, R. Life crisis, control, and health outcomes: A model applied to cardiac rehabilitation and relocation of the elderly. In A. Baum & J. Singer (Eds.), *Advances in environmental psychology* (vol. 2). Hillsdale, N.J.: Erlbaum, 1979.

Lazarus, R. *Psychological stress and the coping process*. New York: McGraw-Hill, 1966.

Lazarus, R., & Cohen, J. Environmental stress. In I. Altman & J. Wohlwill (Eds.), *Human behavior and environment* (Vol. 1). New York: Plenum, 1976.

Lazarus, R., & Launier, R. Stress-related transactions between person and environment. In L.A. Pervin & M. Lewis (Eds.), *Perspective in interactional psychology*. New York: Plenum, 1978.

Lighting for health care facilities, Part 1. *Lighting Design and Application*, 1978, *8*, 19–40. (a)

Lighting for health care facilities, Part 2. *Lighting Design and Application*, 1978, *8*, 36–53. (b)

Lipowski, Z.J. Physical illness, the individual and the coping process. *Psychiatry in Medicine*, 1970, *1*, 91–102.

Lorber, J. Good patients and problem patients: Conformity and deviance in a general hospital. In E.G. Jaco (Ed.), *Patients, physicians, and illness: A sourcebook in behavioral science and health* (3rd ed.). New York: Free Press, 1979.

Marshall, N.S. Privacy and environment. *Human Ecology*, 1972, *2*, 93–110.

Mechanic, D. Physicians. In H.E. Freeman, S. Levine, & L.G. Reeder (Eds.), *Handbook of medical sociology*. Englewood Cliffs, N.J.: Prentice-Hall, 1979.

Mills, R.T., & Krantz, D.S. Information, choice, and reactions to stress: A field experiment in a blood bank with a laboratory analogue. *Journal of Personality and Social Psychology*, 1979, *37*, 608–620.

Mathis, S.A., & Bakeman, R. *Privacy in public: Crowding and sex effects in a laundromat*. Paper presented at the annual meeting of the American Psychological Association, Toronto, August 1978.

Moos, R.H. (Ed.), *Coping with physical illness*. New York: Plenum, 1977.

Moos, R. Social-ecological perspectives on health. In G.C. Stone, F. Cohen, & N.E. Adler (Eds.), *Health Psychology*, San Francisco: Jossey-Bass, 1979.

Moos, R.H., & Tsu, V.D. The crisis of physical illness: An overview. In R. Moos (Ed.), *Coping with physical illness*. New York: Plenum, 1977.

Pastalan, L. *Relocation, mortality, and intervention*. Paper presented at the annual meeting of the American Psychological Association, Montreal, August 1980.

Pastalan, L., Mautz, R.K., & Merrill, J. The simulation of age-related sensory losses: A new approach to the study of environmental barriers. In W.F.E. Pruser (Ed.), *Environmental design research* (Vol. 1). Stroudsburg, Pa.: Dowden, Hutchinson & Ross, 1973.

Parsons, T. Definitions of health and illness in the light of American values and social structure. In E. G. Jaco (Ed.), *Patients, physicians, and illness: A sourcebook in behavioral science and health* (3rd ed.). New York: Free Press, 1979.

Rabkin, J.G., & Struening, E.L. Life events, stress, and illness. *Science*, 1976, *194*, 1013–1020.

Rapoport, A. *Human aspects of urban form*. Elmsford, N.Y.: Pergamon, 1977.

Raven, B.H., & Haley, R.W. Social influence in a medical context. In B. Raven (Ed.), *Policy studies: Annual Review* (Vol. 4). Beverly Hills, Calif.: Sage Publications, 1980.

Reeder, S.J., & Mauksch, H. Nursing: Continuing change. In H.E. Freeman, S. Levine, & L.G. Reeder (Eds.), *Handbook of medical sociology*. Englewood Cliffs, N.J.: Prentice-Hall, 1979.

Reizenstein, J. E. Hospital design and human behavior: A review of the recent literature. In A. Baum & J. Singer (Eds.), *Advances in environmental psychology* (Vol. 4). Hillsdale, N.J.: Erlbaum, in press.

Reizenstein, J.E., & Grant, M.A. *Report Number 1: Schematic design of inpatient rooms.* Ann Arbor, Mich.: The University of Michigan, Office of Hospital Planning, Research and Development, 1981(a).

Reizenstein, J.E., & Grant, M.A. *Report Number 2: Patient activities and schematic design preferences.* Ann Arbor, Mich.: The University of Michigan, Office of Hospital Planning, Research and Development, 1981(b).

Reizenstein, J.E., & Grant, M.A. *Report Number 3: Videotape study of the main entrance.* Ann Arbor, Mich.: The University of Michigan, Office of Hospital Planning, Research and Development, 1981(c).

Reizenstein, J.E., & Grant, M.A. *Report Number 6: Spontaneous design suggestions by patients and visitors.* Ann Arbor, Mich.: The University of Michigan, Office of Hospital Planning, Research and Development, 1981(d).

Reizenstein, J.E., & Grant, M.A. Unpublished working notes, The University of Michigan, 1981(e).

Rodin, J., & Langer, E. Long-term effects of a control relevant intervention with the institutionalized aged. *Journal of Personality and Social Psychology*, 1977, 35, 897–902.

Rosengren, W.R., & Devault, S. The sociology of time and space in an obstetrical hospital. In E. Friedson (Ed.), *The hospital in modern society*. London: Free Press of Glencoe, 1963.

Saegert, S. High density environments: Their personal and social consequences. In A. Baum & Y. Epstein (Eds.), *Human responses to crowding*. Hillsdale, N.J.: Erlbaum, 1978.

Schaefer, C., Coyne, J.D., & Lazarus, R. The health-related functions of social support. *Journal of Behavioral Medicine*, in press.

Searles, J. *The nonhuman environment.* Unpublished dissertation, The University of Michigan, 1979.

Seligman, M.E. *Helplessness.* San Francisco: Freeman, 1975.

Selye, J.H. The evolution of the stress concept. *American Scientist*, 1973, 61, 692–699.

Shapiro, J., & Shapiro, D. The psychology of responsibility: Some second thoughts on holistic medicine. *New England Journal of Medicine*, 1979, 301, 211–212.

Shumaker, S.A. *Perceived discomfort and behavior strategies of privacy attainment: An experimental simulation.* Unpublished dissertation, The University of Michigan, 1979.

Shumaker, S.A. *Adjusting the physical environment: A response to the discomforts of inadequate privacy.* Paper presented at the annual meeting of the American Psychological Association, Montreal, August 1980.

Shumaker, S.A., & Shapiro, J. Unpublished working notes: The Johns Hopkins University, 1981.

Simmons, D., Reizenstein, J.E., & Grant, M.A. Considering carpets in hospital use. *Dimensions in Health Services*, 1982 59(b), 18–21.

Sklar, L., & Anisman, H. Stress and cancer. *Psychological Bulletin*, 1981, *89*, 369–406.

Sommer, R. The ecology of privacy. In H. Proshansky, W.H. Ittelson, & L.G. Rivlin (Eds.), *Environmental psychology: Man and his physical setting*. New York: Holt, Rinehart and Winston, 1970.

Sommer, R. *Personal space: The behavioral basis of design*. Englewood Cliffs, N.J.: Prentice-Hall, 1969.

Sommer, R. *Tight spaces: Hard architecture and how to humanize it*. Englewood Cliffs, N.J.: Prentice-Hall, 1974.

Sommer, R., & DeWar, R. The physical environment of the ward. In E. Friedson, (Ed.), *The hospital in modern society*. London: Free Press of Glencoe, 1963.

Spivack, M. Sensory distortions in tunnels and corridors. *Hospital and Community Psychiatry*, 1967, *18*, 24–30.

Steele, F.I. *Physical settings and organization development*. Reading, Ma.: Addison-Wesley, 1973.

Stewart, A. *Coping with serious illness: A conceptual overview*. Rand Corporation Publication, P6640, October, 1980.

Stokols, D. A congruence analysis of human stress. In I.G. Sarason & C.D. Speilberger (Eds.), *Stress and anxiety* (Vol. 6). Washington, D.C.: Hemisphere Press, 1979.

Stokols, D., & Shumaker, S.A. People in places: A transactional view of settings. In J. Harvey (Ed.), *Cognition, social behavior and the environment*. Hillsdale, N.J.: Erlbaum, 1981.

Stone, G.C., Cohen, F., & Adler, N.E. *Health psychology*. San Francisco: Jossey-Bass, 1979.

Sundstrom, E., Burt, R.E., & Kamp, D. Privacy at work: Architectural correlates of job satisfaction and job performance. *Academy of Management Journal*, 1980, *23*.

Tagliacozzo, D.L., & Mauksch, H. The patient's view of the patient's role. In E.G. Jaco (Ed.), *Patients, physicians, and illness: A sourcebook in behavioral science and health* (3rd ed.). New York: Free Press, 1979.

Taylor, R.B. Human territoriality: A review and a model for future research. *Cornell Journal of Social Relations*, 1978, *13*, 125–151.

Taylor, S.E. Hospital patient behavior: Reactance, helplessness, or control? *Journal of Social Issues*, 1979, *35*, 156–184.

Thompson, S.C. A complex answer to a simple question: Will it hurt less if I can control it? *Psychological Bulletin*, 1981, *90*, 89–101.

Trites, D.K., Galbraith, F.D., Jr., Sturdevant, M., & Leckart, J.F. Influence of nursing unit design on the activities and subjective feelings of nursing personnel. *Environment and Behavior*, 1970, *2*, 303–334.

Vernon, D.T., & Bigelow, D.A. Effect of information about a potentially stressful situation on responses to stress impact. *Journal of Personality and Social Psychology*, 1974, *29*, 50–59.

VerSteeg, D.F., & Croog, S.H. Hospitals and related health care delivery settings. In H.E. Freeman, S. Levine, & L. G. Reeder (Eds.), *Handbook of medical sociology*. Englewood Cliffs, N.J.: Prentice-Hall, 1979.

Vogel, M.J. *The invention of the modern hospital*. Chicago: University of Chicago Press, 1980.

Weisman, J. Evaluating architectural legibility. *Environment and Behavior*, 1981, *13*, 189–204.

Westin, A. *Privacy and freedom*. New York: Atheneum, 1967.

Willems, E.P. Behavioral ecology, health status, and health care: Application to the rehabilitation setting. In I. Altman & J. Wohlwill (Eds.), *Human behavior and environment: Advances in theory and research* (Vol. 1). New York: Plenum, 1976.

Wolfe, M. Room size, group size and density behavior patterns in a children's psychiatric facility. *Environment and Behavior*, 1975, *7*, 199.

Wolfe, M., & Laufer, R. The concept of privacy in childhood and adolescence. In S. Margulis (Ed.), *Privacy*. Stroudsburg, Pa.: Dowden, Hutchinson, and Ross, 1974.

Wortman, C.B., & Brehm, J.W. Response to uncontrollable outcomes: An intergration of reactance theory and the learned helplessness model. In L. Berkowitz (Ed.), *Advances in experimental social psychology* (Vol. 8). New York: Academic Press, 1975.

Wortman, C.B., & Dunkel-Schetter, C. Interpersonal relationships and cancer: A theoretical analysis. *Journal of Social Issues*, 1979, *35*, 120–125.

Zimring, C.M. Stress and the designed environment. *Journal of Social Issues*, 1981, *37*, 145–171.

8.   School environments and stress

Sherry Ahrentzen, Gregory M. Jue, Mary Anne Skorpanich, and Gary W. Evans

Children spend a large portion of their waking hours in educational settings. The average student spends approximately 7,000 hours in school from kindergarten to sixth grade. Except for the bedroom, there is no single enclosure in which the young child spends a longer amount of time than in the classroom (Jackson, 1968). Although there is considerable research on educational programs, surprisingly little attention has been given to the impact of the physical setting of schools on children and teachers. In this chapter, we propose that the effects of school settings on children and teachers can best be understood from an interactionist perspective that emphasizes the concept of person–environment fit. Stress is conceptualized as an outcome reflecting the lack of congruence between individual needs and goals with the opportunities and constraints afforded by the school setting. When environmental constraints directly or indirectly thwart such goals or expectations, the individual attempts to cope with the stressful situation. Manifestations of this process in the school setting may include changes in teaching methods, class disruptions or participation, persistence, spatial utilization patterns, task performance, or attention and distraction.

Potential sources of environmental stress in schools are reviewed in the first section of this chapter. These environmental characteristics may be stressful when they hinder or deter students and teachers from achieving their goals in the classroom. For instance, sociopetal seating arrangements tend to facilitate interaction; however, such seating arrangements may be stressful for those students who seek and need privacy from others during study. Windowless classrooms may produce claustrophobic reactions, resulting in decreased attendance or attention to tasks in the classroom.

The amount of aural and visual stimulation in open-plan classrooms may deter students from performing class activities efficiently and speedily. Most research of the physical environment of schools is in preliminary stages and/or suffers from serious methodological shortcomings. It is difficult to draw many firm conclusions on the ways in which the classroom environment can lead to dissatisfaction and discomfort in teachers and children.

Therefore, our review of the research literature on sources of environmental stress in school settings is followed by a discussion of methodological and theoretical problems. Methodological problems include fundamental issues such as nonrandom assignment of subjects and absence of control groups, as well as more complex issues such as overreliance on self-report data and standardized achievement tests.

There is also a paucity of conceptual work on the issue of school settings. We develop the concept of person–environment fit within the context of a stress model and, in the final section of this chapter, we propose a framework, incorporating this perspective, for understanding human behavior in school environments.

Environmental sources of stress in schools

Various features of the physical environment of schools have been examined by researchers. Early research focused on seating position and climatic conditions. Changes in the design and construction of schools in the last two decades have led to concern over school features such as windowless buildings, noise, and open classroom construction. The postwar baby boom and subsequent large school populations piqued research interest in the effects of classroom density and school size. In addition, studies of the school environment have examined a diversity of social and psychological outcomes: class participation and disruption, task performance, achievement, teaching time and style, attention and distraction, persistence and motivation, privacy, perceptions of crowding and noise, patterns of space utilization, and satisfaction.

In this section we discuss research on seating position and arrangement; amenities such as windows, decorations, and secluded study areas; classroom density; school size; climatic and luminous conditions; noise; and open school designs. Our review is not exhaustive (an exhaustive review is provided by Weinstein, 1979). Instead, we review representative research in the field and discuss limitations and restrictions of research methodology and theory on school settings and behavior. Laboratory experiments are included only when further refinement or interpretation of the findings of a particular field study is needed. In addition, our review is limited to studies in elementary and high school settings. Studies in college settings, although quite extensive and informative, are excluded. In addition to differences in cognitive skills and age of the students, the postsecondary and elementary–secondary school settings differ markedly in the amount of student control typically encountered. As control appears to be a strong mediator of stress and coping (Averill, 1973; Cohen, 1980; Glass & Singer,

1972), our intention is to focus on those individuals who have little choice and control in their educational settings.

Seating position and arrangement

Seating position in the classroom has been studied extensively since 1934. At that time Sumley and Calhoun (1934) discovered that the distance between pupil and teacher was a significant factor in the child's ability to remember word groups. Since then a number of studies have found that the front-and-center row seating positions are significantly correlated with high class grades, positive attitudes, and a higher degree of participation for those predisposed to speak in class (see Weinstein, 1979).

One of the most extensive studies of seating position was conducted by Adams and Biddle (1970), who observed verbal interaction between teachers and students in 32 classes at the primary and secondary levels. They found the greatest amount of verbal interaction among those students sitting in desks in the front and center rows. They consequently labeled this area the "action zone." It may be that teachers attend more to students in the front and center of a class, as Adams and Biddle discovered that the "targets" of teacher-initiated conversation were overwhelmingly located in the "action zone." Delefes and Jackson (1972), studying a fifth-grade class and an eighth-grade class, did not find any differences in teacher–student interaction due to seating position. However, they did find that teachers called on students in the front more often than those in the back. Examining 14 elementary school classrooms, Schwebel and Cherlin (1972) found that students who were assigned seats in the front rows were more attentive and engaged in more task behavior than those students in other rows. When students were then randomly assigned seats, these differences disappeared. However, those students who moved forward received more favorable teacher ratings on attentiveness and likability than they received before the change of seats. Students who moved from front to back seats received less favorable teacher ratings.

Although the conflicting findings in these studies may arise from methodological differences, together these studies do reveal an interesting connection between the environment and students' reactions, namely, the teacher. Teacher-initiated conversation and teachers' perceptions of student attentiveness were associated with students' seating positions. Further research needs to address the causes of such phenomena and the consequences to students of these teacher practices, especially over a long time span. Such findings have important implications for classroom practices involving the frequency of changing seating positions during the school year.

Unlike the extensive research on seating position, that on seating arrangements is quite slim. The traditional seating arrangement of rows and columns is still common in many classrooms. However, new arrangements, such as horseshoe patterns or desks clustered together so that students face each other, also are prevalent in many classrooms. Winett, Battersby, and Edwards (1975) investigated the effects of change from a traditional row and column to cluster seating arrangement. Examining academic and social behaviors of a sixth-grade classroom, they found no significant differences. However, their sample size was small, their time span for baseline observations quite limited, and their postintervention observations confounded with academic interventions; thus, no lagged effects could be noted. Further research needs to be undertaken, focusing on the effects of sociopetal seating patterns at the grade school level and of students working in close proximity to their classmates. Potential effects include increased distraction, withdrawal as a form of privacy seeking, helping behaviors among students, and aggression.

Amenities: Windows, decorations, secluded study spaces

Schools today typically contain the standard provision of desks, chairs, and chalkboards, but they often vary in other classroom amenities such as decorations, types of furniture, and separate study spaces. Advances in technology and construction have even made the presence of windows an amenity in school design. Windowless schools are often the focus of heated debates in the community. Proponents mention freedom from excessive heat, glare, and distraction, and a decrease in vandalism, and opponents speak of the lack of visual access to the outside and claustrophobic reactions (Brown & Hult, 1967; Burts, 1961; Nimnicht, 1966). In a review of the research, Collins (1975) concluded that windowless classrooms had little impact on students. Demos, Davis, and Zuwaylif (1967), for example, found no significant differences in achievement test scores, grade point averages, health records, or personality test results for fifth-grade students in two classrooms, with and without windows, respectively.

Larson (1965) conducted a 3-year longitudinal study of a school in which, for 1 year, the windows were removed. Performance and class behaviors of the same students were studied in settings with and without windows. He found no significant differences in school performance or overall absenteeism. A grade-by-grade analysis did reveal that kindergartners were more frequently absent from the windowless school, perhaps indicating that an adaptation process to windowless schools occurs after the first year in a windowless building. Unfortunately, in these studies the absence of random assignment of students to schools or classes and the covariation of other environmental features with the presence or absence of windows make it difficult to draw firm conclusions about the effects of windows on behavior.

Attitude surveys of children in windowless schools reveal less consistent conclusions. Survey results range from positive evaluations of windowless classrooms (Chambers, 1963), evenly divided opinions (Tikkanen, 1970), to increased displeasure toward windowless classrooms as length of tenure in school increases (Demos et al., 1967).

Laboratory studies of the aesthetic appeal of surroundings were undertaken in the 1950s by Mintz (1956) and Maslow and Mintz (1956). These early studies revealed that adults working in "ugly" environments felt more discontent, fatigue, monotony, and a greater desire to leave than those working in more "beautiful" rooms. In an elementary school setting, Santrock (1976) demonstrated that the "affective" quality of a setting can influence students' task persistence. Approximately 100 students were taken individually to rooms that were decorated with "happy," "sad," or neutral posters. Those students in the "happy" room persisted longer at a motor task than those in rooms with neutral or sad posters. As Weinstein (1979) points out, these findings question prevailing practices characterizing the persistence and motivations of students as enduring, personal traits. Situational factors such as room design may have a greater impact on student involvement than is generally recognized. Other aesthetic factors that are feasible for future study include decorating with children's artwork rather than commercial or teacher-constructed decorations (a form of student personalization); bright colors versus dark or muted colors; and carpeting and soft furniture (Sommer & Olsen, 1980) as opposed to tile floors and exclusively hard furniture.

Another classroom amenity, secluded study space for students, is an occasional feature in school classrooms, either constructed by the original contractors, fabricated later by teachers and students, or provided by commercial school suppliers (e.g., cubby corners, hideaway cubes). Secluded study spaces are physically distinct areas, smaller in scale and size than the regular classroom, and intended to accommodate only a few students. They are physically separated from the rest of the classroom either by changes in floor level or by walls and partitions. Ahrentzen (1981) found such spaces to be particularly important to students. When asked where they would like to go when they really needed to concentrate, 60% of the students in classes with such spaces mentioned them; in contrast, 11% of students in such classes reported that they could concentrate at their desks. Unfortunately, the use of such spaces is often restricted by teachers. Environmental features thus may provide opportunities for optimal study, but institutional or class practices may negate these opportunities, possibly resulting in student frustration from coping in less than optimal environments.

Weinstein (1977) used a quasi-experimental, time series design to examine the effects of design changes in an elementary classroom. Additional shelving and writing areas accessible to students, a small private area in the corner of the room, and clear boundary demarcations of specific study areas were added to the classroom. With these changes, Weinstein reports a more even distribution of students across the room, use of previously underutilized areas of the classroom, and an increase in the use of manipulative games and materials. She also found a decrease in the time spent by students "looking at people" in the reading area.

Density

Studies of density in classrooms primarily focus on satisfaction and social behaviors. Krantz and Risley (1972) found that kindergartners who crowded around a teacher to listen to a story were less attentive than when they were more dispersed. Shapiro (1975) found a curvilinear relationship between square foot per pupil and random, noninvolved behavior in a nursery school setting. Noninvolved behavior was high in most crowded (less than 30 ft. per pupil) and least crowded conditions (more than 50 ft. per pupil), and least frequent in moderately crowded conditions (between 30 and 50 ft. per pupil). In a study of 13 elementary school classrooms ranging from 25 to 33 sq. ft. per person, Ahrentzen (1981) found teachers reporting more distractions from physical contacts, difficulty of movement, and perceived crowding in the denser classes. However, these findings did not hold for students.

Ahrentzen (1980) also found that in classrooms with cluster seating arrangements, clusters with more desks were related to decreased distractions from physical contacts and decreased crowding for teachers but to increased distraction and crowding for students. This discrepancy in students' and teachers' reactions to cluster size may reflect their differing uses of space in the classroom. If children spend a large amount of time at their desks, then they spend more time in close contact with others when in large clusters. Such contact may be disruptive. On the other hand, larger clusters of desks usually allow larger areas of floor space. If the teacher spends a great amount of time moving about the classroom, the large areas may provide him or her more area to move around in without bumping into others or squeezing between rows.

A number of researchers have investigated aggressive behavior in dense classrooms. These investigators have distinguished between social density' (changing the number of individuals in the same space) and spatial density (the same number of people in different size spaces). Laboratory studies by Loo (1972) reveal less group involvement, increased time in social play, and decreased aggressive behavior with children in higher spatial density conditions. Hutt and Vaizey (1966) examined the effects of increased social density on normal, brain-damaged, and autistic children. Although their sample size was quite small, they found that higher social density led to increased aggression among normal and brain-damaged children and less aggression in autistic children. Autistic children additionally spent more time along the periphery of the room in the denser setting. Contrary to the findings of these studies, McGrew (1970), examining both spatial and social density in nursery schools during free play, found no significant differences in physical contact under any density condition. However, in conditions of high social density, children adjusted their locations so that the same distance between individuals was preserved.

Availability of resources, however, may mediate the impacts of density in classrooms. Smith (1975), for example, suggested that the amount of play equipment per child is a critical intervening variable in density studies. Since increased social density implies a greater pupil to toy ratio, greater competition for resources may be responsible for aggressive behavior. Smith and Connolly (1972) found no increases in aggressive behavior in high-density, preschool situations when the number of toys per child was held constant. Rohe and Patterson (1974) found increased aggressive behaviors under conditions of high-density/low-resources conditions compared to high-density/high-resources conditions.

Another critical resource in the classroom that may interact with density is the teacher. In a study of eight open education classes, Rivlin and Rothenberg (1976) utilized behavior mapping techniques and interviews to study patterns of classroom space use. They found a convergence of students in only a small portion of the total space – that space generally close to the teacher. Coupled with interview findings of perceived lack of space, Rivlin and Rothenberg suggest the possibility of perceived crowding due not to lack of physical space but rather to uneven utilization of available space.

Also examining perceptions, Ahrentzen (1981) found that teachers in classes with more open perimeter space report less crowding, and teachers in classes with greater ceiling height report less distraction from physical contacts with students, although there were no differences in actual physical contacts during observation periods. Perhaps architectural modifications such as higher ceilings and more open perimeters that have been used by architects to distort perceptions of space may consequently affect perceptions of crowding.

In summary, although spatial density of classrooms is related to various student behaviors and teacher perceptions, a number of factors may mediate this relationship: furniture arrangements, spatial utilization patterns, resources, ceiling hight, and perimeter openings. Further research on the density of classrooms is needed as class populations increase in size, not because of the growing population of young people, as in the fifties and sixties, but because of recent trends in migration patterns, declining school enrollments, and fiscal cutbacks. A number of schools are closing and students are being routed to other schools, thus increasing the classroom density in these accommodating settings. When new school buildings are needed, school funding is scarce. The result is new but smaller schools that are expected to accommodate student populations that are growing tremendously in areas such as the South and the West. Future studies need to account for more than just spatial or social density but also for other factors that pertain to crowding. Class density continually fluctuates because of rotating classes, team teaching, or students' leaving the classroom for other study areas in the school. The temporal duration of crowding needs to be investigated both at the classroom level (density levels throughout the day or school year, activity level of class) and at the level of the individual (e.g., one's prior experience in dense school settings; crowded conditions at home). Cultural differences have been neglected in school density research. Furthermore, the relation between spatial density and resource density needs to be further explored. Other class resources for investigation include the number of learning or "interest" centers in the classroom; availability of secluded study spaces or corners for quiet, isolated study; and access to teacher aides or teaching assistants.

School size

Investigations of school enrollment size have been extensively undertaken by Barker and Gump and their colleagues (Barker & Gump, 1964). Examining over 200 high schools in the Midwest, they found that students from smaller schools were more likely to participate in extracurricular activities, were more satisfied with participation in school, had more positive self-images, showed greater personal responsibility, and were more sensitive to the needs of others. They attributed these differences to different levels of staffing in the schools. If the number of members in a setting falls below a minimum maintenance level, a condition of understaffing exists so that some or all of the members must take on a larger number of roles in order to maintain that setting. If the number of members exceeds the capacity of a setting, then the setting is considered overstaffed (Barker, 1968; Wicker, McGrath, & Armstrong, 1972). Thus, in order to maintain a setting, students in small schools need to take on additional responsibilities and are consequently more valued.

Although the research on size and staffing in secondary schools is quite extensive (see also Baird, 1969; Wicker, 1968), no comparable studies in elementary or middle schools have been undertaken. Other relevant outcome measures such as achievement, vandalism, and social attitudes have been neglected yet seem particularly relevant for future research on staffing requirements of behavior settings.

Climatic and luminous conditions

Temperature, humidity, and air movement all appear to have an effect on academic achievement and task performance. In general, higher degrees of temperature and humidity are associated with greater discomfort and decreased achievement, task performance, and attention span, and cooler temperatures are associated with increased comfort, activity, and productivity. For instance, Flatt (1975) studied high school students in a gymnasium. As temperature in the gym was increased, fitness and endurance performance fell. Ryd and Wyon (1970) studied third-, fourth-, and fifth-grade Swedish students in a laboratory setting. Higher temperatures (27 compared to 20°C) led to decreased performance on oral language tasks for these students. Wyon (1970) describes a series of heat experiments with children that revealed decreases in simple task performance and comprehension at high (27–30°C) compared to low (20°C) temperatures. These results held for 11- and 13-year-old students but not for 17-year-olds. Wyon (cited in King & Marans, 1979) also examined 40 Swedish 11-year-olds in a laboratory situation, looking at the effects of temperature and noise on two types of tasks, one needing a great deal of concentration, the other requiring very little. Noise conditions were either at 65–70 or 85–90 dB; temperature varied from 20 to 23.5 to 27°C. Increased temperatures resulted in decreased performance on the task requiring a great deal of concentration but increased performance in the nonconcentration task. There was no effect for noise.

In a series of studies of thermal conditions on elementary school children (Schoer & Shaffran, 1973), researchers had matched pairs of students perform various tasks under two controlled class conditions: (1) temperature varying from 21 to 24°C, humidity varying from 35 to 61%, and air movement at 20–40 ft. per minute; and (2) temperature at 22–27°C, humidity at 26–48%, and air movement at 15 to 25 ft. per minute. This latter condition was said to reflect the "typical" classroom condition. No differences were found between the two groups in performing a simple task. However, differences between the two groups occurred on a more complex, conceptual task, with those students in the "typical" condition taking more time to complete the task and making more errors. Those students in the experimental condition also reported that they were more comfortable.

In England, Humphreys (1974) interviewed 48 elementary school teachers from six schools. These teachers reported that rain, wind, and cooler temperatures resulted in better attention, concentration, and activity among the students. Heated conditions were reported to be associated with decreased concentration, attention, and student activity. In 1978, Humphreys interviewed over 600 elementary school students. For these students discomfort was related to the change in temperature rather than to the absolute temperature itself. The greater the change in temperature, the greater the number of student complaints.

Unfortunately, most studies examining the effects of heat are undertaken in laboratory settings and not school settings (the Schoer and Shaffran studies were in a contrived classroom setting, students only using these rooms for 2 to 8 weeks). Admittedly, undertaking research on temperature and humidity in natural settings is difficult when one must consider uncontrollable fluctuations in temperature and regional differences, not only in climate but also in economic and social dimensions. However, several outcome factors pertinent to the impact of temperature (e.g., absenteeism, student lethargy, amount of teacher time spent teaching, teacher satisfaction, active versus passive learning tasks) can only be examined in natural settings.

Little research has been undertaken examining lighting in school settings. Research by Mayron, Ott, Nations, and Mayron (1974) was conducted on approximately 100 first-grade students in four windowless classrooms in Florida. Two classes were equipped with cool white fluorescent lights; the other two had Vitalite (full spectrum) fluorescent lights with cathode elements wrapped to shield against X-rays. The fixtures were further shielded against other electromagnetic radiation. First graders were randomly assigned to these classrooms. From observations conducted for 6 months, the researchers found less hyperactive behavior and greater discipline among the students in the experimental classes. There were no differences in absenteeism or visits to the school nurse. Although confounds exist with teaching style and discipline, this study reveals a need to examine whether improportioned lighting and/or radiation are stress-inducing environmental features for students.

Noise

Although the research conducted on noise and stress is voluminous (see Cohen & Weinstein, Chap. 2, this volume), little research has been conducted on the impacts of normally occurring noise in schools. In order to understand noise in school settings, three dimensions are particularly relevant: duration of exposure (long or short term), nature of the noise, and threats of potential noise.

In examining short-term exposure to noise originating within the school, Slater (1968) compared seventh graders' performance on a standardized reading test in (1) a quiet (45–55 dB), isolated classroom; (2) an average (55–70 dB) classroom near hallways and other classes; and (3) an extremely noisy classroom (75–90 dB) near hallways and other classes and supplemented with noise from outside lawn equipment, tape recordings in neighboring classes, and free play in the hallways. No effects on speed or accuracy of performance were found under the difference noise conditions. Weinstein and Weinstein (1979) compared reading performance of fourth graders under quiet (47 dB) and normal (60 dB) noise conditions in classrooms. They found no impairments in task performance between the two groups although they did find a marginally significant decrease in speed of performance in the noisier setting.

Investigators have also examined long-term exposure to noise originating from outside the classroom. Kyzar (1977) studied the amount of traffic noise near various classrooms and discovered a decrease in teaching time where noise from the street was louder. Bronzaft and McCarthy (1975) examined the reading scores of elementary school students who were located near an elevated train. The scores of children on the noisy side of the building were significantly lower than those of students on the quieter sides. This decrement could occur as the result of (1) students' on the noisy side being unable to hear the teacher, resulting in decreased interaction and communication; (2) a decrease in instruction time on the noisy side, similar to findings of the Kyzar study; and (3) students' in noisier setting filtering out relevant and irrelevant sounds, resulting in poor auditory discrimination and, hence, poor reading ability (see Cohen, Glass, & Singer, 1973).

Cohen, Evans, Krantz, and Stokols (1980) examined the effects of long-term noise exposure on third and fourth graders from schools in the air corridor of Los Angeles International Airport and matched, control schools. There were no significant differences on tests of auditory discrimination, mathematics achievement, or reading achievement. However, students in schools under the air corridor displayed greater distractibility with increased years of exposure to noise. Additionally, these students manifested "learned helplessness" or a lack of persistence on a puzzle task and had significantly higher blood pressure. The use of multiple outcome measures (social, cognitive, and physiological) in this study displays the wide range of effects of noise on students' behaviors.

Aside from the duration of exposure to noise, another dimension of noise is its nature or content. Brunetti (1972) found that students in both elementary and high schools (both traditional and open space) reported that they were more often distracted by social conversation than task-oriented conversation or general noise. (These findings were also replicated by Ahrentzen, 1980, in elementary school classrooms.) High school students in Brunetti's study also reported less distraction during lab activities although decibel levels of lab and nonlab activities were similar. Looking at multiple stressors, Brunetti hypothesized that crowded conditions would amplify the effects of aural distraction, particularly in terms of distraction from social conversation. In the schools he examined, density differed in various areas and decibel level remained the same. Students in these high-density areas reported more distraction than those in low-density areas with the same decibel level. These results suggest that both individual and multiple combinations of environmental stimuli in classrooms can affect student activities and performance.

Fitzroy and Reid (1963) investigated acoustical satisfaction in 37 open-space schools. They found that high levels of ambient sound were acceptable to teachers and students although low reverberant spaces were the most acceptable. The conclusions they draw are similar to those of Brunetti: For intruding noise to be acceptable it ought to be of a general nature without easily identifiable components.

That noise in schools may be now "acceptable" to teachers and students has caused growing concern about the impacts of adapting to such noise. Critics warn about the effects of "tuning out" to stimulus overload (Dubos, 1965; Toffler, 1970) although no such studies in schools have been undertaken. However, the threat of potential noise can also produce a stressful situation (Lazarus, 1966), leading to a change in one's behavior. Instead of "tuning out," teachers and students may adapt to potential noise by inhibiting and restricting activities that would create noise and disturbance. Kyzar (1971), in studying teachers' attitudes toward noise in open and traditional schools, found that teachers in open-space schools selected activities that were "quiet producing." Gump and Good (1976) report similar responses by teachers in open-space schools. Teachers reported two dimensions of noise: noise that actually occurred and efforts to prevent noise. Teachers in open-space classrooms did not find the first type of noise much of a problem. However, half of the teachers mentioned efforts they used to prevent noise that restricted or eliminated certain activities. In a study of both traditional and open-design elementary schools, Ahrentzen (1981) found that those teachers who restricted certain class activities for fear of making noise and disturbing others were in classrooms with more demountable, nonstructural walls.

Thus, teachers' coping responses to potential noise may produce behaviors or conditions detrimental to students. The effects of noise-inhibiting practices of teachers may be particularly salient for younger students, who, because of their lack of control or choice, cannot oppose the teacher and because of their need to learn through active interaction with their environment (Leonard, 1968; Piaget, 1952). Unfortunately, many of the activities in which students take an active participant role in learning or work actively together as a group are the activities teachers eliminate in trying to cope with *potential* noise. Pen-and-paper tasks and quiet reading may become the students' standard activities. In a naturalistic observation study, Gump (1978) found that 36% of students' learning time in schools was spent in pen-and-paper tasks and 37% in directed recitation (i.e., the teacher questions, then the student answers). Where teachers feel so threatened by the potential of noise that they change their curriculum and teaching format, these passive modes of learning may become increasingly the primary teaching mode.

Openness

Most of the research on open space in schools concentrates on achievement outcomes. There is no conclusive evidence that either open-space or traditional school design enhances performance. Two large-scale studies, one by the Metropolitan Toronto School Board (1972) entailing 367 teachers and 1,078 students in 24 elementary schools of both traditional and open design, and one in Sweden in 1976 by Gron, Bertil, and Engquist (cited in King & Marans, 1979) involving 4,500 elementary and junior high school students in 160 classrooms (both open and traditional) and 60 testing instruments, show no simple relationship between open space and achievement. Gron et al. did find that students with good academic records performed better on achievement tests in open classrooms and students with poor academic records and with psychological problems scored better on the achievement tests in traditional schools. The Metropolitan Toronto School Board found no differences in achievement.

Examination of the effects of open space on achievement also has been conducted on a smaller scale. Weinstein (1979) reviewed much of this research and noted contradictory findings. For instance, Grogan (1976), Warner (1971), and Olson (1973) found no significant differences in achievement records of students in open space and traditional schools. Townsend (1971), Bell, Switzer, and Zipursky (1974), and Ward and Barcher (1975) found lower scores in open-space schools. Day and Brice (1977) and Killough (1972) found higher achievement for students in open-space compared to those in traditional schools.

These conflicting findings can be explained by major assumptions that permeate this research. First, many studies fail to adequately distinguish between open space (an architectural innovation) and open education (an educational philosophy and approach to learning), which leads to confusion about what is actually being measured. Controlling for teaching style or program when examining open space is frequently neglected. Second, in most studies, schools or classrooms are dichotomized into "open-space" or "traditional," misleading the reader to believe that schools are designed in two patterns only. A glance at schools built in the last 20 years supports the contention that there actually is an openness–containment continuum in school designs. The conventional dichotomous labels make it extremely difficult to compare research findings; that is, is an "open" classroom in one study similar to that of another? In addition, dichotomous labeling of designs that are so diverse compounds within-subject error in any study.

Third, the potentially serious confounds of subject selection have largely been ignored. Parents, teachers, and occasionally students themselves often choose the kind of school program and/or architectural setting the child will participate in. Thus, it is often difficult to distinguish the effects of classroom openness from selection factors that may systematically bias respective subject samples.

Finally, the strong emphasis on achievement scores has often led to the neglect of other outcomes that may be as important to the student. For instance, if there is no difference in achievement scores between open-space and traditional schools, one cannot assume that the students in open-space schools encounter no difficulty maintaining such achievement standing. The previously reported study by Cohen et al. (1980) illustrates this point for a different physical dimension: Although there was no difference in achievement scores, students in the noisier schools experienced greater distractibility and learned helplessness.

Recent studies have tried to correct some of these fallacies. Evans and Lovell (1979) examined class behaviors in an open-space high school in which variable-height, sound-absorbent partitions had been added to redirect traffic and define class boundaries. Using a quasi-experimental design with a nonequivalent control group, they found a reduction in classroom interruptions and an increase in substantive, content questioning with the classroom modifications. They suggest that clearly demarcated classroom boundaries and sharp distinctions between in-class and out-of-class spaces convey a connotative message to students about what set of behaviors is appropriate in a particular space.

Brunetti (1972) found that elementary students in open-space classrooms with conventional education programs reported that their classrooms were three times less noisy and less distracting than did students in open-space classrooms with individualized programs and those in a conventional school with a conventional program. In actuality, noise levels were higher in the open design–individualized program school, the noise levels in the other two schools being similar. Brunetti concluded that both the physical environment (the carpeting and lack of partitions in the open-space schools made the environment less reverberant) and the educational program were influential in students' perceptions of noise and distraction.

Examining students from several open-space and traditional elementary schools, Reiss and Dyhaldo (1975) hypothesized that open space would promote persistent task behavior. They reasoned that the capacity of a stimulus to disrupt ongoing behavior may be expected to habituate with prolonged stimulus exposures. Consequently, a relatively intense external stimulus might be required to distract pupils in open-space schools; they assumed such schools would have high visual and aural stimulation due to the presence of more students in larger rooms. They found that students from open-space schools were more persistent on puzzle tasks than students from traditional classrooms. There were no significant differences between students in open-space and traditional schools on a locus-of-control scale, suggesting that the higher levels of persistence shown by open-space students were not mediated by different attributes of causality. Additionally, for boys, persistence was positively related to achievement. Reiss and Dyhaldo found that those boys who remained relatively nonpersistent learned less in open-space than in conventional schools. Although this study does not effectively address selection bias or several of the problems discussed earlier in research on open design, it does show that when task performance is broadened beyond standardized achievement tests, effects of school architecture may be present.

Gump and Good (1976) examined the amount of time students spent in nonsubstance activity (e.g., moving, waiting, getting organized) at two traditional and two open-space schools. First and second graders in open schools spent a much larger percentage of school time in nonsubstance activity compared to those in the traditional schools. A similar difference was found for fifth and sixth graders, although the difference between open-space and traditional students was not as great.

Ahrentzen (1981) examined aural, visual, and kinetic distraction in classrooms rated along an openness–containment continuum. Perimeter structures were classified into percentage of perimeter occupied by nonpermanent or demountable walls, structural walls, and open perimeter space. For each classroom these three percentages total 100. She found that teachers in classes with higher percentages of demountable walls reported more aural and visual distraction, more crowding, and less satisfaction with the classroom environment. Teachers in classes with a great deal of open perimeter space reported less crowding and greater satisfaction, but students in these classes were less satisfied with their classroom. Additionally, as reported earlier, those teachers who restricted activities for fear of disturbing others were in classrooms with a larger percentage of nonstructural walls (a mean of 36% compared with a mean of 4% for those not restricting activities).

The construction of scales to measure openness meets a major obstacle in open classroom research discussed earlier, namely, the tendency of researchers to dichotomize classrooms as either open or traditional. Ross and Gump (1978) have also developed a continuous measure of openness, described in more detail in the following discussion.

A growing awareness of the problems of misfit between educational program and school facilities has recently evolved. Traub, Weiss, and Fisher (1977) differentiated between openness in architecture and openness in school program in 30 elementary schools in Ontario. They found that teachers in schools with open program *and* open architecture had higher positive attitudes than those in any other schools. Teachers in open-space schools interacted more often with other teachers, and students in these schools had higher positive attitudes toward school, teachers, and themselves. Gump and Ross (1977) found that teacher attitudes were most positive when team teaching programs were in open-space schools.

Ross (1980) looked at classroom modifications made in 21 open-space elementary schools. She found that teachers in these schools attempted to adjust and modify their buildings to be synomorphic or compatible with the type of educational program they employed. When the educational program is traditional, extreme reduction of original architectural openness generally occurs. In her study of fit between teaching program and classroom design, Ross used the "openness quotient" (Ross & Gump, 1978) as a continuous measurement of the degree of openness in these classes. This measure reflects the degree of openness of the entire school by determining the ratio of the building's area to the number of linear feet of walls enclosing the teaching areas. The modified openness quotient is the ratio of building area to enclosure, consisting of walls, original and newly constructed, and screening and marking furniture.

Research on school environments and human behavior needs to examine more carefully the concept of fit between users and settings and between programs and settings. Perhaps openness as an independent variable has yielded few clear effects on student behavior because some children are affected positively and others negatively, yielding a net, nonsignificant change in behaviors. As detailed in a later section of this chapter, research that takes into account individual differences in children and teachers and the instructional characteristics of class activities as they interrelate to environmental characteristics of classrooms may yield more definitive data on school design and behavior.

In summary, most of the past research on open school design is objectionable due to confounds and inadequate measurements of both predictor and outcome variables. Recent studies, however, attempting to rectify many of these problems, reveal the importance of fit between teacher program and classroom environment, perceptions of what is expected to occur in a classroom and the physical features that influence this perception, and the need to study other behavioral outcomes besides achievement (e.g., participation, persistence, substantive activity, and distraction).

Limitations of past research

The research on school environments reviewed here is limited in several respects. Many studies overemphasize achievement as an outcome criterion. Most ignore aftereffects and mediators of stress. Sample biases plague much of the work. Important predictor variables have been problematic, underutilized, or ignored. After reviewing these methodological and conceptual limitations, we will present an alternative research paradigm that addresses many of these problems. Although methodological problems with many studies abound (see Weinstein, 1979, for critique), we will focus most of our discussion on conceptual and theoretical problems in school environment studies.

Methodological limitations

Methodological difficulties of classroom studies include several sample biases. As with most field research, sample selection bias and the inability to randomize pose threats to internal validity. In addition, small sample sizes jeopardize conclusions drawn from many studies. Comparisons are often made between only two classrooms or between two schools that vary on one particular physical dimension. With only one comparison group there is a greater chance that differences observed are due to initial nonequivalence between groups. Two studies mentioned previously employing large samples, Gron et al. and the Metropolitan Toronto School Board, found no main effects for achievement by open versus traditional school design whereas several studies with smaller samples yielded mixed results.

In addition to subject selection bias, several other methodological problems plague many field studies of school design and behavior. Reactivity of measures is a problem, particularly when teachers and students can "guess" the desired outcomes of a particular study. Additionally, many studies of classroom design have not utilized control groups, relying on changes in behavior measured pre- and postintervention. The importance of control groups in school settings, even when nonequivalent, is discussed in detail by Evans and Lovell (1979).

Statistical problems are also apparent. Many statistical procedures assume that observations are independent, in which case the unit of analysis should more appropriately be the class rather than the individual. Another problem is overall experiment error rate. Type I errors, the probability of falsely rejecting the null hypothesis, inflate when multiple dependent measures are analyzed. Appropriate multivariate techniques have generally not been used in previous school environment research.

Conceptual problems

Much of the research, particularly that examining noise and classroom openness, relies solely on achievement or task performance as outcome measures. This is problematic, first, because school achievement depends on a great number of factors other than the physical setting. As such, it is naive to assume that a change in the physical environment could directly affect achievement if other influencing factors (e.g., motivation, teacher expectations, SES) remain the same.

Second, large individual differences in student aptitude or intelligence may obscure tests of the significance of school design on standardized tests. This is particularly true when between-groups study designs are employed, as is often the case in classroom design research. Third, as mentioned previously, if no difference in achievement scores is found, one cannot assume that students encounter no difficulties in maintaining such achievement standings. Decreased speed of performance, passive interest in school work, distractibility, and aftereffects occurring in other settings are undesirable conditions that students may have to endure to maintain achievement status in less than optimal school environments.

Fourth, the sole reliance on achievement tests ignores direct impacts the physical environment may have on behavior other than intellectual performance. Attitudes, health, spatial behavior, satisfaction and comfort, social behavior, and participation have largely been ignored in studies of school settings. As discussed by Weinstein (1979), intellectual achievement is critical, but it is not the sole criterion of school success. Although traditional perspectives view achievement variables as the ultimate ends of schooling, recent critics and researchers (Moos, 1979; Sommer, 1973) have begun to doubt the practicality and adequacy of that perspective. In reviewing the effectiveness of schooling, Averch (1974) found that socialization and the development of creativity and self-reliance were among the most important functions of schooling. Recent evidence (see Moos, 1979) show low relationships between cognitive achievement, as measured by grades and standardized tests, and later success. Epstein and McPartland (1975) found that positive reactions to school increase the likelihood that students will stay in school, develop a lasting commitment to learning, and use the institution to advantage.

Another limitation of previous research is the lack of attention to aftereffects of stress. Harmful effects of stressors may go undetected because they manifest themselves when coping efforts stop or fail (Cohen, 1980). During experimental noise conditions subjects may show no task performance deficits, yet deficits are noted during subsequent quiet testing conditions (Cohen & Weinstein, Chap. 2, this volume). This failure to carefully consider aftereffects is common to nearly all previous classroom studies. One exception is the study by Cohen et al. (1980) in which children from noisy schools were tested under quiet conditions. Evidence of aftereffects in the forms of distractibility and decreased task persistence was found. Aftereffects may occur in the cafeteria, the playground, or at home. The isolation of the school as the only observed setting ignores the possible carry-over of behaviors or aftereffects across settings.

Time is another important variable neglected by past research. Many stressors produce cumulative effects from long-term exposure (Dubos, 1965) that may not be observed in "one-shot" experimental designs. In two studies, length of exposure was associated with decreasing satisfaction in windowless classrooms (Demos, 1965) and with increasing distractibility, decreasing task persistence, and increasing blood pressure in noisy classrooms (Cohen et al., 1980). Additionally, few classroom studies have examined how changes in the physical environment impact student behaviors. Three studies that are exceptions observed behavioral outcomes of systematic changes in seating arrangement (Schwebel & Cherlin, 1972), traffic flow (Evans & Lovell, 1979), and study area boundaries (Weinstein, 1977).

Few classroom studies have investigated mediators of stress. Throughout the stress literature, control, predictability, and adaptation have been observed to mediate the negative impact of most stressors (Baum, Singer, & Baum, Chap. 1, this volume). As mentioned previously, lack of control and choice in the classroom is a primary feature of elementary and secondary schools (Jackson, 1968). However, within schools there is some diversity. Basic options such as student choice of seats, furniture arrangement, and ability to leave the room to study are available in some classes and not in others. The relative availability of such choices may obscure other environmental influences. Unfortunately, situational variables tapping individual's control and predictability of stressors have not been explored.

Besides control and choice, a number of other mediating variables that may have importance for the notion of stress in classroom environments have not been studied. For instance, teachers' attitudes toward the classroom have received only scant attention. Studies of seating position have noted the relation between environmental conditions and teachers' expectations of students' participation and interaction. Kyzar (1971), Gump and Good (1976), and Ahrentzen (1981) report that teachers in open space classrooms restricted activities for fear of creating noise and disturbing nearby classrooms. These behavior restrictions could consequently create stress not only for teachers but also for students. Another neglected dimension is teacher "burnout." In some instances, this problem may be related to the misfit between a teacher's instructional program and the physical environment. Does coping with inadequate or unsatisfactory environmental conditions add to the problem of stress or "burnout," and what are its consequences for students? Failure to include dimensions of teacher satisfaction in the sociophysical context of the classroom may overlook important stress-inducing interactions between the teacher and the physical setting that are eventually reflected in students' behaviors.

A final set of limitations involves the independent variables in classroom research. In particular, the levels of some independent variables have not been adequately construed. As mentioned earlier, the open-space–traditional design dichotomy inadequately describes the continuum of openness–containment in school design today. Only two studies, Ross and Gump (1978) and Ahrentzen (1981), employ interval level measurement of this dimension. In another study on the effects of heat (Azer, 1972), experimental conditions varied by only 2.5°C in relatively high temperatures (32.5 vs. 35°C), and no temperature effects for task performance were found. The use of inadequate levels of these variables may explain the insignificant or conflicting results obtained.

The open–traditional dimension suffers further from a construct validity problem. As noted earlier, openness has not been defined consistently across studies and is rarely differentiated from educational philosophy. This confound may be the cause of discrepant findings among studies in this area.

Person by situation fit

An overriding criticism of classroom environment research is the absence of combinations of predictor variables. Although the study of multiple stressors is almost nonexistent, stressors rarely occur in isolation and frequently display synergistic effects (Baum et al., Chap. 1, this volume). Very few studies of classroom settings have examined more than one isolated source of stress. Furthermore, the combination of personal and environmental variables and their interactions has not been applied extensively. A major reason for the lack of sufficient evidence on the effects on the classroom environment may be that individual characteristics of students have not been taken into account. That is, an interaction between individual characteristics and aspects of the classroom setting may exist, an interaction that heretofore has been ignored by research dealing with the physical environment of the school. Information from the environment is mediated by the individual, and his or her response will be determined by personal factors (e.g., motivational) involved in that mediation process. The situational orientation that runs through much of the classroom research to date fails to recognize that environmental effects are not unidimensional: *All* students do not require private spaces in classrooms, nor are *all* children distracted in open-space classrooms.

We suggest that a person–environment interaction model of behavior be used to guide research in classroom settings. According to this model, an individual is characterized by a reliable pattern of stable *and* changing behaviors across situations of different character (Endler, 1975). Inherent in this construct is the assumption that both personal and environmental aspects must be considered in any understanding of human behavior. Furthermore, the interaction of both aspects provides more explanatory power than is afforded by a separate examination of either person or setting variables alone. Endler (1975) also describes the necessity of employing an interactional framework in behavioral research:

Asking whether behavioral variance is due to either situations *or* to persons, or how much variation is contributed by persons and how much by situations (an additive approach) is analogous to asking whether air *or* blood is more essential to life or asking to define the area of a rectangle in terms of length or width. . . The appropriate and logical question is *"How* do individual differences and situations *interact* in evolving behavior?"

Additionally, a person–environment congruence or "fit" perspective provides a theoretical explanation that meshes with the stress perspective. Less than an optimal match between individual needs and the classroom environment may lead to lowered levels of performance, satisfaction, and health. Stress can be predicted to occur whenever a person is placed into a situation (sociophysical environment) that does not match his or her expectations, degree of goal achievement, or desired amount of satisfaction.

The interaction model of behavior can be extended to assume that persons and environments can interact at an *optimal* level. That is, one can imagine persons and environments as pieces of a large jigsaw puzzle: Pieces that fit together form a stable balance whereas mismatching pieces that are forced together create disharmony. According to this person–environment fit model, a high level of fit would be accompanied by high levels of satisfaction, performance, goal attainment, and health; conversely, person–environment mismatches would be accompanied by dissatisfaction, goal blockage, performance and health deficits, and stress (French, Rogers, & Cobb, 1974; Jahoda, 1961; Pervin, 1968).

Though an interactionist approach to behavior has long been advocated in psychological theory (cf. Brunswik, 1943; Hull, 1943; Lewin, 1951; Tolman, 1938), research in the area (e.g., Pervin, 1968; Wechsler & Pugh, 1967) and new theoretical formulations (e.g., French et al., 1974; Hunt & Sullivan, 1974) have emerged relatively recently. In the educational arena, a body of research categorized as aptitude–treatment interaction (ATI) reflects an interactionist perspective. ATI examines the interaction of student attributes (e.g., anxiety) with various instructional techniques. Educational psychologists have argued that no single instructional process provides all students with optimal learning (Cronbach, 1957, 1967; Gagné, 1967; Glaser, 1967). As an example, a comprehensive study by McKeachie (1961) found that students with strong achievement needs performed best in classes that were highly organized and structured and that those with high affiliation needs did best in classes with "warm teachers." Reviews of ATI research can be found in Cronbach and Snow (1969) and Berliner and Cohen (1973). Much of this research has employed college students as subjects.

Though admirable, aptitude–treatment research to date is noted by several limitations: (1) "treatment" most often refers to a teaching method or the organizational atmosphere of the classroom; the physical environment is ignored; (2) when the physical classroom setting *is* accounted for, it is described as either "open" or "traditional" based on a priori operational definitions; and (3) only a very small number of classrooms are usually employed.

Unfortunately, very few studies have examined the interaction of personal characteristics by classroom setting features. Judd (1974) found that students characterized by an internal locus of control had more positive self-concepts and more positive attitudes toward school in open-space schools, whereas those with an external locus of control had more positive self-concepts and school attitudes when in traditional schools. Schuster, Murrell, and Cook (1980) observed preschoolers across six different behavior settings in their nursery school. In aggregate analysis, they found that person, setting, and person–setting interaction all contributed significantly to social behavior. Individual analyses indicated that younger children, those with lower IQs, those who had attended the school for at least 1 year, and girls had more consistent behavior across settings.

Ahrentzen (1980), in examining the impacts of the physical environment of 13 elementary school classrooms, found that personal characteristics or preferences of the teacher interacted with environmental features to affect distraction. The congruence between a teacher's desired class population size (personal characteristic) and actual class size (physical feature) was examined. Actual class size ranged from 25 to 33, with a mean of 30; teachers' expressed optimal class size ranged from 15 to 30, with 23 being the mean. For each teacher a ratio was constructed between the optimal and actual class size: The higher the ratio the more congruence between actual and desired sizes. The mean ratio was .79, with a range between .47 and 1.0. Large congruence ratios were significantly correlated with less perceived kinetic distraction and more perceived noise. Congruence, however, was not related to general satisfaction with the classroom environment.

Open education programs in open-space schools have been said to improve student self-esteem and positive attitudes. However, there is little evidence of this. Gump (1980) cites a study in open schools by Beck (1979), which found higher self-esteem scores for high SES students and lower scores for the lower SES students. A large-scale study undertaken by Traub and Weiss (1974) showed differences in open space compared to traditional schools for suburban children. In open schools, the suburban students had more positive attitudes toward self, more liking for school, and more autonomy. However, these differences did not hold for urban students. Traub and Weiss also found that, on achievement measures, suburban children in open-space and traditional schools did equally well. However, urban students in traditional schools achieved higher than those in open-space schools.

Solomon and Kendall (1976) used multivariate statistical techniques to assess performance of fourth-grade students with varying motivational and cognitive characteristics in three open-space and three traditional classrooms. Compared to the traditional classrooms, the open classrooms had more accessible materials, more interest centers, more stimuli of various sorts (e.g., plants and posters), and more varied and simultaneously occuring activities; the atmosphere was more spontaneous and informal, and the teacher interacted more with individuals and small groups than with the class as a whole. Cluster analysis of children's characteristics resulted in six clusters. Multivariate analysis of variance revealed that childrens' characteristics (in terms of clusters) showed the greatest bearing on performance but were not the sole determinants. Personal characteristics × class-type interactions revealed significant differences for a number of outcomes: achievement scores, decision-making autonomy, self-direction, undisciplined activity level, and creativity. For instance, those children who were personally motivated and directed, but in a nonacademic direction, were more undisciplined in traditional classes than in open classes. They also reported stronger values on decision-making autonomy and task self-direction when in open classes than in traditional ones. In addition, they had higher achievement test performance when in traditional classrooms. Although attempts to generalize findings must be curtailed because of limited sample size and unequal cell sizes, Solomon and Kendall's study provides a good research example of person–environment interactions in the school setting. Unfortunately, the physical characteristics of the setting are confounded with organizational elements, thus limiting our understanding of what particular features in the environment interact with personal characteristics.

The following section describes an attempt to build on these studies by integrating elements of student characteristics, classroom organization and social climate, and physical setting features into a framework for studying school settings and stress. The primary focus of this framework is not the separate elements but the *interaction* between environmental and personal factors.

A taxonomy for the study of stress in elementary school settings

Because we believe that stress results from unsatisfactory person–environment fit, a taxonomy incorporating both domains – personal and environmental – was developed to guide research dealing with stress in elementary school

Table 8.1. *A taxonomy for the study of stress in elementary school settings*

Personal attributes	Environmental attributes	
	Physical/design	*Social/organizational*
Past classroom setting experience	Class enrollment	Student involvement
Locus of control	Density	Affiliation
Achievement need	Openness/containment	Teacher support
Sensation-seeking tendency	Arrangement of furnishings	Task orientation
	Seating position	Competition
Competitiveness/ cooperation	Territoriality	Order and organization
	Privacy areas	Rule clarity
Coronary-prone behavior pattern	Soft/hard atmosphere	Teacher control
	Wall decorations	Innovation
	Accessibility of materials	Teacher–environment fit
	Audiovisual stimulation	
	Boundary clarity	

Fit indicators	
Attitudinal	*Behavioral*
Satisfaction with classroom	Attendance
Commitment to school work	Questioning behaviors
Quality of school life	Participatory behaviors
	Social disruptive behavior
	Persistence on tasks
	Fidgeting behaviors/nervousness
	Creativity

settings (see Table 8.1). It should be noted at the outset that we by no means envision our taxonomy as being exhaustive; rather we merely sought to include important variables, as determined by the literature, that we predict will interact according to the person–environment fit perspective. A study using this framework and employing a multimethod approach to the collection of the data currently is being conducted.

Environmental attributes

Like all settings, the elementary school classroom is composed of both physical and social elements. Additionally, because these two domains are part of a system, each can influence educational outcomes directly, as well as indirectly through the other domain (Moos, 1979). For example, a classroom may have secluded study spaces (a physical attribute) yet their use may be governed by the teacher (a social attribute); thus, any study of the effects of privacy areas on educational outcome would have to consider both domains.

In recognizing this, our typology of the elementary school classroom contains two dimensions: physical/architectural design and social/organizational.

Many of the physical features chosen are those traditionally examined in classroom research: class enrollment, density, arrangement of furnishings, seating position, decorations, and aural and visual stimulation (e.g., noise). Also included in the taxonomy are physical variables not often studied in the classroom setting. Territoriality is a concept found to be central to the study of environment and behavior relationships (Altman, 1975). Environments can also be classified as being either "hard" or "soft" (Sommer, 1974), that is, the willingness of settings to accept imprints from users. The accessibility of learning materials and the clarity of classroom boundaries have been examined in a few studies (e.g., Rohe & Patterson, 1974; Evans & Lovell, 1979) and are included in our taxonomy. In addition, we have included an objective measure of "openness" (Ahrentzen, 1981) departing from the more conventional a priori determined label, an approach criticized in a previous section.

All but one of the social/organizational elements of the taxonomy originated from descriptors used by Moos (1979) to characterize the social climate of a classroom: student involvement, affiliation, teacher support, task orientation, competition, order and organization, rule clarity, teacher control, and innovation. According to Moos, these elements make up three social climate dimensions: relationship, personal growth, and system maintenance and change. An additional concept included within our taxonomy is teacher–environment fit. A teacher enters a classroom with various expectations, goals, and needs; if these needs are not supported by the setting (i.e., person–environment mismatch), the teacher's behavior, we believe, will most definitely impact educational outcomes and the stress experienced by students.

Student attributes

Although numerous personal characteristics can no doubt be found to influence the amount of stress students experience, those in our taxonomy were chosen because we felt they would interact particularly well with the previously mentioned environmental attributes.

Remembering that stress is defined as the lack of congruence between personal and environmental factors, a student may experience stress if his or her past classroom setting experience differs substantially from the current situation. For example, being placed in an open-plan classroom after years in a more traditional setting may, at least initially, present difficulties for the student. Locus of control in open and traditional classrooms has been examined in at least one study (Judd, 1974).

Need for achievement and the related concept of competition/cooperation, it is felt, will also interact with environmental characteristics. Students with high achievement motivation and/or competitive drives placed in a classroom setting that emphasizes group learning and cooperation, for example, would experience stress according to the person–environment fit model. The same would apply to students with low achievement needs who are placed in highly competitive classrooms.

Persons differ in the amount of stimulation desired from the environment: Some 'people prefer unpredictable life-styles whereas others are attracted to the more routine. We believe this sensation- or arousal-seeking tendency will interact with the setting the person is in and that stress will result if there is incongruence. For example, noisy classrooms or classrooms with many visual distractions (e.g., students moving about) may be perceived as stressful to a student who is low in sensation-seeking tendency and not stressful to a student high in sensation-seeking tendency.

Medical research has characterized a behavior pattern (type A) related to coronary artery and heart disease that is distinguished by extreme competitiveness, strong sense of time urgency, impatience, easily aroused anger, and aggression (Friedman & Rosenman, 1974). In contrast, type B is defined as the absence of type A characteristics. It has been suggested that the health implications of type A behavior in adults can be traced to childhood experiences (Matthews and Angulo, 1980); in other words, the type A adult may have had a similar behavior pattern as a child. Because of this, and due to the prevalence of the health problems associated with type A, this attribute is included in our taxonomy. It is believed that this characteristic will interact with classroom settings: A type A child may not immediately experience stress in a classroom promoting such behavior, but in the long run, promotion of this behavior pattern may prove to be highly stressful (e.g., heart disease).

Fit indicators

Person–environment mismatches are assumed to result in stress, a condition that may exhibit itself as dissatisfaction and performance and health deficits. Thus, attitudinal indicators such as satisfaction with the classroom setting and commitment to school work and behavioral indicators such as attendance and disruptive behavior are included in our taxonomy. Task persistence is also felt to be an indicator of person–environment congruence: Students will expend more effort on a difficult task in settings that are supportive of their expectations and needs. On the other hand, in cases where there are person–environment mismatches, much energy may have been spent in merely coping with the situation so that students will have less to spend on the difficult task. The expression or repression of creativity is predicted to follow the same logic.

Conventional achievement measures such as grades and task performance have been omitted from the taxonomy because of the criticisms surrounding them (see previous sections). Instead, questioning and participatory behaviors are included. Increased student participation would indicate good person–classroom congruence; increased content questioning over process questioning would indicate lower distractibility (Evans & Lovell, 1979) and, hence, a higher level of fit.

Conclusion

We have reviewed basic findings on the school environment, noting potential sources of classroom stress such as the paucity of secluded areas that provide privacy, crowding, noise, and heat. The overall construction of rooms, particularly the degree of openness, can also impact human behaviors. We argue that the lack of strong, consistent environmental effects found in the classroom research literature is attributable to two primary factors. First, many important methodological limitations exist in this research area. For example, most studies have focused solely on school achievement and have operationalized this concept as scores on standardized achievement tests. It is not at all clear that these tests adequately measure school success. Furthermore, even if they do, is it reasonable to suspect that stress produced by environmental causes would have immediate, discernible effects on such measures? Basic research on stress and cognitive performance clearly indicates that stressors rarely cause immediate task decrements; many effects are apparent only after the stressor has been removed. In those few circumstances where immediate task decrements are found, researchers have noted the importance of measurement sensitivity. Only tasks that are very complex and demand large amounts of concentration seem to be immediately disrupted by stressors.

A second reason why most research on the effects of the school setting on behavior is equivocal is conceptual limitations in the work. The physical environment rarely has direct, unmediated impacts on human health and well-being. As we suggest, it is the *interaction* of individual characteristics with physical features of the environment that one must look at to more adequately understand how school environments affect behavior. Perhaps previous research on classroom environments that has focused almost exclusively on situation variables has failed to uncover important, interactive sources of variance in children's behavior. In addition, more careful assessment of classroom physical features such as a continuum of openness, may allow for a richer understanding of how the classroom environment can affect student and teacher behavior.

What practical application does this research perspective have for school policymakers and for architects? The basic message of the person–environment fit perspective is that all students do not learn in the same way. Open-space schools originally were conceived by architects to provide unlimited flexibility for the users of those settings. However, as Krovetz (1977, p. 263) points out, "space that is too flexible may not do the job well...a facility designed to be both a gymnasium and an auditorium is usually not ideal for either." Instead of "flexible" spaces (which, for many reasons, may turn out to be quite inflexible), a diversity of spaces or features in the design of schools seems more compatible with the varied needs of the users. Krovetz advocates a plurality of school design to accommodate the various teaching and learning styles that are in schools. Classrooms that accommodate structured teaching styles, spaces that allow for isolated, individual study, and areas conducive to peer teaching and teacher "consulting" styles, are all necessary to suit the needs of a typical school populace and could be integrated into a single school design.

Several practical consequences are also discernible to school policymakers. In situations that allow a choice between several identifiable educational programs and/or classroom settings, parents and their children may be intelligently counseled regarding a choice between alternative settings. For classes with more homogeneous student bodies (e.g., special education classes), research findings can be extrapolated to optimize individual settings. For those classes composed of the more typical heterogeneous student population, teachers, aware of the pluralistic environmental needs of the class, can modify their own classrooms to more adequately fit their teaching style and to provide a diversity of spaces relevant to the different needs of students.

References

Adams, R. S., & Biddle, B. J. *Realities of teaching: Explorations with video tape.* New York: Holt, Rinehart and Winston, 1970.

Ahrentzen, S. *Environment-behavior relations in the classroom setting: A multi-modal research perspective.* Unpublished master's thesis, University of California, Irvine, 1980.

Ahrentzen, S. The environmental and social context of distraction in the classroom. In A.E. Osterberg, C.P. Tiernan, & R.A. Findlay (Eds.), *Design research interactions.* Ames, Iowa: Environmental Design Research Association, Inc., 1981.

Altman, I. *The environment and social behavior.* Monterey, Calif.: Brooks/Cole, 1975.

Averch, H.A. *How effective is schooling? A critical review of research.* Englewood Cliffs, N.J.: Educational Technology Publication, 1974.

Averill, J.R. Personal control over aversive stimuli and its relationship to stress. *Psychological Bulletin,* 1973, *80,* 286–303.

Azer, N.Z. Effects of heat stress on performance. *Ergonomics,* 1972, *15*(6), 681–691.

Baird, L.L. Big school, small school: A critical examination of the hypothesis. *Journal of Educational Psychology,* 1969, *60,* 253–360.

Barker, R.G. *Ecological psychology.* Stanford, Calif.: Stanford University Press, 1968.

Barker, R.G., & Gump, P.V. *Big school, small school.* Stanford, Calif.: Stanford University Press, 1964.

Bell, A.E., Switzer, F., & Zipursky, M. Open area education: An advantage or disadvantage for beginners? *Perceptual and Motor Skills,* 1974, *39,* 407–416.

Berliner, D.C., & Cahen, L.S. Trait-treatment interaction and learning. *Review of Research in Education,* 1973, *1,* 58–94.

Bronzaft, A.L., & McCarthy, D.P. The effect of elevated train noise on reading ability. *Environment and Behavior,* 1975, *7*(4), 517–527.

Brown, S.W., & Hult, E.E. New York's first windowless air-conditioned school. *ASHRAE Journal*, 1967, *9*, 47–51.

Brunetti, F.A. Noise, distraction and privacy in conventional and open school environments. In W.J. Mitchell (Ed.), *Environmental design: Research and practice*. Berkeley: University of California Press, 1972.

Brunswik, E. Organismic achievement and environmental probability. *Psychological Review*, 1943, *50*, 255–272.

Burts, E. Windowless classrooms: Windows help to promote better classroom learning. *NEA Journal*, 1961, *50*, 13–14.

Chambers, J. A. A study of attitudes and feelings towards windowless classrooms (Doctoral dissertation, University of Tennessee, 1963). *Dissertation Abstracts International*, 1963–1964, *24*, 4498.

Cohen, S. Aftereffect of stress on human performance and social behavior: A review of research and theory. *Psychological Bulletin*, 1980, *88*(1), 82–108.

Cohen, S., Evans, G.W., Krantz, D.S., & Stokols, D. Physiological, motivational, and cognitive effects of aircraft noise on children: Moving from the laboratory to the field. *American Psychologist*, 1980, *35*(3), 231–243.

Cohen, S., Glass, D.C., & Singer, J.E. Apartment noise, auditory discrimination and reading ability in children. *Journal of Experimental Social Psychology*, 1973, *9*, 407–422.

Collins, B.L. *Windows and people: A literature survey* (Building Science Series No. 70). Washington, D.C.: National Bureau of Standards, 1975.

Cronbach, L.J. The two disciplines of scientific psychology. *American Psychologist*, 1957, *12*, 671–684.

Cronbach, L.J. How can instruction be adapted to individual differences? In R.M. Gagné (Ed.), *Learning and individual differences*. New York: Macmillan, 1967.

Cronbach, L.J., & Snow, R.E. *Individual differences in learning ability as a function of instructional variables*. Final Report, U.S. Office of Education. Palo Alto, Calif.: Stanford University, School of Education, 1969. (ERIC Document Reproduction Service No. ED 029 001.)

Day, B., & Brice, R. Academic achievement, self-concept, development, and behavior patterns of six-year-old children in open classrooms. *Elementary School Journal*, 1977, *78*(2), 132–140.

Delefes, P., & Jackson, B. Teacher-pupil interaction as a function of location in the classroom. *Psychology in the Schools*, 1972, *9*(2), 119–123.

Demos, G.D., Davis, S., & Zuwaylif, F. F. Controlled physical environments. *Building Research*, 1967, *4*, 60–62.

Dubos, R. *Man adapting*. New Haven, Conn.: Yale University Press, 1965.

Endler, N.S. The case for person-situation interactions. *Canadian Psychological Review*, 1975, *16*, 12–21.

Epstein, J. L., & McPartland, J.M. *The effects of open school organization on student outcomes* (Report 194). Baltimore: Johns Hopkins University, Center for Social Organization of Schools, 1975.

Evans, G.W., & Lovell, B. Design modification in an open-plan school. *Journal of Education Psychology*, 1979, *71*(1), 41–49.

Fitzroy, D., & Reid, J. L. *Acoustical environment of school buildings: Technical Report 1*. New York: Educational Facilities Laboratories, 1963.

Flatt, D.L. The effects of high temperature upon performance of certain physical tasks by high school students (Doctoral dissertation, North Texas State University, 1975). *Dissertations Abstracts International*, 1975, *35*, 7678A.

French, J.R.P., Jr., Rogers, W., & Cobb, S. A model of person-environment fit. In G.V. Coehlo, D.A. Hamburgh, J.E. Adams (Eds.), *Coping and adaptation*. New York: Basic Books, 1974.

Friedman, M., & Rosenman, R.H. *Type A behavior and your heart*. New York: Knopf, 1974.

Gagné, R.M. Instruction and the conditions of learning. In L. Siegel (Ed.), *Instruction: Some contemporary viewpoints*. San Francisco: Chandler, 1967.

Glaser, R. Some implications of previous work on learning and individual differences. In R.M. Gagné (Ed.), *Learning and individual differences*. Columbus, Ohio: Merrill, 1967.

Glass, D. C., & Singer, J.E. *Urban stress: Experiments on noise and social stressors*. New York: Academic Press, 1972.

Grogan, R. B. A comparative study of the openness of learning environment, student achievement, and student self-concept as a learner in an open space school and non-open space school (Doctoral dissertation, Georgia State University). *Dissertation Abstracts International*, 1976, *37*, 4115A.

Gump, P.V. School environments. In I. Altman & J.F. Wohlwill (Eds.), *Children and the environment. Human behavior and environment* (Vol. 3). New York: Plenum Press, 1978.

Gump, P.V. The school as a social situation. *Annual Review of Psychology*, 1980, *31*, 553–582.

Gump, P.V., & Good, L.R. Environments operating in open space and traditionally designed schools. *Journal of Architectural Research*, 1976, *5*(1), 20–27.

Gump, P.V., & Ross, R. The fit of milieu and programme in school environments. In H. McGurk (Ed.), *Ecological factors in human development*. New York: Elsevier North-Holland, 1977.

Hull, C.L. *Principles of behavior*. New York: Appleton-Century-Crofts, 1943.

Humphreys, M.A. Relating wind, rain and temperatures to teachers' reports of young children's behavior. In D. Canter & T. Lee (Eds.), *Psychology and the built environment*. New York: Wiley, 1974.

Hunt, D. E., & Sullivan, E. V. *Between psychology and education*. Hinsdale, Ill.: Dryden Press, 1974.

Hutt, C., & Vaizey, M.J. Differential effects of group density on social behavior. *Nature*, 1966, *209*, 1371–1372.

Jackson, P. *Life in classrooms*. New York: Holt, Rinehart and Winston, 1968.

Jahoda, M.A. A socio-psychological approach to the study of culture. *Human Relations*, 1961, *14*, 23–30.

Judd, D. E. *The relationship of locus of control as a personality variable to student attitude in the open school environment*. Unpublished doctoral dissertation, University of Maryland, 1974.

Killough, C.K. An analysis of the longitudinal effects that a nongraded elementary program conducted in an open space school had on the cognitive achievement of pupils (Doctoral dissertation, University of Houston, 1971). *Dissertation Abstracts International*, 1972, *32*, 3614A.

King, J., & Marans, R.W. *The physical environment and the learning process: A survey of recent research*. Ann Arbor, Mich.: University of Michigan, Architectural Research Laboratory, 1979.

Krantz, P., & Risley, T. *The organization of group care environments: Behavioral ecology in the classroom.* Lawrence, Kans.: Kansas University, 1972. (ERIC Document Reproduction Service No. ED 078 915.)

Krovetz, M.L. Who needs what when: Design of pluralistic learning environments. In D. Stokols (Ed.), *Perspectives on environment and behavior: Theory, research, and applications.* New York: Plenum Press, 1977.

Kyzar, B.L. *Comparison of instructional practices in classrooms of different design.* Final Report. Natchitoches, La.: Northeastern State University, 1971. (ERIC Document Reproduction Service No. ED 048 669.)

Kyzar, B.L. Noise pollution and schools: How much is too much? *CEFP Journal,* 1977, 4, 10–11.

Larson, C.T. (Ed.). *The effect of windowless classrooms on elementary school children.* Ann Arbor, Mich.: University of Michigan, Architectural Research Laboratory, 1965.

Lazarus, R. S. *Psychological stress and the coping process.* New York: McGraw-Hill, 1966.

Leonard, G. *Education and ecstasy.* New York: Dell, 1968.

Lewin, K. *Field theory in social science.* New York: Harper & Row, 1951.

Loo, C.M. The effects of spatial density on the social behavior of children. *Journal of Applied Social Psychology,* 1972, 2(4), 372–381.

McKeachie, W.J. Motivation, teaching methods, and college learning. In M.R. Jones (Ed.), *Current theory and research in motivation.* Lincoln, Nebr.: University of Nebraska Press, 1961.

McGrew, P. L. Social and spatial density effects on spatial behavior in preschool children. *Journal of Child Psychology and Psychiatry,* 1970, 11, 197–205.

Maslow, A.H., & Mintz, N.L. The effects of esthetic surroundings: I. *Journal of Psychology,* 1956, 41, 333–344.

Matthews, K.A., & Angulo, J. Measurement of the Type A behavior pattern in children: Assessment of children's competitiveness, impatience-anger, and aggression. *Child Development,* 1980, 51, 466–475.

Mayron, L. W., Ott, J.N., Nations, R., & Mayron, E.L. Light, radiation, and academic behavior. *Academic Therapy,* 1974, 10(1), 33–47.

Metropolitan Toronto School Board. *Study of Educational Facilities (SEF)-Academic evaluation. An interim report.* Toronto: Metropolitan Toronto School Board, 1972.

Mintz, N.L. Effects of esthetic surroundings: II. Prolonged and repeated experience in a "beautiful" and "ugly" room. *Journal of Psychology,* 1956, 41, 459–466.

Moos, R.F. *Evaluating education environments.* San Francisco: Jossey-Bass, 1979.

Nimnicht, G.P. Windows and school design. *Phi Delta Kappan,* 1966, 47, 305–307.

Olson, C.A. A comparative study involving achievement and attitudes of junior high school students from an open-concept elementary school and a self-contained elementary school (Doctoral dissertation, University of Nebraska, Lincoln, 1973). *Dissertation Abstracts International,* 1973–1974, 34, 3708A–3709A.

Pervin, L.A. Performance and satisfaction as a function of individual-environment fit. *Psychological Bulletin,* 1968, 69, 56–68.

Piaget, J. *The origins of intelligence in children.* New York: International Universities Press, 1952.

Reiss, S., & Dyhaldo, N. Persistence, achievement and open-space environments. *Journal of Educational Psychology,* 1975, 67, 506–513.

Rivlin, L., & Rothenberg, M. The use of space in open classrooms. In H. Proshansky, W. Ittelson, & L. Rivlin (Eds.), *Environmental psychology: People and their physical settings* (2nd ed.). New York: Holt, Rinehart and Winston, 1976.

Rohe, W., & Patterson, A.H. The effects of varied levels of resources and density on behavior in a day care center. In D. Carson (Ed.), *Man-environment interactions: Evaluations and applications (Pt. 3)*. Stroudsburg, Pa.: Dowden, Hutchinson & Ross, 1974.

Ross, R. P. Modification of space in open plan schools: An examination of the press toward synomorphy. In R. R. Stough & A. Wandersman (Eds.), *Optimizing environments: Research, practice, and policy*. Washington, D.C.: Environmental Design Research Association, Inc., 1980.

Ross, R., & Gump, P.V. Measurement of designed and modified openness in elementary school buildings. In S. Weiderman & J.R. Anderson (Eds.), *Priorities for environmental design research*. Washington, D.C.: Environmental Design Research Association, Inc., 1978.

Ryd, H., & Wyon, D.P. Methods of evaluating human stress due to climate. *National Swedish Institute for Building Research*, 1970, Document 6.

Santrock, J.W. Affect and facilitative self control: Influence of ecological setting, cognition, and social agent. *Journal of Educational Psychology*, 1976, *68*(5), 529–535.

Schoer, L., & Shaffran, J. A combined evaluation of three separate research projects on the effects of thermal environment on learning and performance. *American Society of Heating, Refrigeration and Air Conditioning Engineers. Transactions*, 1973, *79*(1), 97–108.

Schuster, S., Murrell, S., & Cook, W. Person, setting, and interaction contributions to nursery school behavior patterns. *Journal of Personality*, 1980, *48*, 24–37.

Schwebel, A.I., & Cherlin, D.L. Physical and social distancing in teacher–pupil relationships. *Journal of Educational Psychology*, 1972, *63*(6), 543–550.

Shapiro, S. Preschool ecology: A study of three environmental variables. *Reading Improvement*, 1975, *12*(4), 236–241.

Slater, B. Effects of noise on school performance. *Journal of Educational Psychology*, 1968, *59*, 239–243.

Solomon, D., & Kendall, A.J. Individual characteristics and children's performance in "open" and "traditional" classroom settings. *Journal of Educational Psychology*, 1976, *68*, 613–625.

Smith, P.K. Aspects of the playgroup environment. In D. Canter & T. Lee (Eds.), *Psychology and the built environment*. New York: Halsted, 1975.

Smith, P., & Connolly, K. Patterns of play and social interaction in preschool children. In N.B. Jones (Ed.), *Ethological studies of child behavior*. Cambridge: Cambridge University Press, 1972.

Sommer, R. Evaluation, yes; Research, maybe. *Representative Research in Social Psychology*, 1973, *4*, 127–133.

Sommer, R. *Tight spaces: Hard architecture and how to humanize it*. Englewood Cliffs, N.J.: Prentice-Hall, 1974.

Sommer, R., & Olsen, J. The soft classroom. *Environment and Behavior*, 1980, *12*(1), 3–16.

Sumley, F.H., & Calhoun, S.W. Memory span for words presented auditorially. *Journal of Applied Psychology*, 1934, *18*, 773–784.

Tikkanen, K.T. *Significance of windows in classrooms* Unpublished master's thesis, University of California, Berkeley, 1970.

Toffler, A. *Future shock*. New York: Random House, 1970.

Tolman, E.C. The determiners of behavior at a choice point. *Psychological Review*, 1938, *45*, 1–41.

Townsend, J.W. A comparison of teacher style and pupil attitudes and achievement in contrasting schools—Open space, departmentalized, and self contained (Doctoral dissertation, University of Kansas). *Dissertation Abstracts International*, 1971, *32*, 5679A.

Traub, R.E., & Weiss, J. Studying openness in education: An Ontario example. *Journal of Research and Development in Education*, 1974, *8*, 47–59.

Traub, R., Weiss, J., & Fisher, C. *Openness in schools; An evaluation study*. Ottawa: Ontario Institute for Studies in Education, 1977.

Ward, W.D., & Barcher, P.R. Reading achievement and creativity as related to open classroom experience. *Journal of Educational Psychology*, 1975, *67*, 683–691.

Warner, J.B. A comparison of students' and teachers' performances in an open area facility and in self-contained classrooms (Doctoral dissertation, University of Houston, 1970). *Dissertation Abstracts International*, 1971, *31*, 3851A.

Wechsler, H., & Pugh, T.F. Fit of individual and community characteristics and rates of psychiatric hospitalization. *American Journal of Sociology*, 1967, *73*, 331–338.

Weinstein, C.S. Modifying student behavior in an open classroom through changes in the physical design. *American Education Research Journal*, 1977, *14*(3), 249–262.

Weinstein, C. The physical environment of the school: A review of the research. *Review of Educational Research*, 1979, *49*(4), 577–610.

Weinstein, C.S., & Weinstein, N.D. Noise and reading performance in an open space school. *Journal of Education Research*, 1979, *72*(4), 210–213.

Wicker, A.W. Undermanning, performances, and students' subjective experiences in behavior settings of large and small high schools. *Journal of Personality and Social Psychology*, 1968, *10*, 255–261.

Wicker, A.W., McGrath, J.E., & Armstrong, G.E. Organization size and behavior setting capacity as determinants of member participation. *Behavioral Science*, 1972, *17*, 499–513.

Winett, R.A., Battersby, C.D., & Edwards, S.M. The effects of architectural change, individualized instruction, and group contingencies on the academic performance and social behavior of sixth graders. *Journal of School Psychology*, 1975, *13*(1), 28–40.

Wyon, D.P. Studies of children under imposed noise and heat stress. *Ergonomics*, 1970, *13*(5), 598–612.

9.   The office environment as a source of stress

Jean D. Wineman

Concern for the safety and health of workers has historically focused on industrial settings. It has only been in the last 10 years that office work, once viewed as free of health hazards, has been reevaluated. A body of research has emerged concerning environmental impacts on the health and safety of workers in office settings. These investigations have typically focused on physical health and safety and have only recently considered the importance of job satisfaction and psychological well-being. Creating environments that meet workers' needs for physical, social, and psychological well-being is now an accepted goal in both industrial and office settings. With this increased attention to environmental factors that affect mental as well as physical health, occupational stress has been identified as a potent health hazard.

This chapter reviews the role of environmental factors as stressors and mediators of stress in office settings. In the first section, physical environmental stressors are discussed, including the spatial arrangement, dimensions, and furnishings of the workspace; ambient conditions; artificial lighting, natural lighting, and view outside; visual and acoustical privacy; and other direct stressors. The second section provides a review of social and psychological factors that moderate the adverse effects of stress. In this section, social interaction, symbolic identification, and personal control are discussed. Implications for the design of office settings and directions for future research will be presented.

McGrath (1970) has defined stress as "a (perceived) substantial imbalance between demand and response capability, under conditions where failure to meet demand has important (perceived) consequences" (p. 20). In the workplace, this may be a discrepancy between the demands of a job

The author wishes to thank Gary Evans for his editorial guidance. Portions of this chapter will appear in *Environment and Behavior* (in press).

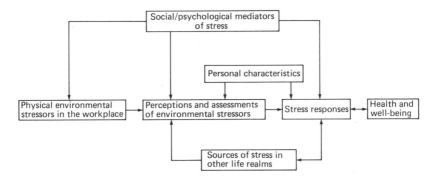

Figure 9.1. Model of the effect of environmental stressors on worker health and well-being.

and a person's skills and abilities to meet those demands, or a discrepancy between a person's occupational goals and needs (including career development, monetary rewards, and physical comfort) and the extent to which these goals and needs are met in the work environment. Misfit in either of these areas poses a threat to an individual's health and well-being (Harrison, 1978).

A model of the stress response

Whether a stressor leads to occupational ill health is dependent upon a number of intervening factors. These relationships are illustrated in the model presented in Figure 9.1. The model suggests that perceptions of stress are based upon, but distinct from, physical environmental stressors. A person's responses are mediated by his or her perceptions of environmental attributes and assessments of these attributes (expectation levels, aspiration levels, needs, and values).

Another important influence on the stress response is a set of variables referred to in the model as "personal characteristics." Included under this general heading are various individual characteristics and experiences that influence perceptions, assessments, and responses: socioeconomic factors such as age, race, income; aspects of personality such as temperament (optimism or pessimism) and response style (type A behavior pattern); as well as background experience and perceptions of available alternative experiences.

The model suggests that there are a number of social and psychological factors that act as mediators of the stress response. These factors may act directly on the source of stress to reduce its effects. For example, the ability to exert control, such as closing one's office door, is a means of reducing noise stress. Or, social and psychological factors may alter the perception of stress or reduce the negative impacts of a stressor. For example, the strong social support of colleagues may act indirectly to reduce the likelihood that environmental factors, such as monotonous tasks, may be perceived as stressful, or to reduce the likelihood that perceived stressors, such as long working hours, will adversely affect mental and physical health. In situations where the level of occupational stress cannot be reduced, it is possible to diminish its impacts by improving an individual's resistance to stress. Research suggests that job satisfaction, good social and work relations, participation, and control are mediators of job stress (Frankenhauser, 1978; Working Women, 1981); that is, these factors may moderate the negative impacts of occupational stress.

Finally, the model suggests that there may be sources of stress outside the workplace such as family problems or financial difficulties that may contribute to the perception of an environmental factor as stressful, or may exacerbate the negative impacts of stress. As indicated in the model, two-way relationships exist between stress responses, health, and well-being, and sources of stress in other life realms. Stress in the workplace may affect responses in other life spaces, shaping a person's relationships with family and friends. Research by Rissler and Elgerot (1978) demonstrates that the major impacts of work overload (as measured by adrenaline excretion) may not be felt until after working hours. Elevated heart rates and reported feelings of irritability and fatigue were also noted.

Responses to job stress may be psychological, such as job dissatisfaction, anxiety, mood changes, or other affective impacts; physiological, such as high blood pressure or elevated serum cholesterol; or behavioral, such as increased smoking, overeating, or frequent health visits (Harrison, 1978). Various types of responses to stressors are reviewed in detail by Baum, Singer, and Baum (Chap. 1, this volume). Sources of stress may accumulate over time and lead to such health problems as chronic depression, coronary heart disease, or peptic ulcer. Strain and illness also affect task performance and social behavior, which will only serve to aggravate the person–environment misfit. For example, environmental noise may cause mild discomfort, which results in irritable and unsociable behaviors. These behaviors may compromise social relationships. The environment is then perceived as unsupportive, and the individual may respond with increasingly aggressive or withdrawn social behavior. Thus, a vicious cycle may ensue, resulting in increasingly poorer fit between the worker and his or her office setting (Harrison, 1978).

Assessment of stress in office settings

Direct measurement of occupational stressors in office settings is difficult due to the subjective nature of the stress response. As described in the foregoing discussion, a person's responses are mediated by perceptions and cognitions of the external physical environment. Therefore, research in the field has largely focused on the investigation of indicators of occupational stress. Cross-sectional studies of morbidity, mortality, and accident rates have demonstrated significant differences in these indicators by occupation (Caplan, Cobb, French, Harrison, & Pinneau, 1975). In office settings, job stressors that are potential causes of these differences include poor working conditions, work overload, repetitive or monotonous work, role conflict or ambiguity, and underutilization of skills (Cox, 1980; Landy & Trumbo, 1976; McGrath, 1976; Smith, Colligan, & Hurrel, 1978; Wahlund & Nerell, 1978).

Although a number of laboratory studies have been conducted using simulated office tasks, the generalizability of these studies to actual office settings is unclear. Relatively little field research has been conducted, and the field research that does exist is based largely on self-report. In part this is due to the subjective nature of many of the stress indicators: job dissatisfaction, job tension or anxiety, low self-esteem. Job performance is difficult to measure directly in office settings because of the cognitive nature of office work. There is often no tangible product with which to assess output. And finally, the nature of the research (largely field research in office settings) often precludes the measurement of physiological responses (Caplan et al., 1975; Frankenhauser, 1978; French & Caplan, 1973; Kahn & French, 1970).

Existing research on stress in office settings has established a base of information from which to identify critical research areas. However, further research is needed to substantiate research results and to develop definitive recommendations for stress reduction through the design and management of the work setting.

Physical environmental stressors

Aspects of the office environment that influence worker comfort and satisfaction include workspace design, conditions of the ambient environment, lighting, and visual and acoustical privacy. Research suggests that these environmental factors can be sources of stress for office workers and may alter physiological responses, work performance, social behavior, satisfaction, and health.

Ergonomics

The adequacy and arrangement of work surface, chair, and storage space have been shown to impact comfort and productivity. Body dimensions and physical capabilities of workers, such as standing and seating heights, reach lengths, arm angles, viewing angles, and distances, affect personal comfort and efficiency in performing office tasks. Even for simple tasks, failures in workplace design can adversely affect health as well as performance (Tichauer, 1973).

Results from a national survey conducted by Harris (1980) indicate that office workers and executives feel productivity can be affected by the provision of proper furnishings (work surfaces, chairs, lighting, and storage space) to support work tasks. For example, a comfortable chair and good lighting were identified by 70% of the workers as factors that affected their personal comfort a great deal. A majority of workers reported experiencing backstrain or a tired back. Of the workers who have experienced problems with their back, most felt the cause was not work related; however, others reported the cause as stress at work or the strain of an uncomfortable chair. Anthropometric and biomechanical studies support these survey results. Optimal chair and desk height had been found to positively affect the accuracy and energy demanded for psychomotor activities such as typing (Burandt & Grandjean, 1963; Kroemer, 1971). In a similar study, Tichauer (1967) found that work surfaces requiring the upper arm to be raised above the relaxed elbow height increased the metabolic costs of work. Long periods of sitting have been associated with health problems such as backache and the aggravation of blood circulation problems, varicose veins, and hemorrhoids (Stellman, 1977).

The adequacy and arrangement of work groups and support services (conference rooms, storage, copy machines, telephones, typewriters, work and display surfaces) also affect work performance. Brookes and Kaplan (1972) report that, in a study of the attitudes and perceptions of 120 office employees, "adjacencies and layout" were major sources of dissatisfaction for office workers in both conventional and open-plan office settings. Workers were disturbed by noise, visual bustle, lack of privacy, and a lack of personal space control. Workspace layout appeared to be controlled by supervisors and supervisory policy.

Office automation

Automation in office environments has caused some additional problems with respect to physical comfort and health. Equipment such as video display units have special requirements for lighting, terminal support surfaces, viewing distances, and work surfaces. Inadequacies in the ability to achieve a satisfactory workstation design can result in discomfort. In a survey of insurance company employees using a computer-inquiry system, Springer (1980) found that 62% of the workers reported some physical discomfort while using display terminals with traditional office furniture. Of these workers, 74% identified back problems as the primary source of discomfort. Dainoff (1979), in a review of the scientific literature on occupational stress factors, reports that among the operators of keyboards (including typewriters, keypunch and accounting machines, and video display terminals), 25% of those studied suffered from occupational cervicobrachial syndrome (OCBS). Approximately 50% of the keyboard operators registered complaints of muscular distress of the arm, neck, and shoulders – symptoms of OCBS. These problems were more pronounced among workers who were involved in rapid work pacing and among the users of video display terminals (Figure 9.2) (Dainoff, 1979).

Figure 9.2. Equipment such as video display terminals has special requirements.

In a study conducted by Smith, Happ, Stammerjohn, and Cohen (1981), video display terminal (VDT) operators at five worksites, including newspaper offices and the clerical departments of Blue Shield in San Francisco, reported experiencing high levels of anxiety, depression, and fatigue. Of the clerical VDT operators, 80–90% reported eye strain or muscle strain. Dainoff (1981), in a review of current research in Austria, Germany, New Zealand, Sweden, Switzerland, and the United States, documents findings of higher levels of reported eyestrain and musculoskeletal discomfort among VDT operators than among non–VDT operators. However, ergonomic analysis indicates that the majority of the worksites studied did not meet current standards for workstation design. Environmental factors identified as potential contributors to discomfort include glare, background-to-surround contrast ratios, gaze angle, and keyboard height. Analysis demonstrated that the use of the VDT was not the only factor contributing to operator discomfort. The jobs of VDT operators often involved rigid work procedures, high production standards, pressure for performance, little operator control over tasks, and little operator involvement with the end product. Dainoff concludes that job demands and a lack of personal control may have significant impacts on the discomfort experienced by VDT operators and often associated with visual or postural problems.

Heating, air conditioning, and ventilation

Good air circulation and the right workspace temperature are among the most important factors for office workers' comfort (Hardy, 1974; Wheeler,

1969); yet these are factors with which many workers are dissatisfied (Harris, 1980). High and low ambient temperatures have been associated with discomfort, physiological arousal, impaired task performance, irritability, and asocial behavior (see Bell & Greene, Chap. 3, this volume, for a more detailed discussion).

The perceived "freshness" of air is of concern to many office workers (Harris, 1980; Parsons, 1976). If the supply of exterior air is inadequate, the percentage of oxygen in the interior air declines, and this may result in headaches, fatigue, or interference with concentration (Working Women, 1981). Air speed has been found to relate positively to levels of arousal (Bedford, 1961).

Sources of air contaminants in offices include vapors from office products or construction materials, fumes from office machines, outdoor pollutants drawn inside the building, and asbestos fibers from insulation or decorative materials. Twenty possible airborne irritants have been identified as potential contributors to office workers' health complaints (Stellman, 1977; Working Women, 1981). Among some of the more common irritants are formaldehyde, asbestos fiber, tobacco smoke, carbon monoxide, microorganisms, and allergens. According to a recent report by the National Research Council's Committee on Indoor Pollutants (1981), problems of indoor air quality could be aggravated by energy-saving efforts to achieve tightly sealed buildings and to reduce ventilation rates. Some of the negative impacts associated with air pollution include lowered arousal, decreased performance on vigilance tasks, and decrements in short-term memory (see Evans and Jacobs, Chap. 4, this volume, for a more detailed discussion). There is increasing evidence that concentrations of pollutants previously not thought to be harmful may have significant effects on mental and physical health (Mehrabian & Russell, 1974).

Artificial lighting

Lighting is ranked highly among the important aspects of the office environment; it is also one of the factors with which office workers are generally satisfied (Elder, Turner, & Rubin, 1979; Elder & Tibbott, 1981; Farrenkopf & Roth, 1980; Goodrich, 1979; Harris, 1980; Kraemer, Sieverts, & Partners, 1977). Optimum illumination levels depend upon task difficulty and required accuracy. For difficult and critical tasks, illumination levels as high as 100–150 footcandles may be appropriate. Barnaby (1980) conducted a systematic study of workers performing a difficult insurance office task under three levels of illumination: 50, 100, 150 fc. Results of this work suggest that productivity and accuracy increased at higher levels of illumination. Workers evaluated the higher illumination levels as more satisfying and reported they were under less stress, more productive, and more motivated in their work under higher illumination levels.

Research suggests that workers respond to the perceived quality of light as well as the quantity of light. Kraemer and his associates (1977) found that workers' evaluations of office lighting, and office conditions in general, were influenced by the level of illumination at workstations and by such qualitative factors as lighting level contrasts and glare.

The relatively recent use of high-pressure sodium lighting in offices has introduced an additional qualitative factor found to influence worker satisfaction: color rendition. High-pressure sodium lamps, which are being considered for office installations because of their low energy consumption, produce light that falls closer to the yellow end of the spectrum than the more common fluorescent lamps.

The impact of color rendition on worker satisfaction is controversial. The work of Williams (1975) indicates general acceptance by workers, whereas in a number of recent studies (Elder & Tibbott, 1981; Flynn, 1977; Wineman, 1981) high-pressure sodium lighting was found to be considerably less acceptable to workers than fluorescent sources. Aston and Bellchambers (1969) suggest that people require higher levels of light to reach a given level of satisfaction, if they feel a light source gives poor color rendition. The research in this area to date is quite limited, and further study would be required to draw definitive conclusions.

A number of studies have been conducted to assess the health impacts of the spectral characteristics of the light source, illumination levels, and duration of illumination (Lucey, 1973; Neer, Davis, Walcott, Koski, Schapis, Taylor, Thorington, and Wurtman, 1971; Vogl, 1976; Wurtman, 1975). Exposure to ultraviolet radiation has been found to influence the formation of vitamin D and the ability of the body to absorb calcium. Light has been used successfully as a treatment for neonatal jaundice. Cycles in environmental lighting are associated with rhythmic changes in biological functions. Although further study is needed, research results underscore the significant effects of lighting on health.

Certain office tasks, such as proofreading and typing, and the use of certain office equipment require special consideration with respect to lighting. The increased use of video display terminals has focused attention on the importance of lighting for comfort and health. Ostberg (1975) estimates that the use of VDTs under typical office lighting conditions will result in discomfort for half of the users. Short-term health effects associated with VDT use include eyestrain, headache, short-term loss of visual acuity, and changes in color perception (Cakir, 1980; Smith et al., 1981; Ostberg, 1975). Current research suggests that these conditions may be the result of either improperly designed display units (causing problems related to image flicker, poor character focus and resolution, and display brightness), or unsuitable lighting conditions (causing problems related primarily to contrast glare and reflective glare) (Stansaab Elektronik AB, 1978).

Natural lighting and view

Related to the issue of artificial lighting are considerations of natural lighting. Both natural lighting and a view to the outside appear in most evalua-

Figure 9.3. Natural lighting affects workers' evaluations of lighting quality.

tions of office settings as highly rated environmental factors (Boyce, 1974; Farrenkopf & Roth, 1980; Goodrich, 1979; Harris, 1978; Wineman, 1978). The research of Goodrich (1979) suggests that people whose office location is closer to the windows rate the quality of lighting more highly than people located farther from windows. Goodrich suggests that, "such things as the color, the temperature, the variation of natural light, its soft texture and its ambience are important but neglected factors of lighting" (p. 9), and these may be some of the reasons natural lighting is so desirable. Natural illumination is not a significant contributor to light levels at distances from the window greater than twice the height of the windows above the floor (Crouch, 1978). However, research by Wells (1965) indicates that if lighting levels are kept fairly constant from the window wall to the interior of a space (by compensating to some degree with artificial illumination), workers will grossly overestimate the amount of natural light reaching their work surface. Because of the high positive value associated with natural light, constant lighting levels from the window wall to the interior of a space would positively affect workers' evaluations of lighting quality (Figure 9.3).

Most people do not have complaints about exterior windows. However, complaints that have been voiced include cold drafts, heat from sunlight, and glare (Wheeler, 1969). Luminance of the sky as viewed through clear glass may range from between 10 to 100 times the optimal luminance required by typical office tasks. Crouch (1978) suggests that viewing areas of higher luminance than the task luminance severely reduce immediate scanning sensitivity and thus task performance for certain tasks. Natural lighting that is controlled, however, and approaches the work surface at wide angles with the vertical, is effective in overcoming veiling reflections (the reflected image of the light source) and provides for high visibility (Crouch, 1978). Recent research has suggested that full-spectrum lighting (lighting with a spectral distribution similar to natural daylight) may increase visual acuity, reduce overall fatigue, and improve work performance (Hughes, 1981; Maas, 1974).

View outside has also been identified in a number of studies as an important factor contributing to environmental satisfaction in offices (Elder & Tibbott, 1981; Farrenkopf & Roth, 1980; Goodrich, 1979; Wineman, 1978). Wineman (1978) found that the desire for a better view and more natural lighting appears to be independent of satisfaction with lighting in general. These findings lend support to the results of previous research, which suggests that, in addition to their value in providing natural lighting, windows provide visual relief and relaxation, contact with the exterior world, and may also reduce perceived crowding (Elder et al., 1979; Evans, 1979b; Farrenkopf & Roth, 1980; Goodrich, 1979). Research indicates that solar radiation activates biochemical events involved in a range of functions including endocrine control, timing of the biological clock, sexual growth and development, immunologic responsiveness, and regulation of stress and fatigue (Neer et al., 1971; Wurtman, 1975). Ne'eman and Hopkinson (1970) have attempted to develop guidelines for window size and placement. Among the factors they found to affect window acceptability were the number of windows within a 60° angle of view and whether the view through the window was near or far (see also Elder & Tibbott, 1981).

Visual and acoustical privacy

The concept of privacy is complex. One important aspect of understanding the need for privacy is to identify the size of the group requiring privacy. Westin (1970) identifies different levels of privacy, including solitary privacy of an individual alone and intimate privacy required by two associates engaged in conversation. As defined by Altman (1975), privacy involves control over access to oneself or one's group. It includes the ability of people and groups to regulate the transmission of information about themselves to others and to control inputs from others.

Several researchers suggest that the interruption of goal-directed activity is a basic stress-provoking situation (Arnold, 1967; Lazarus, 1967; Mandler & Watson, 1966; Saegert, 1975; Weick, 1970), and, in fact, a place to work without interruption has been identified as a principal factor in office workers' comfort (Harris, 1980). Privacy is one of the most important concerns of office workers; yet workers are generally dissatisfied with both visual and acoustical privacy, especially under "open-plan" conditions (Boyce, 1974; Brookes & Kaplan, 1972; Harris, 1978; Hundert & Greenfield, 1969; Zeitlin, 1969). Of these two components of privacy, acoustical privacy has been found to be of more concern to workers than visual privacy (Brookes &

Figure 9.4. Privacy is one of the most important concerns of office workers.

Kaplan, 1972; Harris, 1978; Nemecek & Grandjean, 1973) (Figure 9.4). (See the previous discussion of noise for further information.)

Acoustical privacy. One of the problems most often mentioned with open office planning is noise (Boyce, 1974; Brookes & Kaplan, 1972; Harris, 1978; Nemecek & Grandjean, 1973). Disturbance due to noise has been found to be a function of the sound source, the sound level, and the level of background sound. A certain level of background sound is necessary to mask conversations and other office sounds. Although a sound might be perceived by workers as quite loud, it is not necessarily distracting unless it stands out from or is not masked by background noise.

Frequently cited as the most bothersome types of noise are people talking and phone conversations (Elder et al., 1979; Goodrich, 1979; Nemeck and Grandjean, 1973; Wineman, 1981). Nemecek and Grandjean suggest that the high impact of conversations may be due to their informational content, which distracts attention. As stated by Goodrich, "social distractions are by their nature more distracting because the actions and intentions of people are intrinsically more meaningful to us" (p. 5).

Unwanted stimuli, such as noise, which interrupts activities or task completion, can be stress provoking. When auditory stimuli are unpredictable, uncontrollable, or very intense, excessive arousal interferes with task performance (Carlstam, Karlsson, & Levi, 1973; Cohen, 1978; Glass & Singer, 1972; Mehrabian & Russell, 1974). Noise has been found to have negative impacts on physical health and psychosocial functioning and may affect task performance for some complex tasks (see Cohen and Weinstein, Chap.

2, this volume, for a more detailed discussion). In addition, research suggests that the effects of noise on peformance may continue after the exposure to noise has terminated (Cohen, 1980).

A lack of sound may also be disturbing in the office environment. A certain level of sound helps maintain arousal and masks unpredictable sounds. Thus, a balance must be achieved between task and environment. A moderately arousing setting will be beneficial to boring or monotonous tasks, whereas a nonarousing setting may be more appropriate for a moderately complex task.

A number of physical features affect visual and acoustical privacy in office settings. The orientation of workspaces, the distance between workspaces, and the size of spaces impact privacy. Workspaces located adjacent to major circulation routes may suffer from a lack of visual and acoustical privacy. Walls, partitions, and furnishings may be used to control privacy. The quality of materials and finishes with respect to absorption, reflection, and transmission affects acoustical privacy. However, a worker's experience of privacy and ability to insure privacy may depend upon work tasks, office policy, and position. For example, it may be an accepted procedure to announce one's presence and wait for recognition before entering a workspace regardless of the amount of enclosure provided by walls, partitions, or a door.

Visual privacy. A lack of visual privacy (privacy from the view of others) may be uncomfortable in and of itself (for example, workers prefer to work side by side rather than face to face), or may actually precipitate interruptions to carrying out work tasks when passersby stop to initiate conversation. Research suggests that "visual bustle" is a problem in open office planning (Brookes & Kaplan, 1972).

A lack of privacy does not necessarily have a negative impact on job satisfaction and performance. A person may be motivated to work more effectively if he or she sees others who are working or who are rewarded for increased productivity. Eye contact with either a supervisor or colleague can also function as a motivating factor (Parsons, 1976).

Sundstrom, Burt, and Kamp (1980) hypothesized that for routine tasks, social contact could provide a source of stimulation and function as a facilitator of job performance. In contrast to this hypothesis, Sundstrom's research indicates that even for jobs involving routine tasks, workers preferred private spaces to more accessible work spaces; in fact, job performance was found to be higher in the more private spaces. A number of explanations for these results are plausible (Sundstrom et al., 1980): (1) In private space, one is less vulnerable to noise and distraction; (2) enclosure and visual privacy may reduce the pressure to maintain appearances; and (3) people may prefer private workspaces because of their symbolic status value. It may also be a learned response to seek privacy when one wishes to carry out work tasks. These advantages of privacy may, even for routine tasks, be more important to worker satisfaction and performance than the benefits of social contacts provided in less private spaces. The length of time spent on a task might also be relevant. For example, a worker's desire for privacy may decrease as the length of time spent on routine tasks increases. In order to resolve these issues, further research is needed on the visual and acoustical privacy requirements of workers, and the role of symbolic status indicators.

To the extent that privacy requirements depend upon work tasks, for many office jobs, privacy requirements may vary on different days and during different hours of the day. It is therefore important that opportunities exist for control of the environment in response to privacy needs. For example, in a private office a worker can close the door to control disturbances from passersby. In an open office setting, where flexible control of the boundaries of an office space is more difficult, the availability of a conference room for private telephone conversations or conversations with clients or colleagues may become an important determinant in overall satisfaction with privacy.

Other environmental stressors

A number of other environmental factors act as stressors, affecting worker satisfaction, job performance, and health. Two of these factors, crowding and physical safety, will be discussed briefly within this section.

Crowding. More space, and less crowding, are among the most desired improvements identified by office workers (Harris, 1980). Crowding is a principal complaint about open-plan offices (Brookes & Kaplan, 1972).

In office settings, perceptions of crowding depend upon job tasks. If workers are involved in tasks that take them out of the office, such as salesmen, complaints of crowding may be low even with minimal amounts of space. For different occupations workers prefer different numbers of persons per room. For jobs involving largely routine work and a high demand for information exchange, workers prefer larger numbers per room than those whose work requires careful thought (Boyce, 1974).

Stress reactions under crowded conditions have been demonstrated physiologically. Research suggests that crowding can be detrimental to physical health, psychosocial functioning, and task performance on complex tasks (see Epstein, Chap. 5, this volume, for a more detailed discussion). Results indicate that the effects of short-term crowding may extend beyond the crowded situation and affect a person's ability to cope in other stressful situations (Evans, 1979a; Sherrod, 1974).

Physical safety. Anxiety about physical safety may be another source of stress to office workers. Although more significant in industrial settings, the U.S. Department of Labor estimates a rate of 40,000 disabling accidents per year among office workers in the United States and 200 office-related deaths per year. Most frequent causes include falls or slips, lifting stress, and accidents involving striking against or being struck by objects (Baldwin, 1976). (This is a specialized area of research that will not be addressed further in this chapter.)

In summary the field research on environmental stressors in office settings is limited, and the applicability of laboratory results needs validation. Much of the existing laboratory research is focused on objective measures of quality, without consideration for workers' subjective responses. For example, lighting research is concerned primarily with visibility ratings of lighting for various tasks. Study of the more subjective aspects of lighting, such as color rendition and worker responses to low overall light levels or uneven light levels, is inadequate. Similarly, much of the existing research on privacy concerns the qualities of materials with respect to sound transmission, absorption, and reflection, rather than the levels of privacy appropriate to various work tasks, or the qualitative aspects of visual and acoustical disturbances that are most annoying. In addition, a better understanding of the role of these environmental factors in overall job satisfaction and work performance is needed.

A major limitation of the field research in office settings is the failure to specify and adequately measure both objective and subjective factors that contribute to the success of office environments (Marans & Spreckelmeyer, in press). Much of the existing field research has been conducted within the constraints imposed by office organizations themselves or firms involved in design and planning projects. These constraints include time and budget limitations, limitations on the sample population to be studied, and constraints on the types of measures to be used and frequency of measurement. In addition, due to the proprietary aspects of much of this research, dissemination of findings is often limited.

Mediators of stress

Research indicates that a number of social and psychological factors can modify the effects of stress (see Chap. 1, this volume). As illustrated in the model (see Figure 9.1) some of these factors, such as environmental control, may act directly on the source of stress, reducing its adverse effects. Others, such as social interaction and symbolic identification, may reduce the likelihood that environmental factors are perceived as stressful, or reduce the likelihood that perceived stressors will lead to poor mental and/or physical health. The latter reduction may happen because some mediators enhance individual coping abilities.

The design and planning of office environments influence the mediation of stress. Physical environmental features can support or inhibit social contact; contribute to status identification, wayfinding, and orientation; and/or provide for environmental control. In this section, three social and psychological factors that mediate stress will be discussed: social interaction, symbolic identification, and social control. The influence of physical environmental features on each of these factors will be reviewed.

Social interaction

A major source of stress at work is one's relationships with other workers. Cooper and Marshall (1978) report on work stress caused by the pressure of relationships as well as by the lack of social support in certain situations. "At highly competitive managerial levels it is likely that problem sharing will be inhibited for fear of appearing weak" (p. 90). Mistrust of colleagues has been shown to relate to increased psychological strain (French & Caplan, 1970; Kahn, Wolfe, Quinn, Snoek, & Rosenthal, 1964).

Several studies (e.g., Argyris, 1964; Cooper, 1973) have shown that good relationships within work groups are a significant factor in both individual and organizational health. Supportive social relationships may mitigate initial perceptions of stressful work situations (such as boring tasks or heavy workloads) and may reduce the tendency of perceived stress to lead to harmful physiological, psychological, or behavioral responses (House & Wells, 1978). Unfortunately, there is no direct evidence for the mitigating effects of social support on stress in office settings. Nevertheless, given the large body of data on the ameliorative effects of social support in other contexts, social support in the workplace should reduce occupational stresses such as role conflict and ambiguity, job dissatisfaction, and low occupational self-esteem (House & Wells, 1978).

Conrath (1973) found that face-to-face interactions among office workers are more influenced by spatial arrangement and proximity than by task or authority relationships. Since walking up stairs requires more energy than walking on a level, and waiting for an elevator is inconvenient, office workers are more likely to interact with others on the same floor level than with those on another floor (Parsons, 1976). Research by Brookes and Kaplan (1972) suggests that for both open-plan and enclosed offices, social interactions occur most often in corridors. The location of amenities such as drinking fountains and coffee machines also affects social interaction (see Chap. 6, this volume, for a discussion of interaction nodes). The design and analysis of interaction nodes or focal points have been developed in some detail by Bechtel (1977). His research suggests that the effective design of such spaces requires high visual access plus the opportunity for social contact without extensive social commitment.

Visibility is also an important factor in deliberate social interaction. Hall (1966) reports that two people who work within 10 ft. of each other may feel compelled to talk. Also, when two workers face each other, eye contact and conversation are likely to increase. A worker is more likely to walk over and talk with another worker if he or she can see that the other worker is available (Parsons, 1976).

Figure 9.5. The location of partitions and furnishings affects work group cohesiveness.

Spatial arrangement and the location of walls, partitions, furnishings, and other barriers affect work group cohesiveness and interaction with other work groups. Lawrence and Lorsch (1967) conducted a comparative study of competing organizations that demonstrated the importance of environmental differentiation for activities that require specialization or departmentalization, and environmental integration for activities that require collaboration between individuals or groups. Bobele and Buchanan (1979) report the successful use of partitions and furnishings to achieve greater differentiation among work groups and the use of common work areas and spatial arrangements that enhance visual contact to achieve greater integration among work groups (Figure 9.5).

Open office planning. Proponents of open office systems have suggested that open office planning increases communication among workers. A number of studies have documented an increase in communication associated with a move from a conventional to an open plan office (Allen & Gerstberger, 1973; Brookes & Kaplan, 1972; Hundert & Greenfield, 1969; Nemecek & Grandjean, 1973; Zeitlin, 1969). However, there is no indication from this work that increased communication positively affects work-related outcomes. In fact, recent research by Wineman (1981) suggests that although workers in open plan offices note an increase in conversations, these conversations are perceived as nonwork related, whereas work-related conversations remain constant.

It has been suggested that social interaction increases attraction, a factor that contributes to high task performance (Oldham, 1979). Thus, one would expect enhanced work performance to be associated with open office planing. However, Oldham's research suggests that the open plan office may reduce autonomy, task identity, supervisor and co-worker feedback – factors that have been shown to correlate positively with worker satisfaction, motivation, and productivity. In addition, Oldham's research suggests that the open plan office does not provide sufficient privacy to support the development of close friendships. Consistent with Oldham's findings, Brookes and Kaplan (1972) and Zeitlin (1969) report that workers who move from conventional to open plan office space perceive a decrease in their functional efficiency. Similarly, Hundert and Greenfield (1969) found that workers reported cooperating less with co-workers and accomplishing less in open plan offices than in conventional office space. An important limitation of many of the studies comparing open office plan to conventional design is the time period over which the environment is studied. Studies of office moves need to monitor attitude and performance over longer time periods in order to examine adaptation to changed surroundings at work.

Thus, research suggests that supportive social relationships may mitigate the harmful effects of stress, and the physical environment is an important determinant of both individual and group relationships. Physical features such as spatial arrangement, proximity, and the location of amenities and activity nodes influence interaction and group cohesiveness. In open plan offices, with low partitions and close proximity of workspaces, communication among workers is high. However, research indicates that open offices may lack the privacy required for the development of close friendships, autonomy, and functional efficiency, which affect the satisfaction, motivation, and productivity of workers.

Symbolic identification

Status indicators. A large body of research has established that problems with career development can be significant stressors (Cooper & Marshall, 1978). One such stressor is status incongruence that may result from either overpromotion or underpromotion. Brook (1973) found health impacts associated with status incongruence ranging from minor psychological symptoms to psychosomatic complaints and mental illness.

High status may reduce the impacts of stress on health. In a study of status and conflict in organizational environments, Kahn and French (1970) found that people became healthier as their status improved; also, people whose educational or social class background was higher than would be expected for their job position were less healthy than others in that position. Studies of office executives and navy personnel (Radloff & Helmreich, 1967; Saegert, 1975) suggest that although these workers may experience stressors associated with ill health, such as work overload or poor working conditions, they will not be adversely affected if their job is prestigious. A number of other research studies lend support to these findings (Berry,

1966; Erikson, Edwards, & Gunderson, 1973; Erikson, Pugh, & Gunderson, 1972; Kahn & French, 1970; Kasl & Cobb, 1967).

Physical features that have been associated with status include: (1) the size or square footage of office space (Duffy, Cave, & Worthington, 1976; Manning, 1965; Steele, 1973); (2) the amount of enclosure provided by walls, partitions, and/or a door (Duffy et al., 1976; Manning, 1965; Sundstrom et al., 1980); (3) the location of an office, such as at the corner of the building, adjacent to the window wall, or in close proximity to management (Duffy, 1969; Halloran, 1978); and (4) the amount and quality of furnishings (Duffy, 1969; Steele, 1973). Results of a survey of 529 office workers in government and private sector organizations conducted by Konar, Sundstrom, Brady, Mandel, and Rice (in press) and a national survey of office workers conducted by Harris (1978) confirm the association between these environmental characteristics and status. Both of these studies indicate that the opportunity to personalize workspace may also be an indicator of status.

Konar et al. (in press) investigated the relationship between status indicators and perceptions of status. Their research suggests that appropriate status markers, those that are perceived to reflect the occupant's status, are associated with both workspace satisfaction and job satisfaction. The authors conclude that some elements of the physical environment, such as carpeting, may have symbolic rather than functional value. Thus, symbolic value may be an important factor affecting worker health and well-being.

Other symbolic identifiers. Symbols and cues used in office settings may reduce the stress associated with wayfinding and spatial orientation (see Chap. 6, this volume, for further discussion), and with determining appropriate behavior in unfamiliar settings. Aspects of the physical environment such as signs, scale, location, materials and finishes, furnishings and equipment, and amount of personalization can assist workers or visitors in differentiating territories within an office setting, recognizing ownership (public, group, individual), and determining appropriate behavior. Symbolic identifiers can also be used to control stressful situations such as crowding. For example, a worker may define personal territory with objects or furnishings if existing walls, partitions, or furnishings do not provide adequate boundary control (Davis, 1976).

Thus, research suggests that environmental symbols may be stressors if they are in conflict with perceived or achieved status, or they may mediate stressful situations by defining territory, ownership, and appropriate behavior. Little empirical research is available that identifies environmental elements indicating status and that addresses the question of whether status indicators affect work efficiency and worker health. The physical environment conveys a multitude of status messages, but research has not established a direct link between these messages and office worker well-being (Saegert, 1975).

Personal control

Lack of participation or control in the workplace has been related in a number of studies to job dissatisfaction, job strain, and job-related stress (Buck, 1972; French & Caplan, 1970; Haynes & Feinleib, 1980; Kasl, 1973; Margolis, Kroes, & Quinn, 1974). Karasek (1979) compared job demands with levels of control on the job for a range of occupations. Workers in jobs that have high demands, yet also allow for high control over work, do not experience as much strain as workers in jobs with high demands but low control. Karasek suggests increasing control as a method of improving job-related mental health without sacrificing productivity.

The research linking personal control to job stress generally focuses on control over the pace and organization of work tasks. The relationship between control over the physical environment and stress is less well understood. Workers may exert control over the physical workspace in two ways. If an environment is perceived to be unsatisfactory, it may be changed directly by altering temperature, switching lights on and off, opening or closing windows and shades, opening or closing doors, rearranging furnishings, or personalizing space. Or a worker may exert control indirectly by moving to another workspace (such as a conference area or lounge). Control of the physical environment is therefore dependent upon the availability of and ability to use alternative settings and mechanisms of control (thermostat, doors, opening windows, etc.) (see Chap. 6, this volume, for a further discussion).

Perceived control can be important in and of itself. Glass and Singer's (1972) laboratory study of noise control demonstrated that perceived control (although unexercised) reduced the stressful effects of noise. However, the findings of Weiss (1972) suggest that control may add to the number of decisions required of a worker, potentially contributing to work overload. Thus, for workers suffering from an overload of decision making, control could increase rather than decrease stress.

The perception of control or ability to influence the work environment can act as a direct environmental stressor, or may mediate the adverse effects of other stressors. There are also probably different dimensions of control that may have variable impact on job stress given the particular demands and required physical facilities for particular jobs. Thus, a task requiring concentration would be enhanced by high privacy but would perhaps be in conflict with managerial demands for personnel contact required because of supervisory status. Further research is needed to confirm these results for office settings.

In summary, a better understanding of the role of the environmental factors as mediators of stress appears to be a critical research issue. First, research on symbolic identifiers and personal control is limited and does not adequately address the role of physical environmental factors in stress reduction. For example, studies of status as a stress mediator have not focused on the importance of status messages conveyed by the physical environment. Research linking personal control to stress in office settings has been primarily concerned with control over the pace and organization of work tasks rather than control of the physical environment. Second, research on social support as a mediator of stress does not adequately address the impact of social interaction on task performance for various work tasks. Further research is needed to identify ways of enhancing social support without compromising task performance.

Implications for the design of office settings

A number of stressors have been identified in office settings that can reduce job satisfaction and work performance and lead to harmful physical, psychological, and behavioral effects. Not only are satisfaction and performance at the workplace compromised, but these effects also may carry over to produce negative impacts in other life realms.

Elements of the physical environment can act either as stressors or as mediators of stress. Workspace design, ambient conditions, lighting, and privacy are environmental factors that can function as stressors affecting worker satisfaction, job performance, and health. If workspace design, ambient conditions, and the arrangement of work groups and support services fit the worker and work tasks, potential sources of stress may be reduced. For most workers optimal conditions will allow for choice and control. The types and arrangement of office furnishings should be flexible to adapt to job requirements and work tasks. For example, a job that involves considerable paperwork may require more storage space, more convenient access to storage, and higher illumination levels than a job that primarily involves client communication (Figure 9.6).

Both the quantity and the quality of light should be appropriate to the task. Lighting should be adjustable so that as work tasks or conditions of natural lighting vary, light levels and the position of task lighting could change, providing lower light levels for conversation or higher light levels for close paperwork. Special consideration should be given to requirements for certain office tasks, such as typing and proofreading, and office equipment such as video display units. Windows, providing natural light and view, appear to be important to workers' comfort and health independent of their value as sources of light. Therefore, window placement and the design and planning of interior space should allow a maximum number of workers visual access and proximity to windows.

Privacy is an important concern among office workers, yet workers are often dissatisfied with both visual and acoustical privacy. Of these two aspects of privacy, acoustical privacy is more important to worker satisfaction than visual privacy. In general, a minimum level of background sound is necessary in office settings to maintain arousal and to mask unpredictable sounds. A higher sound level may be desirable for monotonous tasks,

Figure 9.6. Office tasks involving considerable amounts of paperwork require higher light levels and more storage space.

whereas a lower level may be more appropriate for complex tasks. Some of the most annoying types of sound in office settings are telephone conversations and conversations among colleagues. It has been hypothesized that it is the information content of these sounds that results in their high level of annoyance. Within the office space, work groups should be spatially organized according to the acoustical implications of work tasks. For example, work groups whose job involves considerable telephone communication should be separated from other workers.

Privacy needs may vary at different times of the day and on different days of the week depending upon work tasks. A lack of privacy can be a stressor if the performance of work tasks is disrupted. However, too much isolation may lead to monotony and a reduction in work performance. The design of office space should provide privacy control, such as a door for an enclosed office, or the opportunity to move to private space, for example, a common area or conference room, for personal conversations or tasks that require high levels of concentration. Further research is needed to assess the levels of privacy that best suit various office tasks.

Social relationships with colleagues, superiors, and subordinates can be stressors or can act indirectly to mitigate perceptions of stressful situations or to reduce the likelihood that perceived stress will negatively affect mental and physical health. Similarly, social interaction functions as a stressor if it results in the disruption of goal-directed behavior, but it can also be a source of stimulation and work facilitation (Figure 9.7).

Figure 9.7. Low partitions may be appropriate for work tasks requiring a high degree of information exchange.

Aspects of the physical environment such as spatial arrangement and proximity are significant determinants of social interaction and the development of social relationships. For routine tasks or tasks that require high information exchange, larger numbers of people per area with fewer full-height partitions or other visual barriers may be more appropriate than for tasks requiring individual thought. The location of interaction nodes or focal points, such as lounge space, a coffee machine or drinking fountain, within a work group space or adjacent to several groups can enhance communication (Figure 9.8).

Open office planning increases communication among workers, but the impact of increased communication on work performance has not been conclusively demonstrated. Recent research suggests that increased communication may detract from job performance.

Research suggests that environmental symbols may be stressors if they are in conflict with perceived or achieved status. However, further research is needed to identify those environmental elements that are important status indicators and to assess their role in worker health and well-being. Environmental symbols that clearly indicate the function of a space and that differentiate spaces from one another can reduce the stress of way-finding, orientation, and determining appropriate behavior. For example, a manager whose office is furnished and spatially organized to project an image of formality can expect formal behavior of visitors in this office space. Environmental elements such as furnishings and partitions that

Figure 9.8. Interaction nodes enhance communication.

delineate spatial territories may also be useful in the control of crowding (Figure 9.9).

As noted throughout this discussion, the availability of control can reduce environmental stressors or can mediate the perception of stressful situations and the negative impacts of stress. Lack of control over the pace and organization of work tasks is a major stressor in office environments. Further research is required to determine whether this stressor can be moderated by control over the physical environment.

Future directions

Research on the effects of physical environmental factors in office settings is a relatively new area of study. Although research findings from laboratory studies and studies in other settings have relevance to this field, further research is needed in a number of priority areas.

First, there is a need to validate and expand the methods used in evaluating stress in office settings. Current research relies heavily on workers' self-reports of a limited number of indicators, or indirect measures, of stress. Although this is a reasonable measure given the subjective nature of many of the indicators of stress, the difficulties associated with the direct measurement of performance in office settings, and the constraints associated with field research, it is limited in scope. Further research should be conducted to (1) validate the accuracy of self-report; (2) validate the accuracy of stress indicators, especially job dissatisfaction and reduced job performance; and (3) develop supplementary measures of stress. Physiological

Figure 9.9 Environmental symbols should be appropriate to achieved status.

measures for subsamples of the population and observations of behaviors associated with stress, such as eye contact and increased interpersonal spacing, offer considerable potential.

Second, a better understanding is needed of the relationships between certain environmental factors and job satisfaction and performance. A particularly critical problem area in office settings is privacy. Privacy requirements may vary for different people on different days and during different times of the day depending upon job tasks. However, little is known about the levels of privacy that best suit different work tasks. Although research suggests that social interaction can be a source of stimulation and a work facilitator, particularly for monotonous tasks, workers have reported a preference for privacy. Has adequate insulation from noise and distraction not been achieved, or are other aspects of privacy, such as its symbolic status value, of overriding concern? Or do probes about desired privacy need to be more specific about privacy requirements for particular tasks?

Another critical area for research is the relationship between social interaction and job performance. The current trend in the use of open office systems is supported by the contention that increased communication and social interaction will increase satisfaction and job performance. However, recent research indicates that the lack of privacy associated with open-plan offices may result in decreased performance.

Third, further research is needed to clarify the role of a number of environmental factors in stress reduction and in the mediation of stress in office settings. Research is needed on the use of environmental symbols in office settings to enhance wayfinding and orientation. For example, what environmental symbols identify the function of a space and differentiate among spaces? In addition, we need to examine the role of symbolic identifiers in the reduction of stressors such as crowding. Supportive social relationships have been identified as a potentially significant factor in stress reduction in office settings. Research is needed to assess the effectiveness of social support as a mediator of stress and to identify methods of enhancing the formation of supportive relationships without compromising task performance.

Finally, the role of actual and perceived control in stress reduction requires further study. What is the effect of control mechanisms in the reduction of stressors and the moderation of the impacts of stress in office settings? Can control over the physical environment compensate for a lack of control over the pace and organization of work tasks? It is imperative that research on stress in office settings consider the interplay of task demands and other personal needs with the opportunities afforded by the physical setting.

References

Allen, T. J., & Gerstberger, P. G. A field experiment to improve communication in a product engineering department: The nonterritorial office. *Human Factors*, 1973, *15*, 487–498.

Altman, I. *The environment and social behavior*. Monterey, Calif.: Brooks/Cole, 1975.

Argyris, C. *Integrating the individual and the organization*. New York: Wiley, 1964.

Arnold, M. Stress and emotion. In M. H. Appley & R. Trumbull (Eds.), *Psychological stress*. New York: Appleton-Century-Crofts, 1967.

Aston, S. M., & Bellchambers, H. E. Illumination, colour rendering and visual clarity. *Lighting Research and Technology*, 1969, *1*(4), 259–261.

Baldwin, D. Caution: Office zone. *Job Safety and Health*, 1976, February, 4–12.

Barnaby, J. F. Lighting for productivity gains. *Lighting Design & Application*, 1980, February, 20–28.

Bechtel, R. *Enclosing behavior*. Stroudsburg, Pa.: Dowden, Hutchinson and Ross, 1977.

Bedford, T. Researches on thermal comfort, *Ergonomics*, 1961, *4*, 289–310.

Berry, K. J. *Status integration and morbidity*. Unpublished doctoral thesis, University of Oregon, 1966.

Bobele, H. K., and Buchanan, P. J. Building a more productive environment. *Management World*, 1979, January, 8–10.

Boyce, P. R. User's assessments of a landscaped office. *Journal of Architectural Research*, 1974, *3*(3), 44–62.

Brook, A. Mental stress at work. *The Practitioner*, 1973, *210*, 500–506.

Brookes, M. J., and Kaplan, A. The office environment: Space planning and affective behavior. *Human Factors*, 1972, *14*, 373–391.

Buck, V. *Working under pressure*. London: Staples, 1972.

Burandt, M., and Grandjean, E. Sitting habits of office employees. *Ergonomics*, 1963, *6*, 217–228.

Cakir, A., Hart, D. J., & Stewart, T.F.M. *Video display terminals*. New York: Wiley, 1980.

Caplan, R.D., Cobb, S., French, J.R.P. Jr., Harrison, R.V., & Pinneau, S.R. Jr. *Job demands and worker health*. Washington D.C.: U.S. Government Printing Office, 1975.

Carlstam, G., Karlsson, C.G., & Levi, L. Stress and disease in response to noise. *Proceedings of the International Congress on Noise as a Public Health Problem*. Washington, D.C.: U.S. Government Printing Office, 1973.

Cohen, S. Environmental load and the allocation of attention. In A. Baum, J.E. Singer, & S. Valins (Eds.), *Advances in environmental psychology* (Vol. 1). Hillsdale, N.J.: Erlbaum, 1978.

Cohen, S. The aftereffects of stress on human performance and social behavior: A review of research and theory. *Psychological Bulletin*, 1980, *88*, 82–108.

Conrath, D. W. Communication patterns, organizational structure and man: Some relationships. *Human Factors*, 1973, *15*(5), 459–470.

Cooper, C.L. *Group training for individual and organizational development*. Basel: S. Karger, 1973.

Cooper, C.L., & Marshall, J. Sources of managerial and white collar stress. In C.L. Cooper & R. Payne (Eds.), *Stress at work*. New York: Wiley, 1978.

Cox, T. Repetitive work. In C.L. Cooper & R. Payne (Eds.), *Current concerns in occupational stress*. New York: Wiley, 1980.

Crouch, C.L. Lighting for seeing. In G. C. Clayton & F. E. Clayton (Eds.), *Patty's industrial hygiene and toxicology* (Vol. 1). New York: Wiley, 1978.

Dainoff, M.J. *Occupational stress factors in secretarial/clerical work: Annotated research bibliography and analytic review*. Cincinnati: National Institute for Occupational Safety and Health, 1979.

Dainoff, M.J. *Occupational stress factors in video display terminal (VDT) operation: A review of empirical research*. Cincinnati: National Institute for Occupational Safety and Health, 1981.

Davis, G., & Altman, I. Territories at the work-place: Theory into design guidelines. *Man-Environment Systems*, 1976, *6*, 46–53.

Duffy, F. Role and status in the office. *Architectural Association Quarterly*, 1969, *1*, 4–13.

Duffy, F., Cave, C., & Worthington, J. *Planning office space*. London: Architectural Press, 1976.

Elder, J., & Tibbott, R.L. *User acceptance of an energy efficient office building – A study of the Norris Cotton Federal Office Building*. Washington, D.C.: U.S. Government Printing Office, 1981.

Elder, J., Turner, G.E., and Rubin, A.I. *Post-occupancy evaluation: A case study of the evaluation process*. NBSIR 79-1780. Washington, D.C.: U.S. Government Printing Office, 1979.

Erikson, J., Edwards, D., & Gunderson, E.K. Status congruency and mental health. *Psychological Reports*, 1973, *33*, 395–401.

Erikson, J., Pugh, W.M., & Gunderson, E.K. Status congruency as a predictor of job satisfaction and life stress. *Journal of Applied Psychology*, 1972, *56*, 523–525.

Evans, G.W. Behavioral and physiological consequences of crowding in humans. *Journal of Applied Social Psychology*, 1979, *9*(1), 27–46. (a)

Evans, G.W. Design implications of spatial research. In J. Aiello & A. Baum (Eds.), *Residential crowding and design*. New York: Plenum, 1979. (b)

Farrenkopf, T., & Roth, V. The university faculty office as an environment. *Environment and Behavior*, 1980, *12*(4), 467–477.

Flynn, J.E. The effects of light source color on user impression and satisfaction. *Journal of the Illuminating Engineering Society*, 1977, 6(3), 167–179.

Frankenhauser, M. Coping with job stress: A psychobiological approach. Reports from the Department of Psychology, University of Stockholm, 1978 (532).

French, J.R.P., & Caplan, R.D. Psychosocial factors in coronary heart disease. *Industrial Medicine*, 1970, 39, 383–397.

French, J.R.P., & Caplan, R.D. Organizational stress and individual strain. In A. J. Marrow (Ed.), *The failure of success*. New York: AMACOM, 1973.

Galitz, W.O. *Human factors in office automation*. Atlanta, Ga.: Life Office Management Association, 1980.

Glass, D.C., & Singer, J.E. *Urban stress: Experiments on noise and social stressors*. New York: Academic Press, 1972.

Goodrich, R. *How people perceive their office environment*. New York: Citibank, 1979.

Hall, E.T. *The hidden dimension*. New York: Doubleday, 1966.

Halloran, J. *Applied human relations: An organizational approach*. Englewood Cliffs, N.J.: Prentice-Hall, 1978.

Hardy, A.C. A case for reduced window areas. *International Lighting Review*, 1974, 25(3), 90–92.

Harris, L., & Associates. *The Steelcase national study of office environments: Do they work?* Grand Rapids, Mich.: Steelcase Inc., 1978.

Harris, L., & Associates. *The Steelcase national study of office environments, No. 11: Comfort and productivity in the office of the 80's*. Grand Rapids, Mich.: Steelcase, Inc., 1980.

Harrison, R.V. Person-environment fit and job stress. In C.L. Cooper & R. Payne (Eds.), *Stress at work*. New York: Wiley, 1978.

Haynes, S.G., & Feinleib, M. Women, work and coronary heart disease: Prospective findings from the Framingham Heart Study. *American Journal of Public Health*, 1980, 70(2), 133–141.

House, J.S., & Wells, J.A. Occupational stress and health. In A. McLean (Ed.), *Reducing occupational stress*. Washington, D.C.: U.S. Government Printing Office, 1978.

Hughes, P.C. School lighting for the total person: A psychobiological approach. *Council of Educational Facility Planners Journal*, 1981, March–April, 4–6.

Hundert, A.T., & Greenfield, N. Physical space and organizational behavior: A study of office landscape. *Proceedings of the 77th Annual Convention of the American Psychological Association*, 1969, 1, 601–602.

Kahn, R.L., & French, J.R.P. Status and conflict: Two themes in the study of stress. In J. McGrath (Ed.), *Social and psychological factors in stress*. New York: Holt, Rinehart and Winston, 1970.

Kahn, R.L., Wolfe, D.M., Quinn, R.P., Snoek, J.D., & Rosenthal, R.A. *Organizational Stress*. New York: Wiley, 1964.

Karasek, R.A. Jr. Job demands, job decision latitude and mental strain: Implications for job redesign. *Administrative Science Quarterly*, 1979, June, 24, 285–308.

Kasl, S.V. Mental health and the work environment. *Journal of Occupational Medicine*, 1973, 15(6), 509–518.

Kasl, S.V., & Cobb, S. Effects of parental status incongruence and discrepancy in physical and mental health of adult offspring. *Journal of Personality and Social Psychology Monograph*, 1967, 7 (Whole No. 642), 1–15.

Konar, E., Sundstrom, E., Brady, C., Mandel, D., & Rice, R. Status demarcation in the office. *Environment and Behavior*. In press.

Kraemer, Sieverts, & Partners. *Open-plan offices* (translated by J. L. Ritchie). London: McGraw-Hill (UK), 1977.

Kroemer, E.K.H. Seating in plant and office. *American Industrial Hygiene Association Journal*, 1971, *32*, 633–652.

Landy, F.J., & Trumbo, D.A. *Psychology of work behaviour*. Homewood, Ill.: Dorsey Press, 1976.

Lawrence, P.R., & Lorsch, J.W. *Organization and environment: Managing differentiation and integration*. Cambridge, Mass.: Harvard University Press, 1967.

Lazarus, R.S. Cognitive and personality factors underlying threat and coping. In M.H. Appley & R. Trumball (Eds.), *Psychological stress*. New York: Appleton-Century-Crofts, 1967.

Lucey, J.F. The effects of light on the new born infant. *Journal of Perinatal Medicine*, *1*(3), 1973, 147–152.

Maas, J.B., Jayson, J.K., & Kleiber, D.A. Effects of spectral difference in illumination on fatigue. *Journal of Applied Psychology*, 1974, *59*, 524–526.

Mandler, G., & Watson, D.L. Anxiety and the interruption of behavior. In C.P. Spielberger (Ed.), *Anxiety and behavior*. New York: Academic Press, 1966.

Manning, P. (Ed.), *Office design: A study of environment*. Liverpool: University of Liverpool Press, 1965.

Marans, R.W., & Spreckelmeyer, K.F. Evaluating open and conventional offices. *Environment and Behavior*. In press.

Margolis, B.L., Kroes, W.H., & Quinn, R.P. Job stress: An unlisted occupational hazard. *Journal of Occupational Medicine*, 1974, *16*(10), 659–661.

McGrath, J.E. A conceptual formulation for research on stress. In J. McGrath (Ed.), *Social and psychological factors in stress*. New York: Holt, Rinehart and Winston, 1970.

McGrath, J.E. Stress and behaviour in organizations. In M.D. Dunnette (Ed.), *Handbook of industrial and organizational psychology*. Skokie, Ill.; Rand McNally, 1976.

Mehrabian, A., & Russell, J.A. *An approach to environmental psychology*. Cambridge, Mass.: MIT Press, 1974.

National Research Council Committee on Indoor Pollutants. *Indoor Pollutants*. Washington, D.C.: National Academy Press, 1981.

Ne'eman, E., & Hopkinson, R.G. Critical minimum acceptable window size, a study of window design and provision of a view. *Lighting Research and Technology*, 1970, *2*, 17–27.

Neer, R.M., Davis, T.R.A., Walcott, A., Koski, S., Schapis, P., Taylor, I., Thorington, L., & Wurtman, R.J. Stimulation by artificial lighting of calcium absorption in elderly human subjects. *Nature*, 1971, *229*, 255.

Nemecek, J., & Grandjean, E. Results of an ergonomic investigation of large-space offices. *Human Factors*, 1973, *15*(2), 111–124.

Oldham, G.R., & Brass, D.J. Employee reactions to an open-plan office: A naturally occurring quasi-experiment. *Administrative Science Quarterly*, 1979, *24*, 267–284.

Ostberg, O. CRT's pose health problems for operators. *International Journal of Occupational Health & Safety*, 1975, November/December, *44*(6), 24–26, 50, 52.

Parsons, H.M. Work environments. In I. Altman & J.F. Wohlwill (Eds.), *Human behavior and environment: Advances in theory and research* (Vol. 1). New York: Plenum, 1976.

Radloff, R., & Helmreich, R. *Men under stress.* New York: Appleton-Century-Crofts, 1967.

Rissler, A., and Elgerot, A. Stressreaktioner vid overtidsarbete. (Stress reactions related to overtime at work.) Rapporter, Department of Psychology, University of Stockholm, 1978.

Saegert, S. Stress-inducing and reducing qualities of environments. In H. M. Proshansky, W.H. Ittelson, & L.G. Rivlin (Eds.), *Environmental Psychology* (2nd ed.). New York: Holt, Rinehart and Winston, 1975.

Sherrod, D.R. Crowding, perceived control, and behavioral aftereffects. *Journal of Applied Social Psychology,* 1974, 4(2), 171–186.

Smith, M.J., Colligan, M.J., & Hurrel, J.J. Jr. A review of NIOSH psychological stress research – 1977. In U. S. Department of Health and Human Services, *Occupational Stress.* Washington, D.C.: U.S. Government Printing Office, 1978.

Smith, M.J., Happ, A., Stammerjohn, L., & Cohen, B. *An investigation of complaints and job stress in video display operations.* Cincinnati: Institute for Occupational Safety and Health, 1981.

Springer, T.J. *Visual display units in the office environment: Blessings or curses?* Paper presented at Human Factors in Industrial Design in Consumer Products Conference, Tufts University, May 1980.

Stansaab Elektronik AB. The human aspects of office and display lighting. *Datapro Automated Office Solutions,* 1978, October.

Steele, F.I. *Physical settings and organizational development.* Reading, Mass.: Addison-Wesley, 1973.

Stellman, J.M. *Women's work, women's health.* New York: Pantheon Books, 1977.

Sundstrom, E., Burt, R., & Kamp, D. Privacy at work: Architectural correlates of job satisfaction and job performance. *Academy and Management Journal,* 1980, 23(1), 101–117.

Tichauer, E.R. Industrial engineering in the rehabilitation of the handicapped. *Proceedings of the 18th Annual American Institute Conference and Convention,* American Institute of Industrial Engineers, May 1967.

Tichauer, E.R. Ergonomic aspects of biomechanics. *The industrial environment: Its evaluation & control.* Washington, D.C.: U.S. Government Printing Office, 1973.

Vogl, T.P. Photomedicine. *Optical News,* 1976, Spring.

Wahlund, I., & Nerrell, G. Stress factors in the working environments of white-collar workers. In A. McLean (Ed.), *Reducing occupational stress.* Washington, D.C.: U.S. Government Printing Office, 1978.

Weick, K.E. The "Ess" in stress: Some conceptual and methodological problems. In J. McGrath (Ed.), *Social and psychological factors in stress.* New York: Holt, Rinehart and Winston, 1970.

Weiss, J.M. Psychological factors in stress and disease. *Scientific American,* 1972, July, 226(6), 104–113.

Wells, B. Subjective responses to the lighting installation in a modern office building and their design implications. *Building Science,* 1965, 1, 57–67.

Westin, A. *Privacy and freedom.* New York: Atheneum, 1970.

Wheeler, L. *The office environment.* Chicago: Interior Space Designers Incorporated, 1969.

Williams, H.G. High pressure sodium lighting in offices for reduced energy use. *Industry Applications Society (IAS) Meeting,* 1975, 81–87.

Wineman, J. *Building evaluation research: Lighting evaluation*. Research report prepared for Applied Environmental Research Division of Smith, Hinchman & Grylls, Ann Arbor, Mich., February 1978.

Wineman, J. *Office evaluation research: Issues and applications*. Paper presented at the Center for Building Technology Federal Workshop Series of Building Science and Technology, "The office as a work environment: The measurement and evaluation of performance." National Bureau of Standards, February 1981.

Working Women. *Warning: Health hazards for office workers – An overview of problems and solutions in occupational health in the office*. Cleveland, Ohio: Working Women Education Fund, 1981.

Wurtman, R.J. The effects of light on the human body. *Scientific American*, 1975, 233(1), 68–77.

Zeitlin, L.R. *A comparison of employee attitudes toward the conventional and the landscaped office*. Report. New York: Port of New York Authority, 1969.

10. Neighborhood physical environment and stress

Ralph B. Taylor

In the closing pages of *The Hobbit* (Tolkien, 1937), Bilbo Baggins breaks into song as he comes into sight of the land where he was born and raised:

> Roads go ever on
> Under cloud and under star,
> Yet feet that wandering have gone
> Turn at last on home afar. . .
> Look at last on meadows green
> And trees and hills they long have known.

The physical characteristics of the home neighborhood are important for humans as well as for hobbits. The focus, however, may be somewhat different. Instead of "meadows. . .and trees and hills," crucial elements may be "concentrations of buildings, dwelling conditions, the presence or absence of light, air and green open spaces [which] give an area a spatial and aesthetic identity and texture" (Keller, 1968, p. 89).

Although many of us would readily acknowledge the importance of the physical characteristics of neighborhoods (as influences on the quality of life, as significant shapers and containers of early childhood activities, and as symbolic sources of status or collective identity), research and broad theories on this topic are sparse. Reasons for the scarcity may include the following. Until quite recently, the physical environment was not a source of interest to researchers. Whether they shied away from it for fear of being labeled as physical determinists, or whether they truly felt it was not an important source of influence is not altogether clear. There is no question, however, that the social environment, and groups and individual differ-

This paper was prepared while the author was partially supported by Grants 80-IJ-CX-0077 and 80-IJ-CX-0085 from the National Institute of Justice. Points of view and opinions expressed herein are solely those of the author. The author is indebted to Sidney Brower, Sally Ann Shumaker, and an anonymous reviewer for helpful comments on earlier drafts of this article. The author acknowledges the bibliographic assistance of Jim Kearney with the section on delinquency.

ences, were more popular topics than the physical environment. In addition, the concept of neighborhood, like a roller coaster ride, has had up and down periods of popularity. As a consequence of these factors we lack an overall, systematic investigation of the impacts of physical neighborhood characteristics on people.

This chapter summarizes what is known about the relationship between physical neighborhood characteristics and stress-related outcomes. The questions addressed were neatly summarized by Burgess (1925, p. 144) over 50 years ago: "How far has the area itself, by its very topography and by all its other external and physical characteristics, such as railroads, parks, [and] types of housing, conditioned community formations and exerted a determining influence upon the distribution of its inhabitants and upon their movements and life?"

It will readily become apparent that we know more about the effects of some features than others, and more about some outcomes than others. It will also become apparent that there are serious conceptual and statistical problems in this area. The problems have made it difficult to accumulate evidence across studies.

In an effort to sort out what is known I will adopt a framework that is multifunctional, interactionist, and assumes cognitive and cultural filtering. It is multifunctional in that it considers how physical variables may relate to *all* the functions that make neighborhoods important for residents. It is interactionist in that it assumes impacts may be amplified or dampened for some persons or groups. It assumes cognitive filtering in that different social or cultural groups may evaluate or respond differently to particular physical elements due to their own particular viewpoints.

Organization and direction of chapter

The following points are assumed:

1. Neighborhoods may be an important source of influence on residents' attitudes, behaviors, and internal states.
2. Following Popenoe (1973), neighborhoods may promote one or more of the following functions: social interaction, social control, a sense of security and ease, organizational ties, collective identity or sense of place, and socialization.
3. In neighborhoods where these functions are promoted, feelings of satisfaction and attachment ensue; in neighborhoods where these functions are hindered or not met, feelings of dissatisfaction and alienation ensue.
4. To the extent that the physical environment of a neighborhood advances these functions, it reduces stress. To the extent that the physical environment of a neighborhood impedes these functions, it *increases* stress. Thus, stress will be defined in terms of these functions.

Following a section in which basic terms are defined, research on how these functions are influenced by the physical environment is reviewed. Work on security versus fear and crime, and control versus disorder receives the most in-depth treatment as research in this area is most abundant. For each function proposed theoretical contexts as well as empirical evidence are examined. After the discussion of specific functions, work relevant to the more general issue of satisfaction versus dissatisfaction is examined.

The work that is reviewed brings to light some conceptual and methodological difficulties that have not as yet been clearly delineated. Very briefly, these issues are as follows:

1. The neighborhood-level physical environment may influence stress-related functions at the neighborhood, block, or individual level. As outcomes at lower levels of aggregation (e.g., individual instead of block level, block rather than neighborhood level) are considered, the direct influence of the neighborhood-level, physical environment is probably weaker. Indirect effects may come about in that (a) nonphysical neighborhood-, block- or individual-level attributes may amplify or dampen certain impacts of the physical environment, and/or (b) outcomes at the individual level may come "through" block-level impacts. In short, there are various possible causal pathways by means of which the neighborhood-level physical environment may effect stress, and in many studies few of these pathways, and/or the weakest ones, are assessed. A schematic illustrating these pathways is examined.

2. Many studies in this area use "nested" data that is, data from people who are grouped onto blocks that, in turn, are grouped into neighborhoods. Yet, analyses of such data rarely consider how the data should be decomposed, and thus may yield potentially misleading results. To illustrate the point a hypothetical example is worked out.

In a closing section conclusions are drawn and suggested parameters for future research are proposed.

How neighborhoods can promote or alleviate stress

The stress brought about by neighborhood-level features may be considered in relationship to the reasons why a neighborhood is important for residents. Popenoe (1973) has suggested six functions that may be carried out in the neighborhood. These six functions are as follows:

A. *Social interaction* with friends, or other members of the primary reference group, or with neighbors in time of need. Cooley (1902) was the first to suggest that neighbors may constitute a primary reference group. Mann (1954) suggested that the latent function of neighborliness was to proffer assistance in times of need.

B. *Social control* is an extraordinarily diffuse concept with its origins in the sociological and social psychological writings of Ross, Cooley, Durkheim, Simmel, and others at the turn of the century (Janowitz, 1975). In the context of neighborhood research it basically boils down to resident-generated attempts to get other residents and visitors to adhere to existing norms. It is sometimes called "informal control" and is often contrasted with mechanisms of formal control, such as the police and courts. A lack of control is manifested in terms of crime or delinquency, or other problems.

C. *A sense of security and ease* may also be provided by neighborhood. A sense of security is perhaps best recognized by its absence, that is, feelings of fear or concern about the community. Respite may be available only in the actual dwelling unit (Rainwater, 1966), or a very small portion of the neighborhood.

D. *Organizational ties* refers to shared membership or participation in locality-based institutions such as block clubs, neighborhood associations, church groups, and so on.

E. *Collective identity and sense of place* refer to the fact that the neighborhood may be an arena about which residents have positive sentiments. The neighborhood may have symbolic importance for the resident in that it is an appropriate indication of his or her status and social position. It is assumed that such libidinal investment may be variable across residents.

F. *Socialization* refers to the fact that the neighborhood is an arena within which parent–child and child–child interactions are contained. This degree of containment is more prevalent for younger children. The neighborhood may function as a home range (Stea, 1970) circumscribing activity patterns and providing facilities to promote growth.

Each of these functions may be promoted or hindered by physical characteristics. Thus, the physical enviroment may (respectively) alleviate or intensify the stress experienced by residents.

Evidence also suggests that these six functions of the neighborhood are all positively interrelated with each other. For example, the work of Bell and Force (1956) and Kasarda and Janowitz (1974) suggests that participation in locality-based groupings leads to more local friendships (see also Gans, 1967). These positive interrelationships are assumed, and the exact strength of each is not further pursued in this chapter.

All of these needs or functions may have one thing in common. That is, to the extent that the neighborhood satisfies these needs or functions, it probably promotes attachment to the neighborhood, or satisfaction with the neighborhood. In other words:

Attachment/Satisfaction $= F_i$ $\begin{bmatrix} \text{Socialization, Interaction, Control, Security,} \\ \text{Organizational ties, Collective identity} \end{bmatrix}$

The degree to which each need contributes to overall satisfaction or attachment may be highly variable across persons. Thus, the proposed linear function may be quite variable across persons. For example, person P_1 may be satisfied with a neighborhood that strongly reinforces his or her collective identity by providing a very prestigious address. Thus, in his or her satisfaction function (F_{p_1}), Collective identity would have a large weight. An elderly person (P_2) by contrast, might value the security provided by the neighborhood and care less about other needs.[1]

Although the suggestion that the satisfaction of these six needs or functions may contribute to attachment is somewhat speculative, it is grounded in the recent theorizing of Proshansky (1978) and Stokols and Shumaker (1981). They have suggested that the degree to which a locale has characteristics supportive of an individual's or group's needs gives that individual or group a positive sentiment (i.e., attachment or satisfaction) toward that place.

Now look at the reverse side. Each of the six functions or needs previously discussed has a negative side. That is, a neighborhood can promote social isolation *instead* of interaction, nonparticipation *instead* of organization ties, alienation *instead* of collective identity, or delinquency *instead* of socialization. In short, a neighborhood may impose costs instead of serving a positive function. I also expect that such costs are all positively interrelated, on both an individual and an areal basis. Further, these costs are all interrelated in that they may combine or contribute to a general dissatisfaction with place or psychological separation from place. In short:

Dissatisfaction/separation from place $= F_i$ $\begin{bmatrix} \text{Delinquency, Social isolation, Disorder,} \\ \text{Nonparticipation, Fear, Alienation} \end{bmatrix}$

Again, as with the positive function, the contribution of each cost to overall dissatisfaction may be highly variable across persons. One person's dissatisfaction may be largely a function of the belief that the locale does not appropriately reflect his or her status (i.e., alienation), whereas another person's dissatisfaction may be grounded in the fear that the locale will encourage delinquency among his or her offspring.

To discuss this framework differently, these costs, and the resulting overall dissatisfaction or sense of separation, may all be construed as *stress-related outcomes*. These costs, either directly or through dissatisfaction, may also have impacts on health-related outcomes. Such ties have not, how-

---

[1] My suggestion that different neighborhood functions may vary in importance across persons or groups of persons is in keeping with the recent work of Triandis, Fishbein, and others (Triandis, 1977). My suggestion may, however, only apply to attitudes, and not to behavior. Dawes and Corrigan (1974) have concluded that unweighted functions are better predictors of behaviors than weighted ones.

ever, been established (Kasl, 1974). Some of these costs (e.g., lack of local social ties) may make it more difficult to cope with health-related stress.

Preliminary issues

Definitional problems

Neighborhood. Although neighborhoods are a familiar and recognized feature of urban and suburban life, they are difficult to define (Wellman & Leighton, 1979). The uses of the term may be broken down into four types or clusters. The types of uses may be arrayed along a definitional continuum ranging from fairly lax to fairly stringent definitions. Definitions that are more lax would find neighborhoods in many locations, and stricter definitions would discover extant neighborhoods less frequently. (Of course, researchers may, and often do, use definitions that are hybrid and that fall between the four clusters of uses described here.)

The loosest use would be a *minimal, areal* view of a neighborhood. According to this view a neighborhood is simply an area, bounded in some statistical or arbitrary way, where people happen to interact due to their proximity. According to such a use census tracts, school districts, police reporting areas, or planning areas would all qualify as neighborhoods. No strong attachment on the part of the residents to the area is assumed, and neither is outside recognition by political forces assumed. The area may or may not be homogeneous on housing or socioeconomic dimensions. No strong relationships between neighbors are assumed, and neither is an overarching organization assumed.

The reader will see in subsequent discussions that this minimal use of the term "neighborhood" has dominated research. Wellman (1979) and Fischer (1976b) reveal some of the assumptions that go along with this viewpoint.

Moving up the definitional ladder we find what Hunter (1978b) calls *emergent* neighborhoods. These are neighborhoods where some overall bond, of varying number, type, and strength binds residents together such that they share some common identity, purpose, feelings, or fate. Crenson's (1978) treatment of a neighborhood as a polity that advocates for itself, Suttles' (1968, 1972) defended neighborhoods, Hunter's (1974) symbolic communities, or Gans's (1962) notion of urban village, all qualify as an *emergent* treatment of neighborhoods. An emergent neighborhood may exhibit one or more of the following characteristics: presence of a representative organization, similarity among residents on ethnic or value dimensions, extensive networks of voluntary associations, or awareness of area in terms of name and/or boundaries. It is also possible that a neighborhood may become emergent in order to deal with outside issues or agencies (Suttles, 1972; Taub, Surgeon, Lindholm, Otti, & Bridges, 1977).

A harder to fill definition is the *institutional* view of neighborhood. This assumes that people are cemented through the joint use of local facilities – stores, schools, business, theaters, sources of employment, and so on. Probably the best known example of this is Warren's (1963) discussion of community. Governmental or political scholars also may rely heavily on this perspective. For example, Hallman (1973), in his review of the history of the neighborhood as an organizational unit, discusses the roles that precinct committee members, settlement houses, and community centers all played in fostering neighborhood sentiments and local loyalties. Persons adopting the institutional view of neighborhood often draw heavily on the concept of community. Furthermore, these researchers often assume that reliance on or use of local institutions would in turn foster local feelings ("sense of community") and ties between coresidents.[2] For example, in his neighborhood unit plan, Perry (1929) proposed that a centrally located school would help bring the neighbors together.

It is hard to find neighborhood using an institutional perspective because the presence, viability, and importance of local institutions have waned (Warren, 1963). Some recent trends toward street-level bureaucracy and local control may, however, reverse this trend (Altschuler, 1970; Lipsky, 1973).

Most stringent is the *multiple criteria* view of neighborhood. According to this view, every neighborhood has a neighborhood potential. "A knowledge of the prevalent social character of an area, ascertained by various indexes of living conditions, residential stability, and population characteristics, may be used as clues to its neighborhood potential" (Keller, 1968, p. 95). If an area is high enough on these various components that contribute to neighborhood potential, then it may actually be considered a neighborhood.

Local areas that have physical boundaries, social networks, concentrated use of area facilities, and special emotional and symbolic connotations for their inhabitants are considered neighborhood. (Keller, 1968, pp. 156–157)

But, Keller readily admits that such neighborhoods may be hard to find: "The four dimensions do not overlap predictably or significantly in changing urban areas, hence the difficulty of locating neighborhoods and of planning and building effective ones." Nonetheless, such locales have been identified and described in urban areas by Fried and Gleicher (1961), Suttles (1968), Whyte (1943), and Gans (1962). In short, the multicriteria view demands that *both* the emergent *and* the institutional definitions be met, for a single locale to be treated as a neighborhood.

Stress-related outcomes. For the purposes of the present chapter stress-related outcomes are those attitudinal and behavioral consequences that are related to or result from the needs or functions satisfied or not satisfied by

---

[2] Recent research by Hunter (1975) suggests that this linkage may not exist, or may not be as strong as suspected.

neighborhoods. To the extent that an outcome is related to or results from an impediment of the six functions discussed earlier, it is a *stress-promoting* outcome. To the extent that an outcome is related to or results from a promotion of these six functions, it is a *stress-alleviating* outcome. These attitudinal and behavioral consequences may have physiological or mood correlates.

The physical environment. This review will consider the physical environment at the neighborhood and block level. All elements of the potential environment as defined by Gans (1970) are relevant. Thus, I will focus on characteristics such as housing quality, density, boundaries, distance, amenities, building size, street traffic and size, and so on. Demographic, sociodemographic, and socioeconomic characteristics are excluded from discussion, except insofar as they interrelate with physical characteristics.

Empirical links

The next sections detail neighborhood impacts and are organized in terms of the six functions of neighborhood. The first section reviews impacts on security versus crime, fear, and concern, and social control versus social disorder. I then take up impacts relevant to socialization versus delinquency, social interaction versus isolation, and organization ties versus nonparticipation. The last specific impact addressed is collective identity versus alienation. Subsequently, I address more general impacts such as feelings of attachment versus separation and satisfaction versus dissatisfaction.

Security versus fear and crime; order versus disorder

Theoretical contexts

There are several theories of varying comprehensiveness that bear on the relationship between the physical environment at the neighborhood level and issues of security and order.

Defensible space theory, originated by Jacobs (1961) and Newman (1972), suggests that physical features in the environment such as real and symbolic barriers, or surveillance opportunities, may strengthen residents' territorial attitudes and behaviors, which in turn will result in a reduction of crime and related outcomes. The development of this theory and the bulk of evidence pertinent to it are reviewed in Taylor, Gottfredson, and Brower (1980).

Hunter's (1978a) mini-theory about *incivilities* was proposed as a partial answer to the question: Why is fear so prevalent in an urban area? Fear is much more prevalent than crime and, on an areal basis, only loosely correlated with crime (Baumer, 1978). The theory proposes the following linkages: social disorder in an area results in crime and incivilities, and incivilities have a greater impact on fear than does crime. Basically, incivilities, physical or social, are clues to the underlying decay of the social order. *Physical incivilities* could include vacant or abandoned housing, vandalism, vacant lots, litter, lack of upkeep, or other evidence of physical decay. *Social incivilities* could include "street hassles," groups loitering on corners, or drinking and drug use in public. Incivilities may be prevalent in changing neighborhoods or in locales where there is a declining concern on the part of the residents themselves.

Density has also been linked to crime-related outcomes. Roncek (1981a) suggests that this linkage holds at the block level, in particular. He suggests that density may cause anonymity in public places, thereby resulting in more crime. These relationships may hold with more force in areas with particular social and physical characteristics (e.g., high proportion of nonfamily households or apartments).

Greenberg, Rohe, and Williams (1981, 1982) develop a *neighborhood environment* theory to explain neighborhood-level variation in crime rates. They suggest that environmental characteristics may facilitate identification and territoriality, thereby resulting in less crime. Brantingham and Brantingham (1975) share a basically similar conceptual approach.

A final heuristic that deserves mention is the *cognitive–symbolic* approach of Brower (1965, 1980), Craik and Appleyard (1980), and Appleyard (1973). The basic idea is that people "read" physical elements in the environment and interpret or decode these using certain cultural or social assumptions.

Results

Defensible space theory. Although there has been considerable research in this area, it is only recently that impacts at the neighborhood level or block level have been adequately analyzed. Such results have sometimes been impressive and have often unearthed unanticipated complexities. In toto the results suggest that (1) there are links between defensible space variables and crime-related outcomes at the block level; (2) linkages are differentially patterned across various outcomes; and (3) the links may be contingent upon other setting conditions such as social climate (Taylor et al., 1980)

Some of the important recent work is as follows. A Hartford demonstration project, carried out in one neighborhood in that city, evaluated the neighborhood-level effects of design changes (Fowler, McCalla, & Mangione, 1979; Fowler & Mangione, 1981). In the demonstration neighborhood organizational, policing, and design changes were phased in sequentially over a period of a few years. The design changes were the last ones to be implemented. The purpose of the physical modifications was to reroute traffic in order to give certain streets a more "residential" character and provide gateways to the neighborhood itself, as well as to several streets within the neighborhood. It was hoped that the changes would result in less nonresidential vehicular and pedestrian traffic. It is interesting to note that these changes are very much in line with the neighborhood unit plan advocated by Perry (1929; Dahir, 1947) to promote community and a residential atmosphere.

Several strategies were used to assess impacts. Observers recorded levels of street activity. Residents in the neighborhood and other areas in Hartford were interviewed. Crime data for the neighborhood and for other areas in Hartford were gathered and assessed. Impacts were assessed 1 year and 3 years after the physical changes were in place.

Findings showed a significant drop in the burglary rate. But, by 3 years after placement, the burglary rate had risen to expected levels based on extrapolation from preprogram data. Survey responses reflecting neighborhood activities (e.g., incidence of walking in the neighborhood) appeared to rise immediately after the changes were in place and remained at that high level. Indexes of informal social control revealed roughly the same pattern. Perception of problems in the neighborhood showed no change soon after the program was in place, but reflected a more positive view 3 years after the changes. It appears then that the program did have many of the desired effects, although some of the effects showed up sooner than others, and some showed decay over time whereas others did not.[3]

The pattern of changes over time may indicate a lagged relationship between crime and perceptions of crime. It is only after crime has decreased for a time that residents actually perceive this to be the case. And, once the crime rate starts to rise it may be a while before people recognize it. Such appears to be the case with actual burglary and perception of burglary in the present study.

Two shortcomings in the Hartford study deserve mention. First, the demonstration boils down to a case study. It tell us about one particular neighborhood in one particular city. Neighborhoods and cities, like people, have their own character. But, with a sample of one you don't know how those characteristics are influencing the outcomes of interest. Second, in assessing changes in crime rates, the authors assume that the expected postprogram changes in crime rate in the neighborhood are identical to the percentage change shown for the city as a whole. In essence, then, this assumes that the neighborhood falls exactly at the city mean in terms of areal crime rates. This is rather a strong assumption.[4] These criticisms, however, should be tempered somewhat by the realization that this study was in effect a demonstration project. In such cases constraints on research design and analysis are often appreciable.

Furthermore, the overall significance of the project, limitations notwithstanding, is considerable. It does suggest several ties between neighborhood-

[3] The inherent weakness of the quasi-experimental design that was used prohibits asserting a stronger conclusion.
[4] An alternative would be to use areal characteristics to predict crime rate (cf. Harries, 1980) and changes in crime rate. This would then indicate where the neighborhood stood relative to the city mean, and adjustments could be made accordingly. Or, a "control group" could have been assessed.

level physical features and neighborhood-level, crime-related outcomes. Perhaps more importantly, it tracks outcomes over time. It is the only study to date that has done so. And, as an area for future research, it points up complex linkages between behavioral and perceptual outcomes.

Moving down to the block level, three recent studies provide support for the defensible space concept and, at the same time, underscore some limitations of theorizing to date.

In the housing development context, Newman and Franck (1980, in press) assessed 63 housing sites in three different cities. The unit of analysis was the site or project building, which I would consider analogous to a block.[5] Key physical variables were building size and accessibility. Outcomes such as personal crime, burglary, fear, and instability (turnover rate) were assessed. The roles of intervening social and behavioral variables, such as use of space, interaction patterns, and perceived control over space, were also assessed. It was hypothesized that physical variables would have a direct association with the outcomes of interest, as well as indirect associations via the intervening variables. The cross-sectional data were analyzed by means of path analysis.

The hypotheses were supported by the results. For example, building size was negatively associated with use of space, social interaction, and perceived control of space, and positively with fear. Accessibility was positively associated with burglary. The size of the direct effects of the physical variables (β = .2–.3) was somewhat smaller than expected, and Newman and Franck (in press) discuss some of the potential reasons for this.

Using a somewhat different perspective and drawing more heavily on notions of territoriality, Taylor, Gottfredson, and Brower (1981) obtained essentially similar results in the standard residential context. Sixty-three blocks within a stratified sample of 12 neighborhoods in Baltimore were assessed. The primary unit of analysis was the block. Prior research (Brower, 1979) and theory (Suttles, 1972) suggested that the block was a viable social unit. Additional analyses of individual deviations from block means (i.e., pooled within block residuals) were also carried out. The basic hypothesis in this study was that defensible space features and local social ties would both serve to reinforce territorial attitudes and behaviors, which in turn would dampen crime-related outcomes. Outcomes of interest were crimes of violence to persons, problems, and fear.

At the block level the data supported the hypothesis quite well. The physical defensible space features of real and symbolic barriers and local social ties were linked in the hypothesized direction with the majority of the outcomes. Physical features revealed direct associations with the outcomes (β = .15–.25). Physical features also demonstrated the desired in-

---

[5] Throughout, unless otherwise mentioned, "block" refers to the two sides of a street (e.g., 2100 S. Michigan Avenue).

direct patterns. Through a strengthening of territorial functioning they dampened crime-related outcomes.[6]

A couple of interesting and unexpected findings from the Baltimore study merit brief mention. First, at the individual level, physical features were completely unrelated to outcomes such as fear and perception of problems. This suggests that the role played by design is much more salient, or relevant, for impacts at particular levels of aggregation. Second, in the path analyses predicting crimes of violence to persons, some significant interactions between physical, social, and territorial variables appeared. These interactions suggested that social or territorial predictors only became prepotent if real and symbolic barriers were lacking. Therefore, physical and nonphysical determinants of resident-based control may be intertwined such that the influence of one is contingent upon the condition of the others. Calhoun (1971) suggests that such a tie is dependent upon the available physical space.

Another examination of block-level impacts appears in Newman's *Community of interest* (1979) in which he describes some private streets in St. Louis. In these locations residents or a residents' organization have taken legal responsibility for the upkeep and maintenance of the street. The blocks are physically distinctive and have narrow "gateway" entrances, special signs or a traffic pattern such as a closing at one end. Although the analysis reported is somewhat sketchy, it does appear that residents' use of the private streets is higher and their fear lower, as compared to control blocks.

In the examination of the private streets in St. Louis it is difficult to clearly specify the role played by the physical environment. The study blocks had distinctive physical features, but residents also had a legally binding custodial relationship with the street that was also distinctive. It is difficult to tell how much of the results were due to the physical arrangements and how much to the custodial arrangements. It is quite likely, however, that the physical environment played some role in influencing attitudes.

The issue of street accessibility and crime is pursued in more detail by Bevis and Nutter (1978), who examined 65 blocks in Minneapolis that had a non–through–traffic arrangement (dead end, cul-de-sac, L-type, etc.). They then compared residential burglary rates for these blocks with rates for the nearest through street. (For each study block the nearest through street served as a control.) Using the block as the unit of analyis they found that burglary rates were lower on less accessible streets, such as dead end, cul-de-sac, and L-type, as compared to the control blocks.

These last four studies appear to confirm that block-level design features such as access, traffic patterns, and boundaries are often relevant to block-

---

[6] The data from this study, like those of Newman and Franck (1980, in press), were cross sectional. Thus, it is not clear if particular associations really are "causal."

level crime and related outcomes. But interpretation of these results is somewhat difficult for the following reason: These studies often report a direct effect, in path-analytic terms, on crime and related outcomes. Yet, unless one accepts a strict architectural determinist model (cf. Broady, 1972), these impacts probably do not work in an unmediated fashion. Intervening between design and the outcomes are two clusters of behavior: residents' behavior and perceptions of potential offenders. It is incumbent upon researchers to assess the degree to which these two clusters relate to design and crime-related outcomes. Carter and Hill (1979) have made a start on examining how property offenders assess areas as crime targets, but they have not actually measured physical aspects of areas.

At the individual level two studies loosely related to notions of defensible space address the issue of surveillance. Ley and Cybriwsky (1974) assessed the locations of 138 stripped cars and land use immediately adjacent to the cars. Stripped cars were found in proximity to land uses that represented little territorial control and little surveillance (e.g., an institution or vacant house). Tien, O'Donnell, Barnett & Mirchandani (1979) evaluated the impacts of lighting programs designed to heighten surveillance opportunities and reduce crime. They concluded that it was uncertain whether the improved lighting had an impact on crime, but it did appear to play a role in reducing individual-level fear.

In sum, there have been many supportive studies of defensible space concepts. Some of the relevant channels that mediate the impacts of physical variables have been established, whereas, at the same time, other channels have been attended to. A singular gap is ignorance regarding offender perceptions.

Incivilities. By comparison, studies relevant to Hunter's incivility hypotheses are far fewer, but the few studies completed have proved tantalizing. Lewis and Maxfield (1980) assessed the relationship between crime, fear, or concern about crime and social and physical incivilities in four Chicago neighborhoods. Analysis was carried out at the neighborhood level. Three findings are of interest. First, residents were by and large aware of the crime-prone areas in their neighborhoods. These areas usually had a distinctive land use (major thoroughfare, factories, or commercial area) or were in a state of dilapidation. Second, if a neighborhood had a high crime rate but not a high level of perceived social and physical incivilities, concern about crime or fear was usually not high. Third, irrespective of crime rate, the correlation between concern about crime and perceived level of incivilities was quite high (.78). This is an important result because it suggests that elements of physical deterioration, abandonment, and dilapidation contribute substantially to fear and concern about crime.[7]

---

[7] The incivilities scale included two social items and two physical items (how much of a problem is vandalism; how much of a problem are abandoned buildings?) Lacking more

Furthermore, the result was obtained at the neighborhood level. If this finding proves sound through replication in other cities, the policy implications would be substantial. Planners and local officials could target neighborhoods where concern about crime is higher than warranted due to actual crime rate and seek to eliminate physical problems such as abandoned housing and vandalism.[8] The consequences may be a much improved image of the community in the eyes of the residents.

Density. Major reviews of recent density work can be found in Roncek (1975), Choldin (1978), and Baldassare (1979). In this section I will focus largely on a very recent block-level study of density and crime.

Roncek (1981a) investigated the relationships between block-level[9] density, block characteristics, and crime, using data from Cleveland and San Diego. Both violent personal crime and property crime were assessed. Several components of density such as areal density, population potential (persons per mile – a measure of potential contact or moral density), and block population were examined.

His results contain a *very* unexpected finding. Increasing areal density was correlated with *lower* crime rates. This relationship appeared in the regressions for both types of crime in Cleveland and for property crime in San Diego. The author conducted additional analyses that suggested that the unanticipated negative correlation between density and crime was due to a positive correlation between block *area* and crime. This finding supports one of Jane Jacob's (1961) contentions about negative consequences of long distances between cross streets. Jacobs proposed that blocks that are larger in areal extent provide more opportunities for antisocial behavior.

Somewhat more expected were the positive correlations obtained between block population, population potential, and crime. Also, in keeping with the concerns raised by Zorbaugh (1929) and others, proportion of multiunit structures was correlated with crime. Furthermore, in a companion paper Roncek (1981b) compares and contrasts results at the tract level and the block level. He found that density and other areal predictors were relevant to explaining outcomes at both levels of aggregation. Thus, density effects *may* be stable at different levels of aggregation.

Roncek's study is particularly significant not only for the somewhat unexpected pattern of results, but also because he decomposed density into

specific information about the contribution of each item, I assume the two social and two physical items contributed equally to concern about crime. If this is so, then the physical elements would explain half of the correlation of .78, or 30% of the variance in neighborhood-level concern about crime.

[8] Although it may sound like boosterism to mention this, it is the case that in Baltimore, the local officials have taken vigorous steps to deal with both of these physical problems. For the past several years the city has helped people buy and renovate vacant, dilapidated housing, on a neighborhood-by-neighborhood basis. Furthermore, the mayor has recently declared "war" on vandalism and is in the process of developing appropriate programs.

[9] In this study, blocks were *census* blocks.

several constituent parts (space per person, group size, interaction level) and found that the different parts functioned differently. Furthermore, his results suggest that density impacts were intertwined with other socio-demographic characteristics. One limitation of the study is that the ano-nymity that is presumed to mediate the interaction potential–crime link is not measured.

Density, although related to crime, does not appear to be related to fear. Verbrugge and Taylor (1976, 1980) found a hypothesized negative relation-ship betwen neighborhood density and individual-level perceived safety, but the relationship was too weak to be significant (ψ = .15). Baldassare (1979) also found a modest but, in his case, significant positive relationship between neighborhood density and fear. Lavrakas (in press) found a very weak positive relationship between density and concern about crime (β = .10) that was nonsignificant. These three studies focused on individual-level impacts and this may in part explain why such weak relationships were observed; stronger links may be observed with block-or neighborhood-level impacts. As far as I know, such studies have not yet been performed.

In sum, ties between density and some aggregate measures of disorder, such as crime rate, appear to be established. The role played by hypothe-sized mediators, such as anonymity, has not yet been assessed.

Neighborhood environment focus. In this section studies are considered that focus on neighborhood-level environmental features. These studies assume that the neighborhood environment is a critical determinant of crime-related outcomes. Some studies that have more loosely assessed facilities or land use in residential areas are also discussed.

A recent study of six neighborhoods in Atlanta assessed the relation-ships between neighborhood boundaries, land use within neighborhoods, and crime (Greenberg, Rohe, & Williams, 1981). The authors developed a general model of neighborhood safety that includes physical, social, and territorial elements. Three matched pairs of neighborhoods were selected. Each pair included a high-crime and a low-crime neighborhood. Both mem-bers of each pair were roughly matched on socioeconomic characteristics. The unit of analysis for physical features was the census block.

The high- and low-crime neighborhoods differed, as predicted, on land use. In low-crime neighborhoods residential land use was more prevalent, and vacant land was less prevalent than in high-crime areas. Also, one-unit structures were more prevalent in low-crime neighborhoods. (This matches Roncek's findings, previously discussed, as well as suggestions made by Zorbaugh.) For two of the three pairs, blocks in the lower crime neighbor-hoods were more likely to have small, neighborhood streets and less likely to have major thoroughfares. (This is congruent with the results of Bevis and Nutter, also previously described.)

Predicted differences in boundary characteristics also emerged. Boundary streets of higher crime neighborhoods were more likely to be major thoroughfares, suggesting that they constituted more permeable boundaries for outsiders and/or potential offenders. A couple of the low-crime neighborhoods were actually quite isolated, being partly surrounded by industrial land use and railroads. This latter finding raises the possibility that high levels of neighborhood "privacy" or isolation may reduce entry by outsiders, or at least make such entries more visible.

Greenberg et al. (1981) hypothesized that land use and boundary characteristics would reinforce residents' sense of spatial identity, local ties, and control, thereby reducing crime indirectly as well as directly. Such indirect paths, however, were not assessed.

The Atlanta study is important on several counts. It is a multineighborhood study. In addition, it examined an important and largely ignored channel of influence: impact of block-level features on neighborhood-level outcomes (In Figure 10.1, this is represented by arrow J_{nb}.) The exact channels through which such influence is mediated remain to be determined. The relevant carriers of the effect may be potential offenders' behavior and perceptions or residents' behaviors and attitudes, or both.

Brantingham and Brantingham (1975) carried out a study in Tallahassee using topological procedures that grouped census blocks into neighborhood sets. "Interior" blocks were those that were similar to the other blocks in the group, whereas "border" blocks were dissimilar. Using parameters such as average rent, percentage of small apartments, and percentage of single-family houses, they found that burglary rates were always lower for the interior blocks as compared to border blocks. If all three variables were used simultaneously, the differences were even more striking. These results underscore, as have some aforementioned studies, the importance of land use. But, in contrast to these other studies the results of Brantingham and Brantingham point out the importance of land use homogeneity. It may not be the absolute level of a certain type of land that is critical; rather, they suggest that the critical factor is how well that block blends in with surrounding blocks. In short, off-block context, or the neighborhood, is a setting condition for the impact of block-level features.

Burglary was also of interest to O'Donnell and Lydgate (1980) in their assessment of land use in Honolulu. The unit of analysis was the police beat or reporting area. They found that burglary was more prevalent in areas with more entertainment locations, transient residences, and places for alcohol consumption. Land uses such as sex-related businesses, retail shops, and bars also correlated well with the frequency of potentially violent crimes such as robbery.

It is clear then that neighborhood land use is related to crime. The exact chain of association, however, is not yet clear. Research is currently under way in Minneapolis, focusing on small commercial areas, which may help lay bare the relevant causal chains (Minnesota Crime Prevention Center,

1980). To date, these researchers have found very solid relationships between commercial land use in small commercial nodes, and these links hold up *a net of* residential characteristics. Also, type of business in the node is related to the crime that occurs there (McPherson, Frey, and Silloway, 1982). A particular problem in this area is the lack of a coherent, broad-based theoretical perspective specifying the roles that land use may play, and why, in relation to crime. If such a perspective were to develop it would probably have to attend to the following issues: (1) type of land use (different types of establishments will be more or less likely, e.g., liquor store versus religious book store) to attract potential offenders; and (2) relationship between land use and local residents. Locals may see an establishment or park as an important positive element in the neighborhood, or a nuisance. This will influence whether or not they attempt to serve as protectors of the property. (3) Size of establishment and proximity to occupied residences will also influence potential protectors. Nonresidential land is unoccupied land, at some time of the day. Protection of such land is therefore dependent upon whether nonoccupants can or will monitor what goes on. Sommer (1972) has suggested that arrangements such as round-the-clock caretakers in a cemetery or school might be very effective.

Symbolic perspective. There appears to be considerable support for the idea that people "read" physical features in the environment and from that information make inferences about the underlying order (Rapoport, 1977).

Taylor, Brower, and Stough (1976), for example, showed pictures of housefronts to inner city residents. The addition of amenities such as flowers and window boxes suggested safer areas where people cared more. Furthermore, people on different blocks in the neighborhood shared this inference, suggesting that it was fairly consistent at the neighborhood level. In a subsequent study (Brower, Dockett, & Taylor, 1981), respondents from a range of neighborhoods assessed pictures of individual backyards with varying physical features. Elements such as planting were construed again as indicators of care and local safety. In high crime areas, however, people were more likely to perceive that multiple physical cues were necessary to achieve safety, (e.g., fencing *and* flowers). Thus, if threat is greater, more (or more blatant) symbols are needed to maintain the social order.

Craik and Appleyard (1980) applied a Brunswikian lens model to the perception of street scenes in San Francisco. They found that residents' concern about crime was associated with environmental features such as dirtiness of facades, length of block, and lack of trees. Furthermore, based largely on physical appearance, judges were able to rather accurately assess residents' level of concern, although judges did vary considerably in their accuracy. Such a policy-capturing approach reveals interpersonal variation in "decoding" physical features. This suggests that block- or neighborhood-level agreement on how to decode may not always be present. It would seem important to determine the conditions under which such consensus may emerge. Value or ethnic homophyly may be a prerequisite.

Socialization versus delinquency

Many different theoretical perspectives have been applied to the problem of delinquency (see Gibbons, 1976, for a review of these). The area has also been fraught with statistical and methodological hazards (e.g., multicollinearity, confusion about meaningful unit of analysis, and synonymity of independent and dependent constructs; see Gordon, 1967, 1968; Hirschi & Selvin, 1967; Baldwin, 1975; or Harries, 1980, for reviews). In this section I will briefly touch on two theoretical perspectives that are particularly attentive to the physical environment and discuss some typical results.

Theoretical contexts

The best known and perhaps most influential theory of delinquency and environment is the ecological theory of Shaw and McKay (1969, 1942). The basic notion is that human communities, which are ecologically valid areas, are constantly in competition with one another for the most valuable land and are often in a state of flux or succession. Although rates of maladjustment among juveniles may be uniform across the city, methods and modes of controlling delinquency may break down in stressed areas (i.e., locations where turnover, decline, or succession is occurring), resulting in delinquency (cf. Maccoby, Johnson, & Church, 1958). Thus, delinquency is endemic to the processes of city growth and community change.

A more recent and very different approach is being taken by Newman and his colleagues in a study that is currently under way (Newman & Franck, 1977). Focusing on housing project environments, they suggest that design features that promote visual contact between the mother and her children when the latter are outside may lessen the likelihood of delinquency. (Results from this project are not yet available.)

Results

Research has consistently linked physical environmental features with delinquency. Shaw and McKay (1969) found, for example, that high delinquency rates occurred in those areas where physical deterioration was present. Whether the physical breakdown was causal or symptomatic is not clear. Comparable findings have been found since. For example, Herbert (1977) found that delinquency in a town in England was associated with substandard housing and shared dwellings. It appeared, however, that the influence of physical conditions was somewhat weaker than the influence of social environment variables.

Three problematic features of this work are of interest for our present topic. First, as Baldwin (1975) pointed out, most of the studies do *not* use ecologically valid areas, that is, places that are perceived or actually operate as neighborhoods, communities, or social units. Thus, the application of ecological principles (e.g., Burgess, 1925) is not appropriate. Second, it is hard to separate the influence of socioeconomic factors from physical, housing-, or land use-related factors, as these elements covary in the natural environment. Third, delinquency and poor physical conditions may both be the result of the same cause – poverty. Thus, the environment–delinquency link may be spurious. And finally, when a link between physical environment and delinquency is found, mediating mechanisms (e.g., more contact with crime-prone persons and pressure to send children out of the household) are often hypothesized, but rarely measured. (And, of course, a simple direct model is not appropriate. Can low housing quality really lead directly to delinquency?) We are therefore in agreement with the suggestion made by Baldwin that areal studies should be used to generate hypotheses, and that follow-up interview or observation studies should be conducted to really *test* hypotheses.

Design does appear to play a role in providing a place for potential delinquents to gather. Brower (1979, 1980; Brower & Williamson, 1974) and his colleagues have intensively studied small, inner-block parks in West Baltimore. The parks are at the backs of houses where few residents relax or recreate. The bulk of activity is at the front. Consequently, wayward teens and social undesirables gather in these parks and residents avoid them. The parks are located between the existing social groupings and thus constitute a no-man's land. Research is currently under way that seeks to make the parks more controllable by reducing access points and by perhaps "locking up" the park at night with fences and gates. The successful implementation of design changes, however, is contingent upon having a resident group to look after the space and act as "gatekeepers" (Brower, 1981). Some residents, on an individual level, already have implemented design changes. The researchers were very curious about one park where residents reported no problems at night. It turned out that one resident, whose house abutted the park, had a large and powerful searchlight in her backyard. When she suspected people were in the park she would turn on the light, "spot" the intruders, and tell them to go home because the park was closed after dusk.

In sum, it appears that neighborhood-level and block-level environmental and housing features are important as a setting condition for areal delinquency rates. It is not as yet clear, however, how the physical variables might interact with social setting conditions (cf. Roncek's density findings), nor is it clear how social and behavioral variables may mediate the impact of the physical environment. Fortunately, there are several delinquency theories that hypothesize these mediating links.

Social ties versus social isolation

Theoretical contexts

Theoretical statements concerning the relation between the physical environment are, with the exception of density theories, conceptually loose. They are as follows.

Density may have negative or positive consequences on local interaction. A negative model would follow from a treatment of density as a stressor, the consequence being that people would seek to ignore or limit social contacts (Simmel, 1971). A positive model would follow from Durkheim's (1960) notions of "moral density." Higher density means more people around with greater chances of meeting with or being helped by them.

Distance can have a positive or negative impact. Festinger, Schachter, and Back (1950) developed a positive model. Short functional distance (i.e., high likelihood of daily paths crossing) may lead to passive (i.e., unplanned) contacts that may, in turn, lead to the development of friendships. Ebbesen, Kjos, and Konecni (1976) developed a negative model that they call an "environmental spoiling hypothesis." The basic notion is that people living close by are potentially the most dislikable because they have the greatest chance of spoiling one's immediate environment through noise, litter, and so on.

There are also some loose theoretical notions revolving around *positive environmental* qualities and *negative environmental* qualities. If there are available places to interact, and they are pleasant, this will facilitate neighboring. If there are no available places, or the places available are unpleasant in some respect, neighboring will be dampened.

Results

Positive density effects. Verbrugge and Taylor (1976, 1980) found positive density effects, particularly at the household level. Increasing household density, for example, was associated with spending more leisure time with household members, or relying on them when ill. At the street level, increasing density had mixed effects. It was positively associated with recognizing coresidents, but negatively associated with getting to know them. At the neighborhood level support for the positive model was also mixed. Increasing neighborhood density meant that more of one's neighbors were also friends (i.e., increasing role multiplexity), but overall, neighbors were liked less as density increased. In this study all outcomes were individual-level measures.

Negative density effects. Some studies have shown negative density effects, but others have not. Booth (1976), for example, in a Toronto study found no effects of neighborhood density on quality of family life, or aggression, although household density was slightly associated with a decrement in the quality of family life. Baldassare (1977) found that increasing census tract density in Detroit was associated with a reduced level of casual neighboring. This is in accordance with Simmel's suggestion that "low-priority" inputs will be cut in the face of higher density. Meaningful ties were apparently not effected.

Verbrugge and Taylor (1976, 1980) also found negative effects although (1) the pattern was different across arenas (household, street, neighborhood density), and (2) personal attributes such as length of residence or feelings of control served as important buffers of negative impacts. The pattern of negative effects was strongest for the household arena and weakest for the neighborhood arena.

Distance. Festinger et al. (1950) found that friendship patterns and communications patterns followed a distance decay function, falling off rapidly with increasing functional distance. They concluded that face-to-face passive contacts were an important mediating variable. The study was carried out in a homogeneous population, and subsequent studies have suggested that in a heterogeneous population perceived value homophyly may be more important than distance for friendship formation.

Case (1981) and Ebbesen et al. (1976) replicated Festinger et al.'s finding, again with homogeneous student populations. Ebbesen et al. also verified the mediating importance of face-to-face contact. More important, they found that the choice of enemies was more heavily dependent upon distance per se than was choice of friendships. Actual contact frequency appeared to have little influence on picking enemies. The authors interpret their results as supporting the environmental spoiling hypothesis.

Physical opportunities and deterrents. These also appear important. For example, Holohan (1978) found that outdoor activity levels were higher in an "innovative" and aesthetically pleasing environment than they were in a traditional and less inviting playground. Furthermore, the bulk of the outdoor activity observed was social or interactional in nature.

On the negative side, Appleyard (1976) found that a heavy volume of street traffic made it unpleasant for people to sit outside thereby discouraging casual neighboring and reducing feelings of territoriality. Along the same lines, Baum, Davis, and Aiello (1978) found that the presence of corner stores was associated with heavier pedestrian traffic, with residents' using their front yards less, and with residents' chatting less with neighbors outside.

Physical variables such as density and distance can have either positive or negative impacts. It would probably be best then to treat these variables, using Heider's (1959) terminology, as media, which, potentially, can transmit any social impact. For example, on a block where value homophyly is high, high density may help bring about greater neighborly helping. On a block where value homophyly is low, high density may just intensify irritation with neighbors.

Comment on neighborhood-level social life. All the studies in this section have examined individual-level social outcomes. Tannenbaum (1948) has suggested, however, that neighborhood designs may also promote neighborhood-level social life. Layouts such as the neighborhood unit play may help combat alienation, anomie, and isolation. Such a view, *in extremis*, is a form of architectural determinism. Nonetheless, it would seem true that neighborhood design can provide opportunities for neighborhood-level social life. I am unaware of the testing of any such relationships.

Organization ties

No theoretical perspectives have been proposed to suggest links between physical features of the environment and levels of social participation. Locational differences, however, have been observed. For example, Tomeh (1964) found that levels of participation in local organizations were higher in suburban than in urban locations, even when socioeconomic influences were partialed out.

Ceteris paribus, the physical environment may be associated with rates of organizational participation in the following ways. Neighborhoods that are physically singular (i.e., very different from surrounding areas) *and* physically homogeneous may be places where there are stronger feelings of in-group solidarity or attachment, and thus local participation. In addition, if the physical environment is valued by residents *and* threatened by outside forces, such as proposed zoning changes, this may be a point over which residents can coalesce. On the other side of the coin is the possibility that local physical *problems* (e.g., bad housing or nearby a noxious factory), may bring people together. Thus, neighborhoods with stronger noxious physical stimuli in their locale may be more likely to join together to deal with the problem.

Collective identity versus alienation

It is commonly understood that where we live reflects who we are. The simple mention of some famous neighborhoods brings their residents to mind: Beverly Hills, Lake Shore Drive, the Battery, Watts, Harlem, and so on. When such (in)famous locations are conjured up, social characteristics of residents, such as income and race, are simultaneously brought to mind. As held by outsiders or nonresidents, these views may be nothing more (or less) than stereotypes (for discussion, see Downs & Stea, 1977; Gould &

White, 1974; Tuan, 1974). But, as held by residents, these views may be critical to their psychological well-being.[10]

Basically, one can identify with or feel "part of" where one lives, or one can disclaim, deny, or be indifferent about such an association. Searles (1961) discusses this issue from a clinical perspective; Proshansky (1978), Gerson et al. (1977), and Stokols and Shumaker (1981) discuss it from a more environmentally oriented perspective.

One of the basic themes in most of these frameworks is the notion of congruence. If the status or other attributes of the neighborhood or place fit with an individual's (or group's) conception of his or her self (or themselves), feelings of identification may develop (cf. Bielby, 1981). Two points are assumed: (1) Identification leads to attachment and desire to stay there, and (2) the physical quality of the environment plays an important role in shaping the local image.

Several studies suggest that the physical environment does indeed contribute to identification. Rapoport (1977) found in Australia that residents would distort how they mapped their own neighborhood so that it would include higher status, physically better-kept areas. McKenzie (1923) has suggested:

The solidarity of the traditional neighborhood included physical as well as social objects. The old swimming pool, the familiar hills and trees, the architecture and location of buildings, all function as sentimental attachments of the neighborhood. The individual becomes so closely identified with all these objects of early and intimate contact that they tend to form a part of the "extended self" (p. 349).

Ross (1962) and Warren (1977) have suggested that areal names and location serve status-ascriptive functions. The physical environment may also aid in identification by providing clear areal boundaries. For example, major thoroughfares or changes in land use quite often are picked as community boundaries (Hunter, 1974; Ross, 1962).

The physical features may even play a role in maintaining continuity in the population of a neighborhood. Firey (1945) has suggested that certain neighborhoods in Boston have maintained a unique and fairly constant type of population, in part because the physical features appealed to a certain type of person. It is difficult, however, to separate the appeal of neighborhoods based on physical characteristics from the economic resources of residents.

In general, the question about neighborhood and identification is particularly frustrating. The area is rich in theory and hunches, but weak in terms of hard results. Also, it is difficult to say where ability to identify with a neighborhood or feel that one's neighborhood is part of one's identity leaves off, and more general issues such as satisfaction pick up. It is to these more general issues that we turn in the next section.

---

[10] The images may also be critical for safe wayfinding (Suttles, 1972).

Satisfaction, dissatisfaction, and related issues

Several studies have found a strong relationship between the physical environment and satisfaction, or the correlates of satisfaction. For example, Taub and Taylor (1980) in an eight-neighborhood study in Chicago found that the perception of physical deterioration in the neighborhood was associated with a lower likelihood of investing (i.e., fixing up) in property among white, black, and Hispanic homeowners. For white renters, perception of physical deterioration was associated with an increased desire to move. Kaplan (1982) found a relationship between presence of nearby open space and neighborhood satisfaction.

Several studies find a strong relationship between satisfaction with neighborhood appearance and overall satisfaction. In a study of four neighborhoods in New York, Miller, Grega, Malia, and Tsemberis (1980) found that satisfaction with neighborhood attractiveness accounted for over 40% of the variance in overall satisfaction. Zehner (1971) in a study of four communities found that satisfaction with levels of upkeep in the micro-neighborhood (area visible from front door) explained about 30% of the variance in overall satisfaction. Peterson (1967) and Wilson (1966) found that pleasant appearance contributed to neighborhood preference. Lansing and Marans (1969) found that ratings of the physical quality of structures, as made by an architect–planner, were the best predictor of how much people liked their neighborhood.

In contrast to expectations, neither availability nor use of local facilities contributes to neighborhood satisfaction (Zehner, 1971; Miller et al., 1980). Use also does not contribute to sense of community (Hunter, 1975). Local facilities may, however, contribute to satisfaction in a community where residents have strong local ties, and where the local facilities are viewed as appropriate places for casual social interaction (Fried & Gleicher, 1961).

Unfortunately, the apparent linkage between neighborhood physical quality and satisfaction is problematic in several respects. First, it is *perceived* physical quality, not *actual* physical quality that is usually measured. (An exception is Kaplan, 1982.) Second, the link between actual physical quality and perceived neighborhood quality is of unknown strength and reliability. Last, it is unclear how satisfaction is related to other behavioral outcomes, such as actual moving.

Kasl (1974) concludes, after an extensive review of the literature, that housing and neighborhood quality are related to satisfaction and other stress-related outcomes (anxiety, disease). He suggests, however, that the link is highly contingent upon intrapersonal and social factors such as length of residence and location of friends.

Interrelationships

To date there have been few attempts to examine linkages between *general* outcomes, such as satisfaction, desire to move, and actual moving. Studies examining this issue have found somewhat surprising linkages. For example, Michelson (1977, 1980) found that although apartment dwellers felt dissatisfied with several aspects of their housing (e.g., unit size, noise), these factors were not "pushing" them to contemplate an imminent move. He concluded that the important mediating variable was their future expectations. Residents employed short-range and long-range criteria, and the latter were determined by expectations about changes in the family life cycle and long-term goals. Certain environments were viewed only as way stations, in effect. Similar ideas were also expressed by Wolpert (1966), who suggested that the relationship between stress and actual moving was conditioned by how much disharmony people anticipate, due to a change in their status or in the actual neighborhood. Thus, linkages between satisfaction, desire to move, and actual moving appear contingent upon a range of extraphysical factors.

Furthermore, links between specific impacts, such as social disorder, and general impacts, such as satisfaction or moving, are also complex and less solid than one might anticipate. Droettboom, McAllister, Kaiser, and Butler (1971) found that perception of crime in the neighborhood was correlated with actual mobility over a 3-year period (ψ = .22). But, the perception was not correlated with actual moving *out* of the neighborhood. (A conceptually similar result was obtained by Frey [1979]. He found that actual crime rates had no effect on incidence of migration. Analysis was at the SMSA level.) Droettboom et al. (1971) did observe, however, a strong correlation between perception of crime as a serious problem and dissatisfaction (ψ = .69) and between perception and the *desire* to move (.48). They conclude that limited resources and/or discrimination may prohibit people from actually satisfying such desires. Along similar lines, Kasl and Harburg (1972) found a strong correlation between perception of a neighborhood as unsafe, dislike of the neighborhood, and desire to move out. The strength of these linkages varied somewhat depending upon race and socioeconomic level. Also similar were Hartnagel's (1979) findings that increasing fear dampened neighborhood satisfaction.

These results suggest that stress-related impacts are interrelated to the extent that they are attitudinal. The transformation of these attitudinal effects into behavioral or social or physiological impacts is a complex process and is dependent upon additional factors, such as goals and expectations.

An assessment of a general research deficit

A conceptual statement of the problem

The reader may have noted that in the studies discussed in this chapter predictors are often measured at varying levels of aggregation. One researcher may measure neighborhood characteristics at the block level (e.g., Roncek, 1981a), and another may measure the same characteristic at the

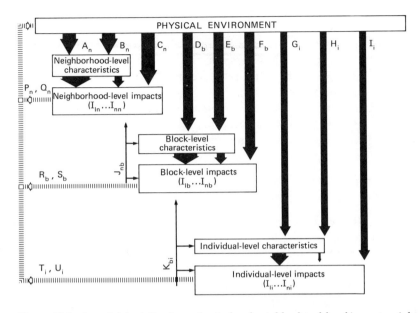

Figure 10.1. A model depicting how physical and neighborhood-level impacts might influence stress-related outcomes.

neighborhood level (e.g., Baldassare, 1977) or individual level (e.g., Lansing & Marans, 1969). The same also holds true for outcomes (cf. Roncek vs. Verbrugge & Taylor). This is unfortunate on two counts: (1) Researchers may be examining only one of the several possible causal paths by which neighborhood-level physical environment influences stress, and (2) paths actually assessed may be weak relative to other possible causal paths.

Figure 10.1 schematically depicts all possible paths by means of which the physical environment may influence stress of residents. The top bar in the figure represents the physical environment. The rectangles beneath represent areal characteristics and impacts at various levels of aggregation. The downward-pointing, solid black arrows represent impacts of the physical environment that occur via different pathways and at varying levels of aggregation. The double-headed, solid arrows represent impacts that may seep upward or downward, across levels of aggregation. The thin, dashed arrows to the left represent subsequent effects of impacts on the physical environment itself.

The *physical environment* includes buildings and land use variables, as well as presence or location of neighborhood facilities. All of the following would qualify as neighborhood-level physical variables:

> Neighborhood size in terms of area
> Nature of boundaries (narrow street versus wide street; adjoining
>   land use residential versus commercial versus industrial versus

vacant; presence or absence of major barriers such as railroads
or highways)

Type of housing (relative prevalence of multiunit versus single
unit; rowhouses versus detached housing; lot sizes)

Condition of housing (age, value, quality, frequency of vacant or
abandoned houses)

Location and pattern of placement of amenities (such as parks,
stores, and other local facilities)

Traffic volume and circulation patterns

Relative predominance of greenery versus paving

Neighborhood-level characteristics are those nonphysical attributes of the
locale that might mediate physical impacts. These may include:

Ethnicity, education, race, income, length of residence, age, or
occupational level of residents

Number of local organizations and extent of participation in them

Integration or diversity of population on parameters such as ethnicity,
income, values, and length of residence

Historicity or "reputation" of neighborhood

These characteristics may mediate impacts in one of two possible ways.
First, in accord with standard notions of person–environment interactionism
(Stokols, 1977), the characteristics may amplify or dampen the consequences
of various environmental features. (See that Impact A_n [in Figure 10.1] is
enlarged by neighborhood characteristics, whereas Impact B_n is reduced).
Second, in accord with filtering notions (Rapoport, 1977), the characteristics determine how people actually perceive and respond to particular
impacts. For example, one cultural group may interpret a particular housing stock as substandard, although another cultural group may feel that
the same stock is adequate.

Neighborhood-level impacts include social, behavioral, and attitudinal consequences brought about wholly or in part by the physical environment.
These include processes such as:

Turnover

Racial succession

Decline

Renewal, rehabilitation, or revitalization

Gentrification

Higher or lower crime, fear, or problem levels

Changes in satisfaction

Grief or other influences on mental health

Impacts that are perhaps less obvious, but that may be component parts
of the foregoing impacts, would be consequences such as an elevation or

decline in housing prices or increased community concern or stress due to an issue such as a proposed highway or a change in zoning.

Block-level characteristics, as with neighborhood-level characteristics, may amplify or dampen particular physical impacts. Relevant block-level characteristics may include:

> Block heterogeneity on issues such as tenure, race, length of residence, education, income, or type of occupation
> Degree of neighborliness or local social ties between various residents on the block
> Presence or absence of a local leader or block captain
> Number of "problem" families on a block.

Block-level impacts may include many smaller-scale counterparts to neighborhood impacts, such as:

> People moving out or not investing in the maintenance of their property
> High turnover rate, with many people rapidly moving in and out
> Loss of community, in the form of deterioration of friendships or local helping networks
> Revitalization in the form of people fixing up properties or desiring to move in
> Higher or lower crime, fear, or problem levels
> Changes in satisfaction or levels of attachment.

A couple of features of these characteristics and impacts deserve attention. A characteristic can operate at many different levels. For example, we can speak of stability in terms of length of residence at the individual, block, or neighborhood level. But, although we are measuring the same variable, the *meaning* or conceptual significance of the item varies across levels of aggregation. Block-level stability is quite a different construct from individual-level, long-term residence. The same may apply to impacts. A neighborhood-level impact, such as dissatisfaction, may be measured using the same variable as was used for block-level dissatisfaction and individual-level dissatisfaction. But, again, the meaning of the construct varies dramatically across levels of aggregation.

Having discussed the "boxes" in Figure 10.1, I move on to a discussion of the "arrows" in the figure. All of the unidirectional downward arrows (A_n through I_i) represent influences due, in part, to the physical environment. These influences may be mediated by characteristics at a particular level of aggregation. These characteristics may amplify (e.g., A_n, D_b, G_i) or diminish (e.g., B_n, E_b, H_i) that particular source of influence. Alternatively, influences may have a direct impact (e.g., C_n, F_b, I_i). An influence may be direct in that no other variables mediate the influence, or in that other variables that may mediate the influence have not as yet been specified. It may also be the case that the impact of a particular physical variable (e.g., housing quality) has a direct influence on some outcomes (e.g., housing values) and an indirect influence on other outcomes (e.g., satisfaction).

These downward arrows of influence become "skinnier" as we go from left to right. I suspect that features of the physical environment at the neighborhood level have the clearest impact at the neighborhood level, a less powerful influence at the block level, and an even less powerful influence at the individual level. For example, for the individual the physical characteristics of his or her own household (number of rooms, size of yard) may be more important than the physical neighborhood characteristics. Note, however, that the impacts at each level of aggregation may "trickle down" or "up." Thus, neighborhood-level impacts may influence block-level impacts and vice versa (arrow J_{nb}). And block-level impacts may influence individual-level impacts, and vice versa (arrow K_{bi}). These "trickle down" or "trickle up" effects are bidirectional causal processes and may complement or counteract the more straightforward unidirectional causal processes.

Further, the model allows for feedback not only between impacts, but also between impacts and the physical environment itself. That is, impacts, over time, may have a subsequent effect on the physical environment itself (arrows P_n through U_i). For example, if physical deterioration of certain portions of the housing stock in the neighborhood results in a heightened sense of concern on some blocks and in disinvestment in homes, this may result in a further deterioration of housing quality. These feedback loops are indicated as separate causal arrows because the feedback occurs some time *after* the original influence. I do not assume that the process of reciprocal influence is simultaneous.

I do assume noncausal correlations between characteristics at different levels of aggregation. People make up blocks and blocks make up neighborhoods.

A final feature of the model deserving mention is the interposition of block-level dynamics between neighborhood-level dynamics and individual-level dynamics. The block, or the two sides of the street, is an important arena. It is a building block that strongly influences residents' commitment to and feelings about their neighborhood (McKenzie, 1923; Wandersman & Giamartino, 1980). It is a level of community that in low-income or minority areas assumes more importance than the neighborhood itself (Hunter & Suttles, 1972).

As a caveat I admit that the hypothesized model does not reflect the location of neighborhoods in a larger context. Neighborhood characteristics are influenced by the qualities of a sector of a city or suburb, which in turn have been conditioned by overall city or county characteristics. These in turn have been conditioned by regional characteristics. Nonetheless, it is still possible to focus on the neighborhood level, and below.

According to this schematic, much research has focused on cross-level, potentially weak causal impacts, (e.g., arrows H or I). Thus, research to date may seriously underestimate impacts of the physical environment. In addition, this research is often incomplete. Very few studies have simultaneously assessed several causal processes. Furthermore, theories in this area have fallen short in that they have not clearly specified *which* paths of causal influence the neighborhood-level, physical environment will demonstrate.

Statistical statement of the problem

The framework proposed in Figure 10.1 depicts impacts and characteristics at three levels of aggregation: the individual, the block, and the neighborhood. Consider also that researchers in this area almost always deal with grouped or nested data. That is, people are grouped into blocks that are different from each other, and blocks are grouped into neighborhoods that are different from each other. These two factors – interest in relationships that cross levels of aggregation, and the nested nature of data – raise the possibility that researchers in this area will be confronted by problems of aggregation and disaggregation. I will not undertake a detailed discussion of these problems here. The reader should consult Hannan (1971a, b), Robinson (1950), Thorndike (1939), Alker (1969), Taylor (1980), Cronbach (1976), or Blalock (1964) for a general conceptual and statistical treatment of these issues. What I will undertake, however, is to show in two or three ways how these problems can wreak havoc.

Composite nature of correlation. In the case of grouped data, data at the individual level are a composite of many processes. They include between-neighborhood, between-block, and between-person sources of variance. For example, suppose that a researcher was investigating the relationship between observed housing quality (x_1) and attachment to the neighborhood (y_1). He or she has data from 1,000 persons, evenly distributed over 100 blocks, evenly distributed over 10 neighborhoods. He or she probably feels quite confident in the correlation he or she observes between the two variables $(r_{x,y})$ since it is based on 1,000 cases. But, within this correlation are several components of correlation. These components are shown in Table 10.1. Furthermore, it is likely that the correlation due to between-neighborhoods variation $(r_{x, y})$ is the most sizable. It is unfortunate, however, that (1) this component is based only on 10 cases (neighborhoods) and is thus likely to be unreliable, (2) the standard error of the correlation will be large, and (3) it will be unlikely to reach statistical significance. Therefore, individual-level correlations based on grouped data are always somewhat suspect, and, depending upon circumstances, perhaps misleading.

Table 10.1. *Components of overall correlation* (r_{xy}) *in nested data*

Source of variance	Number of cases	Form
Between neighborhood	10	$r_{\bar{x}\bar{y}}$
Between blocks (Pooled within neighborhood residuals)	100	$r_{(\bar{x}-\bar{\bar{x}})(\bar{y}-\bar{\bar{y}})}$
Between persons (Pooled within block residuals)	1,000	$r_{(x-\bar{x})(y-\bar{y})}$

Note: $\bar{\bar{x}}$ and $\bar{\bar{y}}$ represent neighborhood means; $\bar{x}$, $\bar{y}$ block means, and x, y individual scores.

To put some flesh on this argument, consider the following hypothetical example. I have data from 36 respondents who are evenly distributed across six blocks. Three blocks are in a neighborhood where housing quality (x_1) and feelings of attachment (y_1) are low, and three blocks are in a neighborhood where housing quality and feelings of attachment are higher. In each neighborhood respondents on one block yield a strong positive correlation between x_1 and y_1, respondents on another yield a strong negative correlation, and respondents on the third block show no correlation between the two variables of interest.

The hypothetical data generated for this example yielded the following result. The overall correlation ($r_{x_1 y_1}$) was a very robust, significant, positive correlation of .850 between housing quality and attachment. This very satisfying result, however, is quite misleading. The strength of the correlation is due almost entirely to the strong correlation between neighborhood means ($r_{\bar{\bar{x}}\bar{\bar{y}}} = +1.0$). If we remove the influence of neighborhood from the individual scores, the relationship drops to almost zero ($r_{(x_1-\bar{\bar{x}}_1)(y_1-\bar{\bar{y}}_1)} = -.018$).

Suppose we decide to look at the data at the block level. Using block means, the correlation between the six data points is very encouraging ($r_{\bar{x}_1 \bar{y}_1} = .997$). But, again, if we remove the influence of neighborhood the strength of the relationship drops drastically ($r_{(\bar{x}_1-\bar{\bar{x}})(\bar{y}_1-\bar{\bar{y}}_1)} = .548$).

This example indicates how the simple overall correlation based upon grouped data can be quite misleading. Decomposition of the data, such as shown in the foregoing discussion, is probably the most appropriate response. This would include an analysis of neighborhood means, an analysis of block means controlling for neighborhood means, and an analysis of individual data controlling for block means. A variable operationalized at different levels of aggregation, however, means different things. A neighborhood mean of housing quality is quite distinct from a block mean *controlling* for a neighborhood mean (i.e., block-level deviation from the neighborhood mean). Unfortunately, as the review shows, such decomposition of grouped data is rare.

Summary and concluding comments

The present chapter specifies ways in which the neighborhood-level physical environment may influence stress-related impacts, delineates which impacts are theoretically relevant to neighborhood functioning, and reviews studies insofar as they relate to these specific impacts or to more general impacts such as satisfaction. Based on such a review, the following points are warranted.

First, there is no doubt that physical neighborhood features are relevant to stress-related outcomes. In all of the specific areas reviewed, except for social participation, it was possible to delineate studies pointing to these relationships.

Second, our knowledge is quite uneven. We know much more about impacts due to certain physical features (e.g., density) than others. Theoretical development is also more advanced for some types of impacts (e.g., social disorder, delinquency) than it is for others. Nonetheless, certain areas appear quite ripe for further theoretical development. The area of identification provides a case in point. Many intuitive notions and heuristics (e.g., place dependence, place as contributor to self-identity, and so on) provide a fertile medium for further conceptual development. This area could also profit from being tied in with the more general area of satisfaction and dissatisfaction.

Third, although there is much theorizing about block-level and neighborhood-level outcomes, the vast majority of studies report individual-level impacts. In many cases the predictors of individual-level impacts (e.g., desire to move) are aggregate-level variables (e.g., changes in housing values) resulting, in essence, in a context analysis (e.g., arrows G_i and H_i in Figure 10.1). These are problematic to the extent that the researcher fails to measure the mediating variable (e.g., perception of neighborhood decline) that crosses these different levels of analysis. Context analyses are also problematic in that they measure (potentially) some of the weakest causal impacts of neighborhood features. Thus, a move toward concerted assessment of aggregate-level outcomes would be beneficial. In addition, there are many neighborhood-related theories, such as those of decline, displacement, and so on, that suggest additional aggregate impacts to be investigated.

Fourth, locales vary. Consequently, multilocale studies are needed. Many neighborhoods and, if possible, many cities need to be assessed in single studies. This is particularly important if aggregate-level outcomes are the focus of interest.

Fifth, as assessments of aggregate-level impacts become more common, I hope that there will be more of a concerted effort to assess ecologically valid, or at least socially recognized areal units. People perceive their life as contained within meaningful, bounded areas, and such considerations need to be incorporated.

Sixth, it is clear that the ties between physical environment and stress-related impacts are mediated by a host of other variables. This is only fitting and is quite in keeping with an interactionist perspective. It is time, however, to start to come to closure on what the relevant mediators are for various impacts.[11] An endlessly expanding laundry list of mediating variables would seem far less desirable than careful assessment of a few theoretically derived variables.

Finally, there is a real need to find out how various stress-related impacts are interrelated. (What are the relationships between neighborhood satisfaction and incidence of worry? Between attachment and smoothness of family function?) Such linkages must be determined if we are to develop a more holistic assessment of neighborhood impacts.

References

Alker, H. R., Jr. A typology of ecological fallacies. In M. Dogan and S. Rokkan (Eds.), *Quantitative ecological analyses in the social sciences*. Cambridge, Mass.: MIT Press, 1969.

Altshuler, A. *Community control: The black demand for participation in large American cities*. New York: Pegasus, 1970.

Appleyard, D. Notes on urban perception and knowledge. In R. Downs and D. Stea. (Eds.), *Image and environment*. Chicago: Aldine, 1973.

Appleyard, D. *Livable urban streets: Managing auto traffic in neighborhoods*. Washington, D.C.: U.S. Government Printing Office, 1976.

Baldassare, M. Residential density, household crowding and social networks. In C. Fischer, R. M. Jackson, C. A. Stueve, K. Gerson, and L. M. Jones (Eds.), *Networks and places*. New York: Free Press, 1977.

Baldassare, M. *Residential crowding in urban America*. Berkeley: University of California Press, 1979.

Baldwin, J. British areal studies of crime: An assessment. *British Journal of Criminology*, 1975, *15*, 211–227.

Baum, A., Davis, G. E., & Aiello, J. R. Crowding and neighborhood mediation of urban density. *Journal of Population*, 1978, *1*, 266–279.

Baumer, T. L. Research on fear of crime in the United States. *Victimology*, 1978, *3*, 254–264.

Bell, W., & Force, M. T. Urban residential types and participation in formal organizations. *American Sociological Review*, 1956, *21*, 25–34.

Bevis, C., & Nutter, J. B. Changing street layouts to reduce residential burglary. In D. Frisbie, G. Fishbine, R. Hintz, M. Joelson, and J. B. Nutter (Eds.), *Crime in Minneapolis*. Minneapolis: Minnesota Crime Prevention Center, 1978.

---

[11] Some of our common intuitions about relevant mediators may be wrong. For example, Michelson (1966) found that social status did not influence neighborhood preference, but that proximity of friends did.

Bielby, W. T. Neighborhood effects: A LISREL model for clustered samples. *Sociological Methods and Research*, 1981, *10*; 82–111.

Blalock, H. M., Jr. *Causal inferences in non-experimental research*. Chapel Hill: University of North Carolina Press, 1964.

Booth, A. *Urban crowding and its consequences*. New York: Praeger, 1976.

Boyd, D., & Iversen, G. *Contextual analysis*. Belmont, Calif.: Wadsworth, 1979.

Brantingham, P. L., & Brantingham, P. J. Residential burglary and urban form. *Urban Studies*, 1975, *13*, 278–284.

Broady, M. Social theory in architectural design. In R. Gutman (Ed.), *People and Buildings*. New York: Basic Books, 1972.

Brower, S. The signs we learn to read. *Landscape*, 1965, *15*, 9–12.

Brower, S. The design of neighborhood parks. *JSAS Catalog of Selected Documents in Psychology*, 1979, *9*, MS, 1843.

Brower, S. N. Territory in urban settings. In I. Altman, A. Rapoport, J. and Wohlwill (Eds.), *Human behavior in environment: Advances in theory and research* (Vol. 4), *Environment and Culture* (Chap. 5). New York: Plenum, 1980.

Brower, S. *Innovation proposal for Harlem Park inner-block parks management*. Unpublished manuscript, Baltimore City Department of Planning, 1981.

Brower, S., Dockett, K., and Taylor, R. B. *Residents' perceptions of site-level features*. Paper presented at the Annual Meeting of the Environmental Design Research Association. Ames, Iowa, 1981.

Brower, S. N., & Williamson, P. Outdoor recreation as a function of the urban housing environment. *Environment and Behavior*, 1974, *6*, 295–345.

Burgess, E. Can neighborhood work have a scientific basis? In R. Park & E. Burgess, *The city*. Chicago: University of Chicago Press, 1925.

Calhoun, S. Space and the strategy of life. In A. Esser (Ed.), *Behavior and environment*. New York: Plenum, 1971.

Carter, R. L., & Hill, K. Q. *The criminal's image of the city*. Elmsford, N.Y.: Pergamon, 1979.

Case, D. Dormitory architecture influences: Patterns of student social relations over time. *Environment and Behavior*, 1981, *13*, 23–41.

Choldin, H. K. Urban density and pathology. *Annual Review of Sociology*, 1978, *4*, 91–113.

Cooley, C. H. *Human nature and the social order*. New York: Scribner, 1902.

Craik, K. H., & Appleyard, D. Streets of San Francisco: Brunswik's lens model applied to urban inference and assessment. *Journal of Social Issues*, 1980, *36*, 72–85.

Crenson, M. A. Social networks and political processes in urban neighborhoods. *American Journal of Political Science*, 1978, *22*, 578–594.

Cronbach, L. *Research on classrooms and schools: Formulation of questions, design and analysis*. Occasional paper. Stanford, Calif.: Stanford Evaluation Consortium, Stanford University, 1976.

Dahir, J. *The neighborhood unit plan*. New York: Russell Sage Foundation, 1947.

Dawes, R. M., & Corrigan, B. Linear models in decisionmaking. *Psychological Bulletin*, 1974, *81*, 95–106.

Deutschberger, P. Interaction patterns in changing neighborhoods. *Sociometry*, 1946, *9*, 303–315.

Downs, R., & Stea, D. *Maps in minds*. New York: Harper & Row, 1977.

Durkheim, E. *On the division of labor in society*. New York: Macmillan, 1960.

Droettboom, T., McAllister, R. J., Kaiser, E. J., & Butler, E. W. Urban violence and residential mobility. *Journal of the American Institute of Planners*, 1971, *37*, 319–325.

Ebbesen, G. E., Kjos, G. L., & Konecni, V. J. Spatial ecology: Its effects on the choice of friends and enemies. *Journal of Experimental Social Psychology*, 1976, *12*, 505–518.

Festinger, L., Schachter, S., & Back, K. *Social pressures in informal groups*. Stanford, Calif.: Stanford University Press, 1950.

Firey, W. Sentiment and symbolism as ecological variables. *American Sociological Review*, 1945, *10*, 140–148.

Fischer, C. Toward a subcultural theory of urbanism. *American Journal of Sociology*, 1976(a), *80*, 1319–1341.

Fischer, C. *The urban experience*. New York: Harcourt Brace Jovanovich, 1976(b).

Fowler, F., McCalla, M. E., & Mangione, T. *The Hartford Residential Crime Prevention Program*. Washington, D.C.: U.S. Government Printing Office, 1979.

Fowler, F. J., & Mangione, T. W. *An experimental effort to reduce crime and fear of crime in an urban residential neighborhood: Re-evaluation of the Hartford neighborhood crime prevention program*. Draft Executive Summary. Boston: Center for Survey Research, 1981.

Frey, W. H. Central city white flight: Racial and non-racial causes. *American Sociological Review*, 1979, *44*, 425–448.

Fried, M., & Gleicher, P. Some sources of residential satisfaction in an urban slum. *Journal of the American Institute of Planners*, 1961, *27*, 305–315.

Gans, H. *The urban villagers*. New York: Free Press, 1962.

Gans, H. *The Levittowners*. New York: Pantheon, 1967.

Gans, H. J. Planning and social life. In H. M. Proshansky, W. H. Ittelson, and L. G. Rivlin (Eds.), *Environmental psychology*. New York: Holt, Rinehart and Winston, 1970.

Gerson, K., Steuve, C. A., & Fischer, C. S. Attachment to place. In C. S. Fischer, R. M. Jackson, C. A. Stueve, K. Gerson, & L. M. Jones, *Networks and places*. New York: Free Press, 1977.

Gibbons, D. C. *Delinquent behavior* (2nd ed.). Englewood Cliffs, N.J.: Prentice-Hall, 1976.

Gordon, R. A. Issues in the ecological study of delinquency. *American Sociological Review*, 1967, *32*, 927–944.

Gordon, R. A. Issues in multiple regression. *American Journal of Sociology*, 1968, *73*, 592–616.

Gould, P., & White, R. *Mental maps*. New York: Penguin Books, 1974.

Greenberg, S., Rohe, W., & Williams, J. R. *Safe and secure neighborhoods*. Final Report, Research Triangle Institute, 1981.

Greenberg, S. W., Rohe, W. M., & Williams, J. R. Safety in urban neighborhoods. *Population and Environment*, in press.

Hallman, H. W. The neighborhood as an organizational unit: A historical perspective. In G. Frederickson (Ed.), *Neighborhood control in the 1970's*. New York: Chandler, 1973.

Hannan, M. T. Problems of aggregation. In H. M. Blalock, Jr. (Ed.), *Causal models in the social sciences*. Chicago: Aldine, 1971(a).

Hannan, M. T. *Aggregation and disaggregation in sociology*. Lexington, Mass.: Lexington Books, 1971(b).

Harries, K. D. *Crime and the environment*. Springfield, Ill.: Thomas, 1980.

Hartnagel, T. F. The perception and fear of crime: Implications for neighborhood cohesion, social activity and community affect. *Social Forces*, 1979, *37*, 176–193.

Hauser, P. M. Context and consex. *American Journal of Sociology*, 1970, *75*, 645–664.

Hauser, P. M. Contextual analysis revisited. *Sociological Methods and Research*, 1974, *2*, 365–375.

Heider, F. Thing and medium. *Psychological Issues*, 1959, *1*(3), 1–84.

Herbert, D. An areal and ecological analysis of delinquency residence. *Progress in Human Geography*, 1977, *1*, 208–239.

Hirschi, T., & Selvin, H. C. *Delinquency research: An appraisal of analytic methods*. New York: Free Press, 1967.

Holohan, C. *Environment and behavior*. New York: Plenum, 1978.

Hunter, A. *Symbolic communities*. Chicago: University of Chicago Press, 1974.

Hunter, A. The loss of community: An empirical test through replication. *American Sociological Review*, 1975, *40*, 537–552.

Hunter, A. Symbols of incivility. Paper presented at the 1978 Meeting of the American Society of Criminology, Dallas, 1978(a).

Hunter, A. Persistence of local sentiments in mass society. In D. Street (Ed.), *Handbook of contemporary urban life*. San Francisco: Jossey-Bass, 1978(b).

Hunter, A., & Suttles, G. D. The expanding community of limited liability. In G. D. Suttles (Ed.), *The social construction of communities*. Chicago: University of Chicago Press, 1972.

Jacobs, J. *The death and life of the American city*. New York: Vintage, 1961.

Janowitz, M. Sociological theory and social control. *American Journal of Sociology*, 1975, *81*, 82–108.

Kaplan, S. *Nearby open space as a factor in neighborhood satisfaction*. Paper presented at the American Psychological Association, Washington, August 1982.

Kasarda, J. P., & Janowitz, M. Community attachment in mass society. *American Sociological Review*, 1974, *39*, 328.

Kasl, S. V. Effects of housing on mental and physical health. *Man-Environment Systems*, 1974, *4*, 207–226.

Kasl, S. V., & Harburg, E. Perceptions of the neighborhood and the desire to move out. *Journal of the American Institute of Planners*, 1972, *38*, 318–324.

Keller, S. *The urban neighborhood*. New York: Random House, 1968.

Lansing, J. B., & Marans, R. W. Evaluation of neighborhood quality. *Journal of the American Institute of Planners*, 1969, *35*, 195–199.

Lavrakas, P. J. Personal safety in urban and suburban neighborhoods. *Population and Environment*, in press.

Lewis, D. A., & Maxfield, M. G. Fear in the neighborhoods: An investigation of impact of crime. *Journal of Research in Crime and Delinquency*, 1980, *17*, 160–189.

Ley, D., & Cybriwsky, R. The spatial ecology of stripped cars. *Environment and Behavior*, 1974, *6*, 53–68.

Lipsky, M. Street-level bureaucracy and the analysis of urban reform. In G. Frederickson (Ed.), *Neighborhood control in the 1970's*. New York: Chandler, 1973.

McKenzie, R. D. *The neighborhood: A study of local life in the city of Columbus, Ohio*. Chicago: University of Chicago Press, 1923. (Reprint, New York: Arno Press, 1970).

McPherson, M., Frey, D. L., and Silloway, G. *An empirical analysis of the relationships between commercial land use and crime*. Unpublished report. Minneapolis: Minnesota Crime Prevention Center, 1982.

Maccoby, E. E., Johnson, J. P., & Church, R. M. Community integration and the social control of juvenile delinquency. *Journal of Social Issues*, 1958, *14*, 38–51.

Mann, P. H. The concept of neighborliness. *American Journal of Sociology*, 1954, *60*, 163–168.

Michelson, W. An empirical analysis of urban environmental preferences. *Journal of the American Institute of Planners*, 1966, *32*, 355–360.

Michelson, W. *Environmental choice, human behavior and residential satisfaction*. New York: Oxford University Press, 1977.

Michelson, W. Long and short range criteria for housing choice and environmental behavior. *Journal of Social Issues*, 1980, *36*, 135–149.

Miller, F. D., Grega, D., Malia, G. P., & Tsemberis, S. Neighborhood satisfaction among urban dwellers. *Journal of Social Issues*, 1980, *36*, 101–117.

Minnesota Crime Prevention Center. *Commercial land use, crime, and fear of crime*. Unpublished manuscript. Minneapolis: 1980.

Newman, O. *Defensible space*. New York: Macmillan, 1972.

Newman, O. *Community of interest*. New York: Doubleday, 1979.

Newman, O., and Franck, K. *Housing design and children's antisocial behavior*. Unpublished manuscript, Institute for Community Design Analysis, New York, 1977.

Newman, O., & Franck, K. A. *Factors influencing crime and instability in urban housing developments*. Washington, D.C.: U.S. Government Printing Office, 1980.

Newman, O., & Franck, K. A. The effects of building size on personal crime and fear of crime. *Population and Environment*, in press.

O'Donnell, C. R., & Lydgate, T. The relationship to crimes of physical resources. *Environment and Behavior*, 1980, *12*, 207–230.

Olson, P. *Urban neighborhood research: Its development and current focus*. Paper presented at the 75th Annual Meeting of the American Sociological Association, New York City, August 1980.

Perry, C. A. The neighborhood unit. *Regional plan of New York and its environs*, 1929, *7*, 22–140.

Peterson, G. L. A model of preference: Quantitative analysis and the perception of visual appearance of residential neighborhoods. *Journal of Regional Science*, 1967, *7*, 19–31.

Popenoe, D. Urban residential differentiation: An overview of patterns, trends and problems. *Sociological Inquiry*, 1973, *43*, 35–46.

Proshansky, H. M. The city and self-identity. *Environment and Behavior*, 1978, *10*, 142–189.

Rainwater, L. Fear and house-as-haven in the lower class. *Journal of the American Institute of Planners*, 1966, *32*, 23–31.

Rapoport, A. *Human aspects of urban form*, Elmsford, N.Y.: Pergamon Press: 1977.

Robinson, W. S. Ecological correlations and the behavior of individuals. *American Sociological Review*, 1950, *15*, 351–357.

Roncek, D. W. Density and crime: A methodological critique. *American Behavioral Scientist*, 1975, *18*, 843–860.

Roncek, D. W. Dangerous places: Crime and the residential environment. *Social Forces*, 1981(a), *60*, 74–96.

Roncek, D. W. *Blocks, tracts and crimes: Methodological issues in analyzing urban crime patterns*. Unpublished manuscript, University of Illinois at Chicago Circle, 1981(b).

Ross, H. L. The local community: A survey approach. *American Sociological Review*, 1962, 75–84.

Searles, J. *The nonhuman environment.* New York: International Universities Press, 1961.

Shaw, C. R., & McKay, H. D. *Juvenile delinquency and urban areas.* Chicago: University of Chicago Press, 1969 [1942].

Simmel, G. The metropolis and mental life. In D. L. Levine (Ed.), *On individuality and social forms.* Chicago: University of Chicago Press, 1971.

Sommer, R. *Design awareness.* San Francisco: Rhinehart, 1972.

Stea, D. Space, territory and human movements. In H. K. Proshansky, W. H. Ittelson, & L. G. Rivlin (Eds.), *Environmental psychology.* New York: Holt, Rinehart and Winston, 1970.

Stokols, D. Origins and directions of environment-behavioral research. In D. Stokols (Ed.), *Perspectives on environment and behavior.* New York: Plenum, 1977.

Stokols, D., & Shumaker, S. A. People in places: A transactional view of settings. In J. Harvey (Ed.), *Cognition, social behavior and the environment.* Hillsdale, N.J.: Erlbaum, 1981.

Suttles, G. D. *The social order of the slum.* Chicago: University of Chicago Press, 1968.

Suttles, G. D. *The social construction of communities.* Chicago: University of Chicago Press, 1972.

Tannenbaum, J. The neighborhood: A socio-psychological analysis. *Land Economics,* 1948, *24,* 358–369.

Taub, R. P., Surgeon, G. P., Lindholm, S., Otti, P. B., & Bridges, A. Urban voluntary associations, locality based and externally induced. *American Journal of Sociology,* 1977, *83,* 425–441.

Taub, R. P., & Taylor, D. G. *Crime, fear of crime and the deterioration of urban neighborhoods.* Draft, final report. Chicago: National Opinion Research Center, 1980.

Taylor, R. B. *People on a block in a neighborhood: Theoretical and statistical implications of grouped data for community crime prevention, research and evaluation.* Unpublished manuscript, The Johns Hopkins University, 1980.

Taylor, R. B., Brower, S., & Stough, R. R. User-generated visual features as signs in the urban residential environment. In P. Suedfeld and J. A. Russell (Eds.), *The behavioral basis of design.* Stroudsburg, Pa.: Dowden, Hutchinson, and Ross, 1976.

Taylor, R. B., Gottfredson, S. D., & Brower, S. The defensibility of defensible space. In T. Hirschi and M. Gottfredson (Eds.), *Understanding crime.* Beverly Hills, Calif.: Sage, 1980.

Taylor, R. B., Gottfredson, S. D., & Brower, S. *Informal control in the urban residential environment.* Unpublished final report, Center for Metropolitan Planning and Research, Johns Hopkins University, Baltimore,: 1981.

Thorndike, G. L. On the fallacy of imputing the correlations found for groups to the individuals or smaller groups composing them. *American Journal of Psychology,* 1939, *52,* 122–124.

Tien, J., O'Donnell, V. F., Barnett, A., & Mirchandani, P. B. *Street lighting projects.* Washington, D.C.: U.S. Department of Justice, 1979.

Tolkien, J. R. R. *The hobbit.* New York: Ballantine, 1937.

Tomeh, A. K. Informal group participation and residential patterns. *American Journal of Sociology,* 1964, *70,* 28–35.

Triandis, H. *Interpersonal behavior.* Monterey, Calif.: Brooks/Cole, 1977.

Tuan, Y. *Topophilia.* Englewood Cliffs, N.J.: Prentice-Hall, 1974.

Verbrugge, L. M., & Taylor, R. B. *Consequences of population density: Testing new hypotheses*. Occasional paper, Center for Metropolitan Planning and Research, Johns Hopkins University, Baltimore: 1976.

Verbrugge, L. M., & Taylor, R. B. Consequences of population density and size. *Urban Affairs Quarterly*, 1980, *16*, 135–160.

Wandersman, A., & Giamartino, G. A. Community and individual difference characteristics as influences on initial participation. *American Journal of Community Psychology*, 1980, *8*, 217–228.

Warren, D. I. The Functional diversity of urban neighborhoods. *Urban Affairs Quarterly*, 1977, *13*, 151–180.

Warren, R. *Community in America*. Skokie, Ill.: Rand McNally, 1963.

Wellman, B. The community question: The intimate networks of east Yorkers. *American Journal of Sociology*, 1979, *84*, 1201–1231.

Wellman, B., & Leighton, B. Neighborhoods, networks and communities: Approaches to the community question. *Urban Affairs Quarterly*, 1979, *14*, 363–390.

Whyte, W. F. *Street corner society*. Chicago: University of Chicago Press, 1943.

Wilson, R. L. Livability of the city: Attitudes and urban development. In F. S. Chapin and S. Weiss (Eds.), *Social correlates of urban growth and development*. New York: Wiley, 1966.

Wolpert, J. Migration as an adjustment to environmental stress. *Journal of Social Issues*, 1966, *22*, 92–102.

Zehner, R. B. Neighborhood and community satisfaction in new towns and less planned suburbs. *Journal of the American Institute of Planners*, 1971, *37*, 379–385.

Zorbaugh, H. W. *The gold coast and the slum*. Chicago: University of Chicago Press, 1929.

Part III

Environmental stress and public policy

In the final chapter of this volume, DiMento demonstrates how research on environmental stress can be effectively introduced and utilized in a variety of policy settings in the public and private sectors. Environmental legislation and judicial decision making are both discussed. The environmental impact report process and urban and regional planning practices provide arenas where research on environmental sources of stress can be applied. DiMento discusses institutional and philosophical barriers between the research and policy communities and suggests how and where social science research on environmental problems can best influence the making of policy.

11. Much ado about environmental stressor research: Policy implications

Joseph F. DiMento

Recently I was approached by a former student of mine who is an aide to a high-level policy maker in state government. From his report, "a bold, exciting innovation" was being recommended by his employer and others, and the issue was to be considered soon in the legislature. I was given some background material on the subject pro and con, including a few editorials that argued that the idea, rather than being an innovation in the public interest, would have severe and grave impacts on the quality of life in the area in which it would be implemented. I told my student that I would be pleased to review the material and, in due course, make some comments on the issue if I found that my expertise in planning, law, and social ecology was relevant. I began to build a file on the subject and to consider ways of organizing the immense amount of potentially applicable research and theory that exists on the innovation itself and closely related reforms.

The following week I received a phone call from the state asking if I could fly to the capitol the next morning to testify in favor of the proposed policy. I expressed reservations, as I had only begun to formulate some working impressions of the potential effects of the change. And I was hearing more and more about a brewing political battle over the proposal. (That morning a lead article had appeared in the *Los Angeles Times* describing the coalitions forming around the legislation. The headline depicted the side I was asked to speak for as akin to the industrial revolution "robber barons.")

My schedule prohibited my being away at the time of the hearings so I concluded that timing had saved me from a potentially conflictual situation. Later in the day, however, a second state caller suggested that I could telephone in my testimony the next morning in time for consideration in the legislative committee.

I decided to do so within a self-imposed constraint that I would not go beyond any of the information that I thought relevant to the issue. If my statement turned out to be too tentative and overqualified – even to the point of not being classifiable as for or against the bill – than so be it. That evening I typed out my comments and reviewed them. I emphasized the experimental nature of the proposal and the existing nonconclusive evaluations of similar ideas, and I suggested changes that would make the reform's outcomes somewhat more predictable.

I dictated the testimony to the committee secretary the following morning. She transcribed it, read it back to me, and carried the statement to the legislature.

It was at that point that several of the questions that are raised when social policy calls on organized knowledge became very real to me. What was to be done with the statement? Would it be used in full, with all of its qualifications? Would it be dissected and applied to make a certain case? (Legally, could it be submitted other than in full?) Was it understandable? Did I fully capture the complexity of the issue and the variety of positions on the questions raised by the proposed change? Was there anything useful in my analysis? Would affiliation with either side affect my credibility to testify on similar questions in the future? How would this type of involvement be viewed by academic colleagues? Would the statement be introduced as a stimulus to discussion or simply tallied as an argument for or against the reform? Given more time, could I find information that would be more directly related to the proposed change? Would my caveats and disclaimers be passed on to the next stage of consideration?

In this article I explore several types of constraints on the use of social science knowledge about environmental stressors in the making of policy in scenarios like that described and in other settings. These constraints are legal, institutional, organizational, and cultural. I also describe groups for which knowledge about environmental stressors may be useful and suggest several models of application of knowledge to increase the opportunities for productive interactions between the policy and research "communities."

Defining policy implications

Research on the health and behavioral impacts of stressors potentially has a large and diverse audience. In the public and private sectors, in mammoth organizations, and in small groups, a portion of the information produced by social science has relevance. The public sector is one important arena for use of stress research and I address it here first with some examples.

Public sector use

Capacity to create and implement programs on environmental stressors, like other governmental interventions, varies among governments. Present regulatory power makes stressor analysis applicable to many local government functions. Extensions of regulatory control over certain stressors are indicated by flexibility in the legally allowed scope of regulation.

Zimring points out (Chap. 6, this volume) that knowledge-based interventions should occur at two levels: the social system and physical design. Findings on design dysfunction have considerable policy implications; they can be applied to local activities such as site review. Here government negotiates with developers over detailed aspects of proposed projects – from location of shrubbery to regulation of the amount, intensity, and direction of outdoor lighting. Work on predictability of the physical environment and its relationship to individual disorientation may also be integrated into project review and into the general planning function. Concepts of personal space (Hall, 1966), sense of place, and other constructs that describe and predict user preferences can guide assessment activity of local government, much like that now required of economic impacts and effects on the physical environment. Likewise, work on crowding has implications for provision of open space, for clustering of housing sites in a subdivision, for creation of parks in densely populated downtown areas, and the like.

Social system intervention can also be guided by environmental stressor research. The work on "learned helplessness" (Abramson, Seligman, and Teasdale, 1978; Koller & Kaplan, 1978) has been applied to the impacts of statutory and judicial planning reforms (DiMento, 1980). For example, if citizens are involved actively in local government planning activities only to learn – or to perceive – that these efforts are ignored at the decision-making stage, they may "learn" that they are ineffective in controlling local government action. Their motivation for participation in community affairs may be decreased and they may be less capable of learning that they can affect outcomes. Cynicism about the ability to control government may be self-fulfillfing. "You can't fight city hall" may reflect one's sense of lack of control over the social environment. Citizens in states where law requires a close relation between planning and official controls such as zoning may perceive that they make a difference in a planning outcome, and their involvement may continue.

Local governments may be more likely than larger, state or federal entities to incorporate environmental stressor data into policy making. Special interest groups that are not located within a particular local community may be less able or willing to block progressive actions to regulate environmental sources of stress. Oakland and Burbank, California, for example, had strict, detailed local noise ordinances well before the United States government had implemented noise regulations. As well, research findings can more easily be customized to the local level than typically is the case at the state or federal level. Social scientists can convert relationships that are unconvincing at the highly aggregated level to disaggregated findings that may apply in a particular neighborhood or town. Here they may be more applicable and may be statistically significant. An additional constraint on the inclusion of research on environmental stressors at the federal level is the myriad of agencies that may have some interest in or jurisdiction over psychological and physical health effects of environmental conditions.

On the other hand, state requirements may preempt local action and similar state regulations may be operative only within the context of federal requirements (Soper, 1974).

Scientific information may be aimed at branches of government other than the legislative. Since the late 1960s, the courts have assumed an important function in the control of the environment. Under certain legal authorities they establish standards of environmental quality (Haynes, 1976; Sax & Conner, 1972; Sax & DiMento, 1974). For example, under the Michigan Environmental Protection Act of 1970: "When a court finds a standard to be deficient, (it may) adopt a standard approved and specified by the court" Section 2(2)(b). Little systematic knowledge exists about factors that are related to judicial use of scientific information (Collins, 1978).

There are several differences between courts and other branches of government that receive information and translate it to decisions and policies (DiMento, 1977). Some of these are relevant to the utilization of scientific information. The judiciary is more formal in its information-processing functions and frames controversies into issues that are treated extensively in an adversary fashion. Its occupants tend to be generalists, and experts in law, as opposed to specialists on scientific and technical issues. The judiciary is often deficient in analysis of "polycentric" problems (those for which judgments on some issues demand simultaneous judgment on others). Furthermore, the courts generally are less political or accountable to interest group input than the legislative and the executive branches. The salience of these differences for social science research on stress undoubtedly will vary with policy issues and with the objectives of the social scientist. For some purposes (such as the recognition of the importance of creating standards where there is pressure to avoid decisions) the unique characteristics of a court may make it an attractice forum.

Recent use of research on crowding in court cases involving prisons (Sommer, 1978) and on the use of psychological research in court cases (Brodsky & Robey, 1973) suggests that some social scientists are becoming familiar with the institutional idiosyncrasies of the judiciary.

The complicated bureaucracies of national, state, and local government are another arena for consideration of research on environmental stressors. At this level introduction can be in the formal rule-making procedures at several points in the process; or input can come in informal interactions with administrators or in expert testimony at administrative investigations and adjudications (DiMento, 1976; Sabatier, 1978; Caplan, 1979).

Reforms suggested for rule making fit nicely into the state of the art with regard to knowledge of the effects of stressors. Although reformists vary in their descriptions of regulatory problems and in their prescriptions for rule making, the use of the adversary approach (Majone, 1977) is increasingly mentioned. This process-oriented strategy admits there are major gaps in our understanding of the effects of stressors and other social and physical phenomena to be controlled and embraces uncertainty and disagreement, using adversary methods to develop the strongest cases for hypothesized relationships. This honesty about our ignorance is presently warranted. Very few simple, direct relationships between environmental stressors and health outcomes, for example, have been established.

There are other questions facing the social scientist who wants social science work to be used. Which levels or branches of government are most likely to employ information in a form for which it was intended? What should be the vehicle for introducing information and at what stage of the policy formulation process? If legislative action is sought, are research results most effectively introduced by the social scientist or by an advocacy group of one form or another? At what stage in the process are results most effective in forming the type of control that government utimately adopts? When are results sufficiently straightforward and usable to merit introduction into the decision-making calculus?

An example: noise regulation. A summary of the federal noise control framework and its evolution illustrates opportunities for the social scientist to influence policy. The major federal intervention in the field of noise did not come until 1972. The only previous controls were felt through the Federal Aid to Highway Act of 1970 (23 U.S.C. §109(h)(1), (1976), which banned federal aid to highways that did not include plans and specifications to meet certain highway noise levels compatible with specified land uses; certain sections of the Clean Air Act Amendments of 1970; and aircraft noise abatement legislation.

The federal government's attempt to attack noise comprehensively came in The Noise Control Act of 1972. The stated goal of the statute (42 U.S.C. §4901-4908 (1976) or Pub.L. No. 92-574, 86 Stat. 1234) was "an environment for all Americans free from noise that jeopardized their health and welfare" (§4901(b)(1976)). The Act gives to the United State Environmental Protection Agency authority to regulate noise characteristics of new products (§4905), motor carriers, (§4917), and railroads (§4916). Priorities are set for major sources of environmental noise pollution; less concern is to be given to smaller sources such as "blenders, electric can openers and vacuum cleaners" (Congressional Record, 1972). Under this scheme states have the responsibility for setting overall noise levels (§4905 (e)(2)). The actual approach to setting of standards represents a legislative compromise, resolving a significant difference in approaches to control sought by the House and Senate. Standards are to be based on considerations of health and welfare of those exposed to new products *and* on cost and technology factors (§4904(b)(2)). The final version of the Act also calls for "a study of the impact of aircraft noise on public health and welfare."

Congressional concern with protecting the public against adverse effects of noise and providing for the health and welfare of the citizenry leaves considerable leeway to guide the setting of standards. The legislative history of the Noise Act and its subsequent interpretation by the EPA, however, indicate that health and welfare have been narrowly construed by those actors who are instrumental in creating the federal program. Input at the Congressional Hearings on the Act (U.S. Senate, Committee on Public Works Hearings, 1972) was varied but there was little social science testimony on the behavioral and psychological effects of noise. Considerable input on medical and physiological responses to noise was offered, although several of the health dynamics, including interference with behavior and sleep, were characterized as "not so well understood" (U.S. Senate, Committee on Public Works Hearings, 1972). Testimony focused primarily on hearing impacts and outcomes such as the activation of the autonomic nervous system, resulting in changes in heart rate, respiration rate, gastric activity, pupil size, and sweat gland activity.

Representatives of the Environmental Protection Agency did mention some nonphysiological effects, but only briefly. One EPA official stated, for example, "the majority of potential individual effects of community reactions to noise occur at levels well below that threshold of demonstrable physiological insult" (U.S. Senate, Committee on Public Works Hearings, 1972). Another concluded that, "There are also obvious psychological effects, such as frustration and anger, as well as other effects which are less obvious. The latter include fatigue, inefficiency and a heightened tendency to mental illness." (U.S. Senate, Committee on Public Works Hearings, 1972). Furthermore, testimony was offered that noise limits might have to be established based on the psychological feeling of annoyance, rather than to some direct changes in physiological health (U.S. Senate, Committee on Public works Hearings, 1972).

But in the 604 pages of testimony on the Noise Act, very little social scientific research on noise as a stressor is found. There are several rival explanations for the absence of the type of research noted in this volume. One is simply that the research was not available. But there was at least some work on noise and annoyance by that time (see Cohen & Weinstein, Chap. 2, this volume). An alternative explanation is that social scientists were not perceived by policy makers as performing work that related to the "health and other human effects of noise" or as studying outcomes that merit the same consideration as results of "hard" science on physiological effects. Or, the social scientific community may have been unaware of this opportunity for entry into federal policy making. Researchers may have been aware, but cynical about how well the federal government could utilize complex results. Alternatively, social scientists may have been aware of the opportunity for input, but concerned for methodological or other reasons that research results were not ready to be translated into standard setting to protect human health and welfare. Opportunities for input into policy making of social science research on the nonmedical effects of noise have now shifted to the regulatory process.[1]

The example suggests several lessons to those who are interested in making more useful the interface between social scientists working on environmental stressors and policy makers. First, there are formal opportunities for introducing research and theory on environmental stressors into policy-making acitivities at several levels of government, but each of those levels has idiosyncratic policy-making processes. To make effective use of a forum, the intricacies of these policy-making dynamics must be understood. Second, the language the major governmental programs and general environmental protection laws use in discussing control of noxiants, including environmental stressors, is quite imprecise. Imprecision itself, however, offers an opportunity for the research community to shape definitions of control priorities and strategies (U.S. Senate, Committee on Public Works Hearings, 1972). Third, whether a governmental "event" is considered an opportunity to make use of social scientific information depends in part on what the social scientist sees as acceptable, in communicating data that are often imprecise, often conflicting, and sometimes not clearly relevant. Social scientists need to realize that policy decisions on outcomes of interest to them will be made whether data are provided or not. For enlightened policy, some data, or experience-based input, are often better than none (Kaplan & Kaplan, 1978).

An aside: Convergence in the stress sciences?

Recent consideration of changes in mandated approaches to control of air pollution has again brought into focus dynamics of the application of scientific information to major legislative programs and regulations. A major debate on health effects is in progress. One reading of this situation is that if we are having difficulty establishing standards with reference to effects on human physical health, this necessarily means that the introduction of information on mental health and behavior is even more hopeless. But several evolving traditions in the social sciences would conclude that this is not necessarily the case: Links between mental and physical well-being are increasingly appreciated and accepted. A conclusion from this political drama is that we are hopelessly ignorant of the effects of air pollution on people. But another is that our analyses are beginning to converge and that there is greater agreement on the relationships worth exploring. We may be learning from the posturing, politicking, advocating, and editorializing of the adversarial use of scientific information that in the area of stress research the amount of ignorance and uncertainty in the physical sciences

---

[1] The Reagan administration declared in 1981 that noise regulation would be a very low priority. In effect, the United States Environmental Protection Agency decided not to enforce the Noise Act.

may approximate that of the social sciences. The gaps between usable physical and social science data may be shrinking.

Private sector use

Social scientists often influence nongovernmental agents as well. For example, they may discuss functional and dysfunctional aspects of certain design forms with architects; describe to planners the dynamics of human response to settings perceived as crowded; offer insights to social service administrators on macroconditions affecting mental health. These observations, even when not intended as attempts to transfer knowledge, may be significant guides in future decisions.[2] (Interestingly, Dunn [1980] has found some evidence for a conclusion that "[k]nowledge will be utilized more in private organizations with formal profit incentives than in public organizations without such incentives" [528].)

In addressing usability, I employ an expansive definition of policy. I refer to any action taken by an organization that affects a public where there are measured choices for the actions taken. My aim is to address the value of scientific information to a wide range of potential users. I discuss implications, for example, for urban design, office design, and hospital design; for major federal environmental legislation (e.g., pollution control); and for concepts that can be used in planning parks.

Types of influence

Research influence comes in several ways and across differing time perspectives. Most traditional investigations of the influence of social science research on policy development have focused on instrumental uses (Rein & White, 1977). Instrumental influence includes effects on the content of regulations, the provisions of statutes, the details of executive orders, and judgments and decisions emanating from the courts or administrative agencies. Influence is called instrumental when social science findings translate to the establishment of a demonstration program or to an official declaration that a regulatory program is needed. Instrumental influence also comes in the application of "differential prognosis" (Merton, 1949). Here the social sciences provide information that directs a choice among programs a government is contemplating – determining which is more acceptable according to specified criteria. Finally, evaluation research is classified as instrumental when it provides data that can directly influence the future of a social program. The instrumental usefulness of social science has been

---

[2] In its most general sense social science gets used by citizens on a daily basis in a most impactful way. Gergen (1973, p. 310) reminds us that over 8 million students "are annually confronted by course offerings in the field of psychology". Based on several considerations, including those addressed in a later section of this chapter, they will come to use or reject information they derive in these courses.

the subject of an immense controversy recently in the United States as changes in economic policy nationally have led to deep cutbacks in funding of research.

Social science comes to have instrumental influence by various means. Under the "knowledge driven model" (Weiss, 1978) basic research identifies some opportunity that may have relevance for public policy. Then applied research is conducted to connect the findings of basic research to practical action.

Several types of interventions derive from research on stressors. For example, quantification of the detrimental effects of noise can suggest zoning changes, scheduling shifts both of the stressor and those effected, and training programs to teach citizens coping strategies to ameliorate the negative impacts of noise. Research results also may point to interventions that are technology based. Technology development and marketing industries may promote policies that derive from research results. Technology producers comprise an interest group whose very existence depends on the nature of policy choices. Environmental legislation sometimes requires use of best available technology as the means for reaching environmental objectives.

Instrumental impact of social science may result from totally conceptual work, evaluated within the social science community as "highly speculative." Some scholars are eager (or at least willing) to have their ideas structure governmental programs before any empirical work is done to test those ideas. Designers of programs in the War on Poverty are an example. Indeed, some social researchers may have been been unable to supply well-developed theory to support their views (Craig, 1976; Frieden & Kaplan, 1975; Moynihan, 1970).

The state of the art in the design and development enterprises may be particularly receptive to conceptual contributions on the impact of stress. Newman's finding (1973) that the "image of public housing may attract criminals to the site and may lower the self esteem of tenants" has been used to determine policy choices on questions of type and location of housing (whether or not the evidence supports it). Distinctions made between crowding and density; the work on relocation of minority groups and subsequent institutionalization and morbidity; between controllable and noncontrollable stressors on classification of physical environments in terms of their social meanings; and on ecological antecedents of innovation are other conceptual contributions that can be put to use.

Instrumental impact occurs in a more homely way when information generated by social science drives the administrative decisions on individual or organizational programs. The conclusion that assigning personal responsibility for the care taking of plants effectively reduces passivity and feelings of helplessness among institutionalized elderly persons (Langer & Rodin, 1976) may have led to no executive orders that state departments of forestry work with the county care facilities for the elderly, or no administrative regulations about the essentials of a properly equipped room in county institutions. But individual administrators, familiar with such findings and concerned about the behavior and degree of satisfaction of their clients, may have directly acted on them (Roos, 1973).

Instrumental use has been described by more radical analysts of the science-policy relationship. In one model social scientists would act *along with the citizenry* to use science to define the directions of social and environmental policy. Roos (1973, pp. 216, 217) describes "a truly democratic model which would deny the need for specialized 'scientists' and 'policy makers,' but would substitute for them a collectivity of people gathering and analyzing information by scientific methods and making national collective decisions on the basis of this analysis, thus being, in reality, *a people for itself* and not merely *a people in itself*." Here the distinction between generator and user of information becomes blurred.

Influence of social science knowledge on policy may be conceptual. Both hard and soft data, highly regarded theory and highly speculative distinctions, can promote public consideration of issues not previously of concern. Berg (1978) defines conceptual utilization as "an impact on the *thinking* of a policy maker without necessarily leading to an identifiable impact on a policy decision" (p. 11). A research finding may promote consideration of a problem in a way that no organized interest group had suggested. Direct action may not follow immediately; rather, an idea enters public dialogue as one in good currency.

Conceptual influence of research on environmental stressors, at this time, may be most significant. To researchers, conceptual distinctions are perhaps second nature; yet to those who design government programs to promote environmental quality, the distinctions may be provocative and useful. Examples are analyses of the differences between noise and sound, and between crowding and density; identification of mediating factors, such as the predictability of a stressor, in its effects on an individual; the notion of adaptation to stressful phenomena; and the concept that behavioral change from alterations in the physical environment may antedate attitudinal change (Taylor, Chap. 10, this volume). Policy makers may not readily grasp all the implications of such distinctions. Nor may they recognize their applicability to a problem facing them. But they may add this information prior to "common sense" notions, without relating their awareness to any learning event or to any identifiable or memorable research product. Later, they may act on the knowledge, or some translation, perversion, extension, or refinement of the concept.

Rein and White (1979) identify another type of conceptual impact. They address how policy makers acquire knowledge:

By focusing on the variegated nature of practice, we come to propose that a reflective social knowledge informs the actions of a professional practitioner. Knowledge is contained in practice, much of it unrealized and unarticulated. When research "brings" knowledge to practice, something rather subtle occurs. The basic function of the research is the raising of latent knowledge to consciousness, that is, to a system of human cognition that allows it to be deliberately and rationally addressed.

Knowledge may also be "used" like an innocent and naive agent. Weiss describes a political model of use of information, "impressment of research results into service for a position that decision makers have taken on other grounds" (p. 8). Kissinger has put it bluntly: "In short, all to often what the policy maker wants from the intellectual is not ideas but endorsement" (1959). Sabatier (1978) has argued that, "it is quite likely that administrative agencies devote a considerable portion of their resources to the *acquisition* of technical information but that this information is often *utilized* to legitimate, rather than to influence policy decisions" (p. 36).

Reasons for calling social science into service for political purposes vary. A statute may require government to consider specificied information before a decision is reached. Under the National Environmental Policy Act of 1970, and under state laws in half the states, environmental impacts (including, in some schemes, environmental stress) of a proposed action must be assessed before governmental action may be taken. But overall, the substantive impact of these laws is questionable: Once information has been collected and assessed the government typically is not compelled to act on the information contained in its assessment. Carefully gathered data on the possible impacts of crowding within a proposed residential development, on the effects of noise from a new freeway exchange, or on the long-range psychological impact of living near a nuclear power plant, may promote an image of thoughtful decision making based on comprehensive information and yet not reflect any commitment of policymakers to mitigate stressful conditions.

Similarly, scientific information may be sought, collected, and even considered up to some threshold point at which a government agency concludes it is protected from legal challenge. Under administrative law, a defendant may be compelled to demonstrate that there was substantial evidence to support its decision – to allow a permit for development for example. Social science experts may be called to meet this test (Sabatier, 1978) or social scientists may simply be called together and counted in a government "theatrical production" in which the side with the most actors will carry the vote on an amendment or a bill or determine the nature of a regulation.

Professional norms may also direct the search for scientific information. Agency personnel, even while being forced to make policy on the basis of external factors, sometimes demonstrate deference to professional communities to which they belong and in which they are socialized. Government actors may pass their analyses to colleagues in their academic discipline, may establish within the agency roles for obtaining scientific advice, may formulate a decision within the context of a scientific issue or debate, or may try to emphasize the ways, even if few, that a policy, once chosen, reflects the best thinking within a field.

Or, a policymaker may seek out information "to establish a visible commitment to and competence in a new area in an effort to gain jurisdiction over that issue from legislative sovereigns" (Sabatier, 1978, p. 405). For the stressors described in this volume, allocation of control authority among and within government institutions is an important ongoing determination. In passing the Clean Air Act of 1970, Congress combined a fear that the automobile industry would "capture" any administrative agency designated to create standards to control automobile pollution, with recognition that there were institutional constraints on legislative time and expertise in setting national ambient air quality standards. The result was legislation that gives the Environmental Protection Agency considerable standard-setting responsibility, with the Act itself setting automobile emission control levels. Jurisdiction over regulation of new noise producing products was assigned to both the Federal Aviation Administration (airplanes) and the Environmental Protection Agency (motor carriers, railroads, and other new products). As similar decisions are made on control of other environmental stressors, agencies possessing information about a stressor and its effects will have an advantage in expanding the reach of jurisdiction. Jockeying for power with the aid of knowledge occurs in a political context where identification of one control agency among several candidates depends on political leanings and approaches to balancing of societal interests. Should the Environmental Protection Agency or the Department of Agriculture be given primary responsibility for control of pesticides? Where should state control functions for noise pollution be lodged? Who should regulate noise levels in occupational settings?

Political considerations may lead to "tactical" use of scientific information. Weiss (1978) points out that in certain cases it is not the content of the findings that is invoked but the sheer fact that research is being done. An agency can point to one of its bureaus – even one doing basic research that has no organizational channel to decision making – to indicate that it is a logical site for a regulatory or development function. For example, planning directors may achieve influence over local decisions partially because they are perceived as having access to information in a master or long-range plan. This document is seen as technical, rational, objective, and scientific by citizen observers. But politically sophisticated planning administrators may simply tolerate the master plan and support it in a *pro forma* manner, while they assess local developmental decisions on the basis of their readings of the external logic of the decisions (DiMento, 1978).

Social scientists may frown on the politicization of their products, but ethical implications are not clear. Certainly, research results can be employed to promote policies that researchers oppose (*New York Times*, 1980). But information may be used to reach an objective that the research supports and that the researcher approves of, but for a program that was developed on the basis of nonscientific considerations. Findings from a study could support an intervention that a legislator had designed in total ignorance of the research. He or she might be searching for a politically attractive rationale for a program that was otherwise marginal. For example, a program that opposed relocation of the elderly might seize upon a rationale found in social science work even though the policy would have been promoted as soon as any acceptable rationale could be discovered. These problems raise classical end–means ethical issues.

Rarely is knowledge influential in only one form. More often, hard data, theory, or sophisticated speculation will influence policy in a combination of ways. The legislative history of the National Environmental Policy Act (NEPA) offers an example (Schroth & Plater, in press). Early versions of the law looked quite different from the NEPA, which has become a model for several states and one of the leading pieces of environmental legislation of the 1970s. The original bill had no environmental impact assessment provisions. However, Lynton Caldwell was called as an expert witness to the hearings on NEPA. He argued that unless the law had an "action forcing" element, such as a mandatory environmental assessment process, its efficacy would be limited. His suggestions had instrumental influence in 1969; they were included directly into the NEPA. He grounded his argument in social scientific knowledge of the behavior of complex organizations. Ideas summarized in his testimony subsequently have been followed in other legislation and rule making. "Action forcing" is now a criterion sought in reform legislation by policy makers, as well as by legal scholars who themselves, in turn, instrumentally and conceptually influence the design of a future generation of environmental laws.

Influence of social scientific knowledge can be long range, nebulous, and difficult to identify. Information enters the policy environment from multiple sources. Ideas filter to individuals in policy making roles through organs of the press, both popular and specialized. Research summaries are themselves summarized and digested. Ways of thinking about social phenomena are shaped (Weiss, 1978). Social science forms the public policy agenda and at the same time complicates the internal logic of policy issues. It generates "complex, varied, and even contradictory views...rather than cumulating into sharper and more coherent explanation" (Weiss, p. 12). External validity is not always a concern, and results may become generalized and then disseminated as hybrids of the original findings. Research may lead to creative ways of viewing the subject of the original data-based investigation.

Stress research now falls within this category. Analyses do not yet converge to narrow policy choices. Rather, they enrich and complicate public understandings of the effects of noise and air pollution, design dysfunction, crowding, and heat. Policy makers may either misapply, or creatively or accurately apply notions like "general adaptation" or some "no effect" conclusion (Evans & Eichelman, 1976). Or they may interpret the inverted

U-shaped curve describing the relationship between "stress" and "performance" to mean that governmental intervention would benefit some while prematurely cutting off positive arousal to others. Indeed, the research product could influence some policy makers to *remove* control of environmental insults from the policy agenda. More frequently, results educate decision makers while not directing instrumental use. Information may promote understandings that lead to readjustments in behavior. Theory and results have nonpublicized implications for policy, for example, through informal experiments with levels of noise in the work environment where a particular adminstrator has control. Utilization is not officially announced to workers. "Use" then comes in the behavior of the well-informed decision maker.

Finally, social science research on stress can have influence as a dependent variable itself. Information generation here is part of the intellectual enterprise of society, "collateral with policy—and with philosophy, journalism, history, law and criticism" (Weiss, 1978, p. 12). Influence is not calibrated according to impact on policy, but rather according to the extent that information defines the decision-making environment of a society or, in blunter terms, determines how a portion of society spends its time. Social science creates a world view to which the populace responds directly, without the mediating activity of translating the results into "policy."

Can and should social scientific research on stress be applied?

Research on stress has focused on fatigue, rate of recovery from surgery, feelings of helplessness, aggression, nervousness and anger, span of attention, signal discrimination, tolerance for frustration, disorientation, "dislike," social interaction, attraction, and mental health. Physiological research has addressed elevated blood pressure, cardiovascular performance, respiratory symptomology, sensory irritation, pulmonary function, skin conductance, mutagenicity, and central nervous system effects. Can and should public policy address the relationships that scientists find interesting, fascinating, significant, or central to an acceptable quality of life? Put differently, are the ways social scientists define problems, and the frames they bring to problem resolution, compatible with the manner in which public policy makers confront problems (Rein, 1973)?

Compatability of present research and present policy agendas

One reading of the foregoing list of outcomes is that social science myopically choses the topics of its investigation. These outcome measures appear overly constrained by disciplinary and exclusively academic orientations quite removed from outcomes that public policy can most effectively control. Government intervention historically has encompassed criminal behavior, negligence, and behavior that violates specific prohibitions.

Government's purpose has been to prevent highly tangible and measurable negative outcome, such as death, sickness, or observable property damage. More recently it has expanded its focus. But even now, regulation is highly controversial when it addresses fairly easily measurable goals such as clean water. Helplessness, negative aftereffects, attraction – these are not the domain of public action. Concern with these outcomes is unfamiliar to government policy, and, some might say, ought to be.

A response to this charge is that immediate acceptability of research interests by policy makers is unimportant. This view is based on a scientific tradition that sees the search for knowledge, regardless of the immediate applicability of information generated, to be the proper domain of science. It holds, in addition, that the policy utility of pure research becomes obvious over time. Knowledge now commonly held in the population was, at one time, the result of the quest of pure research. Furthermore, social scientific investigation is sometimes prescient; the outcomes of scientific interest point toward a quality of life that policy-makers would seek if they were not so constrained by institutional factors.

Organizational stress research is an example. Impact of stressors on behavior of individuals within organizations has been the subject of social scientific inquiry for some years (Kahn, Wolfe, Quinn, Snoek, & Rosenthal, 1964; Katz & Kahn, 1966; McGrath, 1976). Its relevance to policy making within private organizations has been recognized and applied. Recently, organizational stress as a subject of public policy has appeared on the national agenda. Groundwork laid by social science can assist the nation to address problems of organizational functioning and productivity and personnel well-being. Research can suggest whether society can achieve, at the same time, environmental quality, individual satisfaction (or an acceptable degree of stress), and organizational productivity.

When we expand our focus to the nongovernmental sector the chances of finding a match between scientific inquiry – even if pure and not guided by the needs of potential users – are greatly increased. Interior designers, developers, architects, planners, and individual citizens may be quite interested in stressor work related to residential and environmental settings that they create and manipulate.

Legal and philosophical constraints on research-directed public policy

Legal authority for government to address various outcomes of stress can be discussed less speculatively. Government regulation of air and noise pollution, design characteristics, and other environmental stressors is constrained by constitutional (Soper, 1974) and statutory law and judicial doctrine. The extent of these constraints is an area of some uncertainty, but a framework for determining legally acceptable control is in place. Parts of the framework can be used, within limits, to promote strict regulatory activities, both by advocates of control over stressors and by judicial reviewers of government action. On the one hand, at the present time no United States court would uphold a ban on family size, on the basis of a governmental interest in limiting the adverse effects of crowding, no matter what language was employed about promotion of general health, safety, and welfare. Nonetheless, legislatures and administrative agencies have considerable authority (under broad "police powers" on the basis of constitutionally derived powers, and following proper delegation of authority) to protect the citizenry against environmental insult. Even when governmental control conflicts with rights of the citizenry, the state can prevail if it meets certain tests. Either a rational basis, or a compelling state interest in control, will be sought in review by a court, with the actual test depending on the nature of the infringement on the complaining party.

It is difficult to predict the extent of control that will be sanctioned by reviewing courts. Nonetheless, the record of judicial deference to governmental regulation of environmental stressors is strong (Rodgers, 1977; DiMento, Dozier, Emmons, Hagman, Kim, Greenfield-Sanders, Waldau, & Woollacott, 1980). Moreover, the relations that social science research has addressed, between stressors on the one hand and health and behavioral outcomes on the other, will seldom be used as the sole rationale for a government program. More likely they will be accompanied by other reasons for regulating a stressor condition. Research can be received by policy makers at several points. It can be used in the bill-consideration stage of the legislative process, when control proponents seek evidence for convincing skeptical colleagues or to counter antagonistic interest groups. Social scientific evidence can contribute to the background statements (or criterion documents) for regulations or administrative guidelines. Research results can be employed in judicial challenges, to establish a sufficient rationale for government's decision to limit, by one means or another, the stressor.

For other types of governmental use of social scientific information, legal constraints are less significant. Examples are introduction of scientific information on the effects of environmental stressors in investigatory bodies, in public address, in internal decisions by government officials (those affecting their own personnel), and in governmental publications that *recommend* private action.

Legal defensibility does not necessarily equal desirability of public policy on stressors. Views on the wisdom of control of stressors (e.g., to decrease aggression or to increase attention span) depend on philosophy of government. How should quality of life of the individual be weighed against the productive potential of the collectivity? What amount of regulation should be promoted under conditions of uncertainty? Under such conditions, should public policy be the domain of the expert – including the expert who admits to great uncertainty in predictions, immense difficulty in creating rigorous data-generating methods, and questionable external validity to a particular policy focus – or derive more directly from political exchange (Morris, 1979)? What amount of risk to the individual should government tolerate? To what extent is it important to protect the most sensitive members of the population? How important is the privacy interest of a regulatee?

A goodness-of-fit analysis between two communities

The existence of two very distinct communities, of scientists and policy makers, affects the use of knowledge about environmental stressors. Professional lives of researchers and policy makers differ. Each group responds to different reward systems, speaks different professional languages, holds different values, and affiliates with different professional organizations.

The inquiry system of the policy maker

Research is only one part of the data from which policy is created. This is not to assert that policy makers ignore information generated by the sciences. Caplan, Morrison, and Stambaugh (1975) documented that knowledge is used at top levels of government extensively, including in social policy matters. Qualifications on this conclusion, though, are important to an understanding of the policy making environment. Respondents' interests in government careers were negatively related to utilization, suggesting that those policy makers with whom social scientists may have to work in the long run are less disposed to the contributions offered. Those who are sympathetic to the scientific community may soon be returning to that community, or at least leaving policy making. Government officials tended to use knowledge from research either funded by or conducted by the government, and were less favorable to the social sciences than they were to information derived from the natural sciences. They mistrusted the objectivity of the former. Respondents showed most resistance to those findings from the research community that countered their intuitive understandings of social problems (Caplan et al., 1975). Political implications of the research findings was the main factor related to their use.

Conditions that allow for acceptance of scientific information are numerous and rarely converge. Sabatier (1978) has summarized the factors involved:

...technical information is most likely to be influential when it involves high-quality research on a specific issue by a prestigious scientist who has excellent credibility with the decision maker...influence is maximized...[when] there is high consensus concerning the general goals to be pursued but disagreement over empirical questions of moderate scientific complexity. Finally, the agency making the decision should be politically secure and dominated by collegial professionals rather than by managers concerned with formal hierarchy or lawyers preoccupied with procedural due process. Conversely, technical information is most likely to be used for legitimating purposes when presented at a late date on a highly controversial issue dominated by normative or political considerations in which there is little consensus among scientists over empirical questions (pp. 410–411).

If scientific information is not a main factor to which policy makers respond in creating policy, then what is? The answer requires a review of political science findings beyond the scope of this chapter, but factors of particular importance to the social scientist aiming to influence policy can be summarized.

Policy makers (here my discussion focuses on the public sector) respond to demands by their constituents and to their own myths about the nature of societal problems. They respond to perceived crises as well. A crisis is an event that enough significant constituents define as a crisis. Determinations of what is a problem and what is a crisis are made within a shifting context and are influenced in part by the relative importance of one political movement or another. Desirability of a given type of information will vary according to whether the civil rights, women's rights, environmentalist, deregulation, or moral majority influences are presently most salient. Policy makers must acknowledge demands of those whom they perceive put and keep them in their offices. When competition for fulfilling an office is minimal, then internal demands of the institution they occupy become dominant (Jones, 1973).

Multiple environmental forces to which the decision maker reacts translate to short-range attention to individual issues although trends in treatment of similar issues are identifiable. There are some officials who translate personal commitment, including that deriving from familiarity with scientific information to long-range attention to social problems (Jones, 1973) (Senator Muskie's passionate support of environmental controls may be an example), but they do not dominate the policy-making community. Policy makers do not arrive in, nor maintain, the positions they inhabit because of their technical expertise on a given policy topic. On the contrary, they achieve decision-making roles because of their flexible orientations. Many are lawyers or otherwise educated as generalists; they tend to be professionals who assign priorities to scientific knowledge, along with other inputs into decision making, differently from scientists. Effective policy makers are expert at parrying several mutually exclusive constituent requests. They make compelling, in the short run, an issue that later may have little salience. Rewards come for appearing to be concerned with a problem that, politically, demands an immediate answer. The policy environment values the sense of certainty even in areas of immense ambiguity. "The scientist can live indefinitely with the tentative and hypothetical. The administrator wants to act with confidence" (Nagi, 1965, quoted in Berg, 1978, p. 39).

Policy makers need social science results within time periods that are too short from the social scientist's perspective: "Political events are contemporaneous and can occur at speeds that outpace the capacity of researchers to anticipate and to produce data in accordance with the needs of policy makers" (Caplan et al., 1975, p. 49). Furthermore, policy makers are willing to accept information that some social scientists do not consider ready for translation into directives for public action. Research may be welcomed into policy before it has undergone the scrutiny and sometimes obsessiveness characteristic of the social sciences.

Additionally, policy makers often approach social scientists with problems that demand solutions politically (Altman, 1975; Merton, 1949). Such problems are not constrained either by feasibility of resolution or by knowledge of state of the art in the area. Furthermore, the policy maker or practitioner typically addresses issues in a specific jurisdiction whereas behavioral scientists focus attention on process with less attention to the unfolding of process within a particular place (Altman, 1975).

Thus, the scientist will be interested in various effects of noise on children, treating the context so as to extract information of the greatest general applicability; the policy makers will wish to know what were the effects, on his or her constituents, of noise created by this specific flight pattern at this noted time.

A minor but related incompatibility is that some information desired by policy makers and practitioners is not always of terrible interest to the serious social scientist, especially one who feels that his or her research is heady and highly significant. Usable knowledge sought by lawyers was suggested recently in an article in the *American Bar Association Journal*:

Psychology of office layout. Did you know that there are strong places and weak places in an office? Did you know that a desk can be in the authoritarian position? Did you know that there are techniques for reducing the advantage of the person in the authoritarian position? Where is the lawyer's territory in the office and how can it be invaded? Do you reach agreement more often in an informal setting, and what is the significance of a round (as distinguished from a rectangular) conference table? What is the effect when your opposition places himself between you and the door to the office or between you and your telephone? If you are disciplining an employee, where should you sit and where should the employee sit or stand? (Reed, p. 934)

Viewed from the eye of the person of affairs, however, social scientific work may be impossibly abstract. For example, the finding that the fit between the individual and the environment is the most fundamental predictor of the stressfulness of a setting is at first intriguing and engaging. It sounds as if it is a major breakthrough, and indeed it is. But the usefulness of the finding for the policy maker and user of research may be a mystery. Are they being told that we need extensive data on individuals before we can put to work the more general (now questioned?) findings about stressors?

Social science from the view of the policy maker

Several characteristics of the knowledge-creating industry limit usefulness of its results to policy-makers. Political orientations of social scientists are questioned, as are the methods dominant in the scientific community. Policy makers are concerned with objectivity in science and are put off by scientific debate and by several limitations on scientific generalizations. And the modal scientific personality (rigidly methods and theory responsive) is often a barrier to communication with nonscientists.

The personnel. Social scientists are perceived as more willing than most constituents to utilize scarce economic resources to combat what they view as societal ills; others, more conservative politically, might see those same phenomena simply as costs of living in a postindustrial society – costs that do not merit governmental intervention. Policy makers hold that social scientists typically favor an increment of abatement of a stressor over an increment of development accompanied by greater levels of the stressor (noise, density, or ambient air pollution), even if development has considerable economic benefits. Social science norms may be more geared toward protecting the most sensitive, the most vulnerable, whereas some policy makers may wish that these populations remain unheard. Some social scientists, on the other hand, are viewed as conservative politically. They are seen as aligning with forces of authoritarian control or as being physical determinists (Taylor, Chap. 10, this volume). In periods of fiscal conservatism, these perceptions of social scientists may be particularly salient.

It is difficult for the policy maker to walk away from some of the research on environmental stressors without asking, "So what do the social researchers want? The world cannot be as perfect as those who do these research projects would have it. It appears, from the types of phenomena studied and the characteristics of the negative outcomes, that social scientists would have us provide for society an incubator world, an antiseptic environment where there is no stress, no tension, where – with immense costs – we have removed any challenge to the individual psychologically. Frankly, we have more important work."

Often also inexplicable is the position taken by many in the scientific professions that they really have identified what is important in society, what society should attend to, and what outcome measures are critical. In some cases all would agree that the service of keeping our attention on the quality of life is an important function. But in other cases it is quite clear that the choices made (in attending to outcomes) are quite value laden. Yet some analyses are presented as coming forth, compelled by logic and reason.

Some of the differences between the two communities may derive from other aspects of the political phenomenon. A considerable amount of work on environmental stressors (see Wineman, Chap. 9, this volume) focuses on ways of making the work environment more attractive, more pleasing, more satisfying for the worker in a way that seems highly worker oriented, without express concern for the costs to management.

The dominant methods. Policy makers consider laboratory approaches to some problems as irrelevant to policy questions, or even absurd. Bronfenbrenner (1974, p. 3) has addressed the perception as it applies to developmental

psychology, but his comment is more generally applicable: "[m]any...
laboratory situations [exist] in which the situation is ephemeral and unfamiliar, the task not only unfamiliar, but artificial (in the sense that its social significance is at best unclear) and the other participants are strangers. . . . Indeed it can be said that *much of American developmental psychology is the science of the behavior of children in strange situations with strange adults.*" Work with unrepresentative samples in surrogate environments is not rare among the studies summarized in this volume.

Other limitations on social science results derive from characteristics of scientific inquiry. McGrath (1976) summarizes several features of social science (within the stress context) that complicate application of scientific results to policy matters. Among these are the methods-variance issue (science cannot specify precisely what "artifacts" in investigations are created by the specific measurement techniques used); the response pattern issue (separate measures of an outcome variable may disagree); the individual differences issue (considerable, for example, in some studies of the effects of noise [Bryan & Tempest, 1973]); the issue of comparability of stressor conditions (an appropriate metric for calibrating and cross calibrating does not exist); and the issue of realism (Cohen, Evans, Krantz, & Stokols, 1980).

For the latter dimension, policy makers may find it difficult (e.g., in the analysis of the effects of noise) to translate proofreading performance and competitive response on a color word task to activities of importance to public policy. Bryan and Tempest (1973), in fact, exclude laboratory studies from the data they employ to investigate variability in noise annoyance susceptibility, "because the laboratory experiments seem to be almost totally unrelated to the real-life situation. . . It seems extremely unlikely that members of a volunteer listening team will exhibit anything like the variation in annoyance shown by people in real life" (p. 221).

Policy makers and the intelligent lay public may have, for some time, understood limitations of traditional methods in the social sciences. Arguments over the value of experimentation are one example. Critics of the use of the experiment contend that the environments that require understanding are not simply standardized independent variables; they "are in large measure a function of our own behavior" (Wachtel, 1980, p. 407). Perhaps overvaluing their insights, nonscientists for a long time have been asking skeptically: "What can I learn from the writings of this professor based on observation of 25 students at a prestigious eastern college when these observations have been made in situations where students were instructed to behave in ways they never would behave otherwise?"

Some of the most interesting and provocative contributions of the social sciences are those that address broadly the manner in which we are living. They describe molar environments and group x place transactions (Stokols, 1981). This perspective may direct ways to treat populations and to design, or to experiment with designing, environments. The next generation of social scientists who address these questions may develop adequate ways to empirically validate critical, policy-relevant variables. Constructs need to be developed and indexes need to be built so that rigorous analysis using state of the art methods can be undertaken. But it is often at this later point that the eyes of the knowledge user begin to glaze over. This is not to say that such follow-up work should not be done, although there are some fairly convincing arguments that at most it should be very low priority (see Wachtel, 1980). Rather, the outcomes need to be incorporated in very communicative and general terms into working statements for policy makers: Tell them what they might consider doing, not the steps used to arrive at suggestions.

Put another way, social scientists may overvalue their own progress, at least when viewed from the perspective of a person who seeks policy-relevant knowledge. The social scientist is often proud that the study was longitudinal, that it tracked behaviors over time (even if nothing can be concluded from the study because of confounds, etc.). Or they call, as if it were a major breakthrough, for a historical dimension in their analyses. Laymen may simply assume that we are farther along than we are. They become incredulous to learn that there has been progress because earlier work was done on white middle-class sophomores on a one-time, paper-and-pencil exercise.

We are faced with a new and immense challenge: "Research and theory up to this point in the environment stressors area leads to the radical conclusion that we are in need of more sophisticated descriptions and understandings of situations, settings, activity systems, life domains and their relationship with behavior and health" (Stokols, 1981).

Finally, on this point, the very rationale for undertaking systematic investigation differs among scientists and policy makers. The policy focus typically is on what the problem is (for example, the extent and severity of the negative effects of a stressor such as air pollution). The research concern is with the questions of causation (the "why" and "how"), or put another way, on the mechanisms that explain some phenomenon that produces a given effect.

Weakness of method. Policy makers also question social science objectivity (Davis & Salasin, 1978). Caplan et al. (1975) report that respondents found the data used in some social science weak, the study design poor. Respondents generalized from "irresponsible and shoddy program evaluations" (Caplan et al., 1975, p. 48); those were cited by respondents to discredit social research generally. "Emergence of large scale social experimentation," on the contrary, was greeted with approval.

An additional trait is sometimes distressing, namely, the positivistic orientation that equates knowing with the most narrow sense of empiricism, that refutes the commonly held understanding that we know in a variety of ways, some of which we cannot interpret or describe, let alone replicate.

Certain traditions in social sciences have made real only what seems very unreal to the ordinary observer (Ackerman, 1977): that which the researcher can dissect, operationalize, count, and aggregate again. Ironically some of the most impressive statements in the social sciences come from those who add to their disciplined, empirical data base the richness of their own life experiences. These observers have moved beyond data that were recorded in the sterile classrooms of the social relations laboratory. Important statements are also made by social scientists who incorporate the classical thinking of the great sociologists, psychologists, and anthropologists. These investigators recognize that our work on stress in urban areas did not begin with environmental psychology of the late 1960s but harks back, for example, to the path-breaking work of the Chicago school (Catalano, 1979). Failure to contextualize laboratory findings within the traditions of urban planning and sociology sometimes makes individual results unnecessarily irrelevant.

Present applicability of the scientific inquiry. Decision makers also find operational direction lacking in social science results. The state of the art in several of the social sciences requires conclusions that are general, tentative, and suggestive of several, sometimes conflicting, courses of action. Study of stressors is no exception. Cohen and Weinstein (Chap. 2, this volume) conclude "that there is *no* simple relationship between sound intensity and the non-auditory aspects of human behavior and health. It is difficult if not impossible to definitively answer questions about the impact of community and industrial noise exposure on humans." Other examples: "on the average, undesirable events have stronger effects on health than desirable events"; the impact of stressful life events is mediated by "financial or other material resources"; social support, values, coping abilities; stress reactions may produce any of the following: "psychological growth," no "notable change," or "psychopathology" (Dohrenwend, 1978, p. 3); and "it is clear that neighborhood land use is related to crime. The exact chain of association, however, is not yet clear" (Taylor, Chap. 10, this volume). These conclusions are prudently tentative and professional. Such works typically proceed to point out future research that will be necessary to guide social intervention (a recommendation that is becoming less persuasive with time). But such statements are often too general for many policy makers to translate into action on a rational, scientific basis.

Also, results often are qualified to the point that they simply are not interesting. Often they are presented to sound like the complete confession of a compulsive penitent. "X may led to Y under conditions of Z. But this cannot be concluded with confidence since several factors with hypothesized explanatory power are exogenous to the relationship and these were measured in the present study with surrogate indicators on which we need additional research."

A related difficulty is that some social science results are considered so obvious by policy makers that they do not really take them seriously. An example offered by Bryan and Tempest (1973) is a British researcher's conclusion that, "those most susceptible to noise in general were more annoyed by aircraft noise" (p. 228). Others tell us that heavy volumes of street traffic make sitting outside unpleasant and that the presence of corner stores has been found to be associated with heavier pedestrian traffic.

Mincing no words, the senate version of the budget of the Reagan administration of fiscal year 1982 concluded that, "some (behavioral and social science) is too esoteric at best and silly or wasteful at worse" (American Psychological Association, 1981).

Furthermore, to many policy makers the conceptual contributions of social scientists appear to be elaborate articulations of commonsensical notions. What the social scientist has frequently done is to formalize and tease out what has already been appreciated by everyone else.

But it must be noted here that part of the asserted weakness of social science information derives from its misuse. Many social science concepts are more sophisticated than policy makers admit or realize. It is not uncommon for lawyers and political leaders to speak of social and organizational phenomena as if they were making scientifically descriptive statements. Oftentimes, their applications are skeletons and the skeletons bear little resemblance to the fully embodied thought. Consider as examples the notions of "bureaucratic turf," "bureaucratic inertia," "group think," and "on-the-job stress." Highly refined understandings are embodied in these terms but they have been lost by legal commentators and decision makers who employ narrow and expedient meanings in order to develop a position or advocate a change.

Stress research is sometimes so broadly conceived as to inhibit translation to policy, especially to direct, instrumental use. The definition of stress still varies among social scientists. One definition is: Stress "occurs as a result of the individual's exposure to excessive environmental demands or stressors. Conditions of the social and physical environment operate as stressors to the extent they *tax* or *exeed* the individual's *adaptive resources*" (Stokols, 1979, pp. 1–2). Consider the variability in the general population of resources and of thresholds. The incidence of stress thus is related to variables for which policy makers lack data. Similarly, elaborations of the stress event offer several potential, but no compelling, places for intervention. McGrath (1976), for example, suggests that the "stress situation" is a four-stage closed-loop cycle. Each of the steps may be the focus of policy interventions: appraisal process, decision-making process, response process, and outcome process – the last of which is outside the domain of the responding individual. Attention to each of these stages promotes quite different action strategies. So, too, may recognition of differences between acute, short-term stress experience and long-term chronic exposure (Evans & Eichelman, 1976).

The inverted U-shaped curve describing the relationship between level of stress and level of performance is another example of a stress result not readily applied. The U-shaped function is said to hold within-individual and within-situation. Increasing arousal may improve performance for one group whereas another group's performance may be debilitated, disorganized, or degraded at the same level of environmental noise, crowding, or heat, or within the same type of physical environment. And, as Cohen and Weinstein (Chap. 2, this volume) point out, response curves for noise made available to policy makers "will need to be based on estimates of the population likely to show particular effects." Whom should the policy maker serve?

Moreover, there exist, quite acceptably and compatibly from the social science perspective, several competing theories to explain the same outcome. (See Epstein, Chap. 5, this volume.) Researchers still are seeking basic concepts, such as "primary hierarchies" (Zimring, Chap. 6, this volume). The direction of the relationship between certain mediating variables and the ultimate outcome of a stress event may vary; in the learned helplessness area, for example, exposure to failure may *facilitate* performance (Stokols, 1979) under certain conditions. As in other areas of the social sciences (Mornell, 1979), stressor research may not be cumulative and may not converge on accepted findings. The work product may be a collection of ways that a problem is understood as opposed to a shrinking number of parsimoniously stated laws of behavior.

Intervention may focus most economically on mediating variables in the relationship between an environmental stressor and outcome (Evans & Jacobs, Chap. 4, this volume). But social science cannot yet direct policy choices among these factors. Furthermore, some of the candidates – such as personality variables – are beyond acceptable governmental intervention. Others raise very difficult public choices. If SES is an important mediating variable, should it be incorporated into stressor control programs? Promoting governmental intervention that tries to discriminate along sociological and personality characteristics is not attractive to those who act in the public sector and may conflict with other public policy objectives such as protection of personal privacy and individual civil rights.

Other dilemmas arise from application of stress research. A stress event may produce negative results for the individual; but when viewed from another perspective, say that of the organization or the collectivity, stress may be beneficial. When different constituents and competing interest groups are affected differentially, should the decision maker emphasize the negative effects (e.g., of high-density living) that accrue to one group (the inhabitants of densely clustered housing) or the positive effects that are bestowed on others (e.g., those who benefit from the resulting availability of open space)? How should state and federal policy makers weigh air or noise pollution outcomes in relation to stresses caused by economic fluctuations resulting from interventions to close or clean up a particular industry (Brenner, 1973; Catalano & Dooley, 1977)? Should public policy discount the long-range outcomes of exposure to certain environmental stressors, such as effects of noise on future performance, or effects of air pollution on future health characteristics, because of the immediate stressful economic effects of regulatory actions?

The conceptual contribution of inquiries into stress effects has been substantial and should not be underemphasized. Even work on noise, which concludes that individual impacts and direct causal links are difficult to establish, may add up to suggest overall policy directions. (Bryan & Tempest, 1973; Cohen, et al., 1980; Cohen & Weinstein, Chap. 2, this volume). But policy makers will not easily find precise instrumental direction in knowledge about effects of stressors.

On disagreement within science. Differences in the manner in which the two cultures approach unproven relationships may cloud the translation of results. Policy-minded individuals, for example, may conclude that factors that explain a certain percentage of variation in some outcome or control variable are candidates for intervention. Addressing several such "modest" explanatory factors can have a measurable cumulative effect on a social concern. The social science community, however, may tend to minimize the importance of studies that explain little variance.

This attitude toward "incomplete explanation" is reflected in another social science activity that may make usable research results appear too controversial or uncertain for application. Social science culture includes peer review and concomitant criticism, continuous offering of alternative explanations, and developing of rival hypotheses to scientific "conclusions." (Recently, even the sacrosanct phenomenon of the "risky shift" was characterized "as the courageous conversion" [Gergen, 1973, p. 312].) Constant evaluation and reevaluation do not necessarily mean that scientific critics devalue the work of the focal researcher. Criticism within the community is aimed, at least in the best of circumstances, at perfecting the explanatory or predictive power of theory. Policy people, however, may perceive scientific exchange as an indication that the debated results are of little utility or are weak. Disagreement among the so-called experts is often equated with disproven results. This is not to assert that the policy community is unfamiliar with an adversary use of facts. Rather, it is an observation on a recent loss of confidence in scientific investigation.

Platt (1964) has recognized another difference in the attitudes toward usable knowledge of scientists and policy makers. Policy makers search for truth that can lead to effective action; they seek information that describes social phenomena in a way that directs decisions. But according to Platt, the most productive scientific thinking consists of strong inference by which multiple hypotheses are offered, and the search for truth occurs by systematically excluding one or more of the hypotheses. This is a process that has promoted great strides in molecular biology and in high-energy physics but is not one that busy practitioners, confronted with daily problems and seeking immediate solutions, find attractive.

Conflicting explanations of scientific results presented in the media make public an honest debate within science. The effect on the creation of scientific knowledge may be positive. But, simultaneously, it may diminish citizen faith in the scientific enterprise. A "public science" no doubt refines scientific inquiry, but disagreement on methods, extent of generalization, views on causation, ethical issues, definition of threshold levels, and the very epistemological value of information gained from the social sciences (Gergen 1973),[3] and the like, may disillusion the nonscientific audience.

The scientific personality and style

Characteristics of those who enter into social scientific careers and aspects of the socialization of the scientists may affect the selection of study topics and how information is presented, which in turn disturbs some in the policy community. Perhaps for social scientists to gain increased importance in the policy making process, they need to unlearn some of what they have considered essential to appearing truly scientific; they will need to be desocialized from other behaviors. The endless clarifications, qualifications, references to what is statistically significant, and the hedging and developing of the immense complexity of relationships sound bizarre to the non-social scientist. It is difficult to make use of work so painfully presented. There is a sense of the exegesist who cannot force himself to reach a conclusion based on information, but feels compelled to demonstrate the flaws in the operating information of others.

Creation of terminology to make an insight sound academic, professional, and significant may erect a barrier between scientists and those who could benefit from interaction with them. We have seen too many examples of formalizing reasonable but not earthshaking conclusions and observations into the most cumbersome forms of jargon: "heteromethodological approaches" and "moral density," to name two.

It is well to keep in mind that policy makers are often quite intelligent and quick to digest information and learn. They are used to processing vast amounts of input. They can discriminate shoddy work from good work. And they are busy. Few things are more embarrassing to the social scientific community and more harmful to its reputation than a narrow, brash social researcher presenting as elaborate and profound – in a lecturing mode – an obvious finding to a high-level policy person.

---

[3] Consider the impact on the uninitiated in the social sciences who might be considering calling on the enterprise for guidance in policy making: "The continued attempt to build general laws of social behavior seems misdirected, and the associated belief that knowledge of social interaction can be accumulated in a manner similar to the natural sciences appears unjustified . . . the psychologists of the future are likely to find little value in contemporary knowledge" (Gergen, 1973, p. 316). It is like telling the potential convert to a highly dogmatic religion that, "by the way, all beliefs are equally valid, and ours have little divine basis."

More significant, perhaps, than this stylistic criticism is the allegation that the scientific enterprise may too often fall on the side of "avoidance of substantive change, imposed homogeneity and control of the many by the few" – that we may be breeding, as well as describing and classifying, the authoritarian personality (Mornell, 1979). See also Kuhn (1970) for further analysis of the overconservative dynamics of the scholar's training and stewardship.

Potential for a policy-oriented social science response

Structural and intellectual impediments. To be responsive to the politically determined needs of the policy maker may benefit neither public policy nor scientific knowledge. Social science cannot respond quickly enough to meet most policy demands, while at the same time maintaining norms regarding quality of scientific information. When science does manage to "produce on time," results may arrive at an administrator other than the one who communicated the initial request. Or the same administrator may be driven by new guidelines or directives. Policy ideas move, with ease, in and out of good currency. Within a 12-year period, for example, interest in economic incentives to meet objectives of control of environmental stressors in the United States Environmental Protection Agency has waxed and waned and waxed again. Extremely high personnel turnover within state and federal government may account, in part, for government's failure to effectively carry out programs. Shifts in staffing may be even more important than defects in design of the programs themselves.

Organization of the knowledge industry in American universities and in think tanks and profit-oriented research centers is also germane. Social scientists may view certain policy questions as pedestrian, expecting that answers to such questions will make little if any long-range contribution to a body of knowledge even if the relevant body is seen as policy science. Requests for proposals (RFPs) often pose tasks less interesting than questions chosen by the academic community unconstrained by concern with present usability. Government-sponsored research programs change with what often appears to be the whim of a new administration. What was important middecade (witness the RANN [Research Applied to National Needs] program in NSF) may be history by the end of the decade.

Conditions favoring usefulness of stressor research. Is the goal of making usable information about environmental stressors then unreasonable? An overall understanding of the circumstances under which the policy maker calls scientific information into service, of the views of policy makers on scientific inquiry, and of impediments to a policy-responsive social science suggests an affirmative answer. But certain conditions may help resolve the general incompatibility between the two communities.

Several characteristics of problems such as air pollution, noise pollution, design dysfunction, and heat stressors may foster the long-term alignment of policy makers and social science researches. First, identification of environmental stressor problems may provoke less disagreement than other areas of social intervention, such as those involving racial differences. Both communities may find preintervention conditions unacceptable, and even be relatively close on assigning a magnitude to adverse stressors. Disagreement on measurement techniques and instrumentation often might be manageable. The chances that a stressor problem will be "defined away" may be less than for problems on which agreement on "objective social conditions" is lacking.

Stress research may fall into that midrange of scientific inquiry about which Merton spoke and which Kalven adapted to our thinking about the use of science in law. "It can only aspire to facts in the middle range. Some premises are too deeply held for actual footnoting, and some facts are too well and accessibly known for professional inquiry. What remains then as the critical area is the middle range where the premises are not that unshakable and where the facts are not that accessible" (Kalven, 1968, p. 67).

Second, research questions in the environmental stress area have historically arisen from the same contexts as policy concerns. Questions that are important in the social scientific community are also faced by those who make decisions about interventions in urban and rural environments. Individuals interested in transportation-related stress, medical-setting difficulties, crimes of violence, urban fear, design of major commercial centers, difficulties in living near unpopular land uses, and pollution of all varieties have distributed themselves between the two communities.

Furthermore, political coalitions surrounding various stressor control policy questions may be a new feature of the social environment. An understanding of stress concepts sufficient to recognize policy implications is now part of the common knowledge of a wide slice of the population. The citizenry now "knows" that environmental characteristics and pollutants can be stressors, and that beyond a certain threshold stressors can produce dysfunctional human behavioral responses and detrimental health effects. Intense smog, perceived density (congestion), and contaminated water are aspects of environmental quality that citizens continually evaluate as important (Resources for the Future, 1978). Adaptation to stressors may postpone the critical time of policy response, but it is likely that outcomes that social scientists address – even those not now of urgent policy need such as aftereffects and span of attention – will, in time, become salient dimensions of governmental concern.

Other advocates of a strong stressor control policy include creators of control technology, the social science community itself, established environmental groups that aim to reduce environmental noxiants and pollutants (even if health and behavioral effects on *human beings* are not verifiable), and business interests that are damaged by uncontrolled stressors. These actors constitute a potentially powerful political force.

The scientific character of the generation of knowledge about stress is another factor that can promote favorable science–policy alliances. Unlike some social science enterprises, there are considerable data on many aspects of stress (e.g., archives of epidemiologic data on mental and physical health conditions), allowing for detailed analysis and prediction. Although there is variability in precision as noted by McGrath (1976), sophisticated instrumentation for objectively measuring the magnitude of certain stressors is available. Also, direct experimentation involving environmental stressors is more practical, and generally raises fewer ethical and legal questions, than experimentation to detect, for example, the effects of racial imbalance or poverty. Furthermore, conceptual contributions on stress may now be valued. Organization of the certainty and uncertainty around efforts to control a social "bad" is essential before approaches to social intervention can be wisely chosen (Coates, 1976, quoted in Berg, 1978).

Finally, value conflicts in stress research may be tractable, although they are not trivial. They appear to be less of an obstacle, for example, than disagreements that have historically made policy makers skeptical and confused about research on bussing and that which has been characterized as "victim blaming" (Caplan, 1979). To be sure, results of noise research, (e.g., the effects of noise on school children) can be politically volatile. Assignment to schools considered plagued by noise pollution can raise issues – as does racial districting – of equal educational opportunity. So, too, laboratory experiments on the health effects of noise, even when animals are used, are ethically objectionable to some. Experimentation that proceeds without a subject's full knowledge or understanding also poses problems. Nonetheless, the value of a less stressful environment is recognized by many who make policy.

Several multidisciplinary academic programs and departments were developed in the 1970s. Emphasis in their research agenda shifted to a problem and environmental orientation as opposed to a disciplinary focus (Binder, 1972). Despite historical failures of multidisciplinary efforts, many of these programs appear to have sustained their effect through the difficulties of early years. Journals receptive to their work have also appeared (for example, the *Human Stress Journal* and *Environment and Behavior*). At this point, institutional incongruence may be less problematic in the stressor area than in other fields of inquiry that have potential policy application. The National Science Foundation and NIH have begun to play a middleman function. Broker agencies play an important role in matching the interests of performers of research and users of results (Biderman & Sharp, 1976). Those interested in policy-relevant research now not only have their journals (*Policy Sciences, Policy Studies Journal, Evaluation Quarterly, Knowledge: Creation, Diffusion and Utilization*, to name a few), but also have their counterparts within state and federal agencies (e.g., offices of technology assessment, science advisors, and program evaluators). Multidisciplinary and interdisciplinary research is a much less lonely, professionally risky, and potentially irrelevant enterprise than it was two decades ago.

Scientific journalism. Whether they are the cause or the effect of increased interest in science, the new science-oriented journals written for the layman are important to understanding the context in which information enters the public domain. They provide existing and latent opportunities for greater use of scientific knowledge. On one level they indicate that the nonscientist is interested in explanations that may increase the complexity of one's understanding of the world. At the very least, they reflect an appreciation of rigorous analysis among a sizable sector of the society. (The size of this phenomenon has to be understood relative to growing attention to nonscientific explanations: the supernatural, the occult, the biblical, and "know-nothing" descriptions of social phenomena.)

Scientific journalism represents an outlet that social scientists can employ if their perspective on increasing the usability of social scientific information on stressors is general and long range. However, the effects of scientific journalism may not always be positive: The type of article that is typically included ("Sex and survival: Our erotic origins"; "Fuel from water: Science says Yes!" "Boost creativity: Stimulate your brain with breath control")[4] is much more sensational than much of the work produced at the present time on stressors. To make some of the present work on stressors publishable in popular science magazines, the researcher may have to emphasize scenarios that are highly unlikely, results that are atypical, and explanations that might not be raised before professional audiences. A further implication is that mainline work of the social scientist may not be of great interest to those whose more common exposure to science is through the tales of wonder that some of these popular magazines run. How can our findings compete with the following?

The subject matter of *Science Digest* is amazing...astounding...astonishing... incredible...unbelievable. And true.

If the new, the improbable, the unlikely and the nearly impossible have any attraction to you, then welcome to *Science Digest*. Ours is a world where words such as "sensational" and "fantastic" have diminished meaning because the sensational and fantastic are often commonplace. It's a world as small as a gluon, as big as the universe. A world that only grudgingly yields its secrets, as if wondering if we can appreciate their value....Much of what you'll learn from our pages every month is eminently useful, some of it is merely fascinating. But all of it is the result of exhaustive research by some of the best scientific brains...[From promotional material on *Science Digest*]

In evaluating the potential for greater cooperation between the two communities, it is enlightening to note that social scientists have only fairly

---

[4] From *Science Digest.*

recently attempted to be involved in policy making on a large scale. Historically for several reasons links have not been necessary. For their part, social scientists have had sufficient response to their work intracommunity: They have had little need to work to generate greater demand. Furthermore, with only a few exceptions, the large funders of research have not paid great attention to application of research findings. And prestige in the scientific community often has been inversely related to present usability of findings.

For their part, policy makers have worked in less complicated, less interdependent, and more homogeneous policy environments. Impact analysis was not generally required, and when done, impacts were assessed only for dominant interest groups. Conditions now are quite different for both communities. Thus, social scientists are at the beginning of a learning curve, and this learning can be aided by growing contributions from the policy-making and policy-analysis sciences. Recent successes with fending off significant budget cuts in the social sciences proposed by the Reagan administration demonstrate that the social scientific community can apply its considerable organizational capacity to political challenges. That experience itself has generated appreciations of the types of knowledge and information that are valued by those who make decisions at the federal and state levels.

Existing important function of social science. Whether or not policy making incorporates social scientific knowledge preventively, contributions already have been recognized by those who work in responsive, curative modes. By working in this after-the-stressor capacity, the scientist can demonstrate that usable knowledge on stressors exists. He or she can win allies among those negatively affected by stressors – those who may benefit from the work on coping with stressors. Those include policy makers who will make subsequent judgments about the value of a social science of stress. Stressors exist, and although some of their effects are long run, others are presently manifest. Increased publicity about scientific considerations of coping and cure can foster an acceptance of the scientific enterprise. Evans's work on the impact of pollution on school children near airports and Novaco's work on stress inoculation (1977) are examples that influential policy makers presently value.

Toward a closer link between research and public policy on environmental stressors

Recommendations can focus on three areas: the process of public policy formulation, the process of dissemination, and implications for education of social scientists.

Social science involvement in the formulation of public policy

Several opportunities exist for creation of a relevant social science on environmental stressors. *Within* the research community research questions can be synthesized in ways that are more valuable from a policy perspective. Catalano and Dooley's work combining analysis of economic change and indicators of psychological stress is an example applicable to decisions surrounding employment legislation (Catalano & Dooley, 1977). Collaboration between architects and environmental and social psychologists (Kaplan & Kaplan, 1978) holds promise for those in the design professions. Work among environmental scientists, psychologists, and lawyers can generate both criteria for control of environmental pollutants and alternative approaches, including incentives-based schemes for controlling stressors. Social ecological investigations of impacts of new towns can be of use to those contemplating changes in state environmental policy.

Collaboration *between* knowledge generators (social scientists) and users (policy makers) also offers several potential benefits. They include perceived relevance of the results; mutual education of participating policy makers and scientists; increased trust among the actors; learning about professional styles and breaking down of cross-professional barriers; increased commitment to the research findings; and mutual clarification of expectations and responsibilities (Berg, 1978). Furthermore, governmental agencies tend to be resistant to information produced outside of the agency so collaboration between social scientists inside and outside of government can help. Also, issues vary with time. A collaborative research enterprise that takes into consideration that a range of perspectives will help determine policy outcomes stands a greater likelihood of being useful. Overall involvement in all phases of policy making, however, does not appear to be a necessary condition for knowledge use. Critical points appear to be the phases of problem definition, goal setting, and evaluation (Dunn, 1980).

Across communities consultation by social scientists with beneficiaries of public policy, the citizens, can also promote coalitions that influence legislators and administrators. It can generate more credible data through field methods. And the processes of science and policy making can be integrated so that both become demystified to the citizen. Scientist–citizen exchanges can create conditions that make policy choices more acceptable or actually can be the breeding place of policy.

Interaction between social scientists and policy makers can be fostered in several ways. The very semantics used in the presentation of research agenda and results are important. For example, describing stress as "bad" triggers a much different policy response than talking about "challenge," or even about positive effects of arousal (McGrath, 1976). Furthermore, policy is not determined by a discrete event, but by a process. So collaboration takes time, removes research scientists from the laboratory, and involves them in activities that will be new and sometimes painful. The social scientist must monitor the policy making process and cannot rely exclusively on formal sources (such as the *Federal Register*) that announce opportunities for input. Resistance to social science input may be decreased if scientists testify at committee hearings, participate on advisory boards of agencies that set research agendas, communicate informally with legislators and administrative officials, and offer services to lawyers who are in need of expert testimony for judicial or administrative proceedings. If social scientists can participate as anonymous private citizens, they may gain insight into how social science knowledge is regarded by the general public.

Dissemination

The literature on dissemination is immense and now sufficiently developed to be of considerable value to those who aim to have their research known and used. That literature cannot be summarized here, but several points about the dissemination process appear particularly important to those who do stress research and those who would care to apply that research.

First, effective dissemination of research results may require the creation of a formal (and boundary-spanning) dissemination role within the research enterprise, a role recognized as professionally distinct from research. Not all researchers have the skill or motivation for dissemination (Glaser & Taylor, 1973). The individual within such a boundary-spanning role might anticipate changes in the agency that implements research results and adjust either the nature of the research or the characteristics of the user–producer relationship. The principal investigator, or another linking person, needs to pay attention to how organizations mediate information communicated through an organization and translated into policy choices (DiMento, 1976; Katz & Kahn, 1966).

Second, the social scientist's understanding of the concept of dissemination itself may be deficient. It would be silly to try to typify the literature on the subject as of one mind. However, one orientation that may be overadopted is that knowledge exists in a completed form and that the social scientist's task is to move it into the field of action and policy. It may make more sense to think of dissemination of social *scientists* as opposed to packaged *knowledge*. Here the aim is to share a wide variety of information and knowledge, to explore whether there is an "interesting fit" between what we have produced and praxis. Perhaps an interactive mode of dissemination is appropriate given the present state of information on environmental stressors. What social scientists know is sometimes limited and what policy makers know is sometimes quite rich. The latter have developed knowledge from doing, from making mistakes and thinking about attempts, from some limited successes, from creating and from being attacked, from trying and sometimes losing miserably, from building or promoting and reflecting upon the Pruitt-Igoes and the Irvines.

Third, clarity about the nature of the research contribution is also important. Specificity may attract audiences that would not be curious otherwise. Stress now carries so many meanings. We speak of it in contexts ranging from the impact of noise and of seating arrangements on children to the impact of neighborhood spatial arrangements on fear of crime and the impact of job position on depression. Different audiences exist for each of these research areas. When we present our findings at their highest level of abstraction, we may miss those most concerned.

Fourth, researchers may wish to present information only when it can be packaged in a direct, simple, and clear way. If the work is so complicated that disclaimers, descriptions of several confounds, and other confusing caveats have to be addended, perhaps the research simply is not ready to be used. Not everyone should be interested in our ongoing excursuses about the nature of behavior in settings.

One fate to which we must not subject social policy makers is to supply them with the almost infinite variety of ways of saying the same thing, of taking a basic finding and spinning it out in myriad forms to meet our own objectives (of publishing and gaining tenure or publishing and gaining intracommunity fame or publishing and gaining supplemental compensation). Much of what we say need not be said again in slightly different forms. We need not disseminate everything we do.

Finally, when all is said and done, it may be the case that the much-maligned activity within the university community, compensated consulting, is an effective way of adapting, translating, and transferring research findings to make them usable. When one works with a client, one has considerable attention; one observes the specific characteristics of the setting in which the research will be used or ignored; and one can communicate in ways directly receivable by the client. These conditions enhance the scientist's capacity to disseminate effectively.

Implications for education

Familiarity with the intricacies of the knowledge industry is also important. We need to understand the various functions, manifest and latent, played by the search for social science knowledge. We also need to understand how knowledge is created and processed; how problems are defined; how the social research industry is organized; and the immense variation in how social problems are perceived and articulated (Lindblom & Cohen, 1979; Rein, 1973).

Self-education can come from systematically following one's own research results. Lazarsfeld, Sewell, and Wilensky (1967) noted that sociologists have only vague ideas about what happens to their work. If the scholar seeks only instrumental impact, and uses narrow standards (e.g., if he or she expects policy to incorporate fully all that the researcher intended), learning may be painful. But these personnel case studies can identify application, suggest approaches to increasing various types of influence, and can spot problems in existing strategies of research creation and dissemination. The researcher who is sensitive to unexpected uses may also encounter dissemination techniques for future efforts.

Thinking about the contribution of research from the perspectives of the policy maker can be invaluable. Clinical experiences, field study requirements, and internships (Dror, 1971; Michael, 1968) should be part of the education of the research scientist whose career plans include work with policy communities. Insights derived from responding to the actual demands on the policy maker are not often produced in classroom activities. Gaming and simulation activities may help as well.

Greater use of exchanges between the university and government and the private sector can allow for ongoing communication among members of the "two communities." The model sometimes employed in law schools of senior partners taking sabbaticals in the university may be appropriate. In the other direction social scientists may benefit from more frequent leaves in decision-making settings.

Substantively, the curriculum of the knowledge producer should address the differing orientations to social problems and research (Caplan et al., 1975); point out the frustrations and rewards of boundary roles filled by the social scientist (Berg, 1978; Michael, 1973; Vickers, 1965); and discuss activities that attempt to "come to grips with the difficulties of bridging the *perspectives* of social scientists and policy makers" (Caplan et al., 1975, p. 51). Caplan identifies these as, "(a) making realistic and rational appraisals of the relative merits of the diversified information which abounds in the social sciences; (b) creating accurate and concise translations of social science research to facilitate communication with the policy setting community [and] (c) recasting policy issues into researchable terms" (p. 51).

Conclusion

Existing frustrations and the relative "policy impotence" of the social scientists should not obscure the fact that there is great power in knowledge and that ignorance sustains social problems. No doubt, the constraints on the creation of a usable knowledge are numerous and powerful and surely the social scientist is more excluded than heeded. But if one accepts the position that society determines many social outcomes by choices it makes – on the basis of information of one kind or another – of the ways to organize itself (to design its micro- and macroenvironments, to produce, destroy, recycle, etc.) then quality information is inherently powerful. Furthermore, information that can provide clear benefits may be divergent from that of public opinion, which, at final look, may now be the single most powerful driving force for many policy choices. Clearly stated, simply presented, and parsimoniously (and infrequently offered) comments on how stressor phenomena are interconnected and how social phenomena *can* be altered in the long run may have a lasting effect on the manner in which the public and private sectors do business. This, after all, is what usable information seeks to influence.

References

Abramson, L.Y., Seligman, E.P., & Teasdale, J.D. Learned helplessness in humans: Critique and reformation. *Journal of Abnormal Psychology*, 1978, *87*, 49–74.

Ackerman, J. The jurisprudence of just compensation. *Environmental Law*, 1977, 7(3), 509–518.

Altman, I. *The environment and social behavior*, Monterey, Calif.: Brooks/Cole, 1975.

American Psychological Association, Memorandum to Research Support Network Members, from Michael S. Pallak, Alan Kraut, and Gary VandenBos, Re: Federal Budget Information: *The National Science Foundation* (SF), July 10, 1981.

Berg, M. *The uses of technology assessment in policy making*. Center for Research on the Utilization of Scientific Knowledge, Institute for Social Research, Ann Arbor, University of Michigan, 1978.

Biderman, A., & Sharp, L. The selection of performers of social research. In E. Crawford & S. Rokken (Eds.), *Sociological praxis*. London: Sage Publications, 1976.

Binder, A. A new context for psychology: Social ecology. *American Psychologist*, 1972, *27*, 903–908.

Brenner, M.H. *Mental illness and the economy*. Cambridge, Mass.: Harvard University Press, 1973.

Brodsky, S.L., & Robey, A. On becoming an expert witness: Issues of orientation and effectiveness. *Professional Psychology*, 1973, *3*, 173–176.

Bronfenbrenner, U. Developmental research, public policy, and the ecology of childhood. *Child Development*, 1974, *1*, 1–5.

Bryan, M.E., & Tempest, W. Are our noise laws adequate? *Applied Acoustics*, 1973, *6*, 219–232.

Caplan, N., Lecture given to the seminar in Urban and Regional Planning, University of Michigna, Ann Arbor, Michigan, November, 1979.

Caplan, N., Morrison, A., & Stambaugh, R.J. *The use of social science knowledge in policy decisions at the national level*. Ann Arbor: University of Michigan, Institute for Social Research, 1975.

Catalano, R. *Health, behavior and the community: An ecological perspective*. Elmsford, N.Y.: Pergamon Press, 1979.

Catalano, R., & Dooley, D. Economic predictors of depressed mood and stressful life events. *Journal of Health and Social Behavior*, 1977, *18*, 292–307.

Coates, J. F. Technology assessment: A tool kit. *Chemtech*, 1976, June 372–383.

Cohen, S., Evans, G.W., Krantz, D.S., & Stokols, D. Physiological, motivational, and cognitive effects of aircraft noise on children: Moving from the laboratory to the field. *American Psychologist*, 1980, *35*, 231–243.

Collins, S. The use of social research in the court. In Study Project on Social Research and Development. *Knowledge and policy: The uncertain connection*. The National Research Council, National Academy of Science, Washington, D.C.: 1978.

Congressional Record, United States of America, Vol. 118, Part 28, October 18, 1972.

Craig, R. Why academic research fails to be useful. In F. Levinsohn & B. Wright (Eds.), *School desegregation: Shadow and substance.* Chicago: University of Chicago Press, 1976.

Davis, H., & Salasin, S. Strengthening the contribution of social R & D to policy-making. In Study Project on Social Research and Development. *Knowledge and policy: The uncertain connection.* The National Research Council, National Academy of Sciences, Washington, D.C.: 1978.

DiMento, J. *Managing environmental change.* New York: Praeger, 1976.

DiMento, J. Citizen environmental litigation and the administrative process: Empirical findings, remaining issues and a direction for future research. *Duke Law Journal,* 1977, 2, 409–448.

DiMento, J. Improving development control through planning: The consistency doctrine. *Columbia Journal of Environmental Law,* 1978, 5, 1–68.

DiMento, J. *The consistency doctrine and the limits of planning.* Cambridge, Mass.: Oelgeschlager, Gunn & Hain, 1980.

DiMento, J., Dozier, M.D., Emmons, S.L., Hagman, D.G., Kim, C., Greenfield-Sanders, K., Waldau, P.F., & Woollacott, J.A. Land development and environmental control in the California Supreme Court: The deferential, the preservationist, and the preservationist-erratic eras. *UCLA Law Review,* 1980, 27, (4, 5), 859–1066.

Dohrenwend, B.S. Social stress and community psychology. *American Journal of Community Psychology,* 1978, 6, 1–4.

Dror, Y. Applied social science and systems analysis. In I.L. Horowitz (Ed.), *The use and abuse of social science.* New Brunswick, N.J.: Transaction, 1971.

Dunn, W. The two-communities metaphor and models of knowledge use. *Knowledge: Creation, diffusion, utilization,* 1980, 14, 515–536.

Evans, G.W., & Eichelman, W. Preliminary models of conceptual linkages among proxemic variables. *Environment and Behavior,* 1976, 8, 87–116.

Federal Aid to Highway Act of 1970, Pub. L. 91-605, 84 Stat. 1734, 23 U.S.C. §109(h) (1) (1976).

Frieden, B., & Kaplan, M. *The Politics of neglect.* London: MIT Press, 1975.

Gergen, K.J. Social psychology as history. *Journal of Personality and Social Psychology,* 1973, 26, 309–320.

Glaser, E.M., & Taylor, S.H. Factors influencing the success of applied research. *American Psychologist,* 1973, 28, 140–146.

Hall, E.T. *The hidden dimension.* New York: Doubleday, 1966.

Havelock, R. *Planning for innovation through dissemination and utilization of knowledge.* Institute for Social Research, Ann Arbor, University of Michigan, 1969.

Haynes, J.V. Michigan's Environmental Protection Act in its 6th year: Substantive environmental law from citizens' suits. *Journal of Urban Law,* 1976, 53, 589–700.

Jones, B. Competitiveness, role orientations, and legislative responsiveness. *The Journal of Politics,* 1973, 35, 924.

Kahn, R.L., Wolfe, D.M., Quinn, R.P., Snoek, J.D., & Rosenthal, R.A. *Organizational stress: Studies in role conflict and ambiguity.* New York: Wiley, 1964.

Kalven, H. The quest for the middle range: Empirical inquiry and legal policy. In G. Hazard (Ed.), *Law in a changing America.* Englewood Cliffs, N.J.: Prentice-Hall, 1968.

Kaplan, S., & Kaplan, R. *Humanscape.* North Scituate, Mass.: Duxbury Press, 1978.

Katz, D., & Kahn, R.L. *The social psychology of organizations.* New York: Wiley, 1966.

Kissinger, H. *The Reporter,* 5 March 1959, 30 quoted in G.E. Brown and R. Byerly, Jr., "Research in EPA: A congressional viewpoint," *Science,* 1981, *211,* 1385–1390.

Koller, R., & Kaplan, A. A two-process theory of learned helplessness. *Journal of Personality and Social Psychology,* 1978, *36,* 1177–1183.

Kuhn, T. *The structure of scientific revolution* (2nd ed.). Chicago: University of Chicago Press, 1970.

Langer, E. J., & Rodin, J. The effects of choice and enhanced personal responsibility for the aged: A field experiment in an institutional setting. *Journal of Personality and Social Psychology,* 1976, *34,* 191–198.

Lazarsfeld, P., Sewell, W., & Wilensky, H. (Eds.), *The uses of sociology.* New York: Basic Books, 1967.

Lindblom, C., & Cohen, D. *Usable knowledge; Social science and social problem solving.* New Haven, Conn.: Yale University Press, 1979.

Majone, G. Technology assessment and policy analysis. *Policy Sciences,* 1977, *8,* 173–175.

McGrath, J. Stress and behavior in organizations. In M.D. Dunnette (Ed.), *Handbook of industrial and organizational psychology.* Skokie, Ill.: Rand McNally, 1976.

Merton, R. The role of applied social science in the formation of policy: A research memorandum. *Philosophy of Science,* 1949, *16,* 161.

Michael, D. *The unprepared society: Planning for a precarious future.* New York: Basic Books, 1968.

Michael, D. *Learning to plan and planning to learn.* San Francisco: Jossey-Bass, 1973.

Michigan Environmental Protection Act of 1970, Michigan Comp. Laws Ann. §§691.1201 to 1207.

Mornell, E.S. Social science and social policy: Epistemology and values in contemporary research. *SchoolReview,* 1979, *87*(3) 295–313.

Morris, R., Unpublished comments on a conference held at The University of Bath, January 1979.

Moynihan, D.P. *Maximum feasible misunderstanding.* New York: Free Press, 1970.

Nagi, S.Z. The practitioner as a partner in research. *Rehabilitation Record,* 1965, July-August, 1–4.

Newman, O. *Defensible space.* New York: Macmillan, 1973.

The Noise Control Act, Pub. L. No. 92–574, 86 Stat. 1234, 42 U.S.C. §§4901 (1976); The National Environmental Policy Act of 1969, Pub. L. No. 91–180, 83 Stat. 852, 42 U.S.C.A. §§4331 et seq.: The Clean Air Amendments of 1970, Pub. L. No. 91–604, 84 Stat. 1676, 42 U.S.C.A. §1857 et seq., as amended.

Novaco, R.W. Stress inoculation: A cognitive therapy for anger. *Journal of Consulting and Clinical Psychology,* 1977, *45,* 600–608.

The New York Times. Social scientists as policy-shapers. January 8, 1980, C1, C4.

Platt, J.R. Strong inference. *Science,* 1964, *146,* 347–352.

Reed, R.C. The compleat lawyer: Reviewing your skills. Amercan Bar Association Journal, 1981, *67,* 932–935.

Rein, M. *Social science and public policy.* New York: Penguin-Viking Books, 1973.

Rein, M., & White, S. Policy research: belief and doubt. *Policy Analysis,* 1977, *3,* 20–32.

Rein, M., & White S. *Knowledge for practice.* Unpublished manuscript, MIT, June 1979.

Resources for the Future. The public speaks again: A new environmental survey. *Resources,* 1978, 60.

Rodgers, W. H., Jr. *Handbook on environmental law*, St. Paul, Minn.: West, 1977.

Rogers, E. M., & Shoemaker, F. F. *Communication of innovations: A cross cultural approach*. New York: Free Press, 1971.

Roos, J. P. Welfare theory and social policy: A study of policy science. *Commentations Scientiarum Socialism*, 1973, 4, 207–225.

Sabatier, P. The acquisition and utilization of technical information by administrative agencies. *Administrative Sciences Quarterly*, 1978, 23, 394.

Sax, J., & Conner, R. Michigan's Environmental Protection Act of 1970: A progress report. *Michigan Law Review*, 1972, 70, 1003.

Sax, J., & DiMento, J. Environmental citizen suits: Three years' experience under the Michigan Environmental Protection Act. *Ecology Law Quarterly*, Winter, 1974, 4, 1.

Schroth, P., & Plater, Z. *Environmental law: An introduction to the American legal system* (in press).

Sommer, R. *Are crowded jails harmful? Field and laboratory on trial*. Invited address, Western Psychological Association, San Francisco, April 1978.

Soper, P. The constitutional framework of environmental law. In E. Dolgin & T. G. Guilbert (Eds.), *Federal environmental law*. Chicago: West Publishing Co., 1974.

Stokols, D. A congruence analysis of human stress. In I.G. Sarason & C.D. Spielberger (Eds.), *Stress and anxiety* (Vol. 6). Washington, D.C.: Hemisphere Press, 1979.

Stokols, D. Group X place transactions: Some neglected issues in psychological research on settings. In D. Magnusson (Ed.), *Toward a psychology of situations: An interactional perspective*. Hillsdale, N.J.: Erlbaum, 1981.

United States Senate, Hearings Before the Subcommittee on Air and Water Pollution of the Committee on Public Works, Ninety-Second Congress, Second Session of S.1016, A Bill to Control the Generation and Transmission of Noise Detrimental to the Human Environment, and for Other Purposes, S.3342, A Bill to Amend Tital IV of the Clean Air Act, and for Other Purposes, H.R. 11021, A Bill to Control the Emission of Noise Detrimental to the Human Environment, and for Other Purposes, March 29, 1972; San Francisco, California, April 12 and 13, 1972, Washington, D.C. (1) Serial No. 92-H3J. Printed for the Use of the Committee on Public Works.)

Vickers, G. *The art of judgment*. New York: Basic Books, 1965.

Wachtel, P. Investigation and its discontents. *American Psychologist*, 1980, 35(5), 399–408.

Weiss, C. *The many meanings of research utilization*. Public Administration Review, October 1979.

Name index

Subject index

This index is organized around the main topics of the book: particular stressors (e.g., noise), particular settings (e.g., schools), and policy issues. Cross-references among these main topics are located under *setting* and *policy* main entries, as subentries for each stressor.